CAMPAIGN
MONEY
Reform and Reality
in the States

Edited by

Herbert E. Alexander

THE FREE PRESS
A Division of Macmillan Publishing Co., Inc.
NEW YORK

COLLIER MACMILLAN PUBLISHERS
LONDON

Copyright © 1976 by The Free Press
A Division of Macmillan Publishing Co., Inc.

The Free Press
A Division of Macmillan Publishing Co., Inc.
866 Third Avenue, New York, N.Y. 10022

Collier Macmillan Canada, Ltd.

Library of Congress Catalog Card Number: 76-21180

Printed in the United States of America

printing number

1 2 3 4 5 6 7 8 9 10

Library of Congress Cataloging in Publication Data
Main entry under title:

Campaign money.

    Includes index.
    1. Elections--United States--Campaign funds.
I. Alexander, Herbert E.
JK1991.C35   329'.025'0973   76-21180
ISBN 0-02-900410-1
ISBN 0-02-900420-9 pbk.

CONTENTS

FOREWORD

John W. Gardner

After Clarence Darrow had won a court case for a woman client, she said to him rather effusively, "Oh, how can I ever thank you?"

"Madam," Darrow responded dryly, "Ever since the Phoenicians invented money there has been a ready answer to that question."

His reference to the Phoenicians wasn't quite correct, but his point was clear. And certainly it wouldn't have surprised Darrow that when special favors flow from government to individuals or groups, what generally flows in the opposite direction is money.

All governments have favors to hand out or withhold. They cannot escape the making of decisions that benefit particular individuals or bring advantage or hardship to whole classes of individuals. They levy taxes, issue licenses, let contracts, award grants, regulate commerce, prosecute, decide not to prosecute, subsidize, and so on and on. As a consequence, some people gain, others lose. No doubt since the beginning of organized society, a number of the people potentially affected have sought to bend government decisions to their advantage. In a money economy, one doesn't have to look far to find a handy means to that end.

The first Federal attempt to regulate campaign financing did not involve the problem of influence-buying but concerned the problem of protecting government employees from pressures to contribute. In 1867, a naval appropriations bill included the following: "And be it further enacted, that no officer or employee of the government shall require or request any workingman in any navy yard to contribute or pay any money for political purposes." The Civil Service Reform Act of 1883 extended the rule to protect all Civil Service workers. (Yet today Indiana still permits the party in power to require that state employees make political contributions equal to 2 percent of their salaries—a piece of political primitivism that Hoosiers are hard put to explain.)

By the end of the century, attention was being focused on the more difficult problem of how to regulate political gifts from wealthy interests outside government. Theodore Roosevelt said in 1905, "All contributions by corporations to any political committee or for any political purpose should be forbidden by law." Laws were enacted in 1907, 1910, 1911, and 1925 that included disclosure provisions and bans on corporate contributions. There followed roughly 60 years in which these laws remained on the books but were unenforced. It is an incredible and shocking fact that, with rare exceptions, attorneys-general simply did not enforce the law.

By the 1960's, campaigns gifts had become the broad and heavily traveled avenue for those seeking to buy political outcomes. There are a lot of ways to skin a cat—or a taxpayer—and a politician's vote can be corruptly influenced by other routes than campaign giving. But campaign giving had become such a wide-open and easy game that it was the preferred mode; only old-fashioned or stupid people resorted to bribes any longer. Even in those cases in which campaign giving was clearly illegal, it was a reputable illegality.

An observer might have predicted that nothing could possibly shatter a system so comfortably hypocritical. But the old pattern of campaign financing was moving swiftly toward its moment of disaster. Money was flowing in vaster and vaster quantities. And the soaring costs of campaigns were making candidates more than ever desperately needful of dollars. Alexander Heard, a distinguished political scientist, called attention to the gravity of the problem; and Herbert Alexander initiated a research program which provided important early insights on the subject. Many of us who have been most active in campaign-finance reform in the past half-dozen years were introduced to the subject by Heard and Alexander.

By 1970 a new wave of reform was beginning. It proceeded at both state and Federal levels, and the states were often more forward-looking and experimental than the Congress. Over the generations, believers in our Federal system have often expressed the view that the states should (and would) function as seedbeds of governmental improvement, testing a diversity of patterns that would enrich our understanding of self-government.

For most of our history, the states have not lived up to that ideal; but no one could fault their performance in the reform wave of the past several years. Not only in campaign financing but in reforms relating to open government, lobbying disclosure, and personal financial disclosure, they have shown impressive vitality, often putting Congress to shame in their willingness to face a difficult reform issue.

Since adoption of citizen initiatives in Colorado and Washington in November of 1972, 47 additional states have taken significant action to reduce the influence of money and secrecy on their political processes. The high points of this unprecedented reform effort were the overwhelming voter approval of California's historic Proposition 9 in 1974 and the rigorous Political Reform Act enacted by the Michigan legislature in 1975.

At the Federal level, the current burst of campaign-finance reform began in 1970, when a fairly narrow reform statute passed both houses of Congress. Few observers were overly upset when President Nixon vetoed it, especially since he promised to support an improved statute in the following session of Congress.

In 1971, Common Cause, a citizens' lobby that had come into existence in September 1970—just in time to join the last stages of the fight for the 1970 Act—sued both the Republican and Democratic parties for violating the Federal Corrupt Practices Act of 1925. The parties moved for dismissal, but the judge rejected their motion and granted Common Cause standing in the suit. The historic significance of the suit was that after the long decades of nonenforcement by successive attorneys-general there now existed for the first time an alternative path of enforcement of campaign-financing statutes—namely, citizen litigation.

Members of Congress were quick to see the alarming possibilities of the judicial decision. For more than 30 years they had lived comfortably with a ceiling of $5,000 on political contributions from any individual, secure in the knowledge that the Department of Justice would not enforce the law. Now, with the possibility of enforcement by another route, Congress took steps to repeal the 30-year-old ceiling!

When Congress passed the Federal Election Campaign Act of 1971, which was to take effect on April 7, 1972, no one could have foreseen the sinister and spectacular events that would be associated with that date. Many candidates, seeing that the old game of secret money-raising was certain to end on that day, greatly intensified their efforts to round up gifts before the deadline. Maurice Stans and Herbert Kalmbach, raising money for President Nixon's re-election campaign, plunged into what was no doubt the most effective, remunerative, and disastrous fund-raising performance in political history. In the weeks preceding April 7, they swept through the nation's top corporate suites like Sherman marching through Georgia, and vast sums of secret money poured into the Finance Committee of the Committee to Re-elect the President (CREEP).

Focusing on the imminence of the new law, no one gave thought to the already existing law, the Federal Corrupt Practices Act. Since it had never been seriously enforced, it was generally thought to be a toothless statute. But it clearly required reports on contributions from some candidates, reports that had not been turned in. In September 1972, Common Cause sued CREEP for failing to report under the Corrupt Practices Act contributions made prior to April 7, 1972. Common Cause was successful in forcing disclosure of this secret list of contributions; among the gifts disclosed were funds that financed some of the most unsavory episodes of Watergate. Disclosure of the list also led to many guilty pleas and convictions of corporate executives who had made illegal gifts.

In 1974, Congress passed a historic and far-reaching reform law, including comprehensive provisions for public financing of Presidential elections. The concept of public financing had first been raised by Theodore Roosevelt, and now, almost 70 years later, it was established on the statute books and the Presidency was removed from the auction block.

Campaign-financing reform not only moves to eliminate the scandalous capacity of money to buy political outcomes; it also encourages competition and increases public participation in election campaigns. Competition has been almost entirely missing from the contemporary political scene. The re-election rate of incumbent members of Congress and state legislators who ran again has been in excess of 90 percent; and it is the disproportionate flow of campaign dollars to incumbents that stifles competition. So it is a vicious cycle—incumbents win because they get the money, and they get the money because they are incumbents.

Proponents of public financing argue that it offers the only means of breaking the cycle: By providing adequate funding for serious candidates, it would ensure more competitive elec-

tions, increased public interest, and greater citizen participation. Under public financing, they argue, the importance of the
small contributor and the volunteer citizen is substantially
magnified.

On January 30, 1976, the Supreme Court handed down a
decision on the constitutionality of the 1974 law, which had
been challenged by Senators James Buckley and Eugene Mc-
Carthy. It ruled affirmatively on three historic reforms that
drastically alter the old patterns of campaign financing: *disclosure, limits on individual contributions,* and *public financing.* It also kept the door open for another historic reform by
giving Congress a time limit within which it could reconstitute
the independent Federal Elections Commission to conform to
constitutional requirements. In upholding the disclosure requirements and contribution limits, the Court noted: "These
limitations, along with the disclosure provisions, constitute the
Act's primary weapons against the reality or appearance of improper influence stemming from the dependence of candidates
on large campaign contributions." In determining that public
financing was well within the authority of Congress, the Court
said: "In this case, Congress was legislating for the 'general
welfare'—to reduce the deleterious influence of large contributions on our political process, to facilitate communication by
candidates with the electorate, and to free candidates of the
rigors of fund-raising."

The Court ruled, however, that limits on expenditures are
an unconstitutional restriction on the First Amendment right
of free speech. It found that such limits could be imposed as a
condition of receiving public financing, provided that the
candidate has the alternative of rejecting public financing, but
a candidate who raises all his money privately would have *no*
expenditure limits. Under this ruling, there is no limit to the
amount of his own money a candidate can spend to further his
campaign. And "independent expenditures"—that is, expenditures made in behalf of a candidate but without being requested
and without any collusion with the candidate or his campaign
officials, by individuals totally unconnected with the campaign
—may be made in unlimited amounts.

Many of the problems created by the Court's decision on
expenditure limits are solved by public financing of election
campaigns. The Court not only gives public financing a chance
to prove its worth but places it at the top of the reform agenda.

The crimes of Watergate and the role of big money in those
crimes are known to all of us. The system of financing state
campaigns is less well known but hardly less disturbing. State

politics is too often written off as petty and inconsequential, despite the fact that the states raise and spend billions of our tax dollars and provide the great bulk of the domestic law that governs countless aspects of our daily life. The recent return of money and power to the states increases the need for concerned citizens to pay attention to this long-ignored level of government. The contributors to this book, who have closely examined the processes by which politics works in our states, have helped to expose the urgent need for continued campaign reform at the state level.

The material brought together here will be of great value as we continue the learning process that is at the heart of all workable social change. Few of us are Utopians any more. We don't expect humans to be perfect, and we don't see society as perfectible. No significant and far-reaching social change can be blueprinted ahead of time. We proceed as a baby learns to walk—trying, failing, trying again, falling down, getting up again, and finally learning what we set out to learn. In campaign-finance reform, we still have not completed that process. There will be further legislation, litigation, amendments, and administrative rulings.

But one thing is certain. We shall never return to the old corrupt system. We are moving toward something far more in line with our original conception of what this country is about.

EDITOR'S ACKNOWLEDGMENTS

This book was made possible by a grant of funds from the Carnegie Corporation to the Citizens' Research Foundation. We are especially indebted to Eli N. Evans and Avery Russell of the Carnegie Corporation for their interest and cooperation.

Thanks are due to the authors, each of whom did a remarkable job in writing about a difficult subject with understanding and insight. In each of the states studied, a researcher was employed to extract and summarize data from the available campaign-fund reports. The data, comprising a wealth of information, were used by the individual authors and now are filed in the offices of the Citizens' Research Foundation, 245 Nassau Street, Princeton, New Jersey 08540, where they are available for inspection. The researchers could not have completed their work without the assistance of the election officials, in most states in the office of the Secretary of State, where the political fund reports are filed.

Project managers at the Citizens' Research Foundation, first Katharine C. Fischer, then Barbara D. Paul, recruited the authors and researchers and supervised throughout. Carol Weiland assisted in early editing, in some cases substantially rewriting chapters in order to make them uniform in the information presented and comparable in length. Gladys Topkis of The Free Press ably did final editing. Others who contributed importantly to the final product were Lynn Fielden-Smith and Gloria Cornette.

The officers and members of the Board of Trustees of the Citizens' Research Foundation gave their encouragement and cooperation.

THE CONTRIBUTORS

HERBERT E. ALEXANDER is currently Director of the Citizens' Research Foundation, a position he has held since 1958. He has a B.A. degree from the University of North Carolina, an M.A. from the University of Connecticut, and a Ph.D. in political science from Yale University. He has taught at Princeton University and at the University of Pennsylvania and has served as a consultant to the President of the United States, the Comptroller General of the United States, and the Office of Federal Elections at the General Accounting Office, as well as the New Jersey Election Law Enforcement Commission, the U.S. Senate Select Committee on Presidential Campaign Activities, the New York State Board of Elections, and the Illinois Board of Elections.

Dr. Alexander has written extensively on matters relating to money in politics. His most recent book is *Financing the 1972 Election* (1976).

DAVID S. BRODER, associate editor of *The Washington Post*, was awarded the Pulitzer Prize in 1973 for distinguished political commentary. In 1972, 100 leading political journalists surveyed by American University named him America's most respected political reporter. His twice-weekly syndicated column is carried by newspapers across the nation.

Before joining the national reporting staff of *The Washington Post*, Mr. Broder covered national politics for the *New York Times*, the *Washington Star*, and the *Congressional Quarterly*. He has covered every national political campaign and convention since 1956. He is the author of *The Party's Over: The Failure of Politics in America* (1972) and, with Stephen Hess, of *The Republican Establishment* (1967). He is also a frequent contributor to magazines, a guest on radio and television political panels and interview shows, and a sought-after speaker to college and civic audiences.

WILLIAM ENDICOTT is a member of the staff of the *Los Angeles Times*, attached to that paper's Sacramento bureau. Before joining the *Times*, he was city editor of *The Sacramento Union*, city editor of *The Modesto Bee*, and a staff member of *The Courier-Journal* (Louisville, Ky.). In 1975 he won the Greater Los Angeles Press Club award for the year's top story—on the growing political power of public employees. He is also a winner of the California Taxpayers Association award for reporting on state government finance and the California Association of Retarded award for stories describing the plight of the retarded in California.

JON FORD has been political editor of the *Austin American-Statesman* since 1974. Previously, he was Austin bureau chief of the *San Antonio Express* and the *San Antonio Evening News*. He once served the latter paper as managing editor and was also press secretary to former Governor Price Daniel. Mr. Ford, who has covered Texas and national politics for more than twenty years, has won numerous awards for political and interpretive writing. He has contributed many articles on Texas politics and government to *The Christian Science Monitor*.

JOHN W. GARDNER served as Secretary of Health, Education and Welfare from July 1965 to March 1968. Following his resignation he became Chairman of the National Urban Coalition and, in October 1970, Chairman of Common Cause.

At the time of his appointment to the Cabinet by President Johnson, Mr. Gardner was President of the Carnegie Foundation of New York and the Carnegie Foundation for the Advancement of Teaching. He served on President Kennedy's Task Force on Education and as chairman of President Johnson's Task Force on Education and the White House Conference on Education (1965). In 1964, Mr. Gardner was awarded the Presidential Medal of Freedom, the highest civil honor in the United States.

He was the editor of President Kennedy's book *To Turn the Tide* and is the author of *Excellence, Self-Renewal, No Easy Victories, The Recovery of Confidence*, and *In Common Cause*.

ROBERT HEALY, currently executive editor of the *Boston Globe*, has been covering Massachusetts politics since James Michael Curley occupied the Mayor's office in Boston and has covered many national campaigns as well. A former Neiman Fellow, he was a member of the team that won the *Globe*'s first Pulitzer Prize, in 1966. He has been on the *Globe* staff for over thirty years as an editorial writer, Washington bureau chief, and political editor.

JEROME KELLY writes editorials for *The Baltimore Sun*, specializing in state government and politics. He began covering politics in 1963 and has actively participated, as a reporter or editorial writer, in every major campaign since then. He received a Nieman Fellowship in 1970–71 and while at Harvard University researched "conflict of interest in public life."

WILLIAM MANSFIELD, chief of *Miami Herald*'s state capital bureau since 1965, has also covered local government and politics in Ohio, Kentucky, and Florida. In 1964 the *Herald*'s Palm Beach County bureau, which he then headed, received a national Izzak Walton League award for its conservation coverage, and four years later his stories on failing insurance companies won a state public-service award from the Florida Society of Newspaper Editors. "The Greening of the Legislature," a series of stories on campaign financing written with Bruce Giles, won the 1973 state public-service award and the Green Eye-shade award from the Atlanta, Ga., chapter of Sigma Delta Chi.

GERARD J. McCULLOUGH is a political writer on the staff of the *Philadelphia Bulletin*. He has also worked for United Press International in Philadelphia and in the Harrisburg bureau of the *Philadelphia Evening and Sunday Bulletin*, covering state government.

AL POLCZINSKI has covered city, county, and state government for the *Wichita* (Kans.) *Eagle* since 1955. Previously he was a reporter and managing editor of the *McCook* (Neb.) *Daily Gazette*.

HOWELL RAINES is currently political editor of the *St. Petersburg* (Fla.) *Times*. He has also worked for the *Birmingham* (Ala.) *Post-Herald*, WBRC-Television, the *Tuscaloosa News*, the *Birmingham News*, and the *Atlanta Constitution*, for which, as political editor, he covered the 1974 campaigns in Georgia. He is working on an oral history of the civil-rights movement in the South, to be published in 1977.

SAM ROBERTS is chief political correspondent of *The New York Daily News*, for which he has covered New York City and state government and politics since 1969. He won Honorable Mention in the Newspaper Guild's Page One Awards for investigative reporting for a series on the influence of the banking industry on the legislature, and he is co-author (with Michael Kramer) of *I Never Wanted to Be Vice President of Anything* (1976), an investigative biography of Nelson Rockefeller.

BRIAN T. USHER is a statehouse correspondent in Columbus, Ohio, for the *Akron Beacon Journal*, covering the legislature and state politics. He has covered politics in the Midwest for nine years, the past seven in Ohio. He is also an Ohio stringer for *Newsweek* and *The New York Times*.

ONE

INTRODUCTION

RETHINKING REFORM

Herbert E. Alexander

The Supreme Court decision on campaign financing (in *Buckley v. Valeo*) has reopened some important questions about election reform. While the impact of the January 1976 ruling cannot yet be fully measured, it clearly will affect the direction of future efforts and the fate of recent reforms, in the states as well as at the Federal level.

Before the Court decision, the United States was at the crest of a wave of reform reminiscent of the one at the turn of the century, when the excesses of the party bosses and the corporations fueled the Populist and muckraker movements. The more recent reforms began before Watergate but were catalyzed by it and, in some states, by local scandals as well. The system of financing campaigns with private funds—contributed largely by wealthy individuals and organized groups—had long been criticized on the ground that such donors may thereby gain undue influence with candidates and, if the candidates are successful, with elected officials. In the early 1970's, opposition to these funding practices bore fruit in new election laws on the Federal level and in many states.

In addition to the Federal Election Campaign Act of 1971 and its 1974 Amendments, on which the Court ruled, new laws were passed by 49 states between 1972 and 1976. The Federal law, which applied to Presidential and Congressional elections, instituted strict requirements for the reporting of campaign contributions and expenditures, limited the amount of money that could be collected and spent, made public funds available

1

for Presidential contenders, and established the Federal Election Commission to administer and enforce the law. Although approaches to the regulation of campaign finance differed widely from state to state, as did specific provisions, most states enacted statutes covering at least some of these areas of regulation.

The decision in *Buckley v. Valeo* altered the face of that reform. It upheld public disclosure and public financing—considered by many to be the most desirable features of the Federal law—and rejected limitations on candidates' campaign expenditures and on direct expenditures by individuals and groups, the most restrictive aspects of the law. The Court found that the First Amendment right to freedom of expression was abridged by these limitations on the use of money to promote the nomination or election of a candidate and hence overturned them. The decision closely followed the recommendations of the American Bar Association and adhered to positions expressed in the political science and legal literature over the years.

The Supreme Court's establishment of guidelines means that at least some portions of most state laws will have to be revised or repealed. Where no legislative action is taken to repeal laws that are now unconstitutional, litigation may ensue. Some election commissions may simply stop enforcing the affected election laws. Many existing state laws and bills proposed at both the state and Federal levels will bring further challenges in the courts.

But these guidelines are only one factor in a necessary reopening of the reform debate. The reforms that survive this landmark decision will also need to be studied carefully to consider their possible consequences for the electoral process. Most of the laws recently enacted, even had they been unchallenged, would warrant serious examination. Some were in effect during the 1974 elections for the first time. Some have been enacted since and have yet to be tested. As the chapters in this book demonstrate, some of these statutes were hastily put together, without much understanding of their potential effects, quite apart from questions about their constitutionality. Public demand and political pressure often conflicted, producing laws with strange configurations. This, of course, is a regular occurrence in the framing of legislation, but in election reform, where laws affect the democratic process itself and the legitimacy of governmental actions is at stake, the consequences can be enormous.

It is now up to lawmakers and informed citizens to deal with the implications of the Supreme Court ruling for existing and proposed laws, to correct the imperfections of statutes now in effect, and to enact new legislation. In order to do so intelligently and responsibly, the public and its elected officials will need information on how the campaign-financing system has operated up to now and how effective recent reforms have been. This volume is an invaluable source of such information.

Two years before the Supreme Court considered the issue, the Citizens' Research Foundation embarked upon an exploration of campaign financing at the state level, under a grant from the Carnegie Corporation. The project's objectives were to assemble information about campaign-finance practices in the states, about recent reforms in state campaign-finance laws, and about the effects of these reforms on the state elections in 1974. The long-range objective was to increase public awareness of these issues and thus make more informed political judgments possible. The 10 state profiles in this volume are the result of the CRF project.

The states whose 1974 election practices are examined here represent a cross-section of the nation in terms of population, geography, and character. Each had a gubernatorial contest in 1974, making it possible to examine funding processes at the highest statewide level, and all had some form of campaign-finance disclosure laws, so that information gathering was possible. While the theoretical aspects of election financing are touched on here, this book is aimed instead at providing practical information about how the state systems actually work and how change is (or is not) accomplished. Because the press has access to information about campaign funds and the capacity to articulate it for the public, experienced political reporters in the state capitols were chosen to write the articles.

It was recognized at the project's inception that the new state laws would be scrutinized after the 1974 experience and that modifications were likely. It was also anticipated that court tests at both the Federal and the state levels would require changes in some of the laws. Now that the Supreme Court has ruled on the Federal law, establishing important guidelines for the states, the material in this book takes on added importance. As the need develops to analyze further and to change existing state laws and to enact new ones, the experiences explored in this volume will suggest what is feasible and desirable in the several aspects of regulation: disclosure, contribution and expenditure limitations, public financing, and enforcement.

Disclosure

Disclosure, the most basic element of any attempt to regulate campaign financing, has been upheld by the Supreme Court. The Court found that the value of opening the financing process to public scrutiny outweighed the expressed concern that disclosure might result in retaliation against contributors, especially donors to unpopular minority causes, and thus inhibit participation in the electoral process. As the Court noted, disclosure of campaign contributions and expenditures permits the electorate to make informed choices among candidates, at least as far as financing is concerned, discourages corruption, and is a necessary means to monitor compliance with other campaign laws.

In the past, patterns of political giving were known only partially, for campaign contributions and expenditures were either undisclosed or ineffectively regulated. The outlines of campaign finance could thus be discerned only by plodding research or through the dramatic cases that occasionally came to public attention. Today, every state except North Dakota requires some form of disclosure of campaign money (although as recently as 1972 nine states were without such a law). That the stories revealed in this volume could be told at all is a tribute to the success of the disclosure facet of reform. Great variation exists among the state disclosure laws as to frequency of reporting, amount of information required about donors and recipients, and minimum contributions or expenditures that must be reported. These laws are a major component of the "sunshine laws" which in some states include restrictions on conflicts of interest on the part of government officials, and in some cases combine lobbying registration and disclosure, with laws explicitly prohibiting gifts or campaign contributions of more than a certain value from lobbyists to officeholders or candidates.

Disclosure is the keystone of any attempt to deal with the problem of political money and to make elected officials accountable to the public. As long as the public is kept in the dark about the identity of large contributors or special interests and the extent of their participation, it is impossible to pinpoint cases in which influence on government can be related to campaign donations. Reporting of expenditures as well as contributions is necessary to reveal any possible misuse of funds. So is the prohibition of untraceable cash contributions of any significant size. In order to be effective, disclosure laws must require that reports be filed before elections as well as after to give the public a chance to use the information in making its choice among candidates.

Whether disclosure is required for its own sake—on the principle that abuses can be regulated through an informed electorate—or as the basis for the enforcement of other provisions, it is the essential ingredient of campaign-finance regulation. Disclosure may well take on greater importance in the future, since some of the other methods of regulating political financing have been rejected by the Court.

Limitations

State laws limiting campaign contributions and spending embody the efforts of lawmakers to control large donations, with their potential for corruption, to minimize financial disparities among candidates, and to reduce the opportunities for abuse. A corollary aim is to encourage the participation of ordinary citizens in the financing of campaigns through small donations. In some cases—as in the Federal law—contributions by candidates and their immediate families have also been limited, in an effort to reduce the advantages of the wealthy in the political arena. Expenditures by individuals and groups in support of, but independent of, candidates were regulated because of their potential use to circumvent campaign-expenditure ceilings.

The Supreme Court decision upheld limits on contributions to political campaigns by individuals and groups and on total spending by those candidates who accepted public funds (as many Presidential candidates have done under the 1974 Federal law). It struck down all other limits, reasoning that in this age of mass communications an expenditure for speech is essentially the same as speech, and that First Amendment rights are consequently infringed by limitations. The Court explained that direct spending—by a candidate on his own behalf, and by individuals or groups independent of a candidate but to promote his nomination or election—was so clearly related to speech itself as to come under First Amendment protection. It therefore emphatically rejected the government's right to decide the limits of such activity. "In the free society ordained by the Constitution," the Court wrote, "it is not the government but the people—individually as citizens and candidates and collectively as associations and political committees—who must retain control over the quality and range of debate on public issues in a political campaign."

The Court upheld limits on contributions to campaigns by persons other than the candidates because it found such money less clearly related to free speech. The necessity of eliminating the opportunity for corrupt influencing of politicians by large contributors or special interests was seen as sufficient justification for contribution limits. Furthermore, because the Court permitted persons or groups to express their preferences directly by the independent purchase of advertising, as well as by voluntary service, it did not find the free-speech issue compelling with respect to such contributions.

Extensive discussion, new legislation, and additional challenges will clearly result from these rulings, for they affect a large number of states in addition to the Federal Government. Thirty-five states had enacted campaign expenditure limits, with 31 including ceilings on independent spending; some also controlled the amount of money a candidate could spend on his own campaign; and 23 states limited individual and group contributions. Contribution ceilings ranged from $600 in New Jersey to $10,000 in Missouri, with New York putting a $150,000 overall limit on individual contributions to all candidates. (The contribution limits in New York were calculated as a proportion of permitted candidate spending; since limits on spending have been ruled unconstitutional, the status of the contribution limitation is in doubt.) The most common limit is $1,000 per campaign (primary or election), with a $25,000 limit per person per year; these are the limits in Federal law. There also has been great variation in candidates' expenditure ceilings, but these are now applicable only in the few states in which government funding is provided directly to candidates.

By striking down limits on contributions by a candidate to his own campaign but upholding ceilings on contributions by others, the Court has created an anomaly that Congress and the state legislatures will have to resolve. Candidates will once again be able to inject personal funds into their campaigns, limited only by their ability and willingness to spend them. This puts at a considerable disadvantage the opponents of wealthy candidates, who must depend on contributions from individuals or groups which are limited in the amount they may give to any candidate. Thus the Federal law as altered by the Court increases the traditional advantage of the wealthy.

To rectify this inequality, contribution limits could be raised or repealed entirely. The configuration of the Court ruling may lead legislators to decide that the fairest way of dealing with the potential advantage of wealthy candidates is to abandon recently passed contribution ceilings altogether. This would once again open the way for unrestricted participation by monied interests, checked only by the fact of public disclosure or by the provision of partial government funding. But the opportunity for the re-entry of big money still exists in the form of independent expenditures. By permitting these expenditures, the Court also made it possible for those who are bound by limits to draw on support outside the statutory limit.

The Court's judgment that such independent expenditures are aspects of free speech was an important restatement and extension of First Amendment rights, but it does raise a variety of practical problems. If independent expenditures are used as a device to get around limits, they render those limits meaningless. If independent expenditures are used legitimately, they affect the overall spending picture and call into question the effectiveness of limitations. The Supreme Court insisted that there could be no prearrangement or coordination with the candidate when such independent expenditures are made. Hence many such expenditures may be wasteful or counterproductive, raising the policy question of whether it would not be desirable to increase both candidate expenditure limits and contribution limits in order to make it possible to channel such money into the candidate's campaign, where its utility is greater (because it is within the candidate's control) than if it is spent truly independently.

Public Financing

Public financing, as initiated by the Federal Government to fund Presidential campaigns, was upheld by the Court. Challenges to the system of funding minor parties were rejected, and the system of qualifying to receive matching funds in small denominations was upheld. Spending ceilings continue to apply to candidates who accept public funds, although independent expenditures by individuals and groups may be made to promote them.

This decision by the highest court in the Federal system seems to leave intact the public-financing systems in effect in a number of states that had moved similarly to reduce the roles of large contributors and special interests. Eleven states provide some form of direct public support, eight of them through a tax checkoff; 11 others offer a deduction on state income tax for political donations; and three permit a tax credit similar to the Federal one. The states providing direct public funding require candidates to raise a certain proportion of funds on their own, usually in relatively small amounts, in order to qualify for public funds, which are awarded on a matching basis up to a certain maximum. In some states the money goes to political parties, in others directly to candidates; some help to finance both primary and general elections, some only the general election.

Enthusiasm for public financing up to now has been dampened by the recession and by the opposition in some quarters to so radical a change in the system. These factors can be expected to continue to play a role, and the Court ruling injects still other factors that may either foster or deter action to fund elections with public monies. Because public funding is the only Constitutional route to the control of spending, its attractiveness to reformers may be enhanced in the future. But the form remaining after the Court ruling creates two categories of candidates—those who accept public funds and are bound by spending limits, and those who raise funds privately and are not limited in their spending. It will be very difficult to regulate those two categories of candidates fairly. The built-in potential for disparity makes the private route more attractive, but only for candidates with high confidence in their fund-raising appeal or for wealthy candidates willing to spend their own funds. The private option is risky for candidates without a proven track record in raising big money in small sums, at least where contributions are limited.

If free speech in politics means the right to speak effectively, as the Supreme Court decision implies, the decision is further justification for the use of tax dollars to help candidates and political parties reach the electorate. This strengthens the argument that floors, not ceilings, should be enacted, to provide government funds to ensure all qualified candidates minimal access to the electorate. Above such a minimum, candidates could spend as much private money as they could raise. This concept is accepted in democracies around the world, from the Scandinavian countries to Israel, but in these cases money is provided to political parties rather than to candidates. The notion that too much money is spent on politics is, in my opinion, illusory. In fact, the United States devotes a minuscule portion of its massive resources to politics. Acceptance of the goal of achieving more competition in elections means that we may have to spend more, not less, on politics.

Although public subsidies in campaigns evoke much rhetoric for and against, scant attention has been paid to the implications of the various plans for the political system in general and the two-party system in particular. Questions of fairness, cost, administration, and enforcement need to be asked, assumptions challenged, and understanding developed of the conditions that ought to be met if subsidies are to be provided. Public financing is not a panacea, and it will bring fundamental changes in the political structure and electoral processes.

The main design difficulties in public funding concern who should receive the subsidy, and how and when it should be made. The goal of government subsidization is to permit serious candidates to challenge those in power without supporting with significant tax dollars candidates who are merely seeking free publicity, and without attracting so many candidates that the electoral process is degraded. Accordingly, the most difficult policy problems in working out fair subsidies are definitional: how to define major and minor parties in the general election, and to distinguish between serious and frivolous candidates in the prenomination period, without doing violence to equality of opportunity or to "equal protection" under the Constitution.

While it is desirable to increase competition in the electoral arena, there are certain related considerations. One is whether government funding can effectively induce two-party competition in one-party or one-party-dominant areas. Another is whether government dominance of the electoral process will follow government funding.

As the states enact forms of public financing, the large number of elected officials—a hallmark of this country's political system—will become all too obvious. In the United States, over a four-year cycle, more than 500,000 public officials are elected, and far more than that number campaign for nomination. Long ballots require candidates to spend money in the mere quest for visibility, and the long ballot and frequent elections combined bring both voter fatigue and low turnout. As financial pressures mount, states might give increasing consideration to reducing the number of elective offices, thus diminishing the amounts of money (public or private) needed to sustain the electoral system.

Public funding of political campaigns, made doubly attractive by limits on private contributions, may accelerate the trend toward candidate independence and diminish the role of the

parties. The results may be a diminished ability to produce
coherent majorities in legislatures and the nationalization of
personalized politics. This would seem less of a problem in
Presidential campaigns because the party identification of the
candidate is widely known. If public financing directly to candidates is extended to Senatorial and Congressional campaigns
as well, new factionalism and splinter parties might result. At
a time when there is concern about executive encroachment,
any further splintering of Congress or of state legislatures could
further diminish the status of the legislative branch. The parties
can be an important part of the balancing act and therefore
need continuing, not diminishing, relationships with legislators
carrying the party label. Accordingly, ways should be thought
through in which candidate-funding, as least in general elections, can be channeled through the parties. Ultimately, the
way to get more accountability and responsibility in political
finance would seem to be through democratically reformed,
adequately funded political parties, not through increased candidate independence.

The public financing of campaigns is the ultimate tool in the
election reformer's arsenal. Where there is less emphasis on
private money, there is theoretically less chance for corruption
or favoritism. The ruling of the Supreme Court equating campaign spending with free speech recognized that to be heard
effectively in a society of mass communication, speech needs to
be amplified by means of purchased air time, space in the print
media, or through other methods of formulating and dissemi-
nating it. If free speech in politics means the right to speak
effectively, the decision further justifies the use of tax dollars
for campaign purposes, enabling candidates and political parties to reach the electorate more effectively.

Enforcement

The body established by Congress to monitor and enforce
the Federal election law requires reconstitution as a result of
the Court ruling, as does the enforcement machinery in some
of the states. The composition of the Federal Election Commission was found by the Supreme Court to violate the separa-
tion-of-powers provision of the Constitution, since it included
members appointed by the Congress (as well as by the President),
yet had enforcement powers, which are constitutionally the
prerogative of the executive branch. In order to continue to
enforce the law, the Court held that the FEC must be recon-
stituted as a body whose members are all appointed by the

President; states with commissions partially appointed by their legislatures also may have to modify the makeup of these bodies accordingly, depending on their state constitutional provisions.

That such independent, bipartisan bodies must exist is undisputed. Any system of regulating politics is only as good as the machinery to administer and enforce it—machinery that has been notably lacking in most previous efforts to regulate political money. The political pressures inherent in elected or appointed offices such as that of the secretary of state, who until recently has been responsible in most states for administering the law, had ultimately rendered most campaign funding laws less than effective. In order to isolate the administration of the law from such pressures, the Federal Government and 25 states have established independent commissions, falling somewhere between the executive and legislative branches. Some states have given their commissions—most of which have equal bipartisan membership—the power to issue subpoenas and assess penalties for civil violations. Because responsibility for criminal prosecution must remain with the executive branch, the commissions must refer criminal cases to authorized enforcement agents, such as attorneys-general or district attorneys.

But political pressures have not always been absent even in bipartisan commissions, where trade-offs and agreements between the parties not to pursue complaints can occur. And in any case, the quality of enforcement can only be as good as the commitment to the law on the part of the public and the majority of officials. The power of the commissions is dependent to some extent upon such commitment. Perceptions of excesses by some election commissions, both state and Federal, in recent years have met legislative countermeasures in the form of efforts to reduce the power of commissions or change their rulings by statute. The commissions are at once administrator, investigator, auditor, prosecutor, judge, and jury, at least in civil matters, and the combination may produce conflicts of iterest. Commissions must deal impartially and on an even-handed basis with major and minor parties, incumbents and challengers, and independent candidates. They must provide fair administrative procedures and firm adherence to due process in order to protect individual rights.

The Evidence and the Future

Even the most stringent legislation will not wipe out corruption entirely. Bribery, kickbacks, and payoffs are illegal but not uncommon. The aim of reform must be to insulate the electoral system from abuses while assuring fairness and equity. In the past, the campaign-finance laws tended to be evaded or avoided, and administration and enforcement were lax. Now independent commissions bring hope for more durable improvement in the election-law atmosphere.

It is not yet clear, however, that legislation will greatly alter the traditional system of private giving. Only as we learn more about the laws and the environments to which they apply, through investigations such as those reported in this book, will we know how well the laws work and how they change institutions and processes. The profiles on Maryland, Florida, and Texas, which concentrate on how campaigns are actually paid for, indicate that the traditional channels are still open and functioning.

Model statutes—for example, those drafted by the Citizens' Research Foundation—provided some guidance to the Federal Government and the states in drawing up their laws. Common Cause's national model statute will need revision in the light of the Supreme Court decision. The Citizens' Research Foundation model statute (summarized in the Appendix to this book) includes strict disclosure and enforcement provisions, but instead of contribution and spending limits provides for an institution to encourage wider public participation, both monetary and voluntary, in elections and to channel money to candidates and political parties. The model, published in 1974, did not require any revision in light of the Supreme Court decision.

California, Kansas, and Massachusetts—states whose passage of and experience with new political-finance laws are examined in detail here—used different aspects of regulation to deal with election funding. Some of these provisions will have to be modified or eliminated as a result of the Court decision; others will need to be evaluated as to their effectiveness.

Finally, it must be acknowledged that political opposition to reform is potent and possibly increasing as the memory of Watergate fades. Indeed, this may be the most significant factor in the future of reform. Political pressures were the catalyst for some recent laws, and political pressures may lead to their modification or repeal. Such pressures have succeeded in some states in watering down certain provisions and removing others. Some states have passed no significant reform legislation at all. And the legislation that is passed, no matter what its strength, may not be enforced.

Whether the movement toward reform, rechanneled along lines approved by the Supreme Court, continues to spread or abates depends in part on the political situation in states such as Georgia, where campaign-finance legislation was advanced as a political ploy and turned out to be easily circumvented, and Pennsylvania, where no major reforms were enacted. Much depends on public opinion in states such as Ohio and New York, where the relative importance to voters of cleaning up politics and more traditional bread-and-butter issues was not clear in 1974.

Dealing with corruption, real or perceived, and the possibly pernicious influence of money on politics will undoubtedly be more difficult now for those who write, interpret, and enforce the laws. Blanket controls enacted at the Federal level and by many states are no longer acceptable. Those parts of the law that *are* acceptable—disclosure, contribution limits, and public financing—will take on new importance; the search will be for an acceptable balance among them.

The ambiguity of the evidence in some of the states underscores the value of this book. The political process, of which campaign financing is an integral part, is complex. An understanding of its inner workings is an essential prerequisite to intelligent action to modify the system of political funding. The Supreme Court decision and its aftermath should rekindle an interest in the fundamental issues involved in structuring electoral politics in a democracy. The information this volume provides—which until now has been unavailable even to those most concerned about making our political system more responsive and responsible—should go far toward ensuring that the reforms already accomplished and those yet to come will have desirable effects.

The future of American elections will be greatly affected by developments in the states, some of which have moved more steadily and experimentally than the Federal Government in their efforts to deal with political money. The states have proved, in election law, to be the "laboratories of reform" that Justice Louis D. Brandeis once called them. As Brandeis suggested, the advantage of experimentation by the states is that mistakes made in a few will not significantly harm the entire nation, while successes at the state level can serve as models for other states and for Federal law. An understanding of what is happening at the state level is thus crucial at this time of intense activity and debate about political finance and government funding.

TWO

MARYLAND: MONEY TALKS

Jerome Kelly

The most prominent date on Government Marvin Mandel's 1974 campaign calendar was actually May 22, 1973, the night he virtually sewed up his second four-year term. That was the night a $100-a-plate testimonial dinner, the "Four-Star Salute," raised almost $1 million for the incumbent Democratic statewide slate. About 8,000 people filed into the Baltimore Civic Center to toast Governor Mandel, Lieutenant Governor Blair Lee, Comptroller Louis Goldstein, and Attorney General Francis B. Burch. Each flip of the turnstile put Marvin Mandel closer to the full war chest necessary to pay for television commercials, billboards, and brochures and to provide the election-day cash known as "walking-around money" which Democratic Party workers have come to expect. Perhaps even more important than the fact that the $917,000 raised ensured more than adequate funding was the tremendous psychological advantage it gave Mandel over any potential challenger; the result surely would be to dry up sources that might otherwise be tapped by other candidates. And if 1974 were anything like previous years, a lot of the money would filter down to friendly Democrats in the primary, limiting the possibility that candidates lower on the ticket would run independently of the Governor or, if one were so disposed, support a legitimate challenger.

Mandel knew from experience the power of money to help him stake out the top campaign position. He had been chosen Governor in January 1969 by the Maryland General Assembly, which was required by law to select a successor after Governor Spiro T. Agnew became Vice President. They picked Mandel because he was the most powerful man in the legislature—a politician whose strength came from a political cunning that had helped him climb from Baltimore's rough-and-tumble precinct Democratic organization to Speaker of the House of Delegates. During an eight-year reign as Speaker he dealt smoothly and pragmatically with most public issues and built up an impressive list of political IOU's from his fellow legislators. Outside Northwest Baltimore and the State House in Annapolis, Marvin Mandel was not well known, however, and he faced a statewide election in less than two years.

For that reason, almost immediately after his unique selection in 1969, Mandel's advisors moved to make him electable by holding a fund-raiser for the 1970 campaign. They raised $624,000. Four months later R. Sargent Shriver, effervescent brother-in-law of Senator Edward Kennedy, returned home to Maryland after serving as ambassador to France to challenge Mandel for the party nomination. But by the time Shriver got around to organizing, most sources of campaign contributions had dried up. As a result, Shriver dropped his plans to enter the race, for which he later said he would have needed $1 million to wage a successful campaign. "I did have some promise of support, but I didn't see a million dollars," he told an interviewer.

If money could boost a Mandel and block a Shriver, then the Governor's handlers meant to make the most of it. That was why Mandel's political team was selling $100 tickets to a fund-raiser in 1973, 16 months before the voters went to the polls.

Mobilizing the Troops

The Four-Star Salute, and in fact the entire 1974 campaign, were reportedly planned one gray Sunday in January 1973, when the Governor met in Annapolis with approximately 50 persons who came from all parts of the state to see him and his three incumbent ticket mates. According to one participant, the meeting had actually been called by William S. James, then the chairman of the Democratic Party's State Central Committee, which provides year-round housekeeping chores for the party but relies on gubernatorial fund-raisers for expenses.

"I would like to get a feeling whether I could raise as much money for the primary as I raised for the 1970 campaign," the Governor is remembered to have said. Everybody laughed. "He wanted to know whether people wanted him to run again," was the way Irvin Kovens, one of the intimates, described Mandel's thinking.

Kovens was perhaps the most important person at the January meeting. A business entrepreneur and a political power broker since the early 1950's, he was one of several businessmen who opposed an attempt by the late Governor William P. Lane to impose a small tax on retail sales. Governor Lane was successful, but Kovens, a Democrat like the governor, helped defeat Lane in 1952 by backing the Republican nominee, Theodore Roosevelt McKeldin. The taste of politics and fund-raising has remained with Kovens ever since. He has worked mostly on behalf of Democrats, but he has not ignored Republican candidates; in fact, he was instrumental in Spiro Agnew's winning of Baltimore's well-heeled precincts in the 1966 gubernatorial election.

Kovens is, by all accounts, the most powerful figure in Maryland politics. In 25 years he has helped bankroll the state's last four governors. The money he raises for statewide candidates also has its effect on local elections, since much of it filters down to Democratic candidates for more obscure offices. In a very real sense, Kovens is the Democratic Party of Maryland, since he organizes its troops, finances its needs and countersigns its obligations. Politically, he and Mandel grew up together. They came from the same Baltimore city district, the Fifth, and in fact lived in the same neighborhood. About the time Kovens was building a reputation as power broker, Marvin Mandel was moving through the party political structure into the House of Delegates. As Mandel began establishing himself in Annapolis, the two grew to be more than just neighbors. Kovens helped Mandel to achieve positions of legislative power, and Mandel nearly always repaid the debt by reflecting Kovens' political interests. Finally, in the 1974 election, Kovens outperformed all previous efforts for his good friend and protégé.

The Four-Star Salute—the central fund-raising event of the campaign—was a well-orchestrated project. The state was divided into four specific regions assigned to three of the candidates and one appointed cabinet officer. Lieutenant Governor Lee was given Montgomery County, the richest of America's counties in median family income, and with the help of some of its businessmen Lee managed to raise between $80,000 and $90,000, according to Kovens. Attorney General Burch, with friends everywhere, drew close to $100,000. Frederick Wineland, Mandel's Secretary of State, was in charge of the growing and heavily populated Prince Georges County, and he raised a little less than Lee. Comptroller Goldstein, who comes from rural Maryland, was the best known and most popular of the

candidates on the ticket and thus did not need the financial
resources of the others; he drew under $20,000.

Two of the more prominent ticket salesmen for the Four-Star
Salute were W. Dale Hess and Harry W. Rodgers 3d, but Kovens
was unable to recall whether they actually were at the Governor's Mansion that wintry Sunday. Long-time friends of Mandel, Hess and Rodgers are partners in Tidewater Insurance Associates, Inc., a firm whose business interests have grown and
diversified during the Mandel years in office. Mandel has spent
a great deal of time fishing with Rodgers on his luxurious yacht
and at homes both men own in Southern Florida. Hess served as
majority whip of the House of Delegates when Mandel was
Speaker.

Another Hess and Rodgers holding, Zollman Associates, an
engineering consulting firm, began receiving the largest portion
of contracts for work on a new Chesapeake Bay bridge almost
immediately after Mandel became Governor. Although the firm
was practically unknown in Maryland before then, its assignments on the new bridge increased its public works earning
from $2 million to $5 million. The Board of Public Works, controlled by Governor Mandel, was responsible for awarding the
state contracts. In another instance, Mandel participated with
Rodgers in purchase of a waterfront farm costing a reported
$315,000, of which the Governor put up nothing. By all esti-
mates, the value of the property stood to multiply tremendously
once state health and sewer decisions were made and the land
was subdivided and sold as small lots.

Hess and Rodgers were visibly active in planning and managing the Governor's 1970 campaign. They not only raised
money, they also authorized its spending. But in the years following Mandel's 1970 election, charges of cronyism plagued the
Governor and threatened to become a major campaign issue in
1974. In fact, when Mandel's share in the waterfront land deal
was reported by the *Baltimore Evening Sun* in 1972 and caused
public controversy, the Governor decided to withdraw from the
project. By 1973 Hess and Rodgers had become a political
liability to the Governor's re-election efforts and stayed mostly
in the background of his campaign. Yet, according to the Kovens
ledgers, they raised approximately $90,000 through ticket sales
to the Four-Star Salute.

But Kovens himself was responsible for the largest amount of
money raised by any one person who attended the Annapolis
meeting—$345,000. He gathered most of the money through the
unique sales techniques learned in his family business, which

he has sold but still manages under a contract agreement. The M. Kovens Company carries supplies of men's and women's wear, plus linens and appliances, which are sold by door-to-door salesmen in low-income sections of West Baltimore; the merchandise is paid for on installment, either at the store or to collectors directed by telephone men keeping the accounts current. Kovens conducts his political business from an office on the second floor of the old store.

During an interview, Kovens said his fund-raising activities for candidates begins with a list of 125 names he keeps locked in a desk drawer at his office. In the case of the Four-Star Salute, some of those on the list of 125 pledged to purchase blocks of the $100 tickets outright, which they gave to friends and employees. Others took huge blocks and sold them singly, in pairs, or by tables of ten to their close business associates, according to Kovens. However such sales are handled, a strict watch is kept on who is "buying" what amount, for under Maryland law a ticket sold to a fund-raiser is a political donation and the $2,500 limitation for each election campaign applies.

There are numerous reasons for the willingness of these 125 persons to help Kovens raise such huge amounts. Kovens refuses to divulge those on the list, but from the names he mentions in discussing political contributors and contributions, it is possible to piece together part of the list. Ralph DiChiaro, a successful Baltimore contractor and one-time owner of race tracks in Ohio, for instance, comes up constantly in conversation as a donor. Some of the 125 are long-time business associates like William L. (Little Willie) Adams, who told a Senate investigating committee in 1952 that he had operated a numbers policy but had retired. Adams, a black who now operates several businesses and has a financial interest in a shopping center with the Kovens family, is also a moving force in Baltimore's predominantly black political districts. Joseph H. Rash was also a good bet to have been a member of Kovens select list; a vice president of Food Fair, Inc., before his death in 1974, he was the man who acknowledged delivering free groceries to Vice President Agnew once a week before Agnew was forced to resign. Men like Rash serve on obscure commissions and advisory boards for the state, thus gaining access to government officials and agency heads and a familiarity that may prove useful for zoning, sewer, police, or any kind of attention that could become necessary. Kovens is instrumental in their selection to such bodies.

Kovens himself has achieved more access to the powers of government through political fund-raising than practically any other individual in state history, or so it would seem. For example, Kovens once owned the Charles Town (West Virginia) Race Track; although it theoretically draws on the same bettors' market as Maryland's three powerful horse-racing plants, the Maryland Racing Commission, which regulates the sport, never awarded local tracks conflicting dates with Charles Town during the time it was under Kovens' control.

He has built up legions of friends through his association with racing, and the favors he has performed for them include but are not limited to raising money for their own favorite charities. Ben and Herman Cohen, from whom Kovens purchased the Charles Town Race Track, are owners of the rival Pimlico Race Course in Baltimore. They and members of their families gave a total or $9,000 to the Four-Star Salute. The owners of the Bowie Race Track in southern Maryland gave a total of about $5,600; one of them, Eugene B. Casey, personally gave $1,000; another, Ernest N. Cory, Jr., personally contributed $2,500. The owners of the Laurel Race Course, the third of Maryland's three major tracks, put out $10,000 to the Four-Star Salute fund-raiser. Kovens, a man who counsels the Governor on such things as appointments to the Racing Commission, is difficult to refuse when he comes calling for a political contribution.

The same is true of his power over wholesale and retail liquor and beer operators. Each of Maryland's 24 subdivisions has its own liquor board, a state regulatory agency whose individual members are appointed by the Governor. The huge amount of cash recorded on the Four-Star contributions reports from alcoholic beverage interests was due primarily to Kovens's ability to turn the political screws when and if it is necessary.

By the time all 125 Kovens super salesmen were rolling in early 1973, the success of the Four-Star Salute was assured. Ultimately 1,000 persons bought tickets as a direct or indirect result of Kovens' involvement. One of his helpers sold 180 of these $100 tickets.

One group tapped by Kovens to aid his fund-raising drive comprised the administrators and secretaries of large state agencies; a large number of tickets were sold or distributed by high-ranking officials, including members of Governor Mandel's executive staff, the director of the Maryland Lottery, the chief deputy comptroller, two deputy attorneys general, and the deputy state public defender. The state and corporate bureau-crats who bought or were given the tickets were expected to at-tend. Directly or indirectly they owed their livelihood to the administration, the healthy economy it encouraged, and the man who made it function.

But not all ticket buyers were there. As one purchaser of 10 unused tickets later explained, "It is not important whether you are counted at the Civic Center; what is important is that you be counted on the Governor's contribution list."

The average Marylander probably didn't recognize 99 per-cent of the names on that list when it was disclosed. The big donors, however, were quite familiar to those who functioned in the corridors and closets of the executive and legislative branches of state government. The reasons they gave were prob-ably equally familiar to those who knew Maryland politics and government. There were, for example, James H. Doyle, Jr., and his law partner, Theodore Sherbow, who together gave $2,300. Doyle is the busiest lobbyist in Annapolis, a man whose success depends on access to the administration and the General As-sembly. Irene Pollin is not a big newsmaker either. She ap-peared as a $2,500 contributor, just above the $1,000 donation from her husband, Abe, owner of the Washington Bullets basketball team and Washington Capitals hockey team. A year earlier Pollin had been granted state permits to build the Capi-tal Center, an elaborate home for his sports enterprises in the Maryland suburbs, despite considerable opposition from en-vironmentalists and neighborhood improvement groups in the area.

Some givers managed to slip by the 1968 state law that limits political donations to $2,500 by an individual or firm in the primary and general elections, or a total of $5,000 for both. Generous donors like Abe Pollin legally avoided the limit by having wives or other close relatives donate in their own names. More typical of the split donation for Mandel's fund-raiser was the Kay family, owners of a large development firm that oper-ates in the Maryland suburbs of Washington. Jerome D. Kay and his wife, Barbara, each gave the $2,500 limit; Stanley G. Kay, Jerome's brother, and his wife, Stephanie, also contributed $2,500 each. The family gift thus totaled $10,000, just for the primary. Had they chosen to, the Kays could have legally given another $10,000 to Mandel in the general election campaign.

Some Mandel boosters weren't even Marylanders. Contribu-tors like Kaiser Engineering of Oakland, California, and Irvin F. Mendenhall, of the Los Angeles firm of Daniel, Mann, Johnson and Mendenhall, each gave $2,500 apparently because of their delight with the administration's interest in them. Both companies had won lucrative $22 million consulting contracts from the state for work on the Baltimore Mass Transit System.

Another maximum giver was Max W. Jacobs of Buffalo, whose Emprise Corporation controls Sportservice, exclusive vendor at Baltimore's Memorial Stadium. The Governor's interest in building a new downtown stadium would mean that Sportservice would have to renegotiate its contract with the state.

For years unions and corporations in Maryland were ineligible to give to political campaigns, but the law was amended in 1967, which happened to be Spiro Agnew's first legislative session as Governor. Kovens said it made life for the fund-raiser much easier, since big contributors could then deduct the expense from corporate taxes.

Many on the list of donors are state regulated, and their donations reflect the incumbent's power and influence over special legislation. More than 80 liquor dealers gave $27,000, most through their state trade associations. Developers, who require sewer permits from the state, tossed in $40,000 through more than 30 gifts. Approximately $7,800 came from nursing homes; $9,300 from drug stores, most licensed to sell alcoholic beverages; $5,860 from real estate interests; $9,200 from lending institutions and their executives; and $33,600 from race tracks and the people who make money from them.

Even after accounts for the huge fund-raiser were closed out, contributions from special interests continued pouring in. One belated gift—a total of $4,600, with individual contributions of $500–$700 each— came from a small group of liquor dealers on August 14, 1973, two months after the Governor had vetoed unfavorable legislation that would have severely hampered their operations.

Despite the fact that a few waiters and bartenders picketed the caterer, who had hired nonunion help for the Four-Star Salute, union leaders tossed $80,000 into the kitty for the purchase of tickets. And the governor's friends organized a counter-picket across the street, composed of other AFL-CIO unions eager to express faith in the administration.

Of all those susceptible to the political bite, architects, engineers, and contractors traditionally have given the most in Maryland. But a traumatic upheaval was about to overtake Maryland's well-fed political system and some of its traditions —especially this one.

Investigations and Revelations

For years Marylanders never questioned the huge sums of money raised on behalf of incumbent officeholders. By 1973, however, political developments required a closer and more critical look. Not only was the Watergate saga unfolding in shocking detail; even more immediate was an intensive investigation conducted by the U.S. Attorney in Baltimore—an inquiry that was beginning to indicate that not all donations by special interests to local and state politicians went to their reelection efforts. In the office of George Beall, the Federal prosecutor, a troubling picture was emerging of the relations between elected officials and public works consultants, especially engineers and architects. The inquiry concentrated first on Baltimore County, a large suburban area surrounding Baltimore city that for years had been considered a haven for political grafters, though few had actually been caught and prosecuted. Beall's office wasn't looking for the scalp of any specific politician, or so it said, but sought instead to get to the core of corruption itself, a condition that was later to be described as a "long-standing system" of payoffs in Maryland.

Most area residents accurately speculated that the investigation would lead to N. Dale Anderson, the brash Baltimore County executive. But by early summer a new and surprising name popped up on the political cocktail circuit: Spiro T. Agnew, who had been Baltimore County executive before Anderson and whose swift rise to the Governorship and later the Vice Presidency was based largely on his passionate speeches in support of law and order. Many of Agnew's friends and neighbors found it difficult to believe such a symbol of virtue could be involved in a kickback scheme.

On August 23, the Federal Government indicted Dale Anderson on 39 counts of bribery and extortion from several consultant engineers and architects who sought and received nonbid county contracts. A deeper examination of the charges implied that the practices finally brought to light in the Beall investigations were not just signs of personal weakness, but indicated weakness within the institution of government itself. Most observers realized that the men involved with Anderson were also involved in bidding for contracts in state and other local governments as well. Local law permitted most elected leaders in Maryland to select without bids consultants needed to design bridges, highways, courthouses, and other public works.

At the state level, authority to grant such awards on a nonbid basis rests with the Board of Public Works, which consists of the

Governor, the Comptroller, and the state Treasurer, who is selected by the General Assembly but is often approved by the Governor. Because state projects are more numerous and expensive, the contracts awarded by the Board of Public Works are often much fatter than those handed out in city halls and county courthouses. According to four confessed participants, Spiro Agnew as Governor exacted money from consultant engineers in return for nonbid state contracts issued. The possible extent of such practices is suggested in a statement by Agnew on the day he resigned as Vice President and pleaded no contest to a felonious count of income tax evasion: "My acceptance of contributions was part of a long-established pattern of political fund-raising in the state."

Anderson's indictment and Agnew's resignation affected Mandel's campaign, even though the main fund-raising event was over. Although Maryland law requires that campaign donations be reported 7 days before and 30 days after an election, the Mandel organization had wanted an early accounting of the Four-Star Salute—part of the strategy of scaring potential challengers by showing them the bankbook. During June and July the campaign treasurer, a very busy accountant named Donald Webster, was trying to find time from his many clients to unravel the dinner receipts. The Governor wanted the report out, and Webster was doing his best to comply. No reason was officially stated for the delays, but reporters suspected that the Governor's fund-raisers were concerned about the investigations by Beall's office and the links they might later show to the Four-Star Salute. "We have nothing to hide," Mandel told his weekly press conference more than once. "Believe me, I want the report out as soon as it can be made available, and Don Webster knows it."

The report was still not out when Governor Mandel announced, after the Anderson indictment in August, that he would return all money contributed to his Four-Star Salute by consultants who did nonbid work for the state. All told, the rebates amounted to approximately $54,000 from more than 40 engineers and architects. It was to be two more months, however, before the Webster report was issued and the names of these donors would be known. The list, containing 3,180 names, was finally published in October, a few days after Agnew resigned.

Some of the names turned up again in places that tended to raise questions about the fine line between campaign contributions and bribes of the type attributed to Anderson and Agnew. When the *Baltimore Sun* found that 30 contributors to the

Four-Star Salute had been awarded nonbid state contracts by the Board of Public Works at its November 1973 meeting, it asked Governor Mandel about the possible connection. The 30 ticket purchasers were only a small percentage of the total number of recipients of state awards, but the *Sun* found that they were "regular" recipients.

"There isn't any evidence of anybody using campaign contributions to get anything," Mandel told the *Sun* following the Public Works meeting. "Nobody has ever come to me and said, 'I gave.' If a $2,500 contribution [the maximum under law] can be used to sway someone, he doesn't belong in office." The Governor also stated his belief that most people who give to campaigns do so because they just want to rub elbows with politicians and other businessmen: "People want to be able to tell their friends they were talking to the Governor last night."

Not all of the 3,180 donors to the Four-Star Salute, most of whom do business with the state, share Mandel's view. "You should be friendly with the Governor," said Edward J. Courtney, head of the Baltimore Building and Construction Trade Council, which pumped $2,500 into the Four-Star collection box, probably through Irvin Kovens. "If you have a problem, at least you have a guy you can talk to." Gerald Friedman, an executive with the Atlantic National Life Insurance Company and another $2,500 giver, agreed: "You never know when you might need a favor."

Governor Mandel frequently has said that he never personally has sought a political contribution. That is probably true; Maryland candidates are not in the habit of raising their own campaign funds. However, as Lieutenant Governor Lee and Attorney General Burch did, they will normally pledge to help the "ticket" through fund-raising friends or committees, which in turn funnel the money directly to organizations like the Four-Star Salute. Most candidates do not want to be responsible if anything goes wrong. Mandel, and other governors before him, let brokers like Irvin Kovens collect all the money and treasurers like Donald Webster sign all the necessary reports. But the governor knows who gives.

In the autumn of 1973, before the list of Four-Star contributors was disclosed, both Governor Mandel and Lieutenant Governor Lee were placing heavy pressure on Dr. Neil Solomon, Secretary of Health, to release a special permit to the Kay family for a $25 million apartment complex the Kays wanted to build in Prince Georges County. As it turned out, the Kay donations had come from the Lieutenant Governor's share of total contributions, and Lee himself applied most of the pressure on behalf of the development. When Solomon refused to budge, the request was taken before a health review board appointed by Mandel, and the permit was signed. The Kays' $10,000 contribution was returned, however, after the maneuvers were revealed in the press.

The Reaction

By the end of 1973, Governor Mandel was becoming sensitive to questions relating to the Four-Star Salute, which was being associated in the public mind with Watergate and Agnew. Although no Democratic or Republican challenger had yet emerged, he sensed that money could have a debilitating effect on his campaign as one of the issues the enemy—whoever it turned out to be—was sure to hammer away at.

The Baltimore and Washington press were meticulously combing campaign donations to the Four-Star Salute for evidence of significant relations between the administration and the persons and firms doing business with it. The pressure applied on behalf of the Kays was a case in point. Two Baltimore papers played it on page one, and several follow-up stories resulted from gubernatorial press conferences and the reactions of Mandel's political enemies. Though Marylanders had seemingly become hardened to accounts of *quid pro quo* in government, the Governor had no way of telling what effect the story might have in the light of unfolding scandals in Washington.

Thus, when the General Assembly opened its 90-day session in January of the election year, Mandel had begun to show an outward concern for the corrupting influences money had had on Maryland politics—by which he meant, he said, not genuine campaign contributions to organizations like his own, but payoffs in return for government contracts such as had been revealed in the Anderson and Agnew cases. By executive order, and with great fanfare, Mandel established a task force to study a new system of awarding state work to architects and engineers. The task force's recommendation that contracts be awarded mostly through negotiation and, in some instances, competitive bidding was quickly adopted.

In a state-of-the-state message to the legislature on January 16, Mandel declared his intention to restore the state's good name: "Any honest assessment of our condition must begin with openness and frankness. I neither indict the past nor abridge this solemn responsibility. I do not apologize to the nation, but I pledge the future of this state. Maryland, over the past year, has become a household word to many Americans—a postmark for greed, for corruption, for kickbacks and payoffs, for the quick fix and easy ethical standards, for a way of life that is less than honorable."

The Governor was referring to kickbacks passed in white envelopes to ranking elected and appointed officials. But it is difficult to understand how he could expect lawmakers and their constituents to distinguish kickbacks from large campaign contributions. It may be true that Agnew and Anderson, as alleged, pocketed impressive sums of money for their personal use, and that the Four-Star Salute Committee merely took contributions to finance the campaign of the Governor and his running mates. Still, many of those who give large campaign donations and those who grease the palms of grafters do it with the same goal in mind: to tap the millions of dollars awarded in public works contracts. In either case, the public suffers as a direct result, for no matter what form the money takes, nonbid contracts awarded to a preferred group ultimately cost more in tax dollars, if only because of the additional overhead a group must invest to gain a favored position.

But the Governor, according to reforms he later offered the legislature, was more interested in tightening regulations dealing with architects and engineers, his favorite scapegoats. One of his proposals, to give regulatory agencies the power to revoke or suspend licenses of those who violate ethical standards, had no trouble being enacted into law. The other Mandel bill sought to ban from state business those who admitted, or were convicted of, bribing or attempting to bribe a state official. George Beall went to Annapolis to oppose that bill before a legislative committee, and it failed as a result. Apparently the lawmakers were sufficiently pursuaded by Beall that any punitive threat to architects and engineers would inhibit his ongoing investigation into Maryland corruption. Consultants, he argued, had been instrumental in providing testimony and evidence in his cases against Agnew and Anderson. The argument may have been valid from a prosecutor's point of view, but the Mandel bill requiring ethical standards would have provided a little preventive law.

The only reform the Governor sent to the legislature that dealt directly with campaign financing was a proposal to limit cash contributions to $100. "I'm convinced that cash is the contemporary evil in campaigns," Mandel said, referring to Watergate. In fact, his attempt to set cash limits was a campaign decision already made by Republican Charles McC. Mathias, Maryland's senior U.S. Senator, and by many other candidates for public office in 1974.

The Governor's response to political corruption seemed, to many senators, delegates, and newsmen, to be too timid. He was seeking to limit the activities of a small group of consultants who were not central to the political process but made no moves to restore public confidence by strengthening, or seeking to strengthen, state laws dealing with officials convicted of conflict of interest, malfeasance, and extortion.

The Challengers

The Four-Star Salute had set up the incumbent Democratic administration for the 1974 campaign by tapping most of the state's big contributors—who weren't likely to spend as lavishly on any challengers—and by scaring off the opposition. And if the potential opposition weren't intimidated by this show of strength, they should have been by the fact that Watergate and state scandals helped dry up any remaining money sources. For by the spring of 1974, businessmen and corporations that had given in past campaigns were playing hard to get. Even Governor Mandel must have been glad he collected his $1 million when he did. As John D. Copanos, who had given $500 to Mandel in 1969 but contributed nothing in 1973–74, told the *Baltimore Evening Sun*, "I'm a man who goes by percentages, and the percentage [of bad politicians] in Maryland is a little alarming." Others interviewed by the *Evening Sun* concurred: They were embarrassed by the number of political figures who had solicited their money and gone on to disgrace. And it was noted that architects, engineers, and contractors were particularly reluctant to give, "because of their involvement or because of their fear," as the campaign treasurer for one of the eventual challengers noted.

Under the circumstances, any challenge to Mandel would have been surprising; yet four candidates entered the Democratic primary. They didn't get very far, but they entered.

The most interesting challenger was Wilson K. Barnes, a wealthy 67-year-old associate judge on the state Appeals Court who had resigned in protest of the administration's cronyism and spending policies. He had never run for statewide office before, but boldly vowed to offset the governor's war chest by raising $500,000 to conduct his own media blitz. It was a considerable task, even for a man of Judge Barnes's means. But Barnes, a political novice when he entered the race in May, had learned the hard truth by late summer; he wound up raising only $168,640.

More than $136,000 of Barnes' money was in "loans" from family and friends; most of the rest was contributed by the same

sources. Maryland law permits candidates for statewide offices
or the U.S. Senate to contribute up to $20,000 to their own
campaigns, but there is no limit on the amount a candidate or
members of his family can give in loans. The requirement is not
that a loan must be repaid, only that it be reported in semi-
annual filings in Annapolis until it is repaid. According to
records filed in March 1975, Barnes still had outstanding loans
from his unsuccessful campaign nearly eight months earlier. In
fact, the only loan he was recorded as having returned was one
of $50,000 from his wife.

Under Maryland law the political loan permits the candidate
to circumvent the $20,000 limit on personal donations to his or
her own campaign. It also encourages the wealthy candidate to
transfer funds through family accounts so that they may be used
as loans that go unpaid for years. Thus Barnes could let his
debts run indefinitely if he and his debtors don't mind; or, depending on how accounts are kept, a close family member
could hold him harmless for any debt. Although Barnes probably intends to pay back his political obligations, others may
play footloose with what appears to be a serious loophole in
election law in Maryland and elsewhere.

The only other government figure to announce his candidacy
for the Democratic gubernatorial nomination was George N.
Snyder, then the majority leader in the state Senate and a persistent critic of the Mandel administration who had published
a book entitled *Beyond the Game Plan*, which described what
he considered the reckless abuses of executive power over the
past five years. Synder clearly hoped to exploit the book for
political purposes, which wasn't a bad idea considering its message—that a campaign contribution to the Governor was an investment in the future, and any Marylander who believed that
a contributor was willing to give $2,500 or $5,000, or $10,000
without getting something in return was deluding himself. But
lack of money turned out to be the main reason George Snyder
withdrew from the Democratic contest. After raising only
$10,000, he decided to return the money and quit the race.

Two other Democrats had the temerity—and naïveté—to
challenge the incumbent: One was Morgan L. Amaimo, a Baltimore lawyer and perennial candidate for political office, who
raised a little more than $2,000 and spent a little less. The
other was Howard L. Gates, a home builder in the Baltimore
area, who raised and spent over $4,000.

Though he drew fewer votes than any of Mandel's opponents,
Gates undoubtedly caused the Governor more worry than all
the rest put together. Gates held a dinner-dance June 27 to raise

campaign funds and within a few days Romeo L. Valianti, head
of the state Amusement and Admissions Tax Division, notified
the candidate that he owed 10 percent of the receipts because
an orchestra had entertained.

If Valianti had known what he was getting into, he would
have left Gates, the musicians, and the paltry $110 in taxes he
sought alone. For Gates countered that the Four-Star Salute
had not paid an amusement tax on the $917,000 it raised.
Valianti insisted none was due—that he had personally "stopped
in," as a conscientious tax collector, at the Civic Center the
night of the Mandel fund-raiser and heard no music. But the
Associated Press verified that indeed two musicians had alter-
nated at the organ. "That's news to me," a flustered Valianti
said. "I didn't see anything, I didn't hear anything." It turned
out that Valianti hadn't made a professional stop at the Mandel
affair, but had paid $100 for his ticket like several hundred
other state employees.

Trapped in his own zeal to collect taxes, Valianti spent some
very hot August days hemming and hawing over a decision.
Eventually Attorney General Burch was asked his legal interpre-
tation of the law and back came the unavoidable reply. The
Mandel ticket, which included Burch, owed $85,527. It paid.

Meanwhile, the Republican Party was having a much quieter
but more competitive primary in which money was not a deciding factor. The two candidates were Louise M. Gore and
Representative Lawrence J. Hogan. Gore had spent two terms
in the Maryland legislature, cultivated the Nixon Administration, and wound up as a member of its mission to the United
Nations, after which she became Governor Mandel's token Republican as chairman of his Bicentennial Commission. It surprised some members of the Governor's staff when she entered
the gubernatorial contest, but in hindsight it was probably one
of the best things that happened to him.

By all indications, Gore had little chance against Congressman Hogan. Though they shared basically conservative views,
Hogan seemed bright, aggressive, and articulate in contrast to
Gore, who expressed few opinions, appeared timid, and sometimes stammered. Hogan had also gained national attention as
the first Republican on the House Judiciary Committee to announce his vote for the impeachment of Richard Nixon. But
while this action might please Democratic Maryland, he first
had to get through the primary, and the conservative Republican Party stalwarts considered Hogan a turncoat. His impeachment position no doubt robbed him of the support of some
party functionaries who were vital because of the traditionally

light Republican turnout at the polls. As a result, Gore didn't
have to discuss issues or prove her capabilities. She had the
party's support and won by a comfortable margin.

Hogan outspent Gore, $85,000 to $50,000, and owed $30,000
at the end of the campaign. Judging by the pattern of contributions he received, Hogan's victory had been anticipated as he
commanded broaded financial support, though by no means
could it be compared with the Mandel booty. Even Jerome
Kay, whose family gave $10,000 to Mandel, donated $500 to
Hogan, presumably on the scant possibility that the Republican
might go all the way.

The Mandel ticket spent almost $1 million, raised by the
Four-Star Salute and a few small committees operating more or
less independently, and ended the primary campaign with a
deficit of about $6,000. According to Kovens, the $85,000
amusement tax had jarred the organization. But the lack of
funds didn't worry them greatly, since Gore was not considered
a serious challenger. Nonetheless, "incidental" expenses would
have to be met, and someone estimated that the Governor
needed another $500,000 to carry him past the November 5
election. (His ticket mates had no opposition.)

To avoid the embarrassment of another Four-Star Salute,
Kovens and his friends decided to hold a fund-raiser at the end
of October under the auspices of the Democratic State Central
Committee. To politicians and longtime observers, this was a
transparent maneuver. Though the State Central Committee
provides the party with a kind of working machinery, it has
never been taken seriously as a fund-raising source. It usually
cannot even pay its own bills without the aid of an incumbent
governor like Mandel, who always sees to it that $35,000 or
$50,000 out of the money he raises at election time goes to
party operating expenses.

Ironically, the Republican Party in Maryland has had better
organizational experience than the Democrats, and with it a
greater independence, probably because they hardly ever have
a governor dictating party line or procedures. By 1974, however, Republican Party fund-raising prospects in Maryland
were dim as the result of a disastrous Salute to Ted Agnew
Night two years earlier. According to reports filed in Annapolis
for the event, many local friends of Agnew had paid $100 a
ticket to honor the then Vice President at Baltimore's Lyric
Theater. But the money had in fact come from the Committee
to Re-elect the President and been laundered in an effort to
impress official Washington with Agnew's local popularity.

State G.O.P. leaders, who promoted the Agnew affair, were caught and prosecuted as a committee by the state's attorney in Annapolis.

The Democratic Party acted only as a front for the same old political machine for purposes of raising money in the fall of 1974. In fact, when an important check issued at party headquarters bounced, the recipient telephoned Kovens, who had to make it good. Everyone knew he was the man in charge, still operating a battery of telephones with 125 super salesmen. Unlike his competitors, who had spent many fruitless hours in 1974 trying to raise campaign funds, Kovens had not lifted a dialing finger since early 1973. In September and October of 1974 most of the normally soft touches were not accepting his calls; many were turning their backs on politics altogether, or at the least taking a long recess. As a result the Mandel team rounded up only $200,000, two-fifths as much as they expected.

Louise Gore, of course, was faring much worse. She had already borrowed heavily from her family, and not even loyal Republicans or anti-Mandel Democrats thought she had a chance to win. Her campaign, waged on pin money that dribbled in on a day-to-day basis, showed the effects. Some days she didn't campaign at all. Other days, when her schedulers found appearances, she would turn up unexpectedly.

In view of Gore's handicaps, the results of the election were something of a surprise. She received 340,000 votes to the Governor's 594,000, a respectable showing.

Expenditures

So much attention is—and, regrettably, must be—devoted to the sources of campaign money and the methods by which it is raised that the other part of the campaign equation, expenditures, is often overlooked. The real purpose of a donation on the part of some contributors may be to gain favor with government officials, and not necessarily to ensure that the candidate pays for advertising, a research staff, or travel expenses. An incumbent, especially a popular one in a visible position such as governor, has such an overwhelming advantage merely by virtue of incumbency that a huge campaign chest is not really necessary. For instance, Florida's Governor Reubin Askew imposed a voluntary $100-per-donor contribution limit in his 1974 re-election campaign, and had no problems either raising money or winning the election. But when the money is there, as it was after the Four-Star Salute, ways tend to be found to spend it, even when the expenditures aren't necessary. Some of the ways are relatively harmless, but others seem to constitute a misuse of funds.

Governor Mandel's managers, for example, authorized $205,000, their largest single expenditure, to an advertising firm that was not required to detail how that money was used. All the agency revealed was that, for nearly a quarter of a million dollars, it bought give-away gimmicks such as emery boards, plastic shopping bags, and lapel buttons promoting Mandel and his ticket mates. Such blanket expenditures to advertising agencies are common both in Maryland and elsewhere.

Kovens himself acknowledged that much money was misspent on behalf of the Governor during the primary. He was particularly unhappy with a glossy, multicolored brochure glorifying Mandel produced by the Governor's office. "It cost $50,000 to $70,000 for tons of those things," he complained, "but they only gave away a couple thousand. What ever happened to the rest?"

Some expenditures that might not be considered "wasted" by Kovens seem to be very questionable legally and ethically. Perhaps the most questionable use of Mandel money was its distribution to district and neighborhood political organizations for the formation of tickets. Theoretically, "walking-around money" is used to print sample ballots designating the names and lever numbers of friendly candidates, and to pay polling-place workers who hand out the material. In practice, however, the expense is just another way to buy votes. Usually the money is tapped into working-class neighborhoods, where unemployed and retired men and women are happy to pick up the $20 or $25 for a day's electioneering. With it goes a tacit understanding that the worker and his relatives will vote for the candidates putting up the money. In the September 10 primary, Mandel spent $94,000 for walking-around money, mostly in Baltimore city, though it is not certain whether all of it was circulated. The law requires candidates to report how much they give to local political clubs, but the clubs themselves do not have to report how they distribute the cash. With $10,000 and $20,000 handed out to some political chieftains, it is difficult to ascertain how much actually reaches the streets. Perhaps even more important than the legal implications of walking-around money, however, are its political implications for voters in districts where it is popular—that is, mostly poor or economically static areas. Legislative records are full of friendly votes on virtually any issue by state legislators who have bartered away their political power to the candidate with the most campaign money. A pattern of such voting has been especially evident as a result of Mandel's grip on many members of the Baltimore city and Baltimore County delegations.

No one has a corner on the sleazy uses of money, nor is much always needed to kick up a little dirt. Congressman Hogan, in one of his lower moments, spent $2,000 to hire a private investigating firm that included among its gumshoes John R. (Fat Jack) Buckley, a political spy who once worked for the Committee to Re-elect the President. Buckley's role for Hogan was to investigate Mandel, a dubious assignment given the Congressman's grief over the Watergate scandals. The incident prompted one wit on the Governor's staff to print hundreds of bumper stickers warning, "Fat Jack Is Watching." The expense for this novel little message, if it followed a normal course, was probably buried with thousands of other costs filed by several committees established by the Governor's strategists to create an impression of broad, solid support.

The Move to Public Financing

The atmosphere of Watergate and the revelation of widespread abuses at the state and local levels had led (some would say forced) Governor Mandel to take some action on reform in the three proposals he made to the Maryland General Assembly in January 1974—two aimed at architects and engineers, the other calling for a $100 limit on cash contributions. His campaign-finance measure was swiftly greeted in the legislature by other, much more far-reaching proposals to change the traditional methods of conducting political campaigns in the state.

The difficulty of raising campaign funds and the considerable advantage held by incumbents—as dramatically shown by Mandel's near-$1 million kitty raised a year and a half before the election—persuaded many General Assembly members that public financing was the solution to Maryland's money-in-politics problems. The list of legislators supporting public financing was impressive, as was the list of civic groups who pressed for this type of reform. Cosponsors of a public-financing bill in the Senate were Senate President William S. James and Senator Edward Thomas, then the Democratic and Republican state chairmen, respectively. In the House a similar bill, introduced by Delegate Howard J. Needle (D., Baltimore County), was cosponsored by 26 members. Citizen groups actively supporting public financing were organized in two coalitions, which included such organizations as the League of Women Voters, state and local bar associations, the Maryland Junior

Chamber of Commerce, the AFL-CIO Committee on Political Education, and Common Cause.

There was strong opposition on the part of some members, for a number of reasons. House Speaker John Hanson Briscoe articulated the objection most commonly heard in the capitol corridors: "I don't think my constituents want their taxes used in political campaigns." Some legislators did not want to surrender their share of the large sums raised by statewide candidates; others considered public financing a mechanism to encourage competition; and still others cited limits on campaign contributions as a Constitutional violation of free speech.

The struggle to get the legislation moving was a classic battle in each house between supporters and opponents, and it was not until the waning days of the session that each bill passed its own house of origin. Throughout the session Governor Mandel remained opposed to public campaign financing, but he was by no means willing to commit his administration to defeat the bills. While scaled down from its original scope because opposition forced compromise on many points, the legislation was finally passed in 1974 to go into effect in 1978—the next statewide election year.

It was the Needle bill, considerably modified, that eventually became law. The original bill provided for full public funding of both primary and general elections, limitations on expenditures, elimination of private contributions, qualifications for public funding through petition, and an independent enforcement commission. The program was to be funded by a mandatory $2 additional state income tax. As the bill made its way through the two House committees that considered it, it was amended to provide for partial funding of primary elections through matching public funds in a given proportion to private contributions (seed money), and direct grants to cover 75 percent of general election expenses. The funding mechanism was made a voluntary tax checkoff (as in the Federal return) rather than a mandatory addition. The prohibition on campaign contributions—already limited by 1968 law to $2,500 per individual —was removed.

On the House floor, the bill was further modified to apply only to general elections, not primaries, on a matching-fund basis, and the voluntary tax checkoff in the committee version was changed to a voluntary add-on contribution, or surtax. While the reluctance of some legislators to tap the general tax fund for campaign financing led to this latter change, the prospect of considerably less money raised through such a system (which would increase an individual's tax liability) influenced the decision to confine funding to general elections. These final changes represented crucial limitations on the law in a state where primaries are generally much more important than general elections, because of the almost four-to-one Democratic predominance, and where limited enthusiasm to increase the personal tax burden could severely impede the entire program. But despite these inherent weaknesses, the bill was probably the strongest its adherents could get enacted. It was passed by the House and Senate (which had produced a similar bill that the House did not act upon) and signed into law by Governor Mandel on May 31, 1974, probably because he did not want to be identified as an enemy of reform during an election year.

The 1974 Maryland Fair Campaign Financing Law provides for partial public financing in the general—but not primary—election, limitation on the amount of money a candidate for office can spend, rules limiting the size of private contributions to candidates who wish to qualify for public financing, a Fair Campaign Financing Fund raised by a voluntary $2 addition to the income tax to underwrite all candidates' campaigns, and a Fair Campaign Financing Commission to enforce the new act. Under the new law aspirants for governor and lieutenant governor, who run in tandem on the Maryland ballots, are limited to spending 10 cents for each resident of the state, or a total of about $422,500 per election. This spending limitation applies to primaries as well as the general election, even though public funds are only to be available for the latter. Candidates for attorney general and comptroller are limited to spending 2.5 cents for each state resident, or about $106,000. A candidate for state senator may spend 10 cents for each resident within his district, or approximately $7,500; a candidate for the House of Delegates, 5 cents per resident, or roughly $2,500. Per-voter expenditure formulas were also applied to local offices in Baltimore city and each of Maryland's 23 counties.

To qualify for public funds, a candidate must first collect 15 percent of the total expenditures permitted to him in the general election; statewide candidates would get $3 in public funds for every $1 in eligible private contributions up to 75 percent of the maximum allowed, while candidates for local office would get $2 for each $1 raised, or two-thirds of the total. For a gubernatorial candidate that means that $63,375 of his $422,500 must come from private donors before the candidate is eligible to collect up to 75 percent of the total from the state Fair Campaign Financing Fund. The private donations are limited to $50 from each contributor.

Many senators and delegates, feeling that they had enacted
a patchwork product, decided to establish a Task Force to Study
Campaign Financing to make recommendations for improvements in the law in time for the 1975 session. Because of time
pressures, this Task Force concentrated first on the questions
of funding and of the act's limitation to general elections.

The Task Force's first report, issued in January 1975, made
three major recommendations, which were encompassed in
bills introduced in both the Senate and the House of Delegates. The most important of the study's proposals was that
candidates for party primaries also be eligible for public funds.
In order to extend public financing in this way, making it
"fairer and more appropriate to the pattern of elections in
Maryland," the Task Force recommended that the amount
given each qualifying candidate be reduced from a three-to-one
to a one-to-one ratio. Because it discovered that the $2 add-on
contribution would probably raise only a fraction of the total
needed for the public financing program, as only a small percentage of taxpayers were willing to commit such funds, the
Task Force recommended an income-tax checkoff of $5 for
individuals and $25 for corporations—paid out of, rather than
added to, their taxes.

The Mandel administration was by that time willing to concede that some form of public financing might be necessary to
stop the quadrennial dash for money, although it was still not
ready to support the Task Force recommendations. As an alternative, the Governor proposed that public money be restricted
to the campaigns of statewide candidates, that the three-to-one
ratio for financing be retained, and that the program be applied
only to the general election. These provisions, two of which
merely repeated parts of the law passed in 1974, would tend to
aid the candidate Mandel and Kovens eventually choose as a
gubernatorial successor in 1978, when Mandel ends the two
elected terms to which he is limited under law, for they pre-
serve the present system of raising primary money through
private donations alone, while generously supporting the party
nominee.

When the General Assembly considered these proposals in
its 1975 session, the state was awash with the debris of more
political shipwrecks: Dale Anderson, the Baltimore County
executive, had been sentenced to five years; Joseph Alton, the
chief executive in Anne Arundel County, pleaded guilty to
extortion and went to prison for 18 months; Alan Green and
I. H. (Bud) Hammerman, two men who had admitted handing

payoffs to Agnew, were sentenced to 12 to 18 months, respectively; five engineers were convicted and sentenced to lesser terms, with another four still subject to prosecution, along with three architects.

And trouble seemed to be moving closer to the Governor. After Mandel's re-election in November, Dale Hess and Harry Rodgers were notified by U.S. Attorney Beall that they were targets of the investigation into Maryland political corruption. Their financial records, along with those of the Tidewater company, were subpoenaed. News stories speculated that the Governor, too, was under inquiry, since some of his political friends were being called before the grand jury. Mandel promised to inform reporters of his status, while publicly demanding that the Federal prosecutor tell him whether he, too, was a "target" of the probe.

With such reports, conditions seemed good in early 1975 for strengthening Maryland's new Fair Campaign Financing Law in response to the Task Force's recommendations. Indeed, a survey taken by the Maryland chapter of Common Cause during the late summer showed a large majority of legislative candidates favoring improvements in the law. Since there had been almost a 45 percent turnover in the legislature, most observers anticipated a more active, more progressive approach to the problem. Yet the legislature was not very enthusiastic about either the Governor's or the Task Force's plans. Both bills were defeated, as sponsors and floor managers of the legislation were outmaneuvered by old enemies of public spending.

Another proposal was enacted in the 1975 session by those who sought political reform, but in weaker form. Sponsored by the Governor at the request of the Maryland Bar Association, the original bill was to establish the office of a statewide prosecutor to investigate and prosecute political crimes, the first time Maryland would grant such power to a member of its criminal justice system. (The Attorney General may not under law initiate an investigation or prosecute a crime unless he is specifically requested to do so by the Governor or the state Senate.) Amendments in the hectic last days of the session reduced the "prosecutor's" powers to the area of investigating crimes only. He then must turn his findings over to one of the locally elected state's attorneys, who are mostly products of entrenched political systems and whose commitment to prosecute in potentially embarrassing cases may be less than total.

For the immediate future the center of activity in the probe of Maryland corruption remains with the U.S. Attorney in

Baltimore. George Beall, who had headed the Federal attorney's office throughout the two years of the state scandals investigation, was replaced in the summer of 1975 by Jervis S. Finney, a former Republican state Senator and a longtime critic of Marvin Mandel and his political friends and fund-raisers. Finney, not unexpectedly, continued to press the inquiry into Hess and Rodgers that had begun in November 1974.

Shortly after taking office, Finney and his staff subpoenaed the banking records of the Governor and members of his immediate family. From all indications, the Finney office was compiling a net-worth profile of the Governor. The *Washington Post* reported that the Federal prosecutor was attempting to show "a pattern of favoritism" by the Mandel administration toward certain of his political backers.

One of the deals the U.S. Attorney's office was examining involved the Governor's share of ownership in the waterfront farm in 1972. Shortly after Mandel had acquired his interest, the administration sponsored legislation to lengthen racing dates at Maryland's race tracks, a move that would have greatly benefited holdings by Hess and Rodgers in the Marlboro Race Track, a small operation, now out of business, which was purchased in 1971 by the larger and more lucrative Bowie Race Course. When Bowie eventually bought out Marlboro and obtained a longer racing schedule, the stock held by Hess and Rodgers grew in value.

In mid-September, less than a year after Mandel's re-election, the Governor himself announced that he had been notified by the U.S. Attorney that he was a target of the investigation. Two months later, he and five of his fund-raising friends—Irvin Kovens, Harry and William Rodgers, W. Dale Hess, and Ernest N. Cory—were indicted on a series of mail-fraud and racketeering charges. The Governor was accused of receiving valuable interests in two real-estate deals in exchange for influence favorable to race tracks partly owned by his friends.

The state has endured more than a year of political turmoil, but throughout the period one thing has become clear: lots of money found its way into some important hands. Though many Maryland politicians could say with accuracy that it wasn't campaign money, there are unavoidable comparisons between Agnew's kickbacks and Mandel's war chest. Much of the money given to Agnew and Anderson came from persons who had been contributing to campaigns for years. When money is given in order to secure contracts and favoritism from the state, the occasion of giving doesn't really matter.

THREE

FLORIDA:
THE POWER OF INCUMBENCY

William Mansfield

Governor Reubin Askew had just made his first re-election campaign decision, and as his campaign manager, Jim Smith, recalls it, "Everybody was aghast." For Askew's first move had not been, as most had expected, the selection of a running mate, but instead a commitment to limit the contribution he would take from a single person to $100.

For two days, Askew and 37 of his top advisors had been meeting at the beginning of May 1974 in a secluded lodge on the Sopchoppy River, 20 miles south of the Capitol in Talla-hassee, enjoying the local food (shrimp, chicken, black-eyed peas, okra, and cornbread) and drink (mostly iced tea, because the Governor is, after all, a teetotaler) and the political talk. "Then the Governor made his suggestion that contributions be limited to less than the law allowed [$3,000] and we kicked the idea around," remembers a participant. "Not everybody agreed at first, but finally somebody said it sounded like a good idea and maybe $1,000 would be reasonable." (That figure would have not been unreasonable, because the limit applies once to the primary, again to the runoff period—where, if no one gets 50 percent of the primary votes, the top two candidates meet in another election—and finally to the general election. This meant that a single contributor could still have given $3,000 during the course of a campaign, a couple $6,000.)

"Then the Governor said, 'I was thinking more like $100.' That kind of shook a lot of people. They said, 'Yes, that's a

dandy idea in theory, but what do you do if you get in a bind
and can't make it with $100 contributions?' " No one at the
lodge doubted that Askew, who would have all the power of
the governor's office at his disposal throughout the campaign
and who was heavily favored to win (a recent poll had given
him 72 percent of the vote against his most likely opponent),
could raise all the money needed for his campaign—and if he
wished, the entire $850,000 allowed by the state's new cam-
paign-contribution law. But there was serious doubt that he
could finance the campaign if he fettered himself with a pledge
to accept only contributions of $100 or less. After all, he had
spent $737,548 in his upset victory in 1970. "Those of us who
knew we were going to be running the campaign were really
apprehensive," says Smith. "We were worried about the prac-
ticability of it." And so, although Askew had made his decision,
they did not really believe him. "We left feeling we were going
to think about it more before making a decision," says Smith.

But four days later, on May 6, 1974, Askew cut off any
further discussion, unofficially launching his re-election campaign with a press-conference pledge to hold contributions to
the $100 limit. This would, he maintained, "eliminate even
the slightest appearance of conflict of interest." The decision
may have troubled campaign manager Smith, but it proved to
be an extremely wise political move, one that gave Askew perhaps his most effective campaign issue—that he could not be
influenced by campaign contributors—in a year when the attention of Florida voters was focused on that issue as never
before.

In Florida, 1974 was not just the year of Watergate but the
year of state political scandals unmatched in this century.
Within the year, three of Florida's six elected cabinet officers
and one of its U.S. senators would be indicted, and efforts to
impeach three of the state's seven Supreme Court justices would
be under way. Even before the period to qualify for the 1974
election ended, two of the cabinet officers had stepped aside.
First was Education Commissioner Floyd Christian, accused of
accepting $70,000 in bribes and kickbacks involving state con-
tracts. He resigned on the morning a state House committee
was to begin a hearing that could have led to his impeachment.
Until the Leon County (Tallahassee) Grand Jury issued its
19-count indictment against Christian in April 1974, no Florida
cabinet officer had ever been accused of a felony.*

* After pleading guilty to charges of tax evasion and failure to report unlawful compensation, Christian was sent to a Federal prison, where he

Three months later, U.S. Senator Edward Gurney, who had become familiar to the nation's television viewers as the dogged defender of President Nixon during the Senate's Watergate hearings, was to achieve another unenviable record, becoming the first Senator in 50 years to be indicted while still in office. Gurney had scored other, happier firsts in 1968, when he became the first politician in Florida's history to receive more than a million votes and the first Republican senator from the state since Reconstruction. But just two weeks after a Federal grand jury in Jacksonville charged him with an influence-peddling scheme which prosecutors claimed brought him $233,000 in unreported campaign contributions, Gurney, too, stepped aside. "There is," he said, "no sensible or sound way to conduct a statewide political race and prepare for and go through a major trial."†

That same prospect did not deter Florida's Treasurer and Insurance Commissioner, Thomas O'Malley, when he was indicted, just three weeks shy of the November general election, on three felony charges involving $50,000 allegedly paid him for state favors. "I have not yet begun to fight," he vowed. "I am still a candidate." O'Malley had in fact been fighting the charges all during the primaries, because the events leading to the charges and the comings and goings of witnesses before the grand jury investigating him had been widely reported for months. State Comptroller Fred O. (Bud) Dickinson had the same problem. Officers of the banks he regulated paraded before a grand jury in Tampa throughout the campaign, although he was not to be indicted (on multiple counts of tax evasion, extortion, and violation of Federal banking regulations) until well after the election. He, too, chose to fight. Similarly, Justice Joseph Boyd, one of three Supreme Court justices facing re-election in 1974, did not withdraw in the weeks before the election when newspapers carried stories detailing how he and fellow Justice Hal Dekle had received what the Judicial Qualifications Commission was later to call an "illegal outside opinion" intended to influence the court's decision in a utility tax case that could have cost consumers millions of dollars. Later the charges against the pair, and unrelated charges against Jus-

---

served 135 days of a six-month sentence. He is also on probation after conviction on the latter charges, plus perjury, in a state court.

† Gurney was eventually acquitted on five charges, but the jury could not reach agreement on two other counts. The government has announced a decision to retry him of these counts. The date of the retrial has not yet been set.

tice David McCain, were to lead to hearings by the House Impeachment Committee.*

It was in this atmosphere of official charges—and counter-claims by the politicians involved of grand juries being manipulated by their opponents—that Florida's 1974 election campaigns began. Small wonder that reporters found voter after voter who had decided simply to sit out the election, and unhappiness and frustration among many who did plan to vote. "I'm going to vote," said one citizen. "I'm going to go down and turn the crank—or maybe I'll just walk in and kick the machine. But I'll be there."

The political atmosphere of 1974 was also affected by new legislation regulating campaigns. Florida's 1952 Campaign Contribution Law, widely known as the "who gave it—who got it" law, was a pioneering effort that almost immediately became a model for reformers all over the nation. Its aim was simple: to allow voters to see who contributed to each candidate and how each candidate spent that money. But the law was so riddled with loopholes and so lacking in enforcement machinery that it often had the effect of penalizing the honest, who reported properly, while rewarding the dishonest, who did not.

In reality, no one was even checking for violations, and the candidates knew it. A study of 1972 legislative-contribution reports by the *Miami Herald* revealed that candidates had actually signed sworn statements showing that they had collected and spent more money than the law allowed and had taken money from persons associated with the pari-mutuel industry (at that time barred from contributing). Candidates had so little fear of prosecution that three winners hadn't bothered to file their final reports—due 45 days after the general election—a full five months after the balloting.

In 1973 the Florida legislature, after bitter fights in both houses, passed a campaign-finance law that went considerably further than the old law in disclosure requirements. In addition, it limited the size of contributions and expenditures and introduced the key element of enforcement. Under the new law, candidates for statewide offices could accept no more than $3,000 from an individual, candidates for all other offices no

---

* Boyd was not impeached, but the committee made him agree to a Judicial Qualifications Commission determination of his mental and physical competence to continue on the court. Doctors found him competent, and he is still on the bench. Dekle and McCain both resigned while the committee was hearing charges against them.

more than $1,000 in each election—primary, runoff, and general.

Limits on overall spending vary according to the race involved as well as the three election periods. Spending in the governor's race was limited to $250,000 each for the primary and runoff and $350,000 for the general election—a total of $850,000. All other statewide races have a $550,000 spending ceiling, while candidates in the state Senate were limited to $65,000 and for the House $55,000. Judicial races, which are nonpartisan, operate on a separate two-step scale, ranging from $200,000 for the Supreme Court to $40,000 for circuit, county, and municipal courts.

Candidates who got an early start were to file quarterly reports of all their collections and expenses and a full report once the qualifying period ended. All reports had to be signed by the candidate, who was held accountable for their accuracy. They were required to include job identification for all who gave more than $100. In addition, both state and local candidates were to file disclosure statements revealing all sources that made up more than 10 percent of their personal income and certain other assets and sources of income.

The most important aspect of the legislation was probably the creation of machinery to enforce the new laws: an Elections Commission headed by Stephen O'Connell, a former Supreme Court justice and University of Florida President, and an Ethics Commission headed by Talbot D'Alemberte, a former member of the state House of Representatives, and including among its members former Governor LeRoy Collins. Civil penalties were established that allow for fines and for the withholding of certificates of nomination or election in some cases.

The new law promised to make the 1974 elections more open than those of the past and—ideally—more honest as well. It did at least make it possible to measure the amount of money raised by the various candidates and where most of it came from. How it affected the conduct of the campaigns, if at all, would still be debated after the November elections.

The Governorship

The gubernatorial race was in Reubin Askew's hands from the beginning. "For the incumbent," Askew maintained, "elections are won between the campaigns." Thus his 1974 campaign was of the low-key, no-issue variety, in sharp contrast to four years before, when he had run the most issue-oriented campaign of any candidate. He had pledged a corporate-profits tax and the reduction of other consumer taxes so every Floridian would pay his "fair share." Though some differed as to how "fair" the tax changes were, not even his opponents in 1974 denied he'd kept his pledge, and through his four years in office he had maintained an unusually high personal credibility. He was, as one reporter was told by a Jacksonville voter, "almost too good to be true." Not even the fact that the man Askew had handpicked as his running mate in 1970, former Secretary of State Tom Adams, had been censured by the Florida House for using state employees on his farm had damaged the Governor's reputation. Askew had plenty of opponents, but none could come close to him in either the primary or the general election. The twin problems of money and publicity handicapped them all in their fight against the incumbent.

The first challenger was none other than Tom Adams, who led—unsuccessfully—the attempt to tarnish the Governor's reputation. Adams, who had been in public office since 1956 (first as a state senator, then for 10 years as Secretary of State before becoming Askew's Lieutenant Governor) had the remnants of an organization and, he believed, enough money from his old supporters and from opponents of Askew to finance an all-out attack on the Governor. "He had an awful lot of promises from people who wanted him to get in there and mix it up with the Governor," says Harold (Buz) Rummel, who worked with the Adams campaign briefly in its early stages. "Most of the money never materialized." Campaign manager Randy Schrader recalls that "when I got on board, I was told of several commitments from groups of people which would exceed $20,000–$30,000 each. Adams indicated we'd be operating with the maximum the law allowed for the first primary, a quarter of a million dollars." But the candidate could raise only $119,351, and $16,000 of that came from his running mate for lieutenant governor, 33-year-old developer Burl McCormick. Adams, who had long been identified with labor interests, got some endorsement from unions and at least $5,100 in contributions from them. Other money came, but not nearly as much as he'd expected, from scattered longtime Adams supporters and from equally scattered short-term Askew opponents. "We had to totally cut out all our plans for TV," says Schrader. "You can walk the streets and shake hands all you want, but if you can't afford TV, you're in pretty bad shape." Adams walked the streets and flayed at Askew at rallies and through a series of well-publicized "Dear Reubin" letters accusing the Governor's former law partners and current campaign manager of profiting during Askew's term in office. In the end, he finished third in a four-man primary, beating only Clearwater attorney Norman Bie.

Bie had received fleeting national attention as a leader of anti-McGovern forces at the 1972 Democratic National Convention, where he had been a Florida delegate pledged to George Wallace. He predicted no trouble in raising funds for the race, declaring, "I'll have more $5 contributions than you can imagine." They never came. Bie put $25,650 of his own money into the race, got help from his family and his running mate, Florence S. Keen, and finally was able to spend $47,329, which was more in dollars than the 39,758 votes he got.

The second-place finisher was a surprise entry, former state Senator and millionaire citrusman Ben Hill Griffin, Jr., whom Askew had appointed to the Florida Citrus Commission. Griffin did not make his decision to run until the day qualifications were to end. Jumping into a company plane in Avon Park in central Florida, he flew to Tallahassee and beat the filing deadline by just nine minutes. Griffin had long wanted to make the race for governor and, at 63, had decided this would be his last chance. Besides, he was unhappy with a state government he felt was getting too active. "The legislature," he maintained, "tends to be overactive and the Governor is egging them on."

Griffin did not really have to concentrate on fund-raising. The statement he filed in the Capitol showed his net worth at $9 million, and he was prepared to spend freely of his own money. Before the first primary, he had personally contributed $125,000 of the $232,707 he finally spent. ("We would have spent the limit [$250,000], but we had to be safe so we wouldn't go over; we cut back spending the last few days.") Even with the cutback, Griffin was the biggest spender in the primary, leading Askew by $37,427.

For his efforts, he received 137,008 votes and a firm conviction that it is almost impossible to defeat an incumbent governor unless you can spend much more money than he is allowed to spend. "I think an incumbent, in the governor's race in particular, ought to run on his record and not spend any money," Griffin says. "I don't say that facetiously. I think he ought to be limited because he gets so much free publicity from the office. Everywhere he goes, he's in the papers, on TV. Of course,

I got into the race at the last minute and that makes a lot of difference. Maybe if a guy works on the thing, if he starts a year and a half ahead, works all the areas of the state, gets his campaign organization all lined up . . ."

Jerry Thomas thought that would work. An articulate, conservative banker, Thomas had switched to the Republican Party shortly after he put down his gavel as Senate President in 1972 because, he says, "I could find no home in the national Democratic Party." He found an instant happy home in Florida's Republican Party and immediately began planning his campaign for governor, a campaign no Republican was to challenge. It did not take him long, he says, to discover the problems of the "out" attempting to get "in."

"I found out I could not get early coverage from the news media. Somebody talking about the Watergate problem told me, 'If the Lord ran on the Republican ticket, he would lose.' And I said, 'Yeah, he would lose in Florida, because nobody would know he was running.'" There was, of course, the advantage of having no Republican primary opponents while Askew was getting all the bad publicity three opponents could generate. But that, Thomas maintains, is not enough; the challenger must get exposure, must win name recognition. "The incumbent starts off normally—unless he has some unusual problems—at his peak. He just has a fantastic advantage."

The advantage is not just name recognition; it is fund-raising ability as well, Thomas claims. And much of that advantage, Thomas charges, comes from the sheer size of government, from its regulation of so many facets of the economy. "The more government grows, the more people are subject to regulation," he says. "People would say to me, 'If I contribute to you maybe our development won't get the approval of the sewage treatment plant we have to have.' I ran into that type of thing constantly. If I had run in a race where there was no incumbent, I could have raised a lot more money." That, he says, is why Askew had much of the big business support he, as the conservative candidate, had expected to get. "Calls were made," he charges. "The Governor doesn't have to call, but his people can. I'm not saying that they did anything wrong; that's just the cold, hard facts. I've been an incumbent."

Askew says that no such calls were made. "What I told those people at the Sopchoppy meeting," Askew says, "is that I was Governor as well as a candidate; that I intended to see the [campaign] law faithfully executed, in spirit as well as letter. I warned them that what they did could not only embarrass me but lead to criminal charges against them. I almost invited them not to participate in the campaign."

Whatever the reasons or the methods, it was true that Askew, a lawyer from Florida's rural panhandle, had heavy support from both big business and organized labor, while Thomas, a banker from Palm Beach County in the heart of the Gold Coast, got his biggest donations from agribusiness and rural interests. Despite the fact that Thomas headed a large bank-holding company, many of the banking contributions he received (8 percent of his total just before the election) came not from big city bankers, but from small towns—for example, $1,000 from Valparaiso Bank and Trust, $200 from the National Bank of Niceville, $250 from officers at the High Springs Bank. The large-bank money had gone to Askew.

It was also true, as Thomas charged during the campaign, that the $100-a-person limit imposed by Askew did not mean that corporations and groups, through a series of givers, couldn't make much larger donations to the Governor's campaign. Developers were a case in point. At least $2,200 of the Governor's funds came from those associated with Arvida, $1,200 from Coral Ridge Properties, $880 from Pan American Land Development, and $600 from the developers of Punta Gorda Isles. Similarly, employees of Ryder Truck Rental gave $2,500, employees of Southern Bell Telephone $1,300. The multiple listings also made it difficult for opponents to check just where Askew's support was coming from. It was clear he had widespread labor backing, for he listed $100 contributions from unions representing every occupation from plumbers and painters to elevator constructors, but it was impossible to determine just how much labor money he actually received. His reports, for example, included nearly 13 pages of small ($2 to $25) contributors, many identified as electricians, most probably members of the Brotherhood of Electrical Workers. But since Florida law does not require identification of those who give less than $100, it is virtually impossible to arrive at an accurate total.

"If enough publicity had been given to the Governor's contribution plan, it wouldn't have been effective," Thomas maintains. "It was just a farce. The Askew people would call up a law firm and say, 'We want $1,000, but not more than $100 from each partner. When you finally analyze the contributions, the truth is that contributions were not limited."

The Askew forces deny these charges. "To me, it just didn't add up to a substantial figure," says campaign manager Smith of the multiple giving by certain groups. "It just didn't create a situation where any portion of the business community could have any more input than anyone else.... Besides, what do you do, set limits, say, 'We're not going to take more than $2,000 from doctors'? With Askew, two or three testimonial dinners would have raised the limit. But then some people might have felt they had some special interest. When the collection is spread out over thousands of people, they can't feel that way. The Governor didn't want to go into the second term with any people thinking they owned a part of him." Says Askew of the $100 limit: "It was not only the right thing to do to avoid commitments, to avoid accepting questionable money, but I think it was a good thing politically, too. It literally built an organization. It gave our people a chance to go out and do a lot of groundwork. When they are working, they are not spending—and, generally, much of the money spent on campaigns is wasted."

It may have taken a lot of work, but the system did raise money—$594,510.28 in all. Thomas also raised a considerable sum, $394,141.44, but he was outspent by Askew—$315,372 to $199,023—in the period following the primaries. The vote was equally lopsided—1,118,954 for Askew to 709,438 for Thomas.

Governor Askew's office proudly announced on the eve of the general election that 8,876 different persons had contributed to his campaign. That is very probably a record number of contributors to a statewide campaign in Florida, a record achieved by an extremely popular incumbent Governor, who limited contributions to force "mass" participation and who had an active, aggressive organization in each of Florida's 67 counties. After the election, Askew and Thomas could agree on one thing: Only the incumbent could have financed a campaign with the $100 limit.

Other Statewide Incumbents

The power of incumbency was equally effective in other statewide races, in which five of the state's six cabinet officers, three Supreme Court justices, and two Public Service Commissioners were up for re-election. In different times, many probably would have had no opposition at all, but the Watergate and state scandals made the prospects for challengers in 1974 appear much brighter than usual. They seemed to be attuned to the sentiments of voters such as the Jacksonville man who declared that "the main reason I'd vote is to vote somebody out of office who doesn't belong there."

When qualifying ended, the only unopposed members of the group were Attorney General Robert Shevin and Supreme Court Justice James Adkins. It is quite possible that the major reason Shevin drew no opponent was his early show of fund-raising ability: He amassed $167,324 for a race that never came (and is saving it, most likely for a campaign for governor in 1978).

Agriculture Commissioner Doyle Conner's opposition was only token; American Independent Party member Don Webb had qualified, he said, only so the party would still have someone on the ballot should something happen to U.S. Senate candidate John Grady. Webb collected just $25. Conner, a cabinet member since 1960, only bothered to collect $15,328 himself, most of it from agricultural and agribusiness interests. (He didn't need more, polling more than a million votes to Webb's 302,650.)

The other three incumbents—Comptroller Bud Dickinson and Treasurer Thomas O'Malley (both soon to be indicted) and Education Commissioner Ralph Turlington (who had been appointed by Askew to replace the indicted Floyd Christian) drew a total of 12 challengers. It says something of the money-raising power of an incumbent Florida cabinet officer that of the $951,634 collected in those three races, $553,460 went to the three incumbents, and just $398,174 to all 12 challengers. And on a ballot crowded with candidates for the U.S. Senate and the governorship, the challengers were in desperate need of money to get the media exposure that would bring name recognition on election day.

"Incumbents not only have the great advantage of raising money," says challenger Gerald Lewis, "they have name recognition. The cabinet races don't have any visibility. You have to have a certain amount of money for paid media exposure. If an incumbent keeps his nose clean—sometimes even if he doesn't—he's almost impossible to beat."

Lewis speaks from experience. He is now Comptroller of Florida, the only one of the 12 challengers who won, even though Bud Dickinson outspent him in the primary and runoff $199,244 to $83,474. Lewis had considerable help from the Tampa Grand Jury investigating Dickinson; although Dickinson was not indicted until after the election, his former law partner was indicted before the primary, and—even more damaging—Dickinson himself took the fifth amendment rather than

answer questions before the jury. "We didn't have an indictment [of Dickinson], but we did have the fifth amendment,"
Lewis says. "Even with all Dickinson's difficulties, I think we
were losing until we started with the fifth amendment." This
meant staging empty-chair debates with Dickinson (who refused most joint appearances during the first primary), where
a poster-sized blowup of a newspaper headline proclaiming
"Dickinson Takes the Fifth Amendment" would be displayed.
Lewis drew some criticism, even from supporters, for his melodramatic attacks, but he defends them as necessary. "The kinds
of things I'm criticized for—call it showmanship—are things
you have to do when you're running against an incumbent.
Holding an empty-chair debate, staging a press conference in
front of a bank, you have to get exposure." Gerald Lewis admits now he's glad his opponent didn't take up his early debate
challenges. "The incumbent had a tremendous factual advantage," Lewis explains. "He has got the resources in his office
to get the answer to any argument, to overwhelm you with
statistics. You'd have to have a huge staff to do the same thing
and that's where the money comes in again."

Lewis managed to turn Dickinson's campaign contributions
into a weapon. As is traditional for an incumbent comptroller
in Florida, Dickinson relied heavily on contributions from
people connected with the institutions he regulated, including
banks, small-loan companies, and cemeteries. A survey of Dickinson's contributions shortly before the second primary showed
that of the $43,475 collected, roughly a fourth came from those
groups, and most of that from bankers. Lewis made a pledge
to take no money from bankers and set up a three-member
screening committee to ensure that he didn't. He concedes that
the pledge wasn't very hard to keep. "With a very few exceptions, maybe some personal friends, I don't think I would have
gotten any banker contributions anyway," he says. "From what
I saw, even those bankers who were not for Dickinson and
who really wanted a change, contributed to him. I would
imagine that's the situation in any regulated industry." After
Dickinson was defeated by Lewis, there was some evidence that
the ties between bank contributions and the Comptroller might
sometimes be closer than simple fear of reprisal on the part
of those being regulated. During October Dickinson approved
12 charters for new banks whose directors included not only
a number of legislators and former legislators, but two men
who had conducted fund-raising affairs for Dickinson, and several major donors.

After trailing Lewis by almost 40,000 votes in the first primary (in which there was a third candidate), Dickinson reversed his strategy and adopted the Lewis attack approach, even barging into one of his opponent's Capitol news conferences to call him a "damn liar" and "not a man." But it was too late. Lewis beat him by more than 20,000 votes in the runoff and went on to defeat the Republican by more than 500,000 votes. Dickinson was eventually found innocent of Federal extortion-conspiracy charges. His trial on income-tax evasion charges recessed in March, 1976, after he had suffered an apparent heart attack.

In a personal financial sense, it was a costly victory for Lewis. "I had $40,000 or so in a savings account and I knew it was going to go if I ran," he says. "I really waffled about doing something with it that would bring in a return rather than running." But he ran, and contributed $35,000 of his own money.

That personal contribution was just $3.36 more than former state Representative Jack Shreve was able to collect in his primary campaign against state Treasurer and Insurance Commissioner O'Malley. Although he conceded that "it partially depends on how much the other people in the race have," Shreve feels a challenger needs "a minimum of about $100,000" to take on an incumbent in a statewide race. O'Malley spent even more than that figure ($125,590) to beat both Shreve and a Jacksonville insurance man, Fitzhugh Powell, despite continuing news reports of the grand jury investigation into O'Malley's activities. Unlike Dickinson, who allowed Lewis to put him on the defensive, O'Malley carried the battle in the primary. Running with the theme "Tom O'Malley—when he fights, you win," he showed up at the debates, reminded voters how he'd saved them hundreds of millions of dollars by pushing for no-fault insurance and ordering rate reductions, and buried his opponents under an avalanche of facts and figures.

As Dickinson had done, O'Malley went to those he regulated for his campaign contributions, and had, if anything, even more success. An analysis of O'Malley's campaign reports through August 26 showed that nearly half of the $130,869 collected by then was directly tied to groups he regulated or did state business with. Insurance men gave $47,300; bottled gas companies (he is state fire marshal) added $3,600; bankers (as Treasurer he deposits state funds) gave $8,600; and bail bondsmen (whom he regulates as Insurance Commissioner) contributed $2,700. This pattern of collections brought in $220,807 by the general election. Some of this money eventually went to his legal defense—not a surprising development to observers who had seen him raise a $25,000 fund, largely from those same sources, during his four years in office which he used to pay for, among other things, office furniture, flowers, and club dues.

O'Malley's general election prospects looked dim when the October 19 editions of newspapers across the state pictured him emerging from the Dade County jail, where he had been booked on three felony charges. But two days later he was on top again. Reporters, armed with leaks from O'Malley's office, confronted his Republican opponent, Jeffrey Latham, at a press conference and drew admissions from him that he had actively sought the support of the Ku Klux Klan ("If they'd vote for me, I'd be proud of it really") and had spent eight months in a reform school at age 15 ("It made a man of me"). O'Malley went on to win by just over 65,000 votes out of more than 1.6 million cast.

O'Malley resigned his office in August, after the Florida House voted 11 articles of impeachment against him but before he came to trial either in court or in the House. He pleaded no contest to a charge that he had pressured an insurance company to make a $2.3 million loan for a business venture in which he held a secret interest. In return the state dismissed felony charges that he had taken a $10,000 kickback for depositing state funds in a Winter Park bank and then committed perjury by not reporting the money under the state's gift law (which requires officials to report all gifts of $25 or more). The judge withheld sentencing until O'Malley, who was hospitalized for heart problems at the time of his plea, could appear in court. He was also indicted by a Federal grand jury in Miami on 26 counts, including tax evasion, and mail fraud.

The third incumbent, Ralph Turlington, a 23-year veteran of the legislature when Askew named him Education Commissioner, had been on that job just over five months when he faced four opponents—two former Education Department officials, a college administrator, and a Dade County schoolteacher —in the primary. They were five quite helpful months, however, because they gave him the kind of media exposure that the other candidates could not get. And the fact that he was the incumbent helped Turlington to collect $92,023 by primary time, while all his opponents combined raised just $65,630. His sources were predictable, including $15,991 from teachers, professors, and education groups (he was endorsed by the Florida Education Association) and $11,400 from the legislative lobbyists with whom Turlington had worked for so long. Turlington didn't even need a runoff to eliminate all four opponents, and by the general election he had collected $127,441—compared to $20,283 for his Republican opponent, Carl M. Kuttler, Jr. The result was a 1,046,427 to 576,947 Turlington victory.

The remaining election for a cabinet position—secretary of state—did not include an incumbent, as he had resigned to run for the U.S. Senate. Because the largely ministerial duties of the secretary of state's office (handling such things as corporation and election reports) left the four Democrats and one Republican in the race without any real "captive" donors such as those available in the other contests, candidates and their families did most of the initial financing. As a result, there was relatively little money in the race. One candidate, Don Pride, a newspaper reporter turned press secretary for Governor Askew turned candidate, counted on contributions of a type other than monetary to put him into the runoff: editorial endorsement, considered vital in the extremely low-visibility race. Pride had been a respected investigative reporter for papers in St. Petersburg and West Palm Beach, he had performed well in the often hazardous job of press secretary for four years, and he pledged strict enforcement of the state's campaign laws—something no secretary of state had ever paid much attention to in the past. He got the endorsements of virtually every major newspaper in the state, save the *Miami Herald*, which recommended opponent Beverly Dozier, a former director of the State Division of Cultural Affairs. This may have just made the difference, for she nudged him out of the runoff by 6,042 votes statewide, but by 13,545 votes in Dade County, home of the *Herald*. Leader in the primary was State Senator Bruce Smathers, son of the former U.S. Senator, who went on to defeat Dozier by more than 30,000 votes and, finally, Republican James Sebesta by more than 100,000 votes.

If visibility was low in cabinet races, it was near zero for the three Supreme Court and two Public Service Commission posts. Fewer than 15 percent of Florida's registered voters bothered to pull a lever in any of the three judicial races, and incumbent Justices Joseph Boyd and Ben F. Overton won handily. Voter interest was not even generated by the details of Boyd's highly questionable behavior in the utility tax case (including the fact that he had flushed a crucial illegal memo down the commode in a Supreme Court restroom rather than turning it over to the Chief Justice or the Judicial Qualifications Commission, an act that later was to cause the commission to ask for his ouster.) Attorney contributions apparently were not slowed by Boyd's problems either; of the $19,225 he reported, at least $10,650 was from lawyers who might in the future have cases before him.

Nor did sharply rising utility bills spur voters to take an interest in the selection of the men who were to regulate the utilities; only 23 percent of Florida's registered Democrats voted to nominate PSC commissioners. Incumbent William Mayo won easily over his single challenger, Alcee Hastings, outcollecting him by almost ten to one along the way. Commissioner Bill Bevis had a Republican opponent, N. R. Bacon, who was also easily defeated and easily outspent by nearly four to one.

Attempts to identify conflicts of interest in contributions to the Public Service Commission point up the complexity of potentially unethical relationships between regulators and regulatees. For example, was there conflict when a crushed-stone company gave $500 to Mayo, who was one of three commissioners who regulate the carriers that haul the stone? The same question could apply to a $600 donation from the state's largest food chain, which, as part of its operations, maintains one of Florida's largest truck fleets. It didn't appear to be a conflict when several builders contributed to each incumbent and the Building Industry Political Committee itself gave $100 to Bevis. But these contributions could be seen in a different perspective a few months later, when the PSC considered imposing a capital facilities charge to make each new building pay its share of the utility plant needed to generate the added electricity it would require—and the Florida Association of Homebuilders was a major opponent of the charge.

Even those who regulate the ethics of the regulators weren't sure about such cases. Ethics Commission Chairman Talbot D'Alemberte gave $100 to Bevis, despite the fact that D'Alemberte's law firm represented regulated utilities, including the state's largest power company, Florida Power and Light. D'Alemberte said later that he didn't see anything wrong at the time since he and Bevis were old friends and had served in the legislature together, but he conceded that he wasn't sure if he would, or should, make such a donation again. PSC Public Counsel Woodie Liles was sure he'd found a conflict in the $2,500 contribution Bevis received from members of General Telephone Company's law firm and board of directors and he demanded that Bevis excuse himself from voting on General Telephone's request for a $73.8 million rate increase. But the PSC's General Counsel, William Weeks, said Bevis couldn't legally excuse himself for such a thing. "I cannot see how legal contributions, properly reported, could raise questions," he said. (Bevis could, and he returned the contribution.)

If there were questions about the propriety of contributions from regulated businesses to those who regulate them, one thing was clear: The incumbent regulators, from comptroller through PSC commissioner, can get those contributions, can outspend their opponents, and, unless their image problems are severe, can win.

Incumbents at the Grassroots

State legislators may not have the vast direct regulatory power of cabinet officers or utility commissioners, but their votes on issues of concern to certain groups makes them very desirable objects of special-interest money. As with other officials, it is the incumbent legislators—those with proven records and the likelihood of winning—who get the lion's share of these funds.

While some citizens were reluctant to donate because of the recession and Watergate, and most tend under the best of circumstances to be uninterested in low-visibility legislative campaigns, those with a special interest in the laws to be passed and killed by the 1975–76 legislature were eager to give. As a lobbyist for a business group declared, "The only thing I'm sorry about is that we didn't give twice as much as everyone else did."

In fact, that is just about what lobbies and four special-interest groups—the building industry, attorneys, insurance men, and the medical profession—did for winning legislative candidates in 1974: together, they gave them more than twice as much money as all other contributors. A study of campaign reports by the *Miami Herald* (which had done a pioneering investigation of campaign contributions in 1972) found that of the $1.2 million that the 142 winners received from sources other than their own pocketbooks or political parties, 63 cents of every dollar came from these groups. Of the 63 cents, 31 came from registered lobbyists and lobby groups, and of the 31 cents, 14 came from just 10 lobby groups. Of the remaining 32 cents, 14 cents came from individuals in the building industry, 10 cents from attorneys, and 4 cents each from insurance men and the medical profession. Financial institutions and agribusiness each gave 3 cents of every dollar, and public employes 2 cents. That left just 29 cents for the butcher, the baker, and everyone else.

Direct lobby contributions were apparently heavier in 1974 than in 1972, when only 22 cents of direct lobby money was found. But it may be that this is simply a case of more honest reporting, since in 1974 the lobby groups themselves were required to file reports of their donations, thus providing a cross-check.

It was much easier to trace most contributions in 1974 than it had ever been in the past. "There may still be a lot of room for improvement, but the law certainly did make everyone more conscious and careful in collecting money," says former Representative Elvin Martinez, chief House sponsor of the new code. "I'm not sure all the money that was collected was reported, but we certainly got a much clearer picture of where it came from than we ever had before." In the past, many Florida lawmakers have privately admitted that money reported as coming from the candidate's billfold often started out as cash in a lobbyist's briefcase. "It's a great temptation," conceded former House Speaker Terrell Sessums, "to take money like that and report it as a personal contribution."

How much of the $319,325 of personal contributions and $106,306 in party money reported came from these sources in 1974 is difficult to judge. Also, as much party fund-raising is done through dinners for which lobbyists and special-interest groups buy blocks of tickets, it is impossible to trace such contributions to individual candidates. It is regularly charged that candidates who don't want to report contributions from certain groups—perhaps labor unions or liquor dealers—use party dinners as a money "laundry." Former House Speaker Terrell Sessums, who hosted a Democratic dinner that raised $95,768 for party distribution to House candidates in 1972, admits it is easy enough to do this. "We would think twice before giving a candidate back less money than he generated in ticket sales," he explained. "It's an invitation to launder money."

In the midst of the 1973 and 1974 legislative sessions, Republicans held fund-raising dinners, at which most of the money came from lobbyists and special-interest groups with a stake in legislation. But according to House Minority Leader William James, who has worked in the past for the Republican State Committee, the G.O.P. did not do so for statewide candidates "because we felt it was better to let the candidate go directly to the sources of money on a one-to-one basis." But John French, Jr., Executive Director for the state Democratic Party during the 1974 campaigns, prefers party fund-raising wherever possible: "The party can launder money in the positive—not the negative—sense. We can take $1,000 apiece from 10 industrial sources, split it up and give to 100 legislative candidates, and it loses its identity. Somebody can't walk up and say, 'Hey, guy, I gave you a grand and I want you to do something for me.' "

When giving directly to candidates, the big lobby donors were, as a rule, extremely successful in giving their money to those destined to win and thus make the contribution useful. The Florida Business Forum, the second largest lobby donor, gave to 57 candidates, only 11 of whom lost. The liquor distributors, the next biggest lobby giver, reported a 73 percent win ratio in contested races. And Dr. J. Leon Schwartz of the Dental Political Action Committee (DENTALPAC) said of the races his group had backed: "We didn't lose too many. We had around an 85 percent success."

Affinity for incumbents, who have proved themselves at the polls and who have voting records that can be checked, is one of the reasons lobbies are so successful. "We look at the past record of an incumbent," says Jack Lee of the Florida Wholesale Spirits Committee of Continuous Existence.* "Like any giver, we look to see if he shares our views, feels about government like we do, if he's [sic] our kind of man or woman." Jon Shebel of the Business Forum explained, "The criteria for incumbents was: Do they have a record that makes it reasonable to assume they have an appreciation for and understanding of business? We did an analysis of voting records, past committee assignments. Those were the basic things we looked at." In this checking, according to DENTALPAC's Dr. Schwartz, there is very little room for emotions or personal friendships. "The average person votes emotionally in a way, votes because he likes a person," he says. "Yet sometimes that man may have ideas that don't jibe with your own." Men with ideas that don't jibe with the ideas of a lobby group simply don't get that group's money.

Incumbents—including House members moving up to the Senate—got $291,355 from lobbies, legislative newcomers a paltry $53,857. Tht may help explain why 53 of the 66 incum-. bents involved in contested races won, and why the 66 could collect virtually the same amount of money ($835,485) as all their 188 opponents (many involved in extra races with each other for the right to challenge an incumbent) could gather ($857,641).

Lobbyists also direct their campaign contributions to the lawmakers who will have the most impact on legislation that

---

* A committee of "continuous existence" is one that is in operation for more than one year and thus does not have to reregister with the secretary of state each year.

affects them—that is, members of the relevant committees. Al-though committee assignments in the Florida legislature are de-termined anew after each election by the speaker of the House and the Senate president (there is no seniority system), lobby groups often show an uncanny ability to direct their money to the men and women who wind up sitting on the committees handling the legislation involving their industry. For example, a fifth of all liquor wholesaler contributions went to members of the House Committee on Regulated Industries and Licenses, which is assigned virtually every bill concerning liquor. The committee also gets most of the legislation involving the beer industry—and it received a quarter of the industry's contribu-tions. The same pattern applies to powerful individuals. Lobbies were generous with Senator Ralph Poston of Miami, Chairman of the Senate Transportation Committee, for instance; he got $10,300 from lobby groups and $13,410 from the road-building industry. ("A lot of people have it in their minds that I repre-sent the special interests," Poston once said, "and that just ain't true.")

One great advantage of lobby money for candidates in the midst of an active campaign is that they generally don't have to spend any time gathering it. "No, I didn't solicit lobby money," says Senator Guy Spicola, a Democratic veteran who got $13,650 of his $55,301 campaign chest (the second highest of any legis-lative candidate) from lobbies. "There were no mail-outs, no calls." It was the same with Republican Representative Don Hazelton. (Lobbyists, while they may be respectors of philo-sophic differences, have no regard for party lines.) "Most of the contributions just came in the mail and I turned them over to my accountant," says Hazelton of the $6,050 in lobby contri-butions he received.

All incumbents were not, of course, acceptable to all lobby groups. "Don't quote me on this by name," implored one lobby-ist, "but a couple of incumbents called us when they didn't get a contribution and asked, 'Are you against me?' and we an-swered, 'Yes.' Fortunately, they didn't get elected." But the number of incumbents who did not get gifts—or at least offers of gifts, because some were turning down lobby donations—was very few. In Florida it is the conservative lawmaker who is likely to get the lobby gifts; traditionally, liberal funding sources, such as labor unions, simply are not nearly as active as are the more conservative business-allied groups.

Elvin Martinez, who was a state Representative when he chal-lenged Guy Spicola for his Senate seat, thinks his efforts to get

the 1973 campaign reporting law passed may have been responsible for the fact that lobby groups were considerably more
generous in giving to Spicola's campaign than to his. "They may
have thought," Martinez reflects, "that 'if that guy is so goody-
goody, we're not going to mess with him,' but I was never told
that directly." Spicola feels the lobby decision was simpler than
that and was made solely on the basis of philosophy. "The business community may have felt I was the lesser of two evils," he
says. "I've never been a staunch conservative, but Elvin was
considered one of the most liberal members of the legislature."

In the past, many of these business-oriented donations have
been "directed" to candidates by lobbyists for such groups as
Associated Industries of Florida, which numbers among its
members most of the corporate giants of the state. When a lobby
group "directs" money, it does not collect funds from members
and then pass it along to candidates, but instead informs members which candidates will be most sympathetic to their interests and exhorts them to make individual contributions.

Prior to the 1972 election, Associated Industries members
were mailed a detailed rundown on legislative candidates.
Then, at a luncheon just prior to the elections, each guest had
placed before him a plate with a folded piece of paper attached
to it. "This plate is empty as you can see," was written on the
front, and when the diner lifted the flap, he read: "But you
should fill it with folding money and give it to a candidate for
the legislature whose record shows he understands business
problems, votes against waste in government, isn't carried
away by emotion, doesn't swallow the free-spending liberal line,
and does not lie. Do this for self-protection if for no other reason."

Such efforts no doubt produced considerable financial support for lawmakers friendly to Associated Industries, but they
also made donations extremely difficult to trace back to the
lobby group—difficult not only for opponents and researching
newsmen, but sometimes for the candidates themselves. Thus
the group's lobbyist, John Shebel, faced the danger of not getting credit for all the money he had directed to winning candidates. For this reason, he decided to act as catalyst for a group
effort by his members and similar-minded business interests during the 1974 elections and formed the Florida Business Forum.
Shebel is certain that this will make his job easier. "The key to
the thing is that [the contribution] be identifiable," Shebel says,
"that they know businessmen are giving to them, are interested.
If you don't give as a group, legislators say, 'You never do any-

thing for us and then you come up here and want us to be business-oriented.' Too many times if an individual business-man gives, it doesn't get identified as a business donation. If your next-door neighbor, who may be a businessman, gives you a contribution you don't know if he contributed because he's a businessman or because he likes you as a neighbor." When the check comes from the Forum, he will know and, presumably, will remember when Shebel comes to talk to him about a piece of legislation. Shebel's conversations with lawmakers are now backed by contributions of $24,025.

The only man with more direct lobby money to support his legislative efforts than Shebel is H. G. Cochran, who represents the state's beer wholesalers. In the past, beer wholesalers have been generous to legislative candidates, but cautiously generous because many lawmakers, particularly in rural north Florida, weren't eager to list large contributions from beer interests on their campaign reports. ("We are not," Cochran once lamented, "motherhood and the flag.") So the beer contributions came in small amounts from many distributors and, in most cases, from distributors far away from the home town of the candidate, making identification difficult. A single senator's report in 1972 showed at least 25 beer contributors from all parts of the state, ranging from $50 down to $1 and including several for odd amounts like $3, $6, and $13. That system lost a great deal of its effectiveness when the *Herald* ran a complete list of every beer contributor it uncovered, so in 1974 Cochran's group contributed through a committee, the Beer Distributors Committee for Good Government. For the distributors, good government mostly means government that does not tamper with existing laws affecting the beer industry. "Generally, we're an industry that is so highly regulated that we have to play a survival-of-the-fittest game," Cochran says. "Generally, we're more on the de-fensive than the offense." One of the things the distributors want to defend is the rebate they get for collecting state taxes on beer. This rebate, which Governor Askew has asked the legislature to eliminate, means millions of dollars a year to Cochran's small group of distributors—and helps explain why $24,225 of distributor money was found in the campaigns of winning legislators.

The same desire to continue the rebate is found among liquor wholesalers (together with beer distributors, they shared $4.1 million in 1974), who contribute through the Florida Wholesale Spirits Committee of Continuous Existence. The wholesalers are also concerned about retaining a state law that requires retailers to pay their bills to wholesalers within 10 days. A House committee was considering extending the grace period to 30 days when the 1975 session opened; but the liquor group's lobbyist, Jack Lee, was hopeful that the $22,625 given to legislators by his groups would help him kill the proposal. "We're just like anybody else—labor unions, teachers, anybody else," he said. "We're trying to help people get elected who will give us a fair shake if legislation we're against is introduced."

Dentists, among others, also worry about legislation that may change the status quo, and that is the admitted reason why Florida dentists formed DENTALPAC in 1974, when it was the seventh largest lobby donor. "We hate," says Dr. Schwartz, the group's chairman, "to see other groups pushing while we just sit idly by." DENTALPAC, he says, is worried because "There are several legislators who have been persuaded to pass a law that might allow passage [of licensed dentists] from one state to another." Legislators who favor that change, which would introduce greater competition to Florida dentists, got none of DENTALPAC's money. It went instead to those who believe, as Dr. Schwartz does, that "the [Dental Examination] Board gives an honest examination. Many of the people who fail the exam are older men . . . who want to come to Florida to retire, work half a day . . . take only the easiest patients."

Similar concerns can be found among members of the rest of the top lobby givers: The Florida Medical Political Action Committee, which contributed $22,520; the Real Estate Political Action Committee, $20,900; the Florida Action Committee for Rural Electrification, $14,250; William Herrell, a lobbyist who represents, among others, the American Greyhound Track Owners Association, $8,870; and the Florida Lawyers Action Group, $8,605.

Most lobbyists predicted they'd be back with even more money for the 1976 elections. "I think we'll come back a lot bigger next year because the first effort was so successful," declared Shebel of the Florida Business Forum. "We'll have a nice kitty next year," added DENTALPAC's Schwartz. And few doubt that legislators will take as much lobby money as they can get and the law allows.

The Senate

As easy as it is for some candidates to collect money without even trying, others find it quite difficult. Money problems were experienced by almost all contenders in the crowded race for

U.S. Senate, the one major statewide contest without an incumbent. With Gurney out of the race there was no clear favorite, but there was plenty of competition for funds and votes: 11 Democrats, 2 Republicans, and 1 American Independent Party candidate.

The press soon relegated 6 of the 11 Democrats to the "also running" category. With one exception, their names were unknown statewide; without exception, they had no real organization; and also without exception, they could not collect the money to finance a campaign in a state of 8 million people. Together, they amassed $66,177; the ultimate winner, former Secretary of State Richard Stone, alone collected $378,114 for the first primary, $859,796 by the general election.

The "also-running" traveled in cars, not airplanes, attempting unsuccessfully to cope with the distances between Florida's widely scattered urban cénters (347 miles between Miami and Jacksonville, 434 miles between Tampa and Pensacola, 214 miles between Orlando and Ft. Lauderdale). They took free radio and TV time, turned up at rallies, and searched desperately for the gimmick that would catch the public's fancy. All failed to find it—even real estate salesman Duaine E. Macon, who dropped his pants in the secretary of state's office and qualified in jacket, red, white, and blue garters, and bathing suit in an attempt to draw attention to his candidacy.

The one well-known minor candidate was Glenn Turner, a salesman of mink oil and motivational courses, who was under indictment in states across the nation for fraud, but still supremely confident. Right hand circling, fingers snapping to the rhythm, Turner would tell you: "If I know 'em, I can sell 'em [snap], if I know 'em [snap] I can sell 'em [snap], if-I-know-'em-I-can-sell-'em [snap, snap, snap]." But, without money, not even supersalesman Turner could get to "know 'em," so he did not sell them.

And so the press concentrated on the four "major" candidates —Stone, U.S. Congressman Bill Gunter, former House Speaker Richard Pettigrew, and former State Senate President Mallory Horne—and one dark horse, attorney Burton Young, plucked out of the "also running" group because of his credentials (he was a former President of the Florida Bar), his campaign (he was running as the nonpolitician in a year when politicians were under fire everywhere), and his ability to collect enough money to mount a campaign that included not only adequate transportation but some media as well. Young himself termed "obscene" the $135,606.15 he was forced to spend just for that, but it was not nearly enough. Instead of finishing fifth, as most of the experts had predicted, he ran seventh, bested by Turner, whose name was recognized, and by paint-and-body-shop-owner George Balmer, whose name gave him first-place position on the crowded ballot.

Nor were the major candidates without financial problems. The first to surface was in the campaign of Horne, a Tallahassee conservative who had once bolted the party to manage Goldwater's Presidential campaign in Florida. Horne was an 18-year veteran of the Florida legislature, the only man in this century to be elected both speaker of the House and president of the Senate, an attorney who made a million dollars as a developer. In July, although he had raised $130,000 (only Stone had more at that point), Horne discovered he had money problems. "We realized there was an overrun of expenses over collections and we had to discharged all the paid employees—although most of them stayed with us as volunteers," remembers Horne's campaign co-chairman, former State Senator Louis de la Parte. "Some of the problem, how much you can't tell, was a result of the terrible publicity [Horne] received during the Bud Dickinson hearings." Horne, who had some business dealings with Dickinson, voluntarily appeared before the grand jury investigating the Comptroller. Although he was never accused of any wrongdoing, media coverage of his jury appearance had a chilling effect on potential donors, de la Parte feels. Whatever the reasons, Horne who had planned to collect $400,-000 for the campaign, reset his goal at $200,000 (he was actually able to collect $231,519) and reshaped his campaign to conform. That meant not only no paid employees, but no paid television, radio, or newspaper ads. The most conservative Democratic Senate candidate in a state generally considered conservative (George Wallace walked away with the 1972 Presidential primary), Horne finished fourth in the race.

Of the major candidates, Pettigrew was acknowledged as the most liberal. Armed with statistics ("2 percent of the nation's businesses control 88 percent of its assets"), charts, and a 57-page white paper (complete with 79 footnotes), Pettigrew set out to sell his program "For an America We Can Afford," including tougher anti-trust laws, a ban on conglomerate growth, interest and tax credits for small businesses while big businesses got wage and price controls, and regulation of the oil industry. Pettigrew had a reform image, and as the legislative leader for many of the Governor's programs he was closely identified with the popular Askew. He had been the sponsor of tough ethics legislation, and years before he had severed his relationship with his old law firm because one of its clients, Hialeah Racetrack, was heavily regulated by the state.

He limited his own contributions to $1,000 a person, one-third of what state law allowed, and was careful to screen out certain special-interest money. "I kinda think the Askew [limit on contributions] set the tone for those of us who were representing certain things," he says, "but as a nonincumbent I simply couldn't set a $100 limit. The only thing I could do was make a realistic limit for a nonincumbent."

But Pettigrew had the most sophisticated approach to primary campaigning and the most willing unpaid workers. Using a computerized breakdown of recent elections, his organization targeted 1,000 precincts that had historically turned out a liberal vote. By primary time, volunteers, joined by Pettigrew once a week, had rung an estimated 100,000 doorbells in those districts.

The campaign was good, almost good enough. Pettigrew received 146,728 votes, just 10,574 less than he needed to make the runoff. The money, he says, simply wasn't there for the last, needed media push. While Watergate, state scandals, and the sagging economy cut into his collections as they did those of others, he had a special problem. "My central problem was that Dick Stone and I were mining the same geographic area," says Pettigrew. "He had professional and highly paid staffing, his phone solicitation started very early. There was a tendency for him to either get a commitment [for a contribution] or neutralize someone who might otherwise have contributed to me. I was challenged in my financial base by someone with greater roots and ties." Pettigrew met the vote challenge, leading Stone in Dade County (Miami), the home of both. But he lost the money challenge—and the election.

Although it undoubtedly prevented him from raising some sorely needed last-minute funds, Pettigrew still thinks the limit made political sense. "We didn't get to make much use of it as an issue because the field was so crowded," he says. "In the second primary it would have been far more important. I was gambling I'd make the runoff. I certainly would have made an issue of the large contributions then."

While Pettigrew and Stone grappled for money in Dade County, Bill Gunter was collecting it with efficiency in his central Florida home base. Although a first-term Congressman, Gunter had represented the central Florida area in the legislature for years and was one of the few state Democrats able to carry the traditionally Republican area around Orlando. "Bill Gunter spent his first 39 years getting ready for the next 6," read his tabloid campaign brochure, and it almost seemed as if he had. His image was moderate, his record on ethics good. Gunter had filed a bill in the Florida legislature as early as 1969 to require state officials to file certified copies of their income tax returns (it was killed), and as a Congressman, had filed a bill for full public financing of all national races.

While Gunter did not collect quite as much money as Stone for the first primary ($317,301 to $378,114), he spent more wisely, budgeting carefully toward a final-week media blitz that would send voters to the polls remembering Gunter's name when they faced the crowded ballot. The cost was considerable —about $60,000—but it was effective. Gunter led the 11-man field by nearly 90,000 votes. After that victory, he appeared the sure run-off winner, and money began to flow in. "If you really look like a winner you can collect money with no trouble," says Harold (Buz) Rummel, a Gunter campaign aide.

Stone saluted Gunter's last-minute media blitz, saying of his own campaign, "We started our media too early and we couldn't sustain it. That led to a change in momentum. If the lead horse falters, it's difficult to pick up the momentum again." Stone told a reporter, "I worked for 10 months harder than the rest of them put together, and [Gunter] had more television and got more votes." To pick up the momentum after the primary, Stone needed money to take his message to the voters. His program for the three weeks between primary and runoff, Stone said, was clear: "If it is a chance to see Pettigrew people, I go. If it is a chance to see a newspaper still undecided on its endorsement, I go. In the absence of those two things, it is more important for me to be on the telephone trying to raise money to match him on television. It's more important for me to get the money to do to him what he did to me." So Stone and his wife, Marlene (daughter of William Singer, founder of the Royal Castle fast-food chain), took to the phones, contacting potential contributors and raising $60,000—about $20,000 more than Gunter was to use—for a media campaign.

"Message" ads hit at Gunter, calling him a "do nothing" Congressman who was often absent and missed important votes. Gunter denied the charges, but normally only when asked about them by reporters. As the new front-runner, he was staying above the battle, ignoring what he saw as essentially a challenge to debate. "We thought Stone's media was really bad," says Rummel. "He didn't name his opponent, the charges were very vague. If the ads had been better, more pointed, Gunter would have probably responded, but the decision was to ignore them." It is a decision, Rummel concedes, that would not be made again. "They were vague, but they saturated the area [Gunter's central Florida home base]. The biggest impact was just to turn off a lot of people who would have voted for Gunter. They didn't vote against him, they just didn't vote." And that, figures Rummel, was the difference. "We only had a 14 percent turnout in central Florida. If just Orange County had voted 28 percent he would have made it." He didn't; Stone edged Gunter, by less than 11,000 votes out of 632,727 cast.

Ahead was the Republican challenger, carrying few of the encumbrances of Republicans elsewhere, despite Watergate and despite the Gurney charges. "In Florida, I think the cabinet scandal was like a pox on all your houses," says Public Service Commissioner Paula Hawkins. "It wasn't confined to Washington or any one party." An aggressive, articulate campaigner, Hawkins in 1972 became the first woman as well as the first Republican ever to be elected to the PSC. In 1974, her sights were set higher—on the U.S. Senate. They were set, she learned, too high. "The thing we ran into was just a lack of funds, nobody had any money. It was sad because that leaves it to the special interests."

In Hawkins' case, the most logical special interests were the utilities regulated by the PSC, since she did not have to resign to run for the Senate and still had half of her four-year PSC term remaining should she be defeated. "But we had established a precedent in not taking money from people the PSC regulates, and although it was technically legal to take it for the Senate race, we did not take any." Hawkins, in fact, took too very little money from anyone. She collected only $25,096.78, and $5,200 of that came from her husband. Local Republican groups had done most of the fund-raising for Hawkins' PSC campaign, and the difficulty of raising money became, she says, almost a psychological problem. "When we saw how hard it was to raise money—Eckerd, a multimillionaire got in [the race] . . . there's no way you can outspend a multimillionaire—we just backed away and didn't try as hard as we should have."

With no media and no funds for a planned mass mailing, Hawkins relied on personal appearances and what free media was available. She was swamped by Jack Eckerd, 186,897 to 90,049. Eckerd was, as Hawkins said, a multimillionaire. His income tax return and statement of net worth—filed, like those of many candidates, following the examples of Askew and others who had been making yearly reports to the secretary of state—showed that even after $25 million in debts were deducted, the founder of the drug chain that bears his name still had a net worth of $36 million. Eckerd did not feel that such wealth was an asset for a politician, as he made clear in his announcement press conference at the State Capitol: "If I thought you guys wouldn't accuse me of trying to buy the election, I would offer $5 to the favorite charity of anyone here who reports today without using the words 'millionaire,' 'drug-store magnate,' and so on." No charity benefited.

Eckerd was to find that being a millionaire is no aid in collecting the $25 to $100 "average family" donation he sought. Four years before, in a losing attempt to unseat Governor Claude Kirk in the primary, Eckerd had spent more than $1 million of his own money and, in the process, had been accused of trying to "buy" the office. This time, Federal law limited him to $35,000. Hal Stayman, his campaign manager, cited Eckerd's generosity, his multimillionaire image, and the economy as the reasons fund-raising was difficult in 1974. In the end, Eckerd was to raise $432,785.67, and while that was considerably less than Stone amassed, spending in the general election was fairly even ($262,868.20 for Eckerd to $315,751.36 for Stone) since Eckerd did not have the primary struggle Stone faced.

The general election campaign was lackluster and, so far as the major party candidates were concerned, almost devoid of clear issues because they basically agreed. At one point during a televised debate, after both major candidates had given similar answers to question after question, a puzzled listener called in with the obvious question: How do you differ? Replied Stone, we don't. Eckerd did not disagree.

The third man in the race, John Grady, a physician from the farming community of Belle Glade, a national director of the John Birch Society, and the representative of George Wallace's American Independent Party (Wallace himself never took part in the Florida campaign), did disagree. A forceful, convincing speaker who styled himself the only constitutional conservative in the contest, Grady called for a halving of Federal spending, a return to the gold standard, and an end to trade with Communist countries. He fueled his campaign with contributions from true believers around the state and sometimes far away, most in very small amounts. It may have been Grady's $150,846 that decided the election. He took 15 percent of the vote, carried three counties, finished second in a half-dozen others, and cut sharply into Eckerd's margin in the conservative areas where he had been expected to run strongest. Stone squeeked through again, leading Eckerd by 44,357 of 1,800,539 ballots cast.

"Had he not been a national director of the John Birch Society, Dr. Grady might well have been in the number-one spot," Stone said on election night. "I'm sure he drew more Democratic votes than Republican votes, but I don't think he drew more votes away from me than he did from Mr. Eckerd." Months later, Eckerd's campaign manager was to agree: "Dr. Grady was almost the fatal blow. . . . No, I couldn't say Grady was the reason we lost—there were many other things—but he was a major factor."

The Collectors

The money raised in the 1974 campaigns came from a relatively small group of people. Even the record 8,876 contributors in the broadest-based 1974 campaign, Governor Askew's $100-maximum fund-raising effort, represented tiny fractions of the state population of 8 million and the voter registration of 3.5 million. So with few exceptions, Florida politicians generally follow the fund-raising system described by Ted Phelps, who has collected money for several Florida campaigns, including two for the U.S. Senate: "You go to them what's got."

First there is "the list"—a list that will start with names of those closest to the candidate, those who have given before, those who have given to similar candidates, a list that will grow and grow during the campaign and will continue to include those first names. "People who have given to the candidate in the past will give again; 90 percent of them will give again," says Phelps. "You start with the original list and then you keep adding to it. Then, every two or three months, you cover the same ground again." When money was really tight, Lewis says, he went back to those who had given earlier, who had a stake in the race. "One of the sad things," he says, "is that the same people are giving over and over, and they are the ones with an interest."

Richard Stone, the man elected to the Senate in 1974, decided that raising money during the campaign was more important than campaigning, and he went back to his most basic supporters. "We had to go to our families and our friends and their families and friends," he says.

For the big contribution, personal contact with the candidate is a key part of fund-raising, and not even a popular, powerful incumbent is exempted from this rule. "Sure the Governor spent time fund-raising," says Askew's campaign manager, Jim Smith. "Early in, you gotta spend a lot of time fund-raising."

"Our crunch came three or four weeks out of the first primary," remembers Phelps of the Gunter campaign he managed in 1974. "We were never really desperate, but we came to a point where those of us that were collecting—some 20 of us around the state—just weren't getting it done. So we started Bill on a regular schedule, putting a list of 10 or 20 people in his pocket each day. If he had some time to wait in an airport, he could make a call or two, or if we could get him in a motel room for an hour he could call several people. That's the best way to raise money there is, there is no substitute for a call from the candidate."

Stone noted the importance of candidate contact: "Even the people who don't have anything specific in mind want to talk to the candidate. Sometimes they just distrust the collector, thinking he'll take credit for the contribution instead of giving it to them." And Buz Rummel, who worked his way through the campaigns of Adams, Gunter, and Eckerd in 1974, and now serves Lewis as press secretary, pointed out: "If a staffer calls [contributors] might give $250; if the candidate gets on the phone, tells them that things are tough, but the prospects are great and 'how much I hope you can help,' the man might give $1,000."

It is a rare candidate who will tell you that he enjoys this personal fund-raising, or that it improves the political process. "It's very hard for someone who wants to be an officeholder to ask for money, it's different than asking for a vote," says Stone. "I've been a successful businessman, now here I am out begging for money. It takes you down a peg, I'll tell you that. It's a great leveler." Lewis says, "A lot of times you are literally dunning people, almost like a bill collector. Once you get a commitment, you just keep after them. You're asking people for money," he muses, "but you're not selling them anything."

One hopes that most candidates are not selling anything. But some say this is wishful thinking. "There is no way you can convince me," says de la Parte, "that you can go contrary to human nature, can have someone get elected and not have a feeling of gratitude to those who helped him get elected. And money is always the hardest thing to get."

There are those who maintain that giving seems to be based more on the candidate's personality than on his stated political position. "It's all contacts," maintains Phelps, the man with the

list. "We got money from conservatives and liberals, and so did
Pettigrew and so did Stone." Indeed, candidates often solicit
the same people, and an in-depth survey of contributions early
in the 1974 campaign by Bruce Giles of the *Miami Herald*
showed a striking similarity of funding sources. Askew had gotten 23 percent of his support from the building industry, his
opponent Adams 28 percent. In the U.S. Senate primary, build-
ing-industry support percentages were 24 for Gunter, 16 for
Horne, 14 for Pettigrew and 21 for Stone; and before the runoff,
22 for Gunter and 27 for Stone. Attorneys were another source of
support, providing more than 14 percent of Stone's money and
over 13.5 percent of Gunter's. Whether personality or philosophy was the determining factor in these gifts is not clear. There
is of course a wide range of political viewpoints among attorneys
and builders, certainly when it comes to questions outside of
their particular interests. Furthermore, a candidate's stated
political position may have nothing to do with how he or she
can be expected to vote on a given issue, especially a low-visibility special-interest issue.

There is no question, however, that target groups, those with
interests in common with a candidate, are central to a good list.
The connection may be the candidate's background: Gunter, an
insuranceman and former Future Farmer of America, scored
well with both groups; Pettigrew, "the attorneys' attorney," had
great success with law firms. It can be past activities: Turlington
and Horne got considerable initial support from lobby groups
that had worked with them in the legislature. Or it can be
present activities: Governor Askew had heavy backing from developers, builders, and other groups that must deal with state
government; incumbent state cabinet officers drew much of
their money from the groups they regulated.

One source of candidate funds in Florida is the parties, which
get basic support from the filing fees their candidates pay for the
right to run. (Fees are set at 5 percent of the yearly salary the
candidate will receive if he wins.) For statewide and legislative
candidates, the state retains a small portion for handling fees
and passes the remainder on to the party's state organization. All
fees paid by county-level candidates go directly to the parties,
three-fifths to the state unit and two-fifths to the county committee. In 1974, the Democratic State Committee got $291,245
from state filing fees, $154,774 from county fees. Together, the
fees accounted for well over half its budget, which was also
bolstered by $103,971 from a Democratic telethon and the
proceeds from legislative House and Senate fund drives. All

told, the party at the state level pumped $391,558 into campaigns, with the largest single contribution—$25,000—going to U.S. Senate candidate Stone. (Askew was no drain on the party; the state committee, like other contributors, was limited to $100.)

With fewer candidates and no telethon, the Republicans had less money overall to spend, but they were not, says House Minority Leader William James, in any real financial bind. "I didn't find the money situation being one of our major problems," says James, who in the past has worked for the G.O.P.'s state committee. In Florida, Republicans, much more than Democrats, rely on the efforts of county committees and local clubs. "In our county [Palm Beach] alone," notes James, "the committee was able to give $1,750 to each legislative candidate."

The Republicans have stronger local operations because, in reality, they were the only major political party in Florida for years, although registered Democrats heavily outnumbered Republicans (and still lead them by nearly two and a half to one) and won all the elections. But the battles were in the primaries, not the general election, which meant that the Democratic Party was not one party but hundreds of little parties created by candidates; Democrats pledged to one candidate might well hate his opponents more than they did the Republican in the race. Republicans, on the other hand, needed all the unity they could get, and the party structure provided it.

Republican Claude Kirk's election as Governor in 1966, followed by Edward Gurney's election to the U.S. Senate two years later, almost forced party unity on the Democrats. "There's been a dramatic growth in our party during the past four years," says former Democratic Party chairman Jon Moyle. "The Democratic Party made a lot of strides in growing up and becoming competitive, as opposed to the Republican Party, which grew up competitive in the first place. As a result, both parties now handle some of the campaigning chores that they can do more cheaply than individual candidates. "We did polling on issues, research for position papers. We've got a million and a half names on our computer for mailouts. At one point we did radio tapes for legislators. All available for a heck of a lot less than if candidates had to do them separately," says Moyle.

There is general agreement among Republicans and Democrats, among liberals and conservatives, that the 1974 elections, in Governor Askew's words, "came closer to following the rules of reporting than any election that has ever taken place in Florida." There is, however, no such agreement on the reason.

"My personal experience is that reporting was pretty darn accurate," said Askew opponent Ben Hill Griffin. "All of the Watergate mess was boiling in and everybody was scared to death. Five or ten years from now it might be different, but this year people were really shook up about it." Others felt Florida's own scandals were the major deterrent to false reporting, while some, including Senator Stone, gave major credit to the state's new contribution law, which had its first statewide test in 1974. "I believe the harshness of the new rules produced a generally cleaner campaign," he said, only to be contradicted by Ethics Chairman D'Alemberte, who said flatly, "I don't think the new laws made any difference at all, it was the political climate."

Louis de la Parte had been a chief sponsor of much of the election reform legislation passed during the 1973–74 sessions. Now he feels the new laws may have hurt, not helped the election process. "I'm very disappointed with the laws we passed," he admitted. "I think at the time they looked like the right thing to do, but today I'm not sure how many people who should have run, who would have been good candidates, good officeholders, didn't run because of the need to disclose their sources of income. Or how many people didn't run because of the problem of being responsible for what others in the campaign did [on campaign reporting]. For what someone else did, you could end up in stripes."

There was also agreement on one point: None of the new laws worked exactly as had been intended; all needed revision. Askew claimed that problems and complaints weren't unexpected: "You just don't create a perfect system overnight with a new law. A good system has to evolve." Others were not so generous. "Absolutely the most damnable thing I ever saw," complained Griffin of the contribution law. "It was more of a hindrance than a help," agreed William James. "Unless a candidate is really well funded or has a CPA who will work for nothing, the candidate is tied down. He can't talk about issues; all the voter can find out is that he can fill out a form." Even Pettigrew, a strong backer of election law reform, complained of "a considerable amount of confusion between the state and federal law . . . It's a pretty hairy situation because you as the candidate are responsible for what other people do. It's a very hazardous business."

There are those who maintain that private contributions must be eliminated or severely reduced if the election process is ever to function properly. "If you want to do something more than just have a hypocritical situation, you have to go to public financing," maintained de la Parte, who introduced a pilot-project public financing bill in 1973, only to see it killed by a unanimous vote in committee. "One person might be smoother and more suave and less obvious about it, but he's going to be just as indebted to the people who financed him. Until you have publicly financed elections, that's what you're going to have." The problem, said de la Parte, is that the average citizen rarely takes part in campaign financing. "You can put 1,000 average voters in a room and say 'How many of you have ever contributed to a campaign, any campaign?" and not one of them will have contributed. Then you ought to be able to ask them: 'Then where in the hell do you think the money comes from?' To show any shock or amazement [that special interests finance elections] is stupid. We've always known that."

Pettigrew agreed that public dollars would be well spent to finance elections. "The public," he maintained, "loses so much more money by forcing its elected officials to depend to such an extent on special interest contributions . . . in exchange for either tacit or express commitment." He supports public financing on a matching basis, but thinks the individual contribution allowed should be very small and "the match by the state should be higher than 50–50."

Fund-raiser Phelps is, surprisingly, a public finance supporter too. "I favor it because I don't see any other way to get the people's confidence built back in government," he said. "Clearly the upper classes, the monied classes, have an enormous impact vis-à-vis the poorer people. It's a pain to raise money. The givers are suspect, the candidates are suspect, the system is suspect—and no good comes of it. I think we ought to have 100 percent public financing."

Republican James opposed public financing with language as strong as Phelps uses to support it. "The very thought of it offends me," he stated. "A man that can't spend the time working through one of the party vehicles to get elected doesn't deserve to be elected. If they care enough, they'll build the necessary know-how to get elected—and that includes fund-raising," said James, who, oddly, ran his only losing race (for the state Senate) against a millionaire opponent. "Money may have been a factor, but that's the breaks," he said of the loss. "And besides, I still raised within a few hundred dollars of the limit. We can't let every Tom, Dick, and Harry raise a few dollars and get matching dollars. It'll turn this thing into a circus."

Esther Frieden, a member of Common Cause's national governing board and state legislative coordinator for Florida, found that most Florida legislators weren't nearly so adamant on the subject. "We find public financing is the least exposed of all our issues," she said. "There are just more people who know less about it. I think people just aren't quite ready to grapple with it. What they are telling me is 'It's a great idea if you can tell me how it will work.' So I'm trying to tell them."

House Speaker Don Tucker is one who still has to be told. "I think the election laws are working pretty good in Florida, I haven't seen any problems," he declared. "There are still people advocating public financing and I'm not against the concept. If they could show me a way it would be fairly distributed, I would support it." It is unlikely, Tucker conceded, that he will be convinced before the state's economic situation improves.

Florida began the 1974–75 fiscal year with a healthy surplus and every expectation that taxes would produce even more revenue for the year ahead, as they had done for years in the rapidly growing state. Before the fiscal year ended on June 30, however, the surplus had been spent and state agencies had been forced to take an across-the-board budget cut. It was not, most politicians agreed, a good year to try to sell voters on the concept of spending public money for political campaigns. Explained Tucker, whose district includes the state's capital city and the majority of its state employees: "If it's a choice between public financing and raises for state employees, I imagine the state employees would get the money."

In the immediate future, there is little likelihood that Florida will do more than tinker with its new laws in an effort to make them more workable or that the state will seriously explore more than the most limited forms of public aid to campaign financing—perhaps funding a voter booklet with biographies of all the candidates or expanding the public television time now made available to them.

Still, some tinkering could improve the contribution law, and even those who complain bitterly about the problems it caused do not call for its elimination, simply its improvement. "In all fairness," commented James, "I think Florida has one of the finest 'who gave it—who got it' laws in the nation." Expected changes include dovetailing reporting dates with those in the Federal law, reducing the frequency of reporting, and improving enforcement so that honest candidates aren't penalized for complying with the law. "In the past, our law has been a toothless tiger," said James. "The way the legislature acted was to be very, very careful about [allowing too much] enforcement. . . . now we have to look at the laws from the standpoint of penalties. We need more civil penalties; the attorney general and state attorneys are likely to shy away from a criminal prosecution for most violations . . . they'll think, 'if this guy is guilty, then 30 more are probably guilty.' We have to have more civil penalties, penalties that will be enforced."

D'Alemberte has agreed that more civil, not criminal, penalties are needed. "Civil lawsuits sometimes don't do anything but open up a bunch of facts to the public view, but they may be facts that the voters need," he explains. D'Alemberte would not want to see the Ethics Commission given ultimate power to decide on violations and assess penalties, however. "There are serious constitutional problems, and it's a damn dangerous thing to give that power to an appointed commission." But he didn't like the complicated referral system for investigations under which the commission originally operated. Depending upon who was involved, complaints were first referred to either the speaker of the House, the Senate president, the governor, the heads of scores of state agencies, the state cabinet, or the governing bodies of any of the state's hundreds of cities and counties. D'Alemberte asked, and the 1975 legislature granted, power for the commission to make its own initial investigations and publish reports on its findings. He was not successful, however, in persuading lawmakers to combine the Ethics and Elections Commissions. Elections Commission members were cool to the proposal, and even Governor Askew had mixed feelings. "My only serious reservation to merger is the workload," the Governor said. "While they are essentially in the same field, I have a feeling the Ethics Commission will more and more become a part of Florida government and will not be able to concentrate on elections during campaign periods." Speaker Tucker, also unsure of the need for merger, has asked for a year-long study to determine if consolidation is needed.

It was hard, at the time the 1975 legislature met, to find anyone who really liked the disclosure law, a compromise struck between Governor Askew and Senate President Dempsey Barron in the final hours of the 1974 session. It applied to local officials, including appointed members of groups such as zoning commissions, and already some members of boards at that level have resigned or refused appointments rather than fill out the forms, maintaining that the law is an unwarranted invasion of privacy. Backers of disclosure had just the opposite complaint; they said the law required so little information that it was meaningless.

Certainly the law appeared to require a lot of information, asking a candidate or official to list: any source of income making up more than 10 percent of his gross income; sources of

income for each business in which he had over 10 percent interest and which contributed at least 15 percent of his gross
income; every "privileged" business (such as banks, utility
companies, dog and horse tracks, and any business holding a
state liquor license) in which he had an interest of 10 percent
or more; any public agencies he represented at his same level
of government (a provision many legislator-attorneys didn't
like); any loan on which he had received a preferential rate of
interest; and each asset that contributed at least 15 percent of
his total assets, excluding his home and any property located
outside the state. But the law actually required most candidates
to do little more than list one principal source of income, such
as a law firm or insurance agency. Newsmen sifting through
the stacks of reports in the secretary of state's office discovered
they could often learn more about a legislator's sources of income by looking at the clerk's manual issued by the legislature
each year, which prints only information submitted voluntarily
by lawmakers.

As it had the year before, in 1975 the disclosure law became
the focal point in a power struggle between Governor Askew
and Senate President Barron. A conflict between the two men
over appointments affected the fate of legislation proposed by
Askew to require full financial disclosure. Barron consistently
opposed the Governor's measure, calling disclosure an invasion
of privacy, while Askew appealed directly to legislators in a
letter declaring that "The people need assurances that we are
serving their interests and not those of the special interests
that are the parasites on the people's government." Lawmakers
were failing to give these assurances, Askew charged, because
"the special interests are once again displaying all their greed
and all their guile in a concerted effort to resume their dominance of the legislative process." The Governor vowed to put
a full financial disclosure law on the statute books, even if he
had to go over the heads of the legislators and gather signatures
to put the issue on the November 1976 ballot.

The legislature finally passed an amended, far weaker disclosure law than Askew had asked for. It requires the reporting
of all sources of income exceeding 5 percent (as opposed to 10
percent in the old law); reporting by an official of sources of
income exceeding 10 percent (instead of 15 percent) in a business that contributes 20 percent of his gross income; and listing
of all real property in which an official owns an interest of
5 percent or more and all stocks and bonds with a value exceeding 10 percent of gross income. Askew signed the bill, calling

it "a further step toward full, meaningful disclosure," adding that "it falls considerably short of that goal which I have envisioned." It fell so short, Askew later said, that he would continue with his plans to gather the 206,070 signatures needed to put the issue on the 1976 ballot—as he has since succeeded in doing. Aides said he would be satisfied with nothing less than a law requiring the filing of income tax returns and net-worth statements.

It's just possible the legislature might give Askew the law he wants before it has to go on the ballot. The date of the balloting coincides with legislative elections, when all House members plus half the senators will be up for re-election. Failure to vote for a full-disclosure bill during the 1976 spring session of the legislature would, in effect, make an incumbent a part of the disclosure contest, a contest few doubt Askew will win.

But if there is strong pressure for a tougher disclosure law in Florida, there is little push for more major changes in ethics and campaign contribution laws, even from the Governor's office. More than lack of money is involved in the reluctance to make major changes immediately. Virtually all Florida's election laws have been rewritten during the past two years, and there is an inclination to give them a longer test period, for, even though they are not working perfectly, they are working. Both the Ethics and Elections Commissions have been issuing opinions setting guidelines for conduct, thus creating, in effect, a whole body of ethics law. Campaigns during 1974 were generally cleaner, reporting generally better. And legislative leaders have not forgotten the battles necessary to achieve the new legislation. Few issues generate such intensity and involvement by the entire legislature as do ethics-election questions, since everyone who votes on them will be personally affected by them. And underlying it all is the realization that in simply considering such legislation, lawmakers are conceding that the system is not working, that there is dishonest, unethical conduct. "It's really a tragedy the legislature is now being put to the task of trying to make credible its own existence," complained Senator Kenneth Myers during the 1974 ethics debates. "There's a certain presumption in this type of legislation that legislators are dishonest, and that I take a gut dislike to—that we even have to consider this type of legislation."

FOUR

TEXAS: BIG MONEY

Jon Ford

Not much happened in the Texas campaigns of 1974. All the incumbent Democratic statewide officials except one retiring octogenarian were seeking re-election; most had only light opposition in the primaries, or no opposition at all. The Republicans were in bad shape as a result of Watergate, unprecedented voter apathy, and a slate of candidates little known outside their own communities. Good Congressional scraps could be counted on the fingers of one hand, and even the state legislative races were fewer and, for the most part, less turbulent than usual. The six-man race for speaker of the House of Representatives (which is decided by the votes of 150 legislators) for a while looked like the hottest show on the road. In spite of this sluggish action, more than $8 million was poured into the campaigns by the statewide, Congressional, and legislative candidates and their supporters.

Although it was virtually certain that Governor Dolph Briscoe would be elected to a second term (which he was), more than $3,450,000 was spent on the gubernatorial race by all candidates. Briscoe himself, taking no chance on an upset, was the biggest single campaign contributor of the year, if not of all time in Texas. He advanced as loans $645,000 of his personal funds to his 1974 campaign committees, which spent a total of $2,396,523. This brought the total of loans and contributions Briscoe has made to his campaigns since his first (unsuccessful) race for governor in 1968 to more than $1.3 million.

Some statewide candidates—Lieutenant Governor Bill Hobby, Attorney General John Hill, and Agriculture Commissioner John C. White—appeared to be spending money needlessly since their opposition was token. One probable reason is that new four-year terms for all Texas statewide officials went into effect that year, so there will be no statewide campaigns (except for the U.S. Senate, three judgeships, and a Railroad Commission post) in 1976; Hobby and Hill are expected to run for governor in 1978 and wanted some media exposure in 1974. White, a wily veteran of nearly a quarter-century in statewide office, was also mindful of the fact that he would have no opportunity for statewide advertising again until 1978.

One of the most spectacularly successful fund-raisers was U.S. Senator Lloyd Bentsen, who racked up $620,000 from a December mailing for his ill-fated Presidential campaign. He had raised $457,485 from a single dinner in late 1973 (with some of the contributions still trickling in during 1974). Bentsen's finance director, George Lambert Bristol, estimates that 95 percent of the money came from Texans.

Republicans, outsiders at the state level but usually able to match or better Democrats in financing key statewide races, complained that they had never had so much trouble raising money. At that, the Republican gubernatorial candidate, Dr. James H. Granberry of Lubbock, was able to come up with $738,067.

More than 2,275 contributions or loans of $500 or more to Texas statewide and district-level candidates were made in 1974, according to reports filed with the secretary of state. Easily 1,000 additional contributions of $500 and more went to Congressional and legislative candidates in single-county or less-than-county-size districts, who file their reports with local officials. In addition, there were several hundred $500-plus donations to Bentsen. The number of such contributions was only slightly less than the record 3,700 in Texas for 1972, which led all states. And 1972 was a wide-open year, with most major state offices turning over and hard-fought governor's and U.S. Senate races in both the Democratic primary and the general election.

One wonders how much money might have been spent if 1974 had been a "good" year. For fund-raisers, whether they represented liberal, conservative, or moderate candidates, found common ground on one point: Their jobs in 1974 were harder than ever. And campaign costs had soared, largely as a result of increased reliance on television in a vast state with sprawling, lightly populated rural districts and heavily populated metropolitan areas.

Briscoe's primary opponent, Frances (Sissy) Farenthold, never was able to get her planned series of television appeals aired statewide because of lack of money. "Raising money this year was harder than I have ever seen it," said Creekmore Fath, an Austin attorney who was Farenthold's campaign manager. "People were just skittish about giving to anybody," said Fath. "We raised about 20 percent of the funds in 1974 that we were able to raise for Sissy in 1972 when she was a total unknown." Fath, who has been wrangling political contributions from liberal and moderate Democrats since 1948, cited television as the biggest contributor to campaign-cost inflation, but pointed to other factors, including special efforts aimed at minority groups. "There are just more people to reach," said Fath. "More diverse groups than 20 years ago. Minority groups were active in only a few areas of the state when I started in politics. Now, you have to mount a 'brown' campaign and a 'black' campaign."

Republican gubernatorial nominee Jim Granberry, although more fortunate than Farenthold in his fund-raising, also fell far short of his media budget. Norman Newton, Granberry's campaign director and a Republican money-raiser with a decade of statewide political experience, echoed Fath: He found 1974 "the worst year I ever saw to raise money." Both Fath and Newton saw the "turned-off," "burned-out" attitude of voters in the wake of Watergate scandals as the most formidable enemy. "I had to spend 85 percent of my time in the campaign on fund-raising," said Newton, "but we never could break open the money. It was a most disheartening thing to beat your brains out at this, and then read in the newspapers that Governor Briscoe had dropped in another $200,000 of his own money." Granberry was forced to limit his campaign schedule in order to make personal appeals to GOP supporters for funds. Newton acknowledged, however, that money was not the decisive factor in his candidate's defeat. Briscoe had a built-in advantage in the race as a reasonably popular incumbent, whose boast of having avoided a state tax bill in 1973 and pledges of no new taxes in 1975 were big vote-getters.

Briscoe, who reached for his checkbook rather than make the personal hard-sell appeals that former Governors John Connally and Preston Smith were never reluctant to undertake, also had certain unique problems to overcome. "People won't give a lot of money to a Rockefeller—or a Briscoe," said Fath. "Once stories started coming out that Briscoe was worth $50 million, people worth only a paltry $300,000 or $400,000 said: 'Why should I give my money to this guy?' "

Briscoe reflected later, "In retrospect, I could probably have gotten by spending less money in my 1974 race. As it was, I cut the campaign budget considerably from the original recommendations. You never take anything for granted. If a candidate gets complacent, it's a sure bet that his supporters will become complacent, too." As it turned out, Briscoe wasn't in much of a race in either the primary—in which his rival, Farenthold, failed to generate much interest—or the general election against Republican Granberry.

1973 Reforms

A moderating influence in the 1974 elections might have been the new disclosure laws passed in 1973.

The effort to enact new election laws, which found even the most unreformed legislative oldtimers unabashedly lining up behind such niceties as an overhaul of the code of ethics, was prompted by major scandals in state government. The so-called "Sharpstown scandals" of 1971–72, which have been described as Texas's own "little Watergate," were first exposed by the Federal Securities and Exchange Commission through a lawsuit filed on gubernatorial inauguration day in January 1971. It all began in 1969 when Frank Sharp, a religious, nonsmoking, nondrinking, real estate developer, banker, and insurance-company owner, started pushing for legislation to authorize state-chartered bank-deposit insurance on accounts up to $100,-000. He claimed the plan would aid smaller state banks which had difficulty attracting deposits in amounts exceeding the Federal Deposit Insurance Corporation's (FDIC) $15,000 limit on insurance coverage. Sharp acknowledged, though, that his real aim was to "get the FDIC off [my] back." FDIC examiners were looking into $20 million worth of loans his Sharpstown State Bank had made to or received from other companies and individuals associated with Sharp.

Sharp's two bank-deposit-insurance bills were quickly passed in a September 1969 special legislative session with help from House Speaker Gus Mutscher and Governor Preston Smith (who controlled the special session's agenda and had obligingly submitted for consideration by the lawmakers the general subject of additional bank-deposit insurance). Speaker Mutscher, State Representative Tommy Shannon of Fort Worth (sponsor of the Sharp bills in the House), Rush McGinty, an aide to Mutscher, and several others, meanwhile, had profited handsomely on quickie deals in Sharp's National Bankers Life In-

surance Company stock, purchased largely with loans from the
Sharpstown State Bank. Governor Smith and his sometime
business partner Dr. Elmer Baum—an Austin osteopath and
Smith's choice for State Democratic Executive Committee chairman—also made about $62,500 each on the Sharp stock. How-
ever, at the banking industry's urging, Smith later vetoed the
Sharp bank-deposit bills, thus removing himself from the list
of possible bribery suspects.

Mutscher, Shannon, and McGinty were indicted in September 1971 for conspiracy to accept bribes. Mutscher resigned the
speakership, and all three were later convicted at a lengthy
trial in Abilene and given suspended sentences. Sharp received
immunity from prosecution in exchange for his testimony. A
former State Insurance Board Chairman and chief lobbyist for
the bank deposit bills, John Osorio, served a few months of a
three-year sentence in a Federal minimum-security camp for
embezzlement committed while serving as President of National
Bankers Life. And a former Attorney General, Waggoner Carr,
was also named in the initial SEC suit, but nearly three years
later was acquitted of all charges.

Among those whose defeats in the 1972 primary elections
could be attributed at least in part to the Sharpstown scandals
were these: Governor Preston Smith, who although he had
vetoed the bills had profited from Sharp-engineered stock purchases; Lieutenant Governor Ben Barnes, who was never directly implicated in dealings with Sharp and said he was
defeated in his attempt to become governor "just because he
was there [in state government]"; Attorney General Crawford
Martin, who had implied links with Sharp, although no part
in the stock deals; former Speaker Gus Mutscher and several
state representatives who had been members of his "team."

In their place in January 1973, when the new state officials
took office in Austin, were four men who had run on strong
commitments to reform: political newcomers Dolph Briscoe
and Bill Hobby, as Governor and Lieutenant Governor; state
Representative Price Daniel, Jr., who was chosen House Speaker
after Mutscher's successor was defeated in his home district;
and John Hill, as the new Attorney General. Some efforts
toward reform legislation were thus inevitable, and the new
Legislature quickly produced bills providing for changes in
the ethics and campaign-finance statutes.

Under the new law, all opposed candidates were required to
file reports, but unopposed candidates were not. Statewide and
district candidates filed with the secretary of state, candidates

for offices within one county with county clerks, and for municipal offices with city clerks. Two reports were to be filed before the primaries and two after, two before the general election and one 31 days after. In addition, an annual report was required in January until a campaign account showed no unexpended balance or expenditure deficit (if expenditures were made or contributions received since the last filing).

To be included in reports were all contributions over $10, with name and address of donor, and expenditures over $10 with the name and address of recipient, date and purpose of expenditure. The names of each campaign committee and manager also had to be filed. If a contribution or loan exceeded $100, the donor was responsible for seeing that it was reported as well. An individual could spend up to $100 of his own funds or contribute his own personal services and traveling expenses without obligation of reporting to aid or defeat a candidate or measure provided the donor was not to be compensated or reimbursed.

Under the new ethics law, an official who received more than $250 in gifts had to list them in his personal financial-disclosure statement. And the Lobby Control Law was amended to require more detailed reporting of expenditures to influence legislation. Penalties for violation of these laws included fines, jail terms, and civil penalties up to three times the improper contribution.

An attempt to establish an independent ethics and election commission failed, and enforcement remained with the secretary of state and local prosecutors. The legislature did attach to the campaign finance disclosure act a provision that charged state and county election commissions with reviewing reports of violations and informing county or district attorneys where enforcement action was found needed. The commissions were never activated, however. The Attorney General held that the legislature's directive that judges be named as members was unconstitutional. He reasoned that cases involving violations would be likely to come right back for trial before judges who were charged as commission members, with the original screening of the complaints.

The Special Interests

The political climate of 1973 forced lobbyists and special interests to accept the reform legislation with little more than an indignant whimper. They speculated that it would dras-

tically curtail their political contributions, but since records of
past years are incomplete, it is difficult to determine whether
they gave less in 1974 than before. What is certain is that the
tracks of these groups were more evident than ever in the 1974
campaign, thanks to new requirements for fully itemized reporting and the care taken by most candidates in preparing
these reports. Texas or Texas-based special-interest groups collected about $3,225,000 in 1974 and spent more than $2 million,
about $1.5 million of it in Texas.

Some of these groups are organizations long active in politics; some were formed to advocate or oppose specific measures.
Contribution patterns vary widely, as do income sources. Some
groups contributed only to statewide candidates, others only
to legislative races, still others to candidates and causes all over
the country. The vast bulk of the political action committee
money seems to have gone into the campaigns of legislative
candidates, who are traditionally selected on the basis of recommendations of local committees that screen applicants for assistance.

In some cases, the action groups come forward with donations
without waiting to be asked. All denied that they attempted
to exact any commitments in exchange for their aid, and their
beneficiaries unanimously agreed. Many of the special-interest
groups that sponsored political action committees made no
secret of their clear legislative aims in 1975. Others had no
specific causes, but followed such general policy guidelines as
"protection of a good business climate" and preservation of
"conservative government."

Real estate interests, organized in TREPAC, the political action committee of the Texas Real Estate Association and its local associations, raised $162,465 and spent $145,093. TREPAC's
legislative goals included a land-sales disclosure act, a real estate
syndication act, and changes in the licensing law for real estate
brokers and salesmen. It was opposed to land-use control legislation, which was to come up during the 1975 legislative session.

Liquor interests, represented by the Spirits-Wine Action
Committee and the Beer Wholesalers Political Action Committee (B-W PAC), raised $112,813 and spent $54,157, most of
it B-W PAC funds. Liquor lobbyists had no major legislative
projects in 1975, but as usual would be on the lookout for tax
bills that might affect them. Beer wholesalers were concerned
about anti-litter proposals to outlaw throwaway bottles.

Conservative, business-oriented action groups, including the
Political Action Committee of Texans (PACT), Political Support Association, and Manufacturers PAC, raised a combined

total of $365,739 and spent $158,588. PACT, whose 600 members pay dues of $25 per month, is a Houston-based organization of businessmen dedicated to "sound and fiscally responsible government" and "maintenance of a healthy business and economic climate under the principles of the free enterprise system." It aids only House and Senate candidates and did so in 1974 to the tune of about $72,000; it is not a lobbying organization and does not advocate specific legislation.

The insurance industry was one of the big spenders in statewide and legislative races of 1974. IMPACT, the industry's political action committee, and other statewide and local insurance organizations raised more than $220,000 and spent $143,527. Viewed in light of these figures, the industry's legislative goals were relatively bland. No-fault insurance is regarded as a dead issue in the Texas legislature. One of the bills industry lobbyists applied some muscle against would have provided for direct action against insurance companies in auto damage suits. In addition, many companies were reportedly in sympathy with agents on a bill aimed at keeping bank holding companies out of the insurance business.

Texas bankers, whose groups raised about $80,000 and spent $56,000, got into an inter-family squabble after the elections over holding-company legislation. Major bankers opposed limitations on the holding companies. A group of independents favored a prohibition against any multibank holding company owning more than 25 banks or holding more than 8 percent of the aggregate total of Texas bank deposits. The result: a standoff.

The Texas Mortgage Bankers Association (TMBA), whose political committee spent about $13,000 during the 1974 campaigns, was to work successfully for passage of legislation to allow all interest charges on real estate loans to be spread over the life of the debt, and to permit real estate loans of $500,000 and above to be made to individuals (as well as corporations) at above the 10 percent constitutional interest ceiling. TMBA also advocated legislation to permit VA and FHA home mortgage loans to be made in Texas at the same interest rate authorized by the Federal Government.

Lawyers Involved for Texas (LIFT) raised $167,473 and spent only about $38,000, on candidates recommended by its local committees. LIFT, whose bylaws endorse legislation "to advance the cause of those damaged in person and/or property who must seek redress at law," has traditionally opposed no-fault insurance, but this was not a significant issue in 1974. Two pieces of legislation that did interest lawyers once the session began was a bill to expand the wrongful death statute, governing civil-damage recovery actions for deaths caused through negligence (this failed), and the battle over medical malpractice insurance.

Health interests, including doctors and dentists, hospital pharmacists, and nursing homes, raised $419,097 and spent $249,868. Major goals of the doctors were legislation to curb the rising costs of malpractice insurance, their own favored version of Health Maintenance Organization (HMO) legislation, and a variety of licensing bills for allied health professions. The Nursing Home Administrators Political Action Committee (NAPACT), a new group, was concerned with demands for tough licensing requirements and had its own proposal for a less stringent set of standards.

Organized labor, including Texas COPE, Firefighters PAC, Transportation Political Action League, and others, collected nearly $270,000 and spent $126,167. Labor's current legislative aims include collective bargaining for public employees and such general interest projects as education finance reform, utility rate regulation, and curbs on the increasing flood of illegal migrants from Mexico. Labor's drive for "agency shop" legislation lost its steam when a big majority of the 1974 Texas Constitutional Convention delegates (although not the necessary two-thirds) expressed willingness to place "right to work" provisions in the constitution. A major fund-raising drive by the Texas Right to Work Committee had raised about $15,000 and spent nearly $8,000 when the convention failed by three votes to agree on a document for submission to voters.

The largest political action committee of them all, the Associated Milk Producers Inc. (AMPI) Committee for Thorough Political Education (TAPE), is centered in San Antonio, but draws funds in annual donations that average $40 each from milk producers in eighteen states and contributes to nationwide campaigns. TAPE took in $857,624 in 1974 and spent $520,000, but only a small fraction of it in Texas. Most TAPE money goes to Federal rather than state candidates.

The Texas oil industry has no political action committee as such. Oilmen make contributions in their own names directly to the candidates of their choice. Both Republican and Democratic gubernatorial nominees got plenty of help from this quarter, as did the Democratic incumbents running for re-election to the Texas Railroad Commission, the massive agency that regulates oil, gas, and transportation industries.

The largest amount of money spent by special-interest groups in Texas, more than $532,000, went into campaigns for and against a referendum proposition calling on the legislature to legalize, on a local-option basis, pari-mutuel wagering on horse racing. Only two other Texas statewide campaigns in 1974—those of gubernatorial candidates Briscoe and Granberry—were costlier than this May 4 ballot measure. The issue, a familiar one to Texans, was placed on the ballot for the second time in six years through petitions signed by nearly 200,000 proponents of racing. Had it carried, the proposition would have had no binding effect on the legislature; it was merely a recommendation.

Horse-racing enthusiasts organized in the Texas Citizens for Pari-Mutuel Horse Racing (TCP-MHR), with a young staff and a big budget, conducted a smooth media campaign and spent $403,071, including repayment of loans. On the other side, the Anti-Crime Council of Texas, financed almost entirely by Protestant church groups, waged a far less expensive campaign that cost just under $130,000 but included plenty of stern warnings from the pulpit about the evils of gambling.

The bulk of the TCP-MHR's war chest was raised through 132 individual contributions or loans, while the largest block of opposition funds—$84,000 worth—came from the Baptist General Convention of Texas. Other Baptist and Methodist groups contributed $28,881, and the Lubbock Anti-Crime Council $1,381. The measure was defeated rather narrowly—635,000 to 580,000. It carried south Texas and most of the legislative districts, but couldn't overcome the Bible belt and the rural vote in most sections.

Major political action committees guessed right most of the time, placing their money on legislative winners who, for the most part, were conservative Democrats with known voting records. In some cases, committees hedged their bets by contributing to more than one candidate in the same race. Liberals weren't shut off from the special-interest money, but their cut was certainly smaller than that of the conservatives. The labor committees gave most of their resources to liberal legislative leaders.

The size of donations varied greatly. Some groups measured contributions in servings of $100 each, but it was not uncommon for the major committees to pour $4,000 into a single state Senate race. LIFT donated $9,000 to one Senate candidate who unseated an incumbent.

Quite a lot of special-interest money goes into races for the Texas state Senate, which can be more expensive than some statewide elections. (Some Texas Senate districts, in fact, are larger than a few states.) Conservative Frank Lombardino of San Antonio, for example, raised more than $100,000 and spent nearly that amount defeating liberal former Senator Joe J. Bernal for a San Antonio seat. Identifiable special-interest contributions to the Lombardino campaign totaled $32,850; the candidate and his family gave $16,500. Lombardino stated that his benefactors were not as enthusiastic about electing him as they were about defeating Bernal, whose increasingly liberal stance annoyed conservative businessmen and whose blocking of the appointment of two prominent San Antonio citizens to state agencies also brought him powerful opposition.

Another race that attracted a lot of special-interest money was the one in which Kent Hance of Lubbock defeated veteran Senator H. J. (Doc) Blanchard in the Democratic primary. Their contest was an exception to the rule that the candidate with the most money to spend is the winner. Blanchard spent almost $80,000 in a losing effort to hang onto his job. Meanwhile, Hance, a young attorney without prior political experience, spent just $30,548 in the primary and another $37,824 in the general election against Republican Robert E. Garner of Lubbock (who spent about $20,000). Blanchard got approximately $9,000 in special-interest contributions (including insurance, real estate, savings and loan, beer wholesaler, and nursing home groups). Hance almost balanced this with an $8,000 contribution from LIFT. (Hance says Blanchard stirred up the trial lawyers when he "filibustered some of their bills.") In the general election, the special-interest money was with Hance. He got a dozen major contributions, including those of the conservative PACT of Houston ($3,000), the medical lobby ($2,000), the real estate lobby ($1,000), LIFT (another $1,000), and IMPACT ($1,500). Dentists, nursing homes, mortgage bankers, and beer wholesalers contributed $500 each to Hance, as did an Austin-based group known as Free Enterprise PAC. His Republican opponent got fewer than half a dozen donations of over $500 in a losing effort that ate up $17,000 of his own or his firm's cash.

Strangely enough, little of the plainly labeled special-interest money found its way into the Texas House speaker's race.*

---

* The Texas speaker is elected at the beginning of each new legislature by members of the House, not by the public. In addition to campaigning in their own districts as much as is necessary to secure re-election, legislators running for speaker travel around the state seeking support for their candidacy among other representatives. They assist candidates who agree to back them.

Perhaps the donors thought that would have been just too obvious, in view of the 1973 cleanup of the office after the Sharpstown scandals. There was no lack of money in the wide-open race, however, much of it oil money. Five candidates collected contributions totaling $172,178 and spent $126,952. The race would have been even costlier had it not come to a sudden end (for all practical purposes) on Labor Day weekend, when one candidate, Bill Clayton, a staunch Democratic conservative, formed an alliance with another, Fred Head. Head was slipping in the five-man race and decided to back Clayton to defeat the front-runner, Carl Parker. At that time, Clayton, a wealthy farmer, was far behind Head in expenditures, but the money started rolling in after his victory became apparent. Of $74,503 contributed to Clayton, $42,660 came in after his Labor Day blitz assured him of the speakership. He reported spending $34,125, less than either Parker, who spent $44,493, or Head, who reported spending $39,075. (The money-raising efforts of Representatives David Finney of Fort Worth, James Nugent of Kerrville, and George Preston of Paris were insignificant compared with the big three.)

In statewide races, special-interest groups concentrated their wealth on Briscoe, who got nearly $70,000, and Hobby, who received more than $22,000. Both gained funds in the $500–$5,000 range (and occasionally more) from a wide spectrum of groups. Attorney General John Hill and Bob Bullock, who was elected Comptroller to succeed retiring Robert S. Calvert, also received aid from a broad sampling of the special-interest political action committees.

Big Individual Contributors

The size of special-interest contributions in many races was small in comparison with those from wealthy individuals, many of which could of course be related to the business interests of the givers—oil money, for example. Compare the total special-interest spending in the Hobby campaign—$22,000—with donations totaling $23,050 to Briscoe by Trammel Crow of Dallas, the largest real estate developer in Texas. (Other members of Crow's family provided another $7,000 to Briscoe, while Mr. & Mrs. Crow also donated $4,059 to Senator Lloyd Bentsen.)

Most of the biggest contributors in 1974 professed an interest in "good government" or "a good business climate" while discounting suggestions that they had exacted specific positions or promises from the candidates they agreed to support. The access to politicians that being a large donor secured them was a generally accepted fact, however. The major contributors certainly expended enormous amounts of money in pursuit of "good government," whatever that meant to each donor. Some, like Trammel Crow, concentrated their generosity on a single candidate, but others seemed to be trying to cover as many bases as possible.

One of the most diversified campaign contributors was Houston attorney Charles Sapp, who reported personal contributions of $500 and above totaling $18,000 to nearly a dozen candidates, ranging from a state representative in El Paso to the Governor and Senator Bentsen. In addition, the law firm of Liddell, Sapp, Zively, and Brown gave a total of $10,500 to Briscoe and six other candidates. Liddell, Sapp represents El Paso Natural Gas Company, Houston Endowment, the *Houston Chronicle*, and Texas Commerce BancShares, among other banking, business, and industrial clients. Sapp and his partners picked all winners in the statewide races they contributed to, and they contributed to four of the five major candidates in the speaker's race.

The Sapp firm maintains an Austin office headed by former state Representative Frank Calhoun. Sapp strongly denies any improper connection between campaign donations and legislative interests. "There are no commitments made to me by anybody," said Sapp. "I don't discuss legislation with anybody before contributing. That would be highly improper." Sometimes, said Sapp, he contributes to candidates who do not ask his aid and, on occasion, to those he does not know personally. He said early in the 1975 legislative session that his only direct contact with legislators was a letter urging a $2.9 million appropriation to the State Commission on Arts and Humanities. He is a director of the Society for the Performing Arts in Houston and a Briscoe appointee to the Texas Commission for the Blind.

The name of Houston attorney, campaign consultant, and political power Searcy Bracewell, former state Senator, turns up on so many candidates' finance reports that he seems to be giving a great deal more money than he is. His contributions of $500 and above to candidates reporting to the secretary of state totaled $9,000, including $3,500 to Briscoe. Bracewell gives personally to candidates all over the state, as do some of the organizations (like the conservative PACT) with which he is affiliated. (Bracewell's young Austin law partner, former state Representative L. Dean Cobb, is campaign manager for PACT.)

Bracewell frowns on campaign contributions which are "too large," but he is opposed to statutory limits, questioning their good sense and practicality. "Are we going to say everything is hunky-dory if we give less than $100, but something is wrong if we give more?" he asks. "My thought is to require a full disclosure rather than impose a limit," said Bracewell. "I would say the system lends itself to some evils, and yet I really have every faith in its basic integrity. I feel most candidates and contributors participate in the system with a minimum of evil. Most people are pretty honorable."

Bracewell conceded, "There are some who expect to have pinpointed activity looked on more favorably. Politics is no different than anything else. People do business with their friends. Politicians can't help rationalizing a controversial matter in favor of their friends. They do it unwittingly." But Bracewell maintained that conservative contributors are less likely to expect something in return for their aid than "people on the other side of the street. . . . Most [contributors] from the conservative side of the street will contribute to the campaign of a fellow who espouses the philosophy that corresponds to their own. Eighty percent of the people who contribute are not expecting Joe Blow to vote for or against a specific bill," he said.

"The bigger they are, the more tolerant they are and appreciative of problems politicians have and the fact that they may not be able to vote as they [the contributors] would want them to all the time," said Bracewell. "Most politicians are pretty idealistic and sincere. I don't think they would put up with contributions with ties. Naturally, contributors expect a better entrée to present their case. They establish a rapport with the person being helped."

Another familiar name on campaign finance reports is Herbert J. Frensley, recently retired as President and chief operating officer of Brown and Root Inc., who has continued to put his money on candidates. Frensley gave $3,000 to Briscoe's big October 1973 dinner, $1,000 each to three other candidates, and $500 to the Harris County Committee for Responsible Candidates—a total of $6,500. Like Bracewell, Frensley is a member of PACT, the powerful Houston-based organization of conservative-oriented businessmen. He is now also president of the Texas Association of Taxpayers, a group that helped put over sales taxation in Texas more than a decade ago and strongly opposes a state income tax.

"I look entirely to the type of candidate—if he is business-oriented and wants to maintain a good business climate in the state," Frensley explained. "When I spot a good candidate, I try to help him before he asks for help. It is imperative people take an interest in campaigns." Frensley says he invites candidates he contemplates supporting to visit with him and sounds out their attitude on business and taxation. "I never ask any of them for specific commitments," says Frensley. "I have talked to them about bills [before the legislature]. I give them my ideas and views. If they agree, all right. If not, all right . . ."

A longtime contributor to conservative Democratic candidates (and some Republicans), San Antonio contractor and industrialist H. B. (Pat) Zachry helped to the tune of $8,500 in 1974 campaigns. The bulk of Zachry's money, $4,500, went to state Senate candidate Lombardino in his close race against liberal former Senator Bernal, not one of Zachry's favorite people. (Bernal once defeated Zachry's son-in-law for the Senate and blocked the appointment of Zachry's son to a state regulatory board.)

"I have just one criterion [in assisting candidates]: who will perform in the best interest," said Zachry, who has been a major campaign contributor for three decades and has served on the A&M University Board of Trustees and the Coordinating Board of the Texas College and University System. "I base my decision on that, as sincerely as I know how, without regard to party or other factors. And an important question is if the opposition wins, what would be his direction? I never ride the fence and give to both candidates. I had rather tell them where I stand."

A major Briscoe backer was Roland Blumberg of Seguin, independent oil operator, geophysicist, and director of a large San Antonio bank. His wife, Jane Weinert Blumberg (chairman of the board of the bank), was the Governor's choice for Democratic National Committeewoman. Blumberg made two loans of $25,000 each to Briscoe's Conventions Committee, which was set up to finance a campaign by the Governor to control Democratic Party conventions; he also donated $1,000 to the committee and another $1,000 to the Briscoe central campaign committee, and his wife donated another $500 to the Conventions Committee. Together, Mr. and Mrs. Blumberg purchased $1,500 worth of tickets to the Briscoe dinner.

"We never sat down to formulate a policy" on campaign giving, said Jane Blumberg. "Of course, generally, you contribute to those people who share your point of view. We usually give close to home where we are personally acquainted with the candidates." She emphasized that the $50,000 advanced by her husband to Briscoe's Conventions Committee was a loan, that some of it has been repaid, and that full repayment is expected. Her family's donations to Briscoe's campaign were unsolicited, Mrs. Blumberg said, and no commitments were sought. She did not ask for the job of National Committeewoman, she declared, and finds the position "much diluted" in prestige because of enlargement of the committee.

Another big giver was Rex C. Cauble of Denton, cattleman, oilman, and head of a Western clothing firm, who boasts an air-conditioned barn. He donated $17,850 to politicians in 1974 (Briscoe received $13,150, Attorney General Hill $3,000, Lieutenant Governor Hobby $1,200, and Fred Head $500). He has given plenty in the past to both Republican and Democratic candidates, but claims he is getting "disillusioned" with both parties. "I don't care whether a man is a Democrat or a Republican." says Cauble. "I support the man, not the party. I don't like them to be too liberal, though. I have given more in the past than I intend to in the future. I'm disillusioned with both parties—with the way they treated John Connally." Cauble was named by former Governor Connally to the Texas Aeronautics Commission, which regulates intrastate air carriers and channels funds to small airport building, and on which he still serves.

When queried about whether he ever asked anything in return for his financial aid, Cauble indignantly replied: "I never asked a candidate for nothing in my damned life. I don't want them to do anything but what's best for the job. I pick out a man I think is best for the job and support him. I never asked anything. I don't need them."

Liberals have few major contributors to political campaigns. One of the more conspicuous is Colonel J. R. Parten of Madisonville and Houston, oilman, President of Seven J Enterprises, and former member of The University of Texas Board of Regents.

Another is Bernard Rapoport, head of the Waco-based American Insurance Company and major stockholder in two small-town banks. Rapoport generally contributes to candidates at about the rate of $25,000 per election year, more in Presidential years. His contributions actually were off a little in 1974, although he stuck with his usual pattern of giving more out-of-state than in-state. He gave $1,000 to the Texas Democratic Affirmative Action Committee, $1,000 each to Bullock and Farenthold, plus some small-scale assistance to a few state and local candidates. He also made some 30 contributions to candidates all over the country, including $3,000 to Jerry Brown in the California governor's race, $1,000 to John Gilligan in Ohio, $250 to George McGovern, $333 to Joseph Alioto in California, and $350 to a South Dakota Congressional candidate.

"I'm generally for those people who are interested in preserving the competitive system," said Rapoport. "I'm basically a populist. I'm not in favor of the power flowing to Washington. It's easier to control A.T.&T. than the C.I.A." As for his own situation, Rapoport said, "I'm in a business where politicians couldn't help me if they wanted to. We are not in the group insurance business. I never had any benefits from a political situation."

A Fort Worth grain dealer, grain-elevator operator, farmer, and rancher named James S. Garvey has been a mainstay of Republican candidates' finances. "The basic thing is that the Democrats have lost their party to the radicals," says Garvey. "I want to support conservatives. We need the two-party system." Garvey's contributions frequently were in odd amounts (like $2,293) because he was giving wheat raised on his farm and admittedly attempting to avoid Federal taxes on gifts up to $3,000. His wheat donations, the most unusual donations of the year, were handled through sales in Kansas.

In the hard-pressed closing days of the gubernatorial campaign, Garvey made a $25,000 loan to Jim Granberry. He contributed another $5,000 to Granberry and made donations totaling about $20,000 to other Republican candidates.

There were a host of other big contributors to 1974 races in Texas, most of whom probably would have given reasons similar to those advanced by the men and women discussed above. And this was a "bad" year.

Big Money: Recipients' View

Office-holders and political professionals saw varying degrees of influence on the part of large donors, ranging from entrée to the candidate to scattered favors to direct demands on specific issues, persons, and votes. Never, protested many lawmakers, had they been pressured to vote for or against legislation in exchange for contributions. But others acknowledged that such pressure had been applied, though rarely—perhaps "once, twice, three times" in a long political career.

"We simply must do something about the tremendously accelerating costs of campaigns at all levels," said Attorney General Hill, for example. "It is abusive to donors and lends itself to potential wrongdoing. The more you have to raise, the more temptations are there." But Hill said he has no personal knowledge of undue influence of money on government and had "never directly or indirectly" been asked by a contributor to make a commitment.

Dolph Briscoe offered this assessment: "I don't recall any instance when a contributor asked for something in return for a donation. If he did, I would return his money."

Most people who contribute to campaigns, said Lieutenant Governor Hobby, "want a feeling of participation. They want to be part of the action. They contribute to people they identify with politically. "They want to feel they have the ear of an official and be able to tell their friends 'I talked with the governor about that last week.' There is a lot of money out there," said Hobby. "I guess there are a lot of hedged bets in contributions to a candidate for lieutenant governor. They figure he might be governor someday." (Hobby has made it clear he would like to be.)

Comptroller Bullock, who had experience in campaign fundraising for three statewide candidates, including former Governor Smith, before he decided to run himself, says that few contributors have been so crass as to ask for something before letting go of their checks. "I had one man send word he had a $500 contribution, and when I contacted him, he said he needed to talk to me about his son-in-law who was an employee of the comptroller's office. I told him I was doing fine and didn't really need any more contributions right then. When I took office, I fired the guy [the son-in-law]. Since then, I've had two legislators talk to me about rehiring him. I'm not gonna rehire him," said Bullock.

Bullock offered three explanations for large-scale campaign giving: First, "the donors want to be friendly with the person who regulates their business interests. Second, they like to be able to say to their friends 'I helped elect him. Let me introduce you.' They just like to know people in office on a first-name basis and to introduce their friends on a first-name basis. Third, there are those, and they are in the minority, who simply believe in the same philosophy you have, and they don't really expect anything out of you. I never hear from $10 contributors. Those are the people who like what you have done, what you have said, or what you are doing now."

A candidate, said Bullock, must be "almost as interested in seeing that his opponent doesn't get any big money as he is in getting it himself." He claimed he helped keep one potentially formidable candidate, then state Senator Jim Wallace of Houston, out of the 1974 comptroller's race by working diligently in Houston and other major cities to discourage contributions to him. Wallace did not run and later was appointed by the Governor to a district court bench.

George Bristol, finance director of Senator Bentsen's Presidential campaign, acknowledged that there is "special-interest money," but he said the label is overused and questioned the popular view of such groups. "The special interests are usually regarded as unethical in their activities, but thousands of them are good for this country, or, at least in their opinion, they are," he stated. "They balance each other out in most instances. Of course, I don't think special-interest groups would give to candidates dead-set against their interests."

Campaign spending limitations for Federal races are accepted but not applauded by Bristol. "I'm horrified at $2 million and $3 million contributions, like anybody else," he said. "But campaign spending limits can cause some candidates to die on the vine. Under good, tight disclosure laws, the opposition finds out who is supporting you, and if there is something wrong, they will shoot your guts out."

George Christian, press secretary to President Lyndon Johnson, former aide to a U.S. senator and two governors, and now a campaign consultant, is indignant at questions about the corrupting influence of money in politics. "It is not my experience that people give money in return for anything," said Christian. "Most contributors don't ask for anything. Most of them want to be left alone. People with money give their money, and that's the last you hear from them. Perry Bass, for example, asks nothing from state government unless it's for the arts. But, if these people want to express a view, it gets attention," added Christian. "When Pat Zachry or Herb Frensley have something to say, they are listened to. Usually, they are being asked to help with something—to serve on some advisory or planning committee without pay.

"It's meaningless that [Briscoe] got campaign contributions from people he appointed as regents," said Christian. "Briscoe never had a sophisticated money-raising operation. He is probably the least susceptible politician to [consideration of] campaign donations. He doesn't know who gave what. No governor is going to appoint his enemies. Contributions are less important than having confidence in a man. When appointments come up, an official looks to his friends and people who he knows exercise good judgment."

Christian is concerned about the effect of new disclosure laws. "This new emphasis on candidates having to tell all about their private lives may be one more step toward discouraging participation in government. . . . Conflicts of interest ought to be revealed. That's the key to the whole thing."

The issue of appointments was also discussed by Creekmore Fath, Sissy Farenthold's campaign manager, several months after his candidate had attacked Briscoe's appointments, and after she was out of the race. "It is logical the people a governor appoints to office are those he knows," said Fath. "Contributors are those he knows best, but probably he knows personally only 20 percent of the thousands he appoints during an administration. Chances are 99 percent of the people who put up the money for a candidate have no idea of asking for a thing in the world. They know what attitude the candidate has socially and economically. It's very small people who expect to get something out of their contributions directly."

Former Governor Allan Shivers, who held the Texas governor's office longer than any other man, from 1949 to January 1957, commented frankly: "I took the position while I was in office that I would rather appoint my friends than my enemies." Briscoe's words on the matter: "I don't reward people just because they contribute, but I don't disqualify them either."

Lawmakers who defend the innocence of contributions are simply not leveling, contended one veteran of many state and local campaigns who has been a legislative lobbyist and now occupies a high position in a department of state government. "It is almost a daily occurrence in statewide campaigns for people to give a candidate money for a specific purpose," said the source, who did not want to be identified because of his present position. "After he is elected, a man finds out too often that the reason he got that $500 contribution was that the donor has a problem with the regulatory agency the candidate now heads. A large portion of money given to statewide campaigns has this kind of invisible string attached. They want a relative hired or kept on the job. They want a license or a permit, tax consideration or a vote for a bill that benefits them," he said.

The influence of money on the Texas political scene, as elsewhere, is not less overpowering because it is not frequently held out as a direct bribe—a this-for-that proposition—the source emphasized. "Money is a powerful and sometimes corrupting influence. I know of no official who hasn't had major contributors come to him and say, 'I've never asked you for

anything before, but I must have this favor.' Legislators are
faced with that same problem on many of their crucial votes.
[Contributors] are not above reminding you of their past aid
and even of threatening that they will give no more if they
don't get their way. The influence is there, and there is no use
denying it. Of course, there is a lot of money given without
any idea of a return on the investment . . . but when these political action groups contribute, they don't have any other purpose in mind than gaining influence. The liberal groups are
no different from the conservatives on that."

"There is no question you consider the position of people
who support you financially," said Representative Ray Hutchinson of Dallas, the most capable member of the small Texas
Republican legislative delegation. (He is now state Republican
Chairman and will not seek re-election to the House.) "But,
frequently, by the time I get urgent calls [requesting a particular vote on legislation] from those people, I have made up my
mind," said Hutchinson. "Many people donate to campaigns
without asking anything. Many others donate expecting you
to do as they say. The blame should be on the official who lets
himself get in the position of taking money from the latter. He
should gut up and tell them he doesn't need money that badly."

"Money doesn't buy politicians, but I'll tell you what it does:
It hardens the lines of loyalties," said veteran state Senator
A. R. Schwartz of Galveston, for 20 years a highly vocal liberal
member of the Texas legislature. "As for contributors putting
pressure on legislators on their voting, the lines are drawn long
before the vote. People support candidates because they have
taken positions they agree with. They don't support those whose
positions they don't know. It would certainly be improper for
me to go around soliciting my enemies. They know where I
stand. I'm not going to change—not after 20 years," said
Schwartz. Schwartz identified his main base of financial support
as organized labor, the medical profession (the state's largest
medical school is in his district), and lawyers (he is a successful
attorney). Those groups, said Schwartz frankly, know they can
"depend on" him. "If that is wrong, then the whole system is
wrong," said Schwartz.

Slush Funds and Mystery Money

Some of the money that found its way into the 1974 campaign
came from questionable sources and became the object of considerable attention.

One arrangement that received national publicity involved the Southwestern Bell Telephone Company. A tangled tale of political slush funds, rate-making intrigue with local officials, and charitable contributions charged to operating expenses grew out of a $29 million lawsuit against Southwestern Bell filed in a San Antonio court in November 1974 by a discharged company executive from Bell's San Antonio office, James H. Ashley, and the family of another Bell official, T. O. Gravitt, who committed suicide on October 17, 1974. The charges of libel and slander by the company were based on allegations that Bell was investigating Ashley and Gravitt and implying sexual misconduct with women company employees, as well as diversion of company funds (on Ashley's part) and filing of phony expense accounts for his airplane and improving his home at company expense (on Gravitt's part).

Ashley asserted in the lawsuit that $1,000-a-year salary increases were given some company personnel with the understanding the money was to go to political contributions. Before 1966, said Ashley, Southwestern Bell executives were required to contribute $50 cash each month to selected politicians. After that, he claimed, a "political contact man" would direct the telephone executives where to send contributions made by personal check. "We had no choice. We were required to make these 'voluntary' contributions," said Ashley. He estimated that contributions from 142 executives amounted to about $90,000 annually. Bell executives have been frequent contributors to local, district, and statewide campaigns, mostly with donations in the $25, $50, and $100 range. Six executives in Dallas, including Gravitt, who was head of Texas operations, contributed $100 each to Briscoe's 1974 re-election campaign. Others contributed similar or smaller amounts to Congressional and legislative candidates.

Gravitt's suicide note and other documents referred to a mandatory company slush fund. The eight-page note claimed he was being investigated by the company without cause and hounded out of his key job because he was no longer loyal to the system. He said "Watergate is a gnat" compared to Bell's operations. Gravitt contended that Bell executives were to receive a $1,000 pay raise with the understanding that $50 a month would be kicked into a political slush fund to be distributed to deserving candidates. Gravitt apparently wrote five checks in the spring of 1974, just before the primary election, to five candidates.

The company denied the stories. Bell President Zane E. Barnes acknowledged that company management-level personnel are "encouraged" to make political contributions, indicating that political involvement is as much a part of a Bell executive's job as civic activities, church-going, charitable contributions, and working with the Boy Scouts. But he insisted the donations were personal and not "corporate," and he denied there was any coercion involved. He conceded, however, that contributions might have been turned over to one person by several others for placement. He also denied allegations by some company representatives that employees could get back the amount of their political contributions from the company through expense vouchers.

Is that a political slush-fund arrangement? "You may call it that," Barnes said in a press conference in December 1975 at San Antonio. "I would call it a personal contribution.*

The major point of controversy on the financing of the 1974 elections was the dinner for Dolph Briscoe held on October 30, 1973, in Austin's Municipal Auditorium—the biggest fund-raising event of the campaign. Briscoe planned to use the income from the event to pay off some of his 1972 campaign debts and to get his re-election campaign started with a formidable cash reserve. It was at this $25-a-plate dinner that he formally announced his candidacy for a four-year term.

According to the income report filed on February 4, 1974, nearly 10,000 people attended, and net proceeds were about $455,000, $160,000 of which was to be used to retire about 40 percent of Briscoe's 1972 campaign deficit. The balance would help launch the re-election effort. Reports widely interpreted the dinner as one of the most successful fund-raising events in state political history and speculated that it would make Briscoe opponents think twice about their prospects of matching the Governor in financial resources.

But within a few days of the filing, Sissy Farenthold, who had just announced as a candidate against Briscoe, slapped him with a $2.5 million civil lawsuit charging violations of new election code provisions in solicitation of funds for the dinner. These amendments, which had just gone into effect, directed candidates and political committees to designate their campaign managers before funds could be accepted and dispensed. The Farenthold petition for civil recovery of funds complained that

---

* The Bell suit has been transferred from state to Federal district court and is awaiting trial. A state district court ordered Bell to pay more than $300,000 in pension and death benefits to Gravitt's widow, but the company has filed an appeal to delay the pension payments until after the $29 million suit is disposed of.

campaign funds were asked for and received in the form of dinner ticket sales long before Briscoe named a campaign manager. The Governor designated Jess Hay, a Democratic National Committeeman from Dallas, as manager for the dinner committee on October 19, and Joe Kilgore, an Austin attorney and former Congressman, as his re-election campaign manager the day following the dinner. Preparations obviously had been under way for the event months earlier.

District Judge Herman Jones of Austin, to whose court the case was assigned, expressed considerable impatience with the litigation from the start. The main accomplishment of the lawsuit was to freeze more than $400,000 in funds which Briscoe had counted on for his campaign. Once more, he had to dig deep into his own bank accounts for money to meet his campaign budget. More than a year later, in February 1975, the case was dismissed by agreement, with Farenthold stuck with the tab for court costs. Neither side would disclose the terms of the settlement, but the best information that can be obtained suggests that Farenthold got about $125,000. Most if not all of this probably went to pay court costs and legal fees.

"I feel that this litigation has now accomplished its primary purpose of emphasizing to all candidates, past and future, the importance of strict compliance with the Texas election code," Farenthold said after the ruling. "Neither I nor my attorneys will make any further statement concerning this matter."

Critics claim that the unusual legal action was little more than use of the courts for harassment. Temporarily, at any rate, it placed candidates on notice that they had better beware of even technical violations of new reporting requirements if they wanted to avoid legal fees and embarrassment.

Another effect of the suit was to bring to light two stories of questionable funding in Briscoe's campaigns. One involved a $15,000 cash contribution to Briscoe's 1972 gubernatorial bid by Clinton Manges, an elusive south Texas rancher and banker. The story was not revealed until mid-November 1974, however, two weeks after Briscoe's re-election. Farenthold lawyers heard of the contribution while preparing for the trial of their suit and questioned Briscoe about it at a November deposition hearing.

Manges had reportedly left the contribution—an inch-thick stack of $100 bills—in Briscoe's office at a Uvalde bank in 1972. Briscoe said he never formally accepted the Manges contribution, tried unsuccessfully over a period of more than two years to return it, and for that reason did not report it as a campaign contribution. "I felt it was too much money to take from one individual, and particularly I hadn't known Mr. Manges long," Briscoe told the Farenthold lawyers. The Governor said the money remained in an unlocked walk-in vault at his office from May 1972 to September 1974, when he turned it over to his attorney, Joe Reynolds of Houston.

On June 16, 1975, Briscoe, Manges, and their attorneys met over breakfast at Brownsville International Airport, and the unwanted bundle of cash was returned. Briscoe's attorney presented it to Manges' attorney, Jim Bates of Edinburg. Hours later, the Governor's office issued a one-paragraph statement confirming that the meeting had been held and the money given back to Manges.

The other incident was brought to public attention by Farenthold's attorneys, as well as by newspapers, months after the filing of the dinner report. This involved tickets purchased by 100 persons with the same address—that of the Dallas-based OKC Corporation, a cement firm—who reportedly donated $100 each. Dinner manager Hay said that Cloyce Box, President of OKC, initially turned in the $10,000 to him in cash, representing that his 100 employees had bought four tickets each.

In response to questions, Box admitted that he had advanced the money himself after consulting with the employees and with the understanding that they would reimburse him. Some of his employees did not support Box's story, however. Several denied that they had ever been contacted about buying tickets, two said they were no longer on the OKC payroll when they were listed as purchasers, and one complained to the F.B.I. Some—reportedly management-level or engineering officers— said they had agreed to donate to Briscoe.

In a television interview, Box said of his employees' reported reluctance to participate in the scheme, "Of course, I can appreciate that . . . no one really likes to give away $100. But I'm sure that having thought about it a little, and should I have an opportunity to talk to them, I think that they'll understand that it is to our best interests in our home state to have good government. And I think they trust my judgment. I don't think I've been bad for the company or for them." Whatever his employees felt about their "home state," that home state was not Texas; a reported 99 out of the 100 live and work outside the state.

In late October, Jess Hay amended his original dinner report to show that $10,000 had been contributed by Box and amounted to loans from Box's personal funds to his employees for political contributions. A third amended version of the report, filed in December 1974, indicated that at least 81 of the employees did reimburse Box for the ticket purchases; this named 6 who were not on the original list but who reimbursed Box, 5 who did not originally agree to make a contribution but later said they would give $100 each, 1 who was not on the OKC payroll when dinner funds were solicited, 4 who shouldn't have been on the list at all, and 13 who were no longer OKC employees and did not respond to correspondence reminding them sternly of "commitments."

Hay said the initial list of contributions submitted to the dinner committee was inaccurate due to "an inadvertent mistake." Box reportedly had picked up "a solicitation list which did not reflect subsequent deletions of persons who had declined or otherwise failed to agree to make a $100 contribution or subsequent additions of other persons who had so agreed."

Randall Wood, former Common Cause attorney and lobbyist, called on the Travis County (Austin) District Attorney, Robert Smith (who had jurisdiction in the case), to investigate the matter. "If it is true that some of the listed individuals were in fact not contributors, it raises the possibility that the article of the Texas election code relating to filing a false report may have been violated as well as statutes prohibiting perjury and possibly conspiracy to violate Texas laws," Wood said. Smith, a hard-nosed prosecutor who has won convictions against several erring former legislators, denied the request, stating that he saw no "ulterior motives" in Hay's filing of an amended report. "That must have been embarrassing for him, but he filed it anyway," Smith commented.

The OKC ticket purchases were perhaps the most dramatic and questionable example, but multiple ticket buying to political dinners was standard practice. While nearly 10,000 people attended the Briscoe dinner, just under 3,000 actually bought tickets either in their own names or as representatives of organizations. Of the 3,000, 103 bought $204,814 worth of the $600,000 in tickets actually paid for. At least 138 Briscoe appointees to state boards and agencies—about 25 percent of his first-term appointments—contributed $178,401, while identified lobbyists accounted for less than $25,000 of the ticket purchases. A dozen top University of Texas at Austin executives contributed $50 each to the dinner, and four University regents contributed $2,750.

The ticket list included most of the big contributors discussed above. Some of the major donors were later named to relatively minor positions, like Margaret D. Crow's assignment to the

Texas Commission on the Arts and Humanities. Others were appointed or reappointed to major offices: Joe LaMantia, for example, a McAllen produce company head, who was named to the State Board of Corrections two days after his contribution was recorded, and Dan Williams of Dallas, a $2,000 contributor, who was later to be reappointed to the University of Texas board of regents.

Although Farenthold tried to make an issue of Briscoe's record of appointing contributors to state positions (she compiled a list of such persons, saying that a third of them had given to the Governor within three months of their appointments and one on the same day), her charges had no effect on Briscoe's campaign.

Looking at the Law

After the high-spending, if unexciting, Texas campaign was over, those involved in it looked at the new law under which it had been conducted and came up with mixed reviews.

Disclosure was almost universally endorsed, but some of the practices connected with it were not. For example, a bewildering number of political committees supporting candidates from the legislative district level to governor sprang up in Texas. In part, the growth of the political committee structure was a by-product of a change in the state law intended to make the committee operations more open. The law provided that the committees could spend money for campaign purposes only through designated campaign managers, and made them subject to the same reporting requirements as candidates.

The volume and complexity of the reports, ironically, appeared to offer opportunities for laundering or, at least, confusing sources of political funds. Any useful purpose the record number of political committees may have served (which could not have been served as well or better by a less diversified financial structure) was largely lost on political reporters, who found the multiple reports confusing and sometimes impossible to unravel.

The most notable example was the 46-committee setup used for fund-raising and spending in the Briscoe gubernatorial campaign. The rash of reports filed by the groups—some dealing with a complex series of fund transfers from one to another—defies understanding, save perhaps by a certified public accountant and Briscoe's own campaign treasurer. The latter invariably had to be contacted by reporters each time major new reports were filed and asked: "Just how much did you raise and spend?" Nobody could be sure from the individual committee reports. No balanced totals were available on all, interpreting the intercommittee transfers. Although no other candidate had nearly as many committees as Briscoe, many operated with multi-headed fund-raising organizations that vastly complicated the reporting system.

"The major thrust of the 1973 legislation was to make the committees report. We were trying to tighten the lid," said Representative Ben Bynum of Amarillo, author of the 1973 disclosure act, who sought in the 1975 legislature to strengthen the bill, introducing a series of amendments. "Now, we need to tie the committees to the candidates where they belong. We possibly need to require candidates to list all contributions and spending by their committees in their central report." Although Bynum and others have suggested requiring candidates to file a consolidated report on financial activities of their committees, there was no serious effort toward this in 1975.

The 1975 legislature did revise some of the reporting provisions in the 1973 law to simplify record-keeping and reporting slightly. The requirement for disclosure of contributions of $10 and over was changed to require only that contributions of $50 or more be reported, with names and addresses of donors and recipients. Small contributions (under $50) must now be reported in the aggregate but not individually.

The number of reports was reduced slightly, to require filing by the thirtieth and seventh days before elections and the thirtieth day after. An annual report still must be filed showing all previously unreported contributions and expenditures through the previous year. Penalties for failure to file were lowered from felony status to a Class A misdemeanor (with maximum punishment of two years in jail, a $2,000 fine, or both).

Creation of an independent enforcement commission was the top objective of Texas campaign finance-disclosure law reformers in 1975, and one of Ben Bynum's proposals was for such a seven-member commission. While the 1973 amendments were complied with pretty well, reformers concede, there was room for improvement. They fear that if enforcement remains in the hands of the secretary of state, an appointee of the governor, candidates will grow bolder and more inclined to overstep strict statutory boundaries in the future. As it was, no significant enforcement efforts by state authorities to fine or disqualify erring candidates were undertaken in 1974.

"The law obviously has been a success in that it has made a lot more information available," said former House Speaker Daniel, a leading force in the passage of the 1973 legislation. But, he added, "administration and enforcement obviously have not been too successful." Daniel called failure to approve an enforcement commission "the big disappointment" of the 1973 reform effort.

Former Common Cause counsel Wood is one who agrees with the need for enforcement. "People followed [the law] this year," said Wood. "But this tractability will erode as loopholes and lack of enforcement become apparent. The secretary of state cannot adequately enforce a law like that. The office is too political. A candidate has got to know somebody is going to be looking at these reports his files and demanding that shortcomings be corrected, or the temptation to cheat will be too great." Common Cause, which planned extensive monitoring of 1974 campaign finance-disclosure reports but never got around to it because of time demands on its small staff during the State Constitutional Convention, placed at the top of its 1975 legislative program creation of a disclosure commission to oversee enforcement of campaign finance reports, lobby control, and personal finance-disclosure acts.

Not surprisingly, the chief election officer of Texas and the man designated to administer the disclosure act, Secretary of State Mark W. White, Jr., considers it quite adequate, and he is opposed to creation of an independent enforcement commission. White maintained that his elections division staff moved promptly and effectively to handle complaints and ensure compliance during the 1974 campaign. At legislative committee hearings on Bynum's bill, White stated, "What they are proposing, we are doing already. . . . We have not received one complaint of violation where there has not been compliance or the matter referred to the courthouse. Where there have been deficiencies, we are ready day and night to listen to complaints." White's recommendations for improvement in the campaign finance-disclosure act go largely to simplification of filing requirements. "The main thing that needs to be done is to make it simpler for candidates to comply with the statute," he said. "It is now too complex. Too many filings are required."

Opposition by White and Briscoe, who argued that an election commission would be an unneeded additional layer of supervision that might be used to launch witch-hunts, helped spell defeat for the proposal in 1975. While it was approved by the House, the Senate rejected it, preferring to leave enforcement with the politically appointed secretary of state, as did White and Briscoe. A $350,000 enforcement budget was provided, and the secretary of state's election division was enlarged and moved to more spacious quarters. The legislature also amended the law to provide that venue for prosecution of violations is in the home county of the offender rather than in the state capital, a change that brought mild protest of reform groups who considered that the overall effect of the amendments weakened the law.

The staggering costs of campaigns and the usually crucial role of money in their outcome moved some of Texas's most successful politicians and the state Democratic Party to advocate spending limits. Briscoe, after spending more than $1.3 million of his own money in his election races, reached the conclusion that campaigns are too costly. He recommended to the legislature that contribution and expenditure limits be fixed by law—with care not to set them so arbitrarily low as to give incumbents a runaway advantage.

Not all the reformers—who would like stronger measures in the area of enforcement than Briscoe does—support such limits. "If a man has accepted too much money from a particular lobby and his voting record indicates some connection there, the people of Texas can enforce a limit by just not re-electing him," said Price Daniel. "If the voters are given complete information about who is giving when, they can form their own opinions as to whether there is an obligation on the candidate's part."

Spending limits turned out to be an issue the legislature could agree on, and it adopted a bill setting a total ceiling for statewide offices at $800,000 for the first primary, $400,000 for the runoff, and $800,000 for the general election, or a maximum of $2 million. In other action to limit spending, the legislature passed a bill restricting advertising to charging political candidates the lowest rates.

Legislators were ready to revise the law on lobbyists after a new penal code provision outlawing solicitation or acceptance by a legislator of "any benefit" from anyone with an interest in matters "pending before or contemplated by the legislature" was strictly interpreted by the Travis County District Attorney to bar lawmaker solicitation of lobbyists. Legislators feared that lobbyist participation in fund-raisers would have to be curtailed. "We are at the mercy of every district attorney in Texas whether we are going to be indicted or not," said veteran Representative DeWitt Hale of Corpus Christi at a committee hearing on a bill being introduced to relax the penal code provision. "We overreacted in 1973 and burned down the barn trying to get one or two rats out of the loft."

The amendment as finally enacted was viewed by Common Cause and other reform proponents as strengthening rather than weakening the penal code provision, however. Effective definitions and limits were placed on honorariums, fund-raising events, and other benefits. The new law prohibits "pecuniary benefits" from any person to a legislator or legislative employee other than campaign contributions duly reported.

There are still loopholes in the law that were not closed. One is the failure to curb cash contributions, which Bynum wanted to limit to $100. Briscoe wanted to go even further and advocated that they be limited to $10 to avoid "big cash kitties [which] are an invitation to misuse." Neither recommendation was adopted, however.

Another loophole is the lack of reporting requirement for unopposed candidates (who frequently receive substantial contributions) under campaign finance-disclosure laws, although an annual reporting of contributions and gifts other than standard campaign donations is prescribed under the state Code of Ethics. Such a requirement was proposed by Bynum and by state Representative Ray Hutchinson, who charged that state officials, once elected, can raise money from any lawful source without disclosure. Reporting can be evaded, according to Hutchinson, by delaying announcements as candidates for re-election or by "raising the funds for purposes other than a campaign." Neither Hutchinson's nor Bynum's attempt to deal with this problem got anywhere in 1975.

The Future

Spending limits for statewide candidates enacted by the 1975 legislature, if still in force in 1978, may or may not mean that less money will be spent in some major campaigns.

Few candidates have ever topped the $2 million limit. Of course, Dolph Briscoe did it in 1974, when he spent about $2.4 million in a single primary and the general election. The $2 million limit will apply to three races (including a runoff, which Briscoe did not have in 1974). Briscoe himself advocated such limits, but whether future candidates will welcome them is another question. At any rate, they have little choice but to obey them—or seek new ways to circumvent them, if they remain in force. In view of the U.S. Supreme Court ruling on

Federal campaign limits, Secretary of State White has requested an opinion by the Texas attorney general on the constitutionality of the new state law. At this writing, the opinion has not been written.

The legislature's adoption of spending limits but rejection of strengthened enforcement machinery amounts to a strange kind of "reform." Without individual contribution limits or effective enforcement, the role of heavy political campaign contributors may be changed only slightly. The big "angels" may simply compete more forcefully to get their money on the line first, before the candidate reaches his overall limit. If this is true, the campaign spending ceiling will accomplish little toward the end of encouraging more small donations and fewer big ones.

The movement for an enforcement commission is expected to continue in the 1977 legislature, but the present political climate holds little hope. Reform in the area of campaign finance has gone about as far as it is likely to go—until a new scandal provides a new impetus.

FIVE

CALIFORNIA: A NEW LAW

William Endicott

Edmund G. Brown, Jr., who in 1974 was elected California's thirty-fourth Governor, used his inaugural address to call on members of the legislature and others in public office to help him "regain the trust and confidence of the people we serve." He pointed out that fewer than half of those who could have voted in the election did so, "apparently believing that what we do here has so little impact on their lives that they need not pass judgment on it. . . . The biggest vote of all in November was a vote of no confidence."

To restore that confidence, he urged that both the letter and the spirit of the state's new political reform law—Proposition 9—be followed with enthusiasm. He described the measure as "the biggest vote-getter of all in the primary election," and continued, "The provisions of Proposition 9 will not always be easy to follow. But I honestly believe that they are the surest and most certain path to a government beyond reproach."

Indeed, overwhelming voter approval of Proposition 9—probably the most far-reaching formula for regulating the influence of money on politics ever enacted in the United States—was the highlight of a post-Watergate purging of the California political conscience. Clean government and clean politics were bywords of the 1974 election campaigns, and, though it sometimes was speciously used, campaign financing was without question the year's most fashionable issue. "Candidates wanted to go out of their way to show that they were doing more than the law required," said Daniel Lowenstein, who helped draft

Proposition 9 and now heads the Fair Political Practices Commission it created. "They were charging their opponents with violating the law—keeping things secret, taking improper contributions. In fact, even though I think it's an important question and should play a role in campaigning, you can argue that it was overemphasized. But it played a very significant role in the elections."

In one way or another, every major candidate for governor in the June primary presented himself as a man for campaign reform. Each deplored the heavy cost of campaigning. Each objected to domination of campaign financing by corporate and special-interest groups. Each condemned the influence such domination breeds. Each promised, if elected, to find "a better way."

Maybe next time; not in their races. For even though voters were expressing their distaste for traditional forms of campaign financing by endorsing Proposition 9, the money for California campaigns continued to be raised largely in the same old way— from corporations, other special interests, and wealthy individuals.

It still cost more than $1 million to be nominated for governor by a major party in California, and every candidate except one whom the public-opinion polls put within reach of the nomination raised and spent that much or more. For the November general election, Brown, the Democratic primary winner, amassed nearly $2 million while his Republican challenger, Houston I. Flournoy, who then was State Controller, collected close to $1.6 million.*

The irony of Brown's fund-raising was that he was propelled into the governor's chair as much by his tough stand on campaign financing as by anything else, save perhaps the fact that he bore the name of his famous father, a former Governor. Even before Watergate and all it came to symbolize had focused public attention on the influence of big money in politics, Brown, as Secretary of State, had been cracking down on the reporting of campaign contributions and expenditures and pushing for tougher laws. He was a champion of Proposition 9 from its inception. When he announced his candidacy for governor in January 1974, he listed political reform as one of the major areas of concern to him. He talked about it throughout his campaign. He said he would not take money from lobbyists,

---

* Under Proposition 9, each would be limited to $980,000 in the primary, $1,260,000 in the general election. See p. 118.

and he enjoyed emphasizing his lack of reliance on well-financed special interests. In fact, he took money from almost every conceivable source—from big business and big labor, from public employees intent on winning a collective-bargaining law he favored, from doctors and dentists, from developers and builders, from rich Democratic activists, from movie stars and other performers, from his family.

Yet Brown's role in developing campaign financing into a major issue was undeniable, and he exploited it masterfully. The prominence of the campaign for Proposition 9 helped enhance his reform image and neutralize any potential effects of the source of his campaign funding. The atmosphere of reform was also fostered by the existence of a new law passed by the 1973 legislature which set down the strictest rules governing campaign reporting in California history.

The Waxman-Dymally Law

The new law, which won final passage in the legislature on September 14, 1973, and was signed by Governor Ronald Reagan on October 2, grew out of separate bills sponsored by Assemblyman (now Congressman) Henry A. Waxman (D., Los Angeles) and state Senator (now Lieutenant Governor) Mervyn M. Dymally. It was hailed by Waxman as a "nearly unanimous response of the legislature to the failings and loopholes of the present law." Others suspected it was more an effort to head off Proposition 9, a stronger measure, which was being drafted at the same time. At any rate, the Waxman-Dymally Law, as it came to be known, was a strong replacement of the existing law —which was very weak, requiring little more than that candidates report the names of individuals who gave $500 or more to a campaign, and was loosely enforced.

The Waxman-Dymally Law, which went into effect on January 1, 1974, meant that the 1974 campaigns—including the campaign for Proposition 9—would be more open than ever before. It gave voters an unparalleled opportunity for a detailed look at who pays for campaigns in California and how much. The result, supporters hoped, would be to illuminate links between special-interest largesse and political favors.

Specifically, the law required candidates to:

• register with the secretary of state all campaign committees that collected or expected to collect $500 or more in a calendar year;

- identify individuals who filed campaign statements by name, residential and business addresses, and telephone numbers;
- file campaign statements 10 and 28 days before and 31 days after elections;
- list by name, city, occupation, and employer or principal place of business contributors who gave $100 or more;
- list by name and city those to whom expenditures of more than $100 were made;
- refuse anonymous contributions and those made in the name of another of $100 or more;
- refuse cash contributions of $500 or more; and
- report political contributions and expenditures in nonelection years.

The law also required the secretary of state and county clerks to report violations and provided for stricter enforcement by the state attorney general and local district attorneys. The state Board of Equalization was directed to audit campaign finance statements of all candidates who received 15 percent or more of the vote or spent $25,000 or more, and of all committees that spent $10,000 or more. Another provision allowed plaintiffs in a civil action against violators to receive 50 percent of any campaign money unreported or improperly reported; this came to be known as the "bounty-hunting" provision.

Secretary of State Brown predicted the law would mean an end to "secret political slush funds and backroom payoffs," and, indeed, a larger percentage of campaign contributions was disclosed than ever before. But there were problems.

Ideally, full disclosure should have meant detailed and accurate reporting on what came into a campaign and what went out, and timely, cumulative publication of reports readily accessible to the public. In these respects, the new law fell short. While the documentation produced was the richest ever, the real dollar value of campaigns still tended to remain elusive in the confusion of multiple campaign committees, fund transfers, in-kind contributions, and imprecise reporting.

The *California Journal*, a magazine reporting monthly on state government and politics, noted that the sheer volume of material "makes it difficult, if not impossible in many cases, to ferret out the significant contribution or trend of contributions from the eye-washing detail offered, one suspects, more in faithfulness to the letter of the disclosure law than to the spirit." The *Los Angeles Times* said that in many cases nobody —not even the candidates themselves—knew for certain how much they had raised and spent. When a *Times* reporter called a Flournoy aide for confirmation of a figure after the primary election, the aide said, "That's probably pretty close." It was not uncommon within a candidate's mass of reports to find clerical errors, conflicting figures, and the same committee being referred to by two different names. Such conflicts were blamed on the difficulty of monitoring relatively minor committees over which the candidate had no control.

Every candidate seemed to have his own bookkeeping system. For instance, the secretary of state's office wrote the campaign treasurer for state Senator Mervyn Dymally, the Democratic nominee for lieutenant governor, that one of his reports "lacks a grand total of expenditures, a subtotal in Section C is incorrect, and your grand total receipts is also incorrect." Dymally, cosponsor of the campaign-reporting law, was asked to file an amended statement, and did so. A handwritten note included in the file of state Senator John Harmer of Glendale, Republican candidate for lieutenant governor, said: "This report shows a surplus of $289.29. Actually have $536.44 in the bank and cannot find the error."

Numerous organizations raised funds from contributors and parceled them out to pet candidates—party caucuses and euphemistically named clubs and committees, such as United for California, a business group. A candidate receiving money from said groups did not have to list the original sources of the organizations' funds, although the law did require the organizations themselves to file statements showing both their sources and how they distributed their money.

Another problem was that money was constantly transferred back and forth between various committees for the same candidate, making it extremely difficult to keep an accurate count of what actually was being raised and spent by the overall campaign. Monitoring and enforcement of the law would have been greatly strengthened and simplified if each candidate had been required to have a central campaign committee with a single accounting system to coordinate, control, and report on all contributions and expenditures.

Proposition 9

Some of the problems left unresolved by the Waxman-Dymally Law were dealt with in Proposition 9, which strengthened reporting and enforcement requirements and introduced the key provision of limits on total spending.

The proposition was drafted by an uneasy coalition of Common Cause, the maverick People's Lobby, and top aides on Jerry Brown's staff. People's Lobby, founded in 1968 by the husband-and-wife team of Ed and Joyce Koupal as a non-partisan political reform organization, was an outgrowth of an unsuccessful Koupal effort to recall Governor Ronald Reagan. Ed Koupal, a former used-car salesman, claims that People's Lobby has a mailing list of 20,000, but its actual membership remains elusive. Enemies describe the Koupals as self-righteous zealots, while supporters swear by their uncompromising enthusiasm for reform and, apparently, their populist belief that you can't trust politics or politicians.

A lengthy investigation by Al Martinez of the *Los Angeles Times* of the events that led up to the document's drafting concluded that it almost died before birth in the conflict generated by its sponsors. The coalition came close to collapse several times, and reportedly it usually took a representative from Brown's office, Daniel Lowenstein, acting as peacemaker to resolve the differences between the two political activist organizations. According to one source, "They got along about as well as the Arabs and the Jews."

The precise genesis of the measure is difficult to determine because the major participants, all long-time adherents of political reform and recent proponents of strict campaign reporting and conflict-of-interest laws, traced its roots to the work each already had done in that area. Martinez reported that it probably was People's Lobby that moved first by drafting a tough measure based largely on a successful reform initiative in the state of Washington. Common Cause meanwhile was looking for a proving ground to test its political clout and logically settled on California, where it enjoyed its largest membership.

Brown brought the two groups together early in 1973, but problems emerged almost immediately. Common Cause, fearing that Brown would exploit the measure for political purposes in his race for governor, wanted him to dissociate himself from it. People's Lobby, viewing Common Cause as "the establishment" and suspecting that it might move slowly, demanded an immediate public announcement of the coalition. Common Cause had its doubts about People's Lobby as well. Ken Smith, state director of Common Cause, later stated that "People's Lobby is really not an organization but two people with a lot of true believers who follow. We felt from the start that we could not work with them, but that we had to—because they could qualify the initiative. We also believed that aside from their rhetoric, the Koupals had an honest belief in political reform. They are a monument to what can be done with a low budget and a lot of work."

Although Smith feared that People's Lobby was moving too fast, that it was less interested in giving thoughtful considera-tion to a workable political-reform instrument than in ram-ming hard-line reforms down the throats of politicians, "this," he said, "had to be the year." So Common Cause continued in the coalition, but problems—both substantive and procedural (and often bordering on the absurd)—continued to arise.

A major controversy developed over the issue of limiting campaign spending. "The Koupals felt the only way to clean up politics was to spend no money in elections," said Smith. "That was a joke. We wanted liberal limitations, otherwise you'd create an incumbency party." Joyce Koupal denied that her group wanted to eliminate campaign spending entirely. "The truth is," she told Martinez, "Common Cause wanted no limitation on spending. We almost split up over that. They were adamant on that score, and we were adamant in our posi-tion. Limitations were important to us."

This dispute precipitated serious thought on the part of Common Cause of pulling out of the coalition and even cam-paigning against the Koupal proposal. But cooler heads pre-vailed, and by the spring of 1973, a series of meetings was being held to draft the document and set up a campaign. Most of the drafting was done by members of Brown's staff and Bob Girard, a Stanford University law professor and Common Cause representative. The target date for the first draft of the initiative was June 1, 1973, and the final draft was due August 1. Both deadlines were met.

After another series of crises, including one over the issue of who would announce the drive for the initiative (both sides eventually agreed on Brown, Martin Stone, the state Chairman of Common Cause, and Joyce Koupal), the final document was circulated and approved by all the parties involved. Then there was a dispute over which group would file the measure with the state attorney general's office preparatory to soliciting signatures to place it on the ballot. Martinez reported that both Common Cause and People's Lobby wanted to be the first to file and thereby gain some measure of control over the initia-tive. A Common Cause representative later admitted he con-sidered "a foot race" with the People's Lobby representative to "beat him to the door." As it turned out, Dick Gregory of People's Lobby got there first with the $200 filing fee.

Mike Walsh, who had become chief negotiator for Common Cause, charged that People's Lobby had double-crossed them, while Joyce Koupal said she feared her group was about to be double-crossed and muscled out of the picture by Common Cause. According to Martinez, Common Cause officials actually considered filing a second initiative and discussed a lawsuit against the Koupals "for their capture of the document," but decided that they would try to repair things. According to Lowenstein, if Jerry Brown had not spoken to Walsh and the Koupals and succeeded in reconciling the two groups, "the whole thing might have fallen apart right then." "At the time," said Ken Smith, "everything seemed so serious. Now it seems funny. But we knew we were playing for high stakes."

And they won. Proposition 9 needed the valid signatures of 325,504 registered California voters to qualify for the June ballot. More than 500,000 names were filed. In the end, Smith said later, "all things aside, it was one of the best grass-roots campaigns ever run."

The document that had emerged from this protracted wrangling dealt with the major issues involved in campaigns, elections, and conflicts of interest. It covered the same points as the Waxman-Dymally Law in the area of disclosure but lowered the minimum amounts of receipts and expenditures that had to be reported. It also limited anonymous and cash donations more strictly, shifted the auditing responsibility to another body, and imposed new reporting dates. It broke new ground in the areas of spending ceilings and lobbyist regulation, and it provided for detailed financial-disclosure statements by elected officials. While it retained the prohibition against any official's participating in governmental decisions in which he has a financial interest (unless participation is required by law), it removed the requirement that the specific interest involved be disclosed.

Specifically, the measure's provisions were:
• *Campaign disclosure:* Campaign contributions and spending of $500 or more must be reported for every candidate and ballot measure, with the reports due at specified times: for candidates and committees, 40 and 12 days before the vote and 65 days after it; for proponents of ballot measures, 65 days after qualifying their measure. Committees supporting or opposing ballot measures must report 35 and 7 days before the election and 70 days after it. All reports must identify all contributors of $50 or more by name, address, occupation, and employer's name, and list the amount given each time and cumulatively. Persons

receiving $50 or more and the services they render also must be identified. Anonymous contributions of $50 or more, cash contributions of $50 or more, and cash expenditures of $50 or more are prohibited. Auditing of reports is to be done by the state Franchise Tax Board.

• *Spending limits:* How much can be spent in statewide campaigns is based upon the number of citizens of voting age in the state as of January of the year preceding the election. Using the 1973 estimate of 14 million voting-age persons in California, the spending limits are as follows: governor, 7 cents per voting-age citizen ($980,000) in the primary and 9 cents in the general election ($1,260,000); other statewide offices, 3 cents per voter ($420,000) in both the primary and general elections; incumbents seeking re-election to statewide office, 10 percent less than their challengers' limits; party state control committees and affiliates, 1 cent per voter ($140,000); independent committees, $10,000 maximum; initiative qualification, no more than 25 cents times the number of signatures required ($81,376) to qualify statewide measures; ballot-measure campaigns, 8 cents per voter ($1.12 million) or $500,000 more than the amount approved for spending by the opposition, whichever is smaller. No committee or group of committees can spend more than $10,000 on ballot-measure campaigns without approval of the Fair Political Practices Commission.

• *Ballot pamphlet:* The ballot pamphlet, which is sent to voters before each election, is revised to include more information in a more readable format. The text of all proposed measures and the laws to be repealed are to be included, along with arguments and rebuttals for and against and an analysis prepared by a nonpartisan legislative analyst. In addition, the public will be able to examine the material to be included and test its accuracy in a court action.

• *Incumbency:* Incumbency is not to be a factor in determining the order of candidates' names on the ballot, as it has been in the past, when incumbents have been listed first. Once an elected state officer files a declaration of candidacy, all mass mailings at public expense must cease.

• *Conflict of interest:* Public officials must disclose financial holdings that present "a potential conflict with their official responsibilities" and are disqualified from making public decisions in areas of conflict. Elected state officers, boards of supervisors, city councils, chief administrative and elected officers of cities and counties, and candidates for election to any of these offices are required to disclose any investment worth at least

$1,000 (indicating whether their value exceeds $10,000 or $100,000), any interests in which at least 50 percent is held, income totaling $250 or more in 12 months (indicating if it exceeds $1,000 or $10,000), gifts of $25 or more, and all income from business if more than $1,000 was received for legal or brokerage services or $10,000 for other businesses. All state and local agencies are required to adopt a conflict-of-interest code that contains (1) a list of jobs vulnerable to conflict-of-interest considerations and (2) the circumstances under which an official must be disqualified from acting.

• *Lobbyist regulation:* Lobbyists must register with the secretary of state, rather than with a legislative committee as before, and cannot spend more than $10 a month on a single public official. They cannot make or arrange political contributions. They must open separate accounts to handle lobbying funds. All payments received for their activities must be reported periodically, and must include deposits and expenditures in the lobbying account and expenditures of $500 or more in one year made to any business in which a public official or candidate holds an interest. The legislative and administrative decisions the lobbyist sought to influence also must be reported. Those who hire lobbyists or who spend at least $250 a month to influence legislative or administrative decisions must report expenses over $25, gifts to officials, candidates, or members of their families, business transactions exceeding $1,000 with firms in which an official or candidate has ownership, and the date and amount of political donations. Auditing and investigating of reports filed by lobbyists is to be done by the state Franchise Tax Board.

• *Enforcement:* A five-member appointive Fair Political Practices Commission, no more than three of whose members can be from the same party, is created to enforce the initiative's provisions, issue advisory opinions, and promulgate regulations. The governor is permitted two appointees, including the chairman, and the attorney general, secretary of state, and controller one appointee each. The commission can subpoena records and witnesses, issue cease-and-desist orders, and levy fines up to $2,000. It has a $1 million annual budget.

• *Penalties:* Knowing and willful violation of the law is a misdemeanor, and anyone convicted is to be prohibited from holding elective office or acting as a lobbyist for four years. Fines are possible up to $10,000, or three times the unreported amount for failure to report contributions received or expenditures. Late filers may be fined $10 a day or $100, whichever is greater. Enforcement of criminal provisions is in the hands of the attorney general and local district attorneys; and with the Fair Political Practices Commission or city attorneys for civil penalties, including fines. Any citizen may file for a court injunction to stop violations or enforce the law and claim half of any unreported money, if a violation is proven.

The campaign for Proposition 9 was a confrontation between an unusual alliance of big labor and big business on one side and traditional citizen lobbies such as Common Cause on the other. Some saw it as a power struggle between the organizations that had been most influential in the political process in the past and the organization—Common Cause—that was moving most aggressively to challenge them. It was considered a major test of the strength of citizen-organized action groups, with Common Cause hoping that success would set in motion nationwide changes designed to eliminate the domination of money in American politics. "It is not accidental that labor and business have become unaccustomed allies in this fight," David Broder of the *Washington Post* wrote. "For the first time, both realized that their power is being challenged by that 'upstart' citizens' group."

Lobbyists, whose activities were due to be sharply restricted if Proposition 9 passed, adopted a fatalistic view, many of them deciding that to oppose it merely would generate more votes for it and concluding that it was going to pass anyway. "Our opposition would not be given credence because we are automatically expected to have a selfish viewpoint," said Paul McCarron, lobbyist for the California Builders Council. "I felt on my part that the thing was definitely overregulation, some parts may be unconstitutional, and I also had every confidence the doggone thing would move, because it had a motherhood sound to it. The Watergate syndrome gave all these things a motherhood sound." Indeed, Albert J. Shults, who represents several major oil companies, told associates facetiously that "the best way to defeat this thing is to say Standard Oil is for it." And Donald J. Reisner, who represents the California Railroad Association, said that for his group to take a public position in favor of it "would be the kiss of death for sure."

But labor mounted an aggressive effort to defeat the measure, calling it "deviously contrived, antilabor, antidemocratic." John Henning, state AFL-CIO Executive Secretary, was particularly critical of two sections of the proposed law—the one prohibiting lobbyists from making any personal campaign contributions to political candidates and the one establishing the nonpartisan

Fair Political Practices Commission to enforce the law. Henning, who is registered as a lobbyist with the secretary of state, said the restriction on contributions would deny elected union officials who make such contributions the right to represent their members before the state legislature. He also said the measure was "antidemocratic" because it would give the commission "arbitrary and dictatorial powers over the fundamental political processes of representative government."

Common Cause, with which labor often had worked in the past, was accused by the AFL-CIO of "spreading political poison among the labor movement and the working people of the nation." Common Cause's Walsh countered that such opposition was "reactionary and wrong-headed at a time when our nation is wracked by political scandal." Labor's fears were ludicrous, he said. The proposition defined a lobbyist as anyone who spends a "substantial" portion of his or her paid time trying to influence governmental activity, and, according to Common Cause, most union leaders would therefore be excluded from registering as lobbyists. "Because a union has an agent to represent it in Sacramento is no reason for all officers of the union to register as lobbyists, unless the officers themselves spend a substantial portion of their time directing the agents," said Walsh. "Either the union leader would register as a lobbyist and, therefore, cease being the conduit for campaign contributions or, if he desires to continue making contributions on behalf of the union, he must refrain from exercising a substantial portion of his time lobbying."

Lined up with organized labor in opposition to Proposition 9 were the state Chamber of Commerce, the California Manufacturers Association, the California Bankers Association, the California Taxpayers Association, doctors, farmers, and the Executive Committee of the Republican State Central Committee. They banded together as the California Know Nine Committee and persuaded Robert H. Finch, a former Lieutenant Governor and Cabinet member of the Nixon Administration, and Democratic Assemblyman John T. Knox of Richmond, to be cochairmen.

Finch took to his task with relish and seemed to draw on every possible argument against it. He described Proposition 9 as "a classic example of burning down the temple to flush a thief . . . a multiple overkill effort." Its significant provisions, he said, duplicated reform legislation already passed and not yet tested by experience. Proposition 9, Finch charged, would have the same effect on political reform as Prohibition had had on drinking: making contempt for and violation of the law a national hobby. He zeroed in particularly on the five-member enforcement committee to be created and said it would have powers over political action so sweeping that "it could literally give the green light to candidates and causes it favored while it could bottleneck or give the red light to candidates and issues to which it might be opposed. This means that if an unscrupulous group gained control of the commission . . . it could perpetuate favored men and cliques in power and throttle its critics and opponents."

Just two weeks before the election, Republican Governor Reagan announced—to no one's surprise—that he also opposed the proposition and submitted his own political reform package to the legislature, saying that "surgery is required" to restore public confidence in government because Watergate and other events have spawned a public cynicism that is "a cancer, an ugly growth eroding the public's belief in the honesty and integrity of our very form of government." But as his proposals called for a virtual ban on political activity by business and labor, cynics suspected that the Governor never meant them to be passed but was only attempting to thwart Proposition 9. At any rate, the legislature received Reagan's proposals coolly and promptly scuttled them.

The pros and cons of Proposition 9 permeated all of the primary political races. Candidates rarely escaped taking a position on it, and Democratic gubernatorial candidates Brown and Jerome R. Waldie, then a Congressman, lost the endorsement of organized labor because of their support of it. A lead article in the *California AFL-CIO News* detailing the union's withdrawal of support for Brown and Waldie called it "an anti-worker measure." One proponent charged unions were putting "extraordinary pressure" on candidates to oppose it. But neither Brown nor Waldie backed down. "I helped write the measure, helped get petitions signed to put it on the ballot, and I have been and intend to continue to speak out strongly in favor of Proposition 9," said Brown. "I think labor totally misunderstands the measure. It is not antilabor, and not aimed at unions. But it will stop the wining and dining of legislators and put everything out in the open, limit political spending, and curb the abuses of our political system."

Other Democratic gubernatorial candidates, such as San Francisco Mayor Joseph L. Alioto, took equally strong positions against the measure; some, like Assembly Speaker Bob Moretti,

at least were lukewarm toward it, thus staying in the good graces
of labor. Alioto, for instance, got $50,000 in campaign contribu-
tions from the California Labor Political Action Committee,
plus lesser amounts from scores of other unions.

But opposition to Proposition 9 never translated into the
sums of money necessary in California to mount an effective
campaign. Final spending reports showed that four major pro-
Proposition 9 committees spent close to $600,000, while the
opposition spent less than $170,000. In other words, those
fighting runaway campaign spending outspent its proponents
by almost four to one; in fact, though, their own law would
have permitted them to spend nearly twice as much as they
did.

California Common Cause put up more than $450,000 of the
proponents' total, including a $123,000 loan from its parent
organization in Washington, and there were many private donations ranging from small amounts to the $10,000 given by
wealthy Los Angeles businessman Max Palevsky, a perennial
contributor to liberal causes. Jerry Brown funneled $33,000
to the campaign from three committees supporting his gubernatorial candidacy.

Labor carried the financial load for the opponents, with the
United Labor Against Proposition 9 Committee spending more
than $50,000. Major corporate contributors to the California
Know Nine Committee included the Southern Pacific Transportation Company, $10,000; Pacific Gas and Electric Com-
pany, $10,000; and Atlantic Richfield, $5,000. Several lobbyists
gave in amounts up to $1,500.

In the week before the election, opponents poured their last
remaining resources into a $50,000 radio blitz, put together by
the political public relations firm of Whitaker and Baxter. The
message: "Protect your free speech and right to petition." It
called the proposition "political repression." The proponents,
depending heavily on Common Cause money, countered with
$100,000 worth of radio and television commercials whose
main thrust was a plea to "get tough on corruption in government." Actor Lloyd Bridges volunteered his services as narrator.

The issue was never in doubt, as Common Cause's Walsh
adroitly predicted in a pre-election article in the *Los Angeles
Times*, which vigorously endorsed the proposal: "With a single,
dramatic step—a direct vote of the people—Californians can
make it clear that they want a government at all levels that is
open, accountable, and unbought. The average citizen is fed

up with double-talk and double-dealing. He wants reform, and not rhetoric. . . . It's time we got tough on political corruption in California wherever it exists."

As it turned out, Californians did seem to want reform. They voted 3,224,765 in favor of the measure and only 1,392,783 against it—particularly impressive in view of the fact that California voters traditionally have rejected initiatives as long and complex as Proposition 9. It is doubtful that most of the voters completely understood the provisions of Proposition 9 or had read more than a cursory introduction to the 20,000-word proposition. But it carried the tag of political reform—a "motherhood" issue in the atmosphere of Watergate. The climate for political reform in California had predated Watergate, but Watergate provided the necessary impetus and made it vitually impossible for an effective opposition to be mounted. In the opinion of its sponsors, Proposition 9 would have passed without Watergate, but not as overwhelmingly; and the opposition, almost without question, would have been more intense.

The *Los Angeles Times* editorialized after the election: "The overwhelming decision in the largest state is certain to encourage reform movements in other states and to impel even reluctant members of Congress toward action on the national level." This view of the inevitability of campaign reform was not shared by all, however. The law had no sooner taken effect on January 7, 1975, than it was met with a spate of legal challenges by lobbyists and other special-interest groups. An organization of 35 of Sacramento's top lobbyists filed a suit claiming it infringed on their freedom of speech and right to petition government in behalf of those they represented. The California Bankers Association and several major banks also sought to block the law by claiming it would force them to disclose to the public the private accounts of many state officials and saying the definition of a lobbyist was overly broad. These preliminary efforts were rejected by the courts, however. While lobbyists claimed that the restrictions on their ability to make campaign contributions was unconstitutional, Los Angeles Superior Judge Harry L. Hupp, in a four-page ruling, said, "A compelling state interest is found in the necessity to protect the lawmaking and administrative process against improper influences." He said he doubted that campaign contributions are a form of free speech.

Experience thus far indicates general compliance with the law. The Fair Political Practices Commission Chairman, Daniel Lowenstein, when asked whether its division of enforcement powers would weaken it, pointed to the attorney general's office's extensive experience in criminal prosecution, the Franchise Tax Board's skilled staff auditors, and the specific expertise in the general administration of the law that he expected the commission to develop. "Each really adds a different element," Lowenstein said, "and furthermore, at a given point in time, if one or two of them sort of slack off and don't approach things aggressively, there will be one or two who will be perhaps approaching things aggressively. Setting up enforcement this way strengthens the law, rather than weakens it."

Lowenstein believes that just having Proposition 9 on the books serves as a powerful deterrent because of the threat of penalities, the civil "bounty-hunter" suits, and, most important, public exposure. The chilling, or cautionary, effect stems from the fact that violators must contend with three branches of government, plus reform-minded citizens armed with the right to file civil suits and, as an incentive, to collect half of any unreported money.

The chaos that many foes predicted has not occurred. "People are still complaining about the paperwork, but they no longer challenge the workability," said a commission staff member.

As for its effects on lobbyists, in the opinion of William J. Keese, lobbyist for the California Dental Association, "Proposition 9 has only changed the rules under which lobbying is done. We complied with the old rules which regulated lobbying, and we certainly intend to comply with these rules. We have formed an organization to assist us in understanding and complying, and, hopefully, it will also be successful in working with the commission to make these rules understandable."

But at this writing, Proposition 9—the Political Reform Act of 1974—has not been in effect long enough for evaluation. What has been evident is the schism between the broad terms of Proposition 9 and the pragmatism required in drafting the regulations and operating rules needed to carry out the law's intent.

Vigo Nielsen, a San Francisco attorney and one of California's foremost authorities on political reform law, wrote recently in the *California Journal* that the authors of Proposition 9 were rushed, inclined a plug every loophole—both real and imagined —and pressured by People's Lobby and Common Cause to put in something for everybody. Fortunately, said Nielsen, they also established the Fair Political Practices Commission to make it manageable and to protect it—so far successfully—from constitutional challenge.

Many of the shortcomings in the Waxman-Dymally Law, such as complicated reporting procedures and multiple committees, were not corrected by Proposition 9, but reformers already are discussing changes that could be made by regulations or law to simplify the required reports and provide more useful public disclosure, such as requiring a single campaign reporting committee for each candidate.

Givers in the 1974 Campaign

Although Proposition 9 was not in effect during the 1974 campaign, the Waxman-Dymally Law was, and the mass of information available as a result afforded a new glimpse into campaign financing. Reporters willing to delve into the data had an unusual opportunity to document the extent of corporate contributions, pinpoint the donations of other special-interest groups such as doctors and dentists, and detail the emergence of teachers and public employees as major forces in financing California elections.

By the time final statements were filed after the November general election, newsmen were able to point out with authority that major business and professional interests provided the lion's share of money to both candidates and ballot-measure campaigns. As corporate contributions are legal in California, some money came directly from companies. Big oil firms, with a stake in depletion allowances, other tax advantages, and off-shore drilling permits, spent $480,000. Horse-racing interests, dependent on the state for racing dates and tax advantages, chipped in $234,200. Realtors donated $224,000 through their California Real Estate Association, and doctors and dentists, major beneficiaries of the state's Medi-Cal program for the medically indigent, gave out $640,000.

In one of the more blatant instances of self-interest contributions, a group of general contractors building a giant earth dam on the Stanislaus River pumped $175,000 into the campaign to defeat an initiative measure that might have halted dam construction to keep the river in a "wild and scenic" state. The measure lost. Supporters of the measure, interestingly enough, had paid out close to $200,000, raising the money in large part by selling tickets for raft rides down the white-water stretch.

Howard Hughes, who listed his occupation as "self-employed," turned over $83,800 to lobbyist Donald K. Brown to be disbursed to favored candidates, but a handful of other wealthy individuals far outspent Hughes. Max Palevsky gave close to $200,000, almost a third of it to an unsuccessful Democratic candidate for attorney general, Los Angeles attorney William A. Norris. Palevsky's ex-wife, Joan, handed out about $140,000, $74,338 of it to Norris. Other major individual donors included David Packard, who listed $118,700, including a $100,000 loan to Republican gubernatorial candidate Flournoy; San Diego industrialist Cornelius G. Dutcher, who gave $89,500, mostly to liberal Democrats; and San Francisco socialite Constance Reynolds, who reported $89,500 in donations, most of which went to Flournoy.

The major labor organizations, in support of pet candidates and in opposition to Proposition 9, filed final reports totaling $843,000. Smaller unions kicked in countless more dollars.

Then, of course, there were the lobbyists, who dumped huge amounts of money into campaigns as a last hurrah before Proposition 9, which would prohibit lobbyist donations, went into effect. Several top lobbying groups and individual lobbyists contributed well over $100,000 each, and their reports showed they overwhelmingly favored incumbents, regardless of party or political philosophy. In many cases, lobbyists hedged their bets by giving money to opposing candidates for the same office. For instance, the California Medical Association's Political Action Committee gave $5,000 each to Republican Assemblyman Jerry Lewis and Democrat Ruben S. Ayala in a special San Bernardino County election to fill a state Senate seat. (Ayala won.) The Bankers Responsible Government Committee, through Sacramento lobbyist Frederick M. Pownall, donated $300 each to Republican Assemblymen Newton R. Russell of Burbank and Mike D. Antonovich of Glendale, who opposed each other in a bitter primary race. (Antonovich won.) The wine industry, through Viticultural Associates, gave $5,000 each to Democrat Brown and Republican Flournoy in the governors' race. When the lobbyists did contribute to newcomers they made sure, in most cases, of one thing—none were running against incumbents.

The reporting documents showed how big corporate interests distributed money through dummy committees into the campaign treasuries of friendly politicians. There were the Good Government Committee (savings and loan associations), the Citizens for Responsible Government (Pacific Telephone Company executives), the Committee to Elect State and Local Candidates (big businesses and oil companies), and a long list of others. A group called the Orange County RSVP Committee, for instance, gave nearly $50,000, most of it to Flournoy, the money coming from Orange County business interests. United for California, which drew money from a variety of corporate interests such as Union Oil Company, donated $122,000, mostly to Republican legislative candidates. Gerson D. Ribnick, representing the Professional Astrologers of California, labeled his contributions as being from the Consumer Action Committee, and another committee he represented was the Environmental Action Committee, made up of sandblasting contractors, painting and decorating contractors, and the United Business League. Lewis Keller, lobbyist for the insurance industry, distributed $40,278 through a tongue-twisting committee listed as ACLICPAC (Association of California Life Insurance Companies Political Action Committee). Such a proliferation of dummy committees would not be prevented by Proposition 9, although the committees will have to reveal their sponsors in a separate filing.

Perhaps more surprising than any other disclosures in the mound of contribution reports was the revelation that teachers and public employees were among the biggest investors in 1974 compaigns. Unions, associations, and committees representing state and local government workers and teachers contributed at least $1.7 million to candidates favorable to their views. The 144,000-member California Teachers Association (CTA) gave out $555,956, and the 105,000-member California State Employees Association (CSEA) added another $410,671. Like many members of labor unions, teachers and public employees also volunteered huge chunks of off-duty hours to help out in the campaigns of candidates sympathetic to their drive for collective bargaining, higher wages, and increased benefits.

The growing political awareness of these groups started several years ago, after the teachers lost an initiative designed to give more public money to schools and the state workers lost an initiative measure on salaries. Leonard Kreidt, the CTA's veteran press representative in Sacramento, confirmed that teachers learned to play the money game from traditional special interests. "When you watch how trucking and gravel have had an influence on transportation for so long, you learn a lesson," he said. "Money happens to be a political fact of life. It kind of makes you wonder, though, what's going to happen to you in a democratic society."

When the teachers began their involvement in political campaigns, distributing their money through a CTA arm called Association for Better Citizenship, $500 was a typical gift and

$1,000 was exceptionally large. But in 1974, some legislators were given as much as $10,000 and Brown got $25,000, as did his running mate, Dymally; and gifts of $2,000 to $5,000 were not uncommon. After the election, CTA boasted in its newsletter of its 85 percent win record.

State employees have also become adept at the political game. In 1972 they set up a political action arm to collect money from members (50 cents a month) and disburse it to friendly candidates. "Who gets how much is determined by the need of the individual candidate and how he rates on our list," said Rich Martin, a CSEA public relations officer. "If he's a guy we really feel has been good to us, that figures in how much he gets." Proof of this policy could be found shortly after the 1975 Legislature convened, when a major collective bargaining bill, giving government workers the right to strike, was introduced by state Senator Ralph C. Dills of Gardena and Assemblyman Howard L. Berman of Los Angeles, with the strong endorsement of Assembly Speaker Leo T. McCarthy of San Francisco and Senate President Pro Tem James R. Mills of San Diego, all Democrats. A check of contribution reports showed the four had received more than $50,000 from teachers and public employees. Dills, who was in a tough primary race, got the most—$8,000 from the CTA and $6,500 from CSEA for a total of $14,500.

Only a small share of campaign funds was distributed from the treasuries of the state parties, which are notoriously weak in California. The Republicans, perhaps because they are better organized, raised a little more than the Democrats. There was little laundering of funds through party organizations, certainly not as much as in many other states, and the major responsibility for raising money was left primarily with the individual candidates. In legislative races, partisan caucus committees in both the Senate and Assembly collected contributions, usually from lobbyists, to parcel out to candidates, but the amounts were not great, and the sources were easily traceable through reports filed by the committees. Minor party (American Independent and Peace and Freedom) candidates ran their campaigns on a shoestring and won not a single office.

There were an increased number of candidate-to-candidate donations, which probably began in earnest in 1966 when Ronald Reagan, perceiving that he was about to win by a landslide, put a good deal of his campaign money into helping—successfully—other Republicans who were trailing in the polls. Eight years later, Jerry Brown contributed more than $80,000 to a get-out-the-vote drive for the Democratic ticket and taped a special commercial urging support for William Norris, the candidate for attorney general and the only statewide Democratic candidate trailing his GOP opponent in the polls. Assembly Speaker McCarthy and Assemblyman Willie L. Brown, Jr. of San Francisco, also a Democrat, spent generously on other Assembly candidates in an effort to win loyalties in anticipation of another showdown for the speakership. McCarthy had defeated Brown earlier for the position most political observers regard as the number-two job in California politics. And a continuing effort to unseat James Mills as President Pro Tem of the Senate benefitted some Senate candidates, who got campaign money from both Mills and his chief rival, Senator George N. Zenovich of Fresno.

Recipients: The Primary

Despite complaints by campaign managers about fund-raising problems, there was plenty of money around. In the major statewide races alone—governor, lieutenant governor, secretary of state, controller, attorney general, treasurer, and superintendent of public instruction—more than $12 million was raised and spent in the primary, nearly $8.5 million of it spent by the gubernatorial candidates, making the contest the most expensive in state history.

Perhaps the reason for this was the one put forth by Alexander Heard in his *Costs of Democracy* (1960), that "cash is far more significant in the nominating process than in determining the outcome of elections," because primaries pit candidates of the same political parties against each other, thus blunting normal partisan factors affecting the voter choices and making money a major determining factor in the outcome.

Democrats outsolicited Republicans by more than four to one in the gubernatorial primary for a variety of reasons, including the facts that more Democrats were running for governor; that Republican Ed Reinecke's fund-raising efforts were crippled by his Federal prejury indictment in connection with an investigation into ITT's offer to underwrite the 1972 Republican National Convention (he was later found guilty); and that donors and politicians alike generally felt that 1974 was a Democratic year.

Alioto, unsuccessful in his effort to win the Democratic nomination, led with $1.7 million, trailed closely by the Democratic winner, Jerry Brown, with nearly $1.6 million. Assembly

Speaker Moretti amassed $1.4 million; millionaire businessman William Matson Roth, $1.24 million; Congressman Waldie, $592,000; attorney Herb Hafif, $380,000.

On the Republican side—aid it was not the best of years for the G.O.P.—Flournoy, the winner, collected and spent more than $1.2 million, but his only major opponent, Reinecke, managed to take in only $373,000.

Democrats matched Republicans pretty evenly in contributions from corporations and their wealthy executives, supporting Reagan's claim that "the old stereotype image of Republicans being all rich people and the Democrats being all poor people is not borne out by the facts. The opposition has its affluent people, also. Some very hefty and healthy corporation gifts have found their way into Democratic candidates' hands."

Among all Democratic gubernatorial primary candidates, only Roth turned away from traditional fund-raising to finance his $1 million campaign. A millionaire, he paid for virtually the whole thing with his own money and with the help of a $250,000 donation from his 83-year-old mother.

Because of his strong support for Proposition 9, Brown received no labor contributions in the primary. He sought to bolster his image as a reformer by returning several checks, including a $1,000 donation from the Dow Chemical Company, but did not reject many contributions and drew heavily on a variety of corporate and individual sources.

His biggest individual donor was Joan Palevsky, who gave the candidate $33,250 outright and loaned him another $40,000 through 11 separate Brown committees, most of them set up specifically to receive her contributions and permit her to avoid paying gift taxes on individual donations exceeding $3,000.

Brown relied heavily on borrowing, to the tune of $350,495, in various loans guaranteed by contributors. Although his reports indicated that he finished the primary race with a surplus of more than $200,000, this included nonmonetary contributions such as free office space totaling $100,000, and about $44,000 in pledges of future donations. The nominee's various bank accounts actually had less than $75,000, and there was $131,000 in bank loans to be repaid immediately, according to campaign manager Tom Quinn.

Houston Flournoy collected money from a long and impressive list of corporations and business executives, but none donated spectacular amounts. He also was given substantial loans by many corporate executives, including Leonard K. Firestone, but repaid them out of campaign funds. J. Paul Getty gave him

$200. The difference between Flournoy's total receipts—loans, contributions, and pledges—and his expenditures indicated that he wound up the primary with a slight surplus, but the fact was that he was faced with $287,500 in unpaid loans, including $100,000 from David Packard. In addition, the G.O.P. nominee owed $167,500 to the Bank of America for a loan that was guaranteed for him by a collection of wealthy California Republicans, including many of Reagan's key supporters.

What the money spent—$1.6 million by Brown, $1.2 million by Flournoy—and the votes cast boiled down to was a cost to Brown of $1.29 for each vote he received in winning his party's nomination, compared with 91 cents for each of Flournoy's votes.

In primary races for the other statewide offices, the winners alone ran up expenditures of almost $2.8 million, and at least two losers—Assemblyman Walter Karabian and San Francisco Supervisor Robert H. Mendelsohn, seeking the Democratic nominations for secretary of state and controller, respectively—raised well over $300,000 each. Again, the most successful fund-raisers were Democrats. Kenneth Cory, the Democratic nominee for controller, was the biggest spender in the race for statewide offices below the level of governor—with an outlay of nearly $680,000, 75 percent of which came from two friends in Orange County, Louis Cella and Richard O'Neill.

Recipients: The General Election

The primary campaign barely was over when Flournoy made a proposal that he and Brown voluntarily curb spending in their general election race, in keeping with the limits imposed by Proposition 9. Political reform as represented by the measure was, he said, "obviously the will of the people," even though provisions would not take effect until 1975. Flournoy proposed a spending limit of 9 cents for each voting-age citizen, or about $1.3 million—as in Proposition 9.

Brown eagerly embraced the suggestion as "an excellent idea," but they ran into an immediate snag when the question was raised of who would enforce such an agreement. Aides of both Brown and Flournoy conceded that the enforcers would have no legal power, their only recourse being appeal to public opinion. In addition, both sides worried about independent committees created by others to campaign for the candidate but not actually directed by him—groups like "Lawyers for Brown" or "Teachers for Flournoy"—which might feel no obligation to report to an informal enforcing agent. They also considered such questions as whether a state-committee mailing urging the election of all members of the party ticket would be included in the Brown-Flournoy limit; whether to include in the total spending by potent political forces such as the AFL-CIO's Committee on Political Education, if it should endorse Brown; what to do about the scores of legislative candidates who send out campaign literature featuring the name of the gubernatorial candidate along with their own.

Both sides ultimately decided to discard the limit. But Brown, not to be one-upped by Flournoy, then proposed that the two candidates "set a bold new precedent" by eliminating paid television commercials from their campaigns, engaging instead in face-to-face debates and joint appearances. Brown had spent $702,800 for television and radio in the primary, Flournoy $432,352 for media (including newspaper advertising, which Brown hardly used, and some other publicity functions). "In recent years," said Brown, "politics has been corrupted by the use of slick television and radio commercials which ignore the issues and sell candidates like bars of soap." Brown said a "substantial number" of joint appearances and debates would give voters "a real opportunity to compare the two candidates and their views on the issues." Flournoy rejected a total ban, but both candidates subsequently agreed not to put more than $900,000 each into television and other media advertising, and they stuck to that limit.

By mid-October, Brown not only was loping easily ahead of Flournoy in the public-opinion polls, but was outdistancing him in the crucial struggle for campaign funds as well. "We're having to work at it, but it's not difficult," Tom Quinn told reporters. Reports filed under the Waxman-Dymally Law showed that in the three-month period following the primary Brown raised approximately $1,216,900, in contrast to $968,500 for Flournoy—a difference of nearly a quarter-million dollars. Post-election reports showed that Brown raised nearly $2 million altogether, about $400,000 more than Flournoy.*

More significant than the total figures, however, were the sources of the money. Flournoy raised his from traditional Republican sources—corporations and wealthy business executives —with virtually no financial support from labor unions or pub-

---

* Brown wound up with a surplus of $40,127 and said he used $269,495 of the money he raised in the general election to pay off primary campaign debts and an additional $233,000 to repay general election debts.

lic employee groups. Brown's backing, on the other hand, fanned across the socioeconomic spectrum—from bartenders, waitresses, and bulldozer operators to teachers and civil servants to developers, bankers, and corporate heads to doctors and dentists. Some corporations hedged their bets by giving to both candidates.

The Republican candidate's contributors included then Vice Presidential nominee Nelson Rockefeller, who sent him $5,000, novelist Joseph Wambaugh, who gave $100, and San Francisco socialite Constance B. Reynolds, who gave $70,000, making her his biggest individual angel. Doctors and dentists gave to both gubernatorial candidates through their state political action arms, but were more generous to Flournoy, handing over $17,500 and $22,500, respectively. A last-minute fund-raising dinner in Los Angeles featuring President Ford, which produced about $220,000, numbered among the big donors Atlantic Richfield Company, Rhor Industries of San Diego, the Bank of America, and Continental Airlines. Comedian Bob Hope, who was master of ceremonies, gave $5,000.

In late October, Wes Sawyer, a cattle rancher who headed the Agriculture for Flournoy Committee, sent out a letter to dairymen and farmers with a melodramatic appeal for support of Flournoy. He said Brown "has consistently supported the far-out consumer groups and the Cesar Chavez movement. . . . We are not in a battle of Republican against Democrat. We are fighting for our way of life, for the future of our families and for the future of agriculture." Sawyer, who subsequently was appointed by Governor Reagan to the California Beef Council, said additional funds were needed "to purchase television time to insure a victory on election day. Your contribution of $50, $100, or more would be a tremendous help and greatly appreciated by Hugh. Corporate checks are acceptable under California law." Flournoy wound up with more than $100,000 from agribusiness interests, including more than $50,000 from the Western Growers Association.

He also wound up, after losing the election to Brown by 176,-805 votes, with a debt totaling nearly $350,000. Flournoy's campaign finance director, John A. Tretheway, said he did not know how the deficit, which came from both his primary and general election campaigns, would be paid.

Brown's listing of contributors, a six-inch-thick sheaf on file in the secretary of state's office, left the clear impression that, as the consistent leader in the polls for more than a year, he enjoyed the unique capability to solicit money from any segment of society—a political luxury usually possessed only by an expected victor. It was as if there were a bandwagon fervor among the individual "fat cats" and private institutions that traditionally contribute to campaigns.

While Brown lived up to the letter of his pronouncement that he would accept no lobbyist contributions, he violated the spirit by taking substantial donations from a variety of sources those same lobbyists represented. Organized labor, which had not contributed to him during the primary, swung solidly behind him for the general election and was, collectively, his dominant supporter. In all, organized labor and public employee groups, which increasingly became intertwined, turned over at least $230,000, including $76,800 from the United Auto Workers, $25,000 from the California Teachers Association, and $14,600 from the California State Employees Association. At the other end of the socioeconomic scale, doctors put up $15,000 for Brown through the California Medical Political Action Committee, and dentists, through the California Dental Political Action Committee, chipped in $12,500. Even the sports world got involved. Peter O'Malley, president of the Los Angeles Dodgers, donated $1,000 to Brown, and the San Francisco 49'ers kicked in $500. *Playboy's* Hugh Hefner gave the young bachelor $4,900. The Los Angeles law firm of Republican Robert Finch, a philosophical ally of Flournoy, gave Brown $600. Finch said he was not aware of the donation, was "shocked" by it, and later quit the firm in protest.

Brown's biggest single individual benefactor in the general election was Martin Harmon, a retired builder of hospitals and nursing homes, who accounted for $61,000—a loan of $50,000, a donation of $10,000 through his Auburn Manor Holding Corporation, and a personal gift of another $1,000. Frank Sinatra also gave $1,000.

Such contributions prompted Flournoy to attack the Democratic candidate as a "political streaker" who was posing as an opponent of uncontrolled political contributions on the one hand while filling the other "from any large money sources he can find." Flournoy conceded that he, too, accepted large political contributions but added, "I am not critical of Mr. Brown for accepting political donations but of his political hypocrisy and shallow attempts to deceive the voting public." Brown responded that there were "no strings" on any of the money he collected, that it came from people "interested in getting the best government possible." Indeed, he showed no inclination in his first several months in office to be swayed by the special interests of his major contributors. A case in point: After accepting substantial donations from teachers and various educational associations, he rejected their pleas for more state aid for public schools and ultimately slashed $27 million from a bill passed by the legislature to give financial help to hard-pressed school districts.

Candidates in statewide races below the level of governor raised and spent something less than $2 million in the general election campaign, Democrats leaning on traditional party sources such as organized labor and Republicans drawing heavily from corporate interests. An exception was the Republican incumbent Attorney General, Evelle Younger, who won several labor endorsements and the money that went with them.

Another $4 million was spent in the fall campaign by candidates trying to win legislative seats. Particularly expensive races were those involving incumbents thrown together by reapportionment and the battles for open seats in several southern California areas.

A few, but not many, legislative candidates imposed restrictions on contributions. Senator Arlen Gregorio, for example, a San Mateo Democrat, refused all group contributions and would take only a maximum of $500 from any one individual source. Democratic Senator Anthony Beilenson of Los Angeles turned down all lobbyist and special-interest donations. Assemblyman Willie Brown, Jr. of San Francisco returned, on principle, contributions from the California Automobile Wholesalers Association and the League of California Milk Producers. But such actions were the exception, rather than the rule. One candidate told a *Los Angeles Times* reporter that he would like to eliminate the fund-raising of which he had been critical but could not if no one else did. "You know what they'll call you after the election if you do that this year?" he asked. "They'll call you a loser."

It was business as usual for a number of state Senate candidates who did not even face re-election races in 1974. For example, Senator Jack Schrade, a San Diego Republican whose term extended to 1976, added $65,000 to his campaign treasury with a Salute to Jack Schrade dinner patronized heavily by lobbyists. Similarly, the Friends of Senator Whetmore and the Whetmore Booster Committee kept active in 1974 on behalf of noncandidate Senator James Whetmore of Anaheim, a Republican. The Whetmore boosters, many of them lobbyists such as

Daniel J. Creedon of the California Brewers Association ($500) and James Garibaldi of the Wine and Spirits Wholesalers and Hollywood Park Race Track ($2,000), gave $14,375 to Whetmore in 1974. Whetmore's "friends" added another $11,723.

Let the Sunshine In

Money—especially money traceable to lobbyist and "fat cat" sources—could be a liability in the reformist atmosphere of 1974. The effect of the Waxman-Dymally Law—which required much more thorough disclosure than before—and of the debate on Proposition 9, which focused attention on campaign finance reform, was to help turn a handful of incumbent legislators out of office when their opponents were able to exploit campaign financing as a major issue against them. Others had narrow escapes.

Early in the primary race for a state Assembly seat in the Sacramento area, for example, Democratic challenger Eugene Gualco ran newspaper advertisements listing the contributors to his incumbent opponent, Walter Powers. "Each election more and more lobbyists appear as contributors to Walter Powers' campaign," read the Gualco ad. "In 1972, the names of lobbyists and special-interest groups made up approximately 65 percent of his contributors. Here is a partial list (note that many lobbyists try and hide behind misleading committee names). Check the contributions from lobbyists with the bills Powers has killed, authored, or supported."

The ad went on to list donations to Powers from banking and financial interests, oil companies, utilities, the funeral industry, transportation and moving industries, and liquor and food dealers and distributors. It also said that Powers' largest contributor at that point in 1974 was United for California, the euphemistically named business group, which gave the incumbent $2,500. Gualco called United for California "a front organization" that gets its money from major California corporations. Throughout the campaign, Gualco continued to pound away at Powers' ties to special interests. He won in the primary and went on to gain an Assembly seat in the November general election.

The legislative race in which the most money was spent (a total of $230,000), between Assemblymen Joe Gonzalves of Cerritos and Robert McLennan of Downey in a newly reapportioned district, was also affected by an awareness of campaign practices and abuses. McLennan enjoyed an advantage because of the attention he had received earlier in the year for his leadership in repealing a controversial pension bonus plan for legislators.

Just a few days before the November election, a *Los Angeles Times* story by Steven C. Smith noted that Democrat Gonzalves was being investigated by the attorney general's office for alleged campaign reporting violations. Gonzalves had admitted failing to report roughly $130,000 in campaign funds raised during 1973 and had been characterized as "one of the worst offenders" of campaign reporting laws by Common Cause, which had been unable to trace the disposition of almost $80,-000 in campaign funds raised by the veteran legislator over the past three years. Despite a flurry of complaints against a number of major candidates, Gonzalves was reportedly the only candidate for state office under "active investigation." And although Attorney General Younger stated that an investigation "doesn't mean that we have any conviction that any wrongdoing has been committed," the reports proved to be Gonzalves' undoing. He lost to McLennan by 2,536 votes and subsequently was cleared of any reporting violations.

In probably no other race did the issue of campaign financing take on as much significance as in the contest for state controller between Assemblymen Kenneth Cory of Garden Grove, the Democrat, and William T. Bagley of San Rafael, the Republican. Conflict centered on Cory's receipt of more than half a million dollars from two wealthy Orange County supporters and on Cory's charge that Bagley was accepting contributions from his own legal clients, who were subject to state regulations.

Dr. Louis J. Cella, Jr. of Santa Ana and Richard J. O'Neill, a Mission Viejo rancher and developer, were the men Bagley described as Cory's "financial angels," and indeed they virtually underwrote his successful primary campaign with more than $500,000 in donations, loans, and payment of campaign bills. In appearance after appearance, Bagley charged that in accepting the Cella-O'Neill money Cory was "spawning another Watergate" in California. He said such huge donations from only two individuals were "ethically improper." "This situation," Bagley stated, "two people trying to buy an office, has never occurred in the history of the state of California. Never have so few given so much for so little. Ken Cory has conducted a campaign financed by two individuals. It is ugly. It is sick. It is obscene."

Cory insisted there was nothing wrong in his taking the money. "My campaign is supported by friends of mine, business associates, very close personal friends," he said. "They are people who have not been involved in prior controller's races. They have been active liberal Democrats, contributing money to liberal candidates throughout the state of California, throughout the nation. "That's the kind of contributions they are—good, clean, emotional political money."

But Orange County voting records showed that Cella was a registered Republican. O'Neill was Chairman of the Orange County Democratic Central Committee and was a partner in several business ventures with Cella. Cory's assertion that neither man wanted anything from him as controller brought this rejoinder from Bagley: "Richard O'Neill owns 53,000 acres of land in Orange County. That's a bigger land mass than the city and county of San Francisco. He's quoted as saying, 'I don't have any problems with the state government. The county assessor is my problem.' If Mr. Cory were to sit on the Board of Equalization (as controller) he has supervisory and supervening powers over the practices of assessment by county assessors. Then, by gosh, if I owned 53,000 acres of land in Orange County, I'd get Ken Cory's ear and that's exactly what's going to happen."

Cory, for his part, accused Bagley of working in the legislature to advance the interests of oil companies, utilities, and other big corporations that either were clients of his law firm or contributors to his legislative campaigns. "I would suggest to you," he told an audience, "that Pacific Gas and Electric Company is a client of Bagley's law firm. P.G.&E. is a contributor, and go through the major issues affecting P.G.&E. in this legislature and you can't find Bill Bagley voting once against P.G.&E. I think it's very clear that Mr. Bagley has done well by his law clients, well by his contributors, and I think that's the issue in this campaign."

Bagley denied being beholden to corporate or other interests and said oil companies and utility firms had used his law firm "in a very, very minor way." He also said: "The question is whether you should be a legislator totally dependent on the public trough for your groceries. . . . I would rather see somebody have a base at home, have his farm, have his insurance agency, which Cory has, have his law firm or his grocery store—if he can run it while he's in Sacramento—and have a base in the community—political, social, and fiscal."

Though it was clear that Cory had accepted unprecedentedly high individual contributions for an office that had never been contested in such costly fashion before, Bagley never was able to

establish a quid pro quo; his challenge primarily was based on
the appearance of impropriety. Cory won a relatively easy
victory.

After the election, Cella and O'Neill said they expected to get
half their money back, the repayments coming over a period of
the next eight years from fund-raising events for both Cory and
the Democratic Party. Both men also said they did not expect
anything in return for their support of a winning candidate.
"We sometimes get a lot of lip service," O'Neill told a group of
newsmen, "but they usually do what they please. We don't have
to like it, but we're stuck with them and we have to support
them. Some people think we have a lot of influence afterwards,
but it isn't true. About the best you can expect is that they
might send a car to the airport to pick you up."

He and Cella explained that they had estimated they might
have to spend up to $200,000 in support of Cory. "When we
got to $200,000," said O'Neill, "we found out the Cory was still
behind. We don't like to lose, so we decided we had to put in
some more money. But we didn't expect that kind of expense
and we didn't expect it to be so lonesome out there." O'Neill
said he and Cella reached a point where they were so deeply
into the campaign that they had to put in more in order to
save their investment. He also said he and Cella were sometimes goaded into making heavy contributions by attacks against
them, either by other candidates or in the press.

In an ironic twist, O'Neill early in 1975 ran successfully for
a southern California Democratic Party office and told guests at
an opulent cocktail party, "Thank God, the big spenders are
out of California politics." His main message was that Proposition 9 would make his type of contributor obsolete.

Public Financing

The net effect of the 1974 election year was a growing enthusiasm among politicians of both major parties for at least
partial public financing of campaigns. Common Cause late in
November reported that it had commitments from a substantial number of legislators, including a majority in the state Assembly, to vote in 1975 for a mixed system of public and private
campaign financing, plus strict limits on private donations and
total campaign expenditures.

Similar legislation had been defeated in a Senate committee
in 1973, but a proponent, Senator Anthony Beilenson, opti-

mistically stated that the momentum had shifted in its favor. "It is somewhat more appealing as time goes on," he reflected.

Common Cause's Michael Walsh noted several factors that had enhanced chances of partial public financing legislation: First, "Congress enacting a system of public financing for the 1976 Presidential race has taken a little of the scare out of the topic. Secondly, the post-Watergate scrutiny and the fact that more and more voters are aware of the relatively small base of financial support for many political candidates and officeholders tends to make some politicians a little wary of what the future holds." For example, some California candidates heavily financed by special interests were embarrassed by the detailed press accounts of campaign solicitations in their 1974 races. Walsh said the passage of Proposition 9 was a "sign of the times" to politicians that the public was dissatisfied with conventional campaign financing.

Under a Common Cause public financing proposal, to qualify for public funds in a primary election, candidates would have to demonstrate a base of support by collecting a substantial amount in small private donations or a large number of signatures. In the general election, the major party candidates would be guaranteed a substantial percentage of their expenditure limit in public funds, and minor party candidates would get funds in proportion to their party registration figures. The primary goals of Common Cause in this area, according to Walsh, are to provide adequate campaign funding for challengers as well as incumbents and "break the stranglehold wealthy private interests maintain on elected officials through large campaign donations."

But despite interest in it, the push for public financing has run up against a shaky economy. Assembly Speaker Leo T. McCarthy, who had been a proponent, said he no longer would support public financing "unless the economy comes bounding back" and told reporters he wanted no action on any bills that cost money "unless they create jobs or feed hungry people."

Consequently, public financing bills, including the Common Cause proposal, were put in limbo, and Common Cause officials indicated that if the Legislature continues to reject public financing efforts they would take the issue to the voters via the initiative process, perhaps in November 1976.

SIX

MASSACHUSETTS:
CORRUPTION AND CLEANUP

Robert Healy

Each day, as Michael Dukakis drove from one stop to another in his 1974 campaign for governor of Massachusetts, he would inspect a folder in his lap containing a packet of checks. They were campaign contributions, and the law required that they be deposited in a monitored campaign account within 72 hours after receipt. Dukakis examined each check carefully, sometimes telling an aide to return one because it came from a state employee or from a contractor who did a lot of business with the state and thus might be looking for something after the election.

Forty-one-year-old Michael Dukakis was not the ordinary Massachusetts politician. Part of a new breed, he had cut his teeth in politics during John F. Kennedy's run for the Presidency in 1960. Dukakis had seen Kennedy win in Massachusetts by a landslide while the Democratic candidate for governor lost to a former plasterer who had become a wealthy contractor, Republican John A. Volpe. Immediately after that election, Dukakis formed a committee of young Democrats to reform the party. In the state legislature, he led the way to no-fault insurance and worked for a campaign-financing disclosure law. Dukakis ran his 1974 campaign to conform to both the spirit and the letter of the campaign-disclosure law passed by the legislature in 1973, which, in comparison with other states' disclosure laws, would have to be given high marks. And a year later the legislature came close to passing the first state law in the nation for public financing of the gubernatorial election.

Massachusetts had come a long way. It was only a few decades since the legendary days of Boston's Mayor James Michael Curley, whose campaign workers (and those for the mayors and governors who followed him) used to sit in the old "boiler rooms" at the Parker House on School Street. Before the decisions were made for the final radio and newspaper advertising blitzes, they would factor into expenditures vacation trips to Florida for themselves, whether their candidate won or lost the election. In these same rooms, they ran poker and gin-rummy games, where favored journalists competed with campaign workers. Curley had once sent a campaign aide to a legislative leader with a bag of money for distribution to his colleagues in return for a promise that Curley's "official" slate would not be challenged in a Presidential primary. (The money was refused, but Curley prevailed anyway.) And if Massachusetts was not the site of the first $100-a-plate fund-raising dinner, it takes a back seat to few other states in the number of such events held since.

Election corruption—and efforts to stamp it out—are an old business in Massachusetts. One can point to the mix of scandal and reform as early as the so-called Boston Plan of 1915, when Boston's "good" people, headed by E. A. Filene, one of the city's leading merchants, hired muckraker Lincoln Steffens to develop what they called "a vision" for Boston. Steffens was given seven years to bring together a plan for business, political, religious, and social reform.

Steffens' principal call in the city was to the old leader of the ninth ward, Martin Lomasny. Like all bosses, Lomasny made the collections and delivered the votes. He gave Steffens his view of the system: "I think," said Lomasny, "that there's got to be in every ward somebody that any bloke can come to—no matter what he's done—and get help. Help, you understand; none of your law and your justice, but help." That was the rock on which the trades for corruption and votes were built. Steffens was deeply impressed, and in his autobiography he called Lomasny "one of the best men I met in Boston. He was honest; he had intellectual integrity. He saw things straight and talked straight about them. He had the mind and the imagination to do that. And he had a heart, both for daring and kindness."

Perhaps the most radical idea advanced by Steffens when he unveiled his plan for Boston was that the leading grafters themselves should lead the fight against graft, because it was only they who totally understood the system and how it worked. Another aspect of Steffens' design was to convince people that they should resent political or business corruption, not only because it was a "steal," but because it delayed the advance of the program for the city.

But when Steffens, the intellectual, tried to pull together the reformers and social leaders and make them work with Lomasny to change the political system, the plan failed. Working with Lomasny was simply beyond the comprehension of most of Boston's reform-minded citizens, who said that theoretically the plan looked good but it wouldn't work in practice. As Steffens recounted it, the reformers instead sought out the advice of the next mayor, whose "theory of reform was to limit the suffrage to property owners and college graduates."

That, of course, was not the last reform effort any more than it was the end of corruption. There has been general acceptance, for example, of walking-around money. After a fund-raising affair in St. Louis for John Kennedy in 1960, the organizer of the event, Thomas P. O'Neill, Jr., now the House Majority Leader, was asked by Kennedy how they did. O'Neill ticked off the amount raised, and Kennedy told O'Neill to give his aide Theodore Sorensen the checks and give him the cash. O'Neill, an old hand at Massachusetts politics but new to a Presidential campaign, said to Kennedy: "It really doesn't make much difference whether you're running for President or city council, it all works the same, doesn't it?"

Reform Efforts in the 1960's

Some changes in the way things worked came about through legislation passed in 1962, after the recommendation of a blue-ribbon commission to study campaign financing. It was the kind of bill that a crafty legislature sometimes puts together: It looked good but it had more holes in it than a screen. Its one useful provision was establishment of a campaign depository system for Congressional and statewide candidates and political committees. But a candidate could have 40 political committees and transfer funds from one committee to another, so that it would take a team of accountants to run down expenditures accurately. Testimonials or "friendship" dinners did not have to be reported, either. Edward Kennedy, running for U.S. Senator that year, funneled all his campaign expenditures through an advertising agency that had represented his father, Joseph P. Kennedy, for years. The agency protected disclosure of the individual vendors used in that campaign the way a Catholic priest protects the seal of the confessional. Furthermore, the law provided for the secretary of state to make complaints to the attorney general, which meant—according to the Massachusetts political code, in which one politician does not turn in another —that enforcement was not going to occur. The law didn't work. Despite its weaknesses, however, having a law on the books gave the reformers something to amend, and it eventually brought about a better bill.

That legislation was the product of an effort that probably had more impact on the recent course of campaign-financing reform in Massachusetts than any other: the work of the Massachusetts Crime Commission in the mid-1960's. The commission began its work after a series of revelations coming from a tax case involving a distinguished engineering contractor, Thomas Worcester, a graduate of Harvard who was well-placed socially. Unfolded in grand jury transcripts were stories of crooked accountants, of brown bags of money being passed in cars near Boston's old Faneuil Hall, of a bipartisan payoff system of legislators with both jobs and money, and of a direct 10 percent relationship between the bribes delivered by a bag man for Worcester and the contracts received by Worcester's firm. The Crime Commission developed a good deal more, including cases involving architects that showed a pattern of campaign gifts, delivery of services, and pieces of helpful legislation. The investigation reached into the governor's office and into the judiciary and resulted in a number of convictions and jail sentences.

In its final report to the state legislature on May 17, 1965, the Crime Commission, which was headed by Alfred Gardner, a stern Yankee lawyer, described the quality of corruption the group had uncovered. Campaign contributions played a central part:

> Those who assume the powers and responsibilities of government must get elected and to do so they usually spend large amounts of money. The moral standard set by the methods used in raising money continues after the candidate is elected.
>
> Corruption in government in a large part consists of the sale of contracts, privileges, appointments and other benefits that may be dispensed through the power of office. If a candidate or a group in a party that controls a candidate promises contracts, privileges, offices or other benefits to those who provide sizable campaign contributions, or if there is a threat to withhold such benefits unless contributions are forthcoming in

requested amounts, the moral standard that makes it wrong to exercise governmental authority for a cash consideration has been discarded in advance. The first dollar has been taken from the till.

The thin line that separates bribes from campaign contributions provided by those seeking preferential treatment is emphasized by the fact that several of those accused of accepting bribes on information uncovered by the commission have contended that the amounts paid were campaign contributions.

The Crime Commission pointed firmly to the need for reform of campaign financing, and cash contributions were seen as a particular problem:

> Corruption in the state government may be reduced by remedial legislation and by administrations that are vigilant in preventing corruption and prosecuting those who are guilty of corrupt activities, but the moral force that is needed to eliminate or minimize corruption on a long-term basis will be lacking as long as campaign funds are raised by the improper methods referred to above. The staggering costs of conducting statewide campaigns and the relatively few sources from which substantial contributions can be obtained have made adherence to sound moral principles increasingly difficult. But these principles cannot be abandoned. . . .
>
> An additional evil of the present campaign contribution system is the personal use by some candidates of a part of the contributions made to their campaigns. The commission has found that in many cases, campaign contributions have been solicited in cash rather than by check. All or parts of the cash so contributed can be retained by the candidate for his personal use without much risk of exposure. When a candidate asks for contributions in cash rather than by check he can have no motive other than the concealment of the use to be made of the cash received. Contributions by check can sometimes be traced to their ultimate destination; contributions in cash can go to the traditional tin box to be used for any purpose that the needs or desires of the candidate may determine.

The work of the Crime Commission had great impact on the public and fired the need for reform in the state legislature. It was, if there is a place in time for such things, the beginning of a substantive effort to tighten things up, and it was critical in bringing about change in the campaign spending law. Among the proposals made by the commission and ultimately adopted as amendments to the Massachusetts statute on campaign contributions were regulations on the makeup of political committees and their statements of accounts, the filing of candidate statement by advertising agencies; on inspections, penalties for violations, and election inquests; on court procedures to compel statements and provide immunity for witnesses. Amendments were also passed prohibiting political contributions by corporations, prohibiting certain nonelected public employees from soliciting campaign contributions, and providing that public employees not be required to contribute or render political services.

But there were still gaps. The *Boston Globe* in 1966 editorialized about $100-a-plate testimonial dinners that were not being reported. Professor Murray B. Levine of Boston University, a student of election practices, spoke out about the faults of the law. He said that Edward J. McCormack, who ran against Edward Kennedy in 1962 for the Senate nomination, reported spending only $78,000 "but it is obvious he spent at least $750,-000." Persons wishing to contribute more than the $3,000 statutory limit could get relatives to contribute.

The 1973 Campaign Reform Bill

During the early 1970's, efforts were made to limit spending on certain campaigns, to bar money raised under the guise of compiling a campaign chest, and to limit giving by lobbyists. Each time, these efforts succeeded to a certain extent—in committee or in one of the two bodies of the legislature—but never enough to achieve passage into law. It was not until 1973 that there was a substantial redraft of the law, and it was under these new provisions that the campaign of 1974 was to be run.

The drive actually began in 1972, and the men who were to meet in the gubernatorial election two years later—Republican Governor Francis Sargent and Democrat Michael Dukakis—both took part. Sargent asked to be heard on the Democrats' reform proposals in the legislature. Before the legislature scheduled a public hearing, however, Sargent appeared on statewide public television and radio to press for campaign reform with his own proposals, which he said he hoped would allay "suspicion" and restore "confidence" in government. His major proposals were to limit overall campaign spending, to prohibit lobbyists and public employees from making contributions, to limit contributions to $500, and to tighten the reporting system and the enforcement procedure.

Michael Dukakis, who was not about to give Sargent an edge, even at that early stage of the race, criticized the Governor's plan before a legislative committee. Dukakis pointed out that the proposal to prohibit state, county, and municipal employees from contributing to political campaigns had been the law for 80 years; and he added that the Governor had been conspicuously silent about solicitation of contributions by state officials for political purposes. (One of Sargent's major fund-raisers during the campaign was Albert P. [Toots] Manzi, a Sargent appointee to the Massachusetts Turnpike Authority.)

The bill that was finally signed in December 1973 by Governor Sargent covered disclosure, lobbyist regulation, and oversight. Candidates were prohibited from having more than two financing committees. All expenditures had to be made by check and reported in detail by the candidate, with contributions above $15 itemized as to the amount and the source. To get around the early testimonial (or "friendship") dinners, a precise description of "candidate" was drawn: All officeholders were considered potential candidates, and any funds raised in their behalf, including those from testimonial functions, had to be reported as campaign contributions. Candidates also had to file full financial reports before both the primary and the general election. The law also restricted and provided for disclosure of the spending for political purposes of the lobbyists who practiced their trade on Beacon Hill. (Before the Governor put his signature on the bill, there were dozens of testimonial dinners to give candidates access to the lobbyists' money without having to pay the public price of disclosure.)

The biggest change in the law was oversight. The new bill provided for a full-time, politically independent director of campaign and political finance, who was armed with broad powers to investigate campaign funding and to oversee the funding of all of the candidates. The director would be chosen for a six-year term by the unanimous votes of a bipartisan panel composed of the secretary of state, the chairmen of the Democratic and Republican State Committees, and the dean of a Massachusetts law school, who would be appointed to the board by the governor. The director was given the power to bring abuses to the attorney general for prosecution, and it was assumed that the public citation of an abuse would have the potential effect of making the attorney general move on the complaint even if he might be reluctant to do so for political reasons.

While the legislature had passed what most people felt was a good bill, there was some question about motivation. At the same time that the legislature was wrestling with the campaign reform bill, state Senator John Quinlan, a Republican who was to run unsuccessfully in the 1974 campaign for secretary of state, was collecting signatures for an initiative petition to establish an independent Corrupt Practices Commission to oversee campaign expenditures—a proposal that had even stricter provisions for the vendors' reports and gave the commission broader powers. Quinlan's group got more than the 56,038 signatures needed to get the proposal before the legislature and the additional 9,340 signatures to put in on the November ballot, where it was overwhelmingly adopted by the voters. The petition drive died in 1975, however, mainly because Quinlan, the moving force behind it, was out of politics when he lost in November.

There was one final piece of campaign-financing business to be disposed of before the campaign oratory would finally begin in 1974: a move for public financing of the gubernatorial campaign. All the important people appeared to be for it, including House Speaker David M. Bartley, other legislative leaders, and Governor Sargent. Sargent—who was being criticized in newspapers around the state for running a series of $100-a-ticket fund-raisers before the new law requiring reporting of money collected at such events went into effect—called fund-raising "the most repugnant part of the job." He said he would not only support a good bill but would return all the funds he had collected at the fund-raisers if public financing was instituted. "We've got to get into public financing of political campaigns," said Sargent. "I hate it. I hate the business of people passing the hat for you." Attorney General Robert Quinn, a candidate for the Democratic nomination for governor, gave public financing lukewarm verbal support. Michael Dukakis was not enthusiastic, but indicated that he would be willing to participate in a public financing experiment. Dukakis said, however, that he did not want to see "public financing used as a cop-out for those who don't want to obey the law. . . . Enforcement will still be necessary by both government and the press."

But even with all the big names in both parties in favor of the bill—at least for the record—it was defeated in late May in the House on a 115-to-109 roll call and later in the Senate by a 22-to-12 count. Despite their statements of support, none of the candidates really worked for it.

The 1974 Gubernatorial Election

With campaign-finance legislation out of the way, the time came to collect the money for the 1974 election. The amount needed to get elected as governor of Massachusetts in recent years has generally been about $1 million; if the candidate was an incumbent with a tough fight and the ability to raise money, the figure was more in the neighborhood of $1.5 million.

The big expense, of course, is television. The media market of Boston (which has three VHF and two UHF stations) reaches more than an effective majority of the state's electorate, but a worried candidate has to spend a few dollars in Worcester, Springfield, and New Bedford as well. In recent years there has been some switching of the concentration in the final media blitz to radio and newspaper advertising, but it is still television that moves the image and the polls. Candidates try to anticipate the polls run by the *Boston Globe*, which they claim influence elections, and they spend money on organizational efforts in the early part of the campaign and on television in the last days to affect these polls.

Governor Sargent had raised $1.6 million for his successful campaign against Boston's Mayor Kevin White in 1970. Knowing that there was going to be trouble in the business of raising money in the post-Watergate year of 1974, he set his campaign goal at $1 million. Sargent actually raised a little more—$1,156,866, according to his own figures filed with the director of campaign finances—and spent $1,160,240. While there is less than $4,000 difference between these figures, in fact the Sargent campaign ended up rather deeply in debt. In the figures he filed, Sargent noted two loans of $40,000 and $47,000; in addition, other contributions between May and November 1974 that must have been loans would place the campaign deficit at over $200,000. For Sargent worked off over $100,000 of personal debt by April 1, 1975, but he still owed another $100,-000, which, he said, he would never be able to work off. Officially, his loan balance is listed at $153,000.

Sargent began the election year with a healthy $233,008 bankroll and a black eye for the testimonial dinners he had held before signing the new law. Sargent admitted, at the same time that he acknowledged sponsoring the fund-raisers, that he had raised $412,000 in the two and a half years he had been in office. He used this money to set up a separate political office staffed by one or two full-time people and to finance things "that the public should not pay for," such as a number of expensive polls and trips by the Governor and his wife and staff to such affairs as the Republican governors' conference. (Some governors do use public funds for such expenditures.)

Sargent defended his record: "We have always made out reports in complete openness and in full. . . . I haven't adopted the policy since it has become fashionable in Washington. That's my personality. That's the way I have always operated."

Sargent's offer to return all the money he had collected in the pre-December fund-raisers, if the legislature passed a bill to make public funds available for the financing of the gubernatorial election, became irrelevant when the bill failed. Without public financing, the Governor naturally had to continue raising money. The main recipient of revenue raised in 1974 was the Sargent Committee. A second committee raised funds for Lieutenant Governor Donald Dwight, who was running for re-election with Sargent. The Dwight Committee, which raised a total of $140,649 and spent only $22,769 on its own campaign, funneled most of its money to the Sargent Committee.

If there was a pattern to the Sargent campaign, it was that he received a number of large gifts, many of which came from what is considered the Boston "establishment." On the Sargent lists for contributions over $500 were such names as Richard Saltonstall and his brother Leverett, the former Senator; Forrester A. Clark, an investment banker; Gerhard D. Bleicken, head of the John Hancock Mutual Life Insurance Company and an old friend of Nixon's; George Macomber, a contractor and former Olympic skier; C. Vincent Vappi, a builder; and David Rockefeller, Jr., of Cambridge, one of the many Rockefeller children who has settled in Massachusetts. Out-of-state contributions came from Laurence Rockefeller of New York and Indiana industrialist Irwin Miller, and from many of Sargent's relatives. There were two small contributions from the National Republican Governors Association, and only one from a union, Local 25 of the Teamsters, which gave $1,000. Sargent also took a campaign contribution from a member of his cabinet, Mary Newman.

Despite the kind of support he attracted, Sargent was not a traditional Republican in important ways. He was independent, he was not considered a friend of business, he had spoken out against Nixon on a number of issues, and, although he was an incumbent, he had challengers within his party for the gubernatorial nomination. Late in January 1974, a group of dissident Republicans met in Boston with the express purpose of fielding a candidate against Sargent. For a time they had rallied around Peter Fuller, a wealthy New England Cadillac dealer and son of the late Governor Alvan T. Fuller, once a power in Republican politics. But Fuller seemed to have his own ideas about running, so the Republican conservatives settled for Carroll Sheehan, who had been eased out of the Sargent administration as Commissioner of the Department of Commerce, supported President Nixon, and had little chance of even making it through the primary. Sheehan's great accomplishment in campaign financing was in nailing down Lloyd Waring, who was important not so much as a generous giver (although he was that) as because he was the man with the list. Waring was honest, wanted no power for himself, and was the perfect fund-raiser. Sheehan's records have not been filed correctly, but the figures that are available indicate he spent about $50,000 to $60,000.

Sheehan won all the votes the conservatives could muster, or 32.5 percent, in the Republican state nominating convention in June. In the September primary, Sargent buried him by almost a two-to-one margin. In a way, Sargent had made Sheehan a straw man, hoping the thrust of his victory would help him in November. But it did not work out that way.

Sargent had trouble both raising money and gaining support in the general election. He said later that he had been hurt by Watergate and his own reaction to it. One of the most outspoken critics of President Nixon at the national conferences of Republican governors, and a critic in Massachusetts of Nixon's conduct of the Vietnam war, Sargent said, "The traditional sources of money in the Republican party were sore as hell at me. People like Lloyd Waring felt initially that I was unfair to Nixon, when I was critical of him. Then all of a sudden they were embarrassed by Nixon and they crawled away from politics. I guess I just griped them," Sargent went on, "and when the roof fell in [on Nixon] it didn't make any difference. They didn't say that Sargent was right about Nixon, they were still sore as hell with me and, of course, they had been let down by Nixon."

Sargent's record on other issues, and the strength of his opponent, Michael Dukakis, hurt him as well. The polls showed Sargent as much as 25 points behind Dukakis. "The *Globe's* polls hurt me plenty," Sargent said. "When they showed me way off during the campaign, fund-raising was tougher and the organization took a nosedive. But I had other problems, too," he reflected. "I had worked against more highways in the inner cities and I was considered antibusiness by a lot of people in the business community. Believe me, I got damn little money out of the business community." Furthermore, he said that he thought the recession was a large factor because the ability of his friends and associates to make political donations was markedly affected by the stock market decline. Still, Sargent was philosophical about his 1974 campaign, and he does not blame money or the lack of it for his defeat. "Just as in 1970, there was no way I could lose, in 1974, there was no way I could win." As an incumbent Republican, even one who had a record of being anti-Nixon, Sargent could not overcome Watergate sentiment.

In fact, Sargent could hardly blame money for his defeat because he spent about $350,000 more than Dukakis. From the first of the year to the end of 1974, according to the statement he filed, Dukakis received $846,509 in contributions and spent $817,497 on his winning campaign.

Dukakis used only one committee to receive funds, although, as Sargent did, he transferred funds into his committee from the committees to elect his running mate, Thomas P. O'Neill III. But O'Neill, unlike Dwight, had serious opposition in the primary, and his records show that he spent more than two-thirds of the $154,535 he raised on that campaign. The transfers into the Dukakis campaign thus totaled only about $37,000.

The Dukakis campaign worked to raise funds from small contributors and refused money from those whose donations might create a conflict of interest. Whereas Sargent found fund-raising depressing, Dukakis was rather stimulated by it and, perhaps more important, stimulated his supporters. For this reason, the Democrat has mixed feelings about public financing. He believes that those who contribute a dollar are committed and will work hard for their candidate. "We had 15,000 individual contributors," said Dukakis, "and it helped to build our organization. We had the small fund-raisers where there would be 10 people in a living room or 150 people in someone's backyard." He pointed specifically to a backyard party in the town of Reading, where they sold 400 tickets at $5 each. "Those 400 people in that town made a difference in the primary and ultimately in the election."

The campaign's self-imposed regulations were apparently observed. "We decided from the outset that we would take no money from state employees or their relatives, and it was the best thing we ever did," said Dukakis. "I decided that the $1,000 statutory limit [on contributions] was okay, that we would not have to make it less than that, that is. But we took no money from lobbyists and there were selected cases where the relationship between the individual contributor and the state was so clear that I said no, we can't take that," said Dukakis. The practice of soliciting from lists of those who do business on a regular basis before state regulatory agencies was also rejected.

"There were people who would be before these agencies and
I had to say, 'no dice.' We returned a lot of money because of
that. We went over the list every day. I mean personally, and
toward the end of the campaign that is kind of tough to do,
and you know I would say this guy is a state employee or this
one is married to so and so and he has business before state
agencies and I would say send it back," said Dukakis.

Dukakis was amazed, he said, at the people who would come
to his headquarters with an envelope in their hands asking
about prospective appointments to such things as Racing Commission jobs. Despite his clear position on campaign contributions, "they still come to campaign headquarters looking for
something," said Dukakis.

Dukakis did not have the advantage of holding office during
his fund-raising effort, yet he was almost always ahead in the
polls—first in the primary against Attorney General Quinn
and then in the general election against Sargent. Quinn had all
the traditional political muscle to raise money as former Speaker
of the Massachusetts House and present Attorney General. In
the end, though, these ties to the party machinery seemed to
work against Quinn. In the September primary, he was able
to carry Boston over Dukakis by only 5,000 votes, while Dukakis piled up a plurality of more than 100,000 in the other
Massachusetts cities and towns to win by a four-to-three margin.
Quinn spent $497,452 in his unsuccessful campaign, and he
reported raising $474,962. He had some business support in
Boston and unusually strong labor support for a primary campaign. The name of Quinn appeared 16 times in campaign gifts
of $500 and over, a way to avoid the campaign gift limit. And
if there was any distinctive pattern to the Quinn contributors,
it was that in the $500-and-over list there were many lawyers,
some of whom had business before state agencies.

In the general election, Dukakis got the large union contributions. (Sargent had had considerable difficulty with the trade
unions represented by the state AFL-CIO labor council because
state agencies were holding up the building of the multimillion-
dollar Park Plaza project in central Boston.) Though he ran
as a reformer, Dukakis received support from a great number
of the traditional Democratic sources in addition to labor.
There were contributions of $500 and over from Edward J.
McCormack, a lawyer and nephew of the former Speaker of
the U.S. House of Representatives; Joseph Curnane, Director
of the Port of Boston in the Kennedy Administration; E. J.
Carroll of Longmeadow, a western Massachusetts businessman;

and Jerome Rappaport, a Boston real estate developer. Although Dukakis did not accept contributions from state employees, he did take gifts from legislators. Dukakis also had some help from Republicans and from several contractors who had given to Republican candidates in the past.

Two other gubernatorial candidates—Donald Gurewitz of Boston, who ran on the ticket of the Socialist Workers Party, and Leo F. Kahian of Middleboro, who ran as an antibusing candidate of the American Party candidate—raised little and got few votes. The Socialist Workers Party reported spending $10,534 on Gurewitz, who received 15,011 votes, or less than 1 percent of the 1,896,421 votes cast; Kahian spent $8,872 and gained 63,083 votes.

Two incidents involving campaign financing were brought to light in connection with the gubernatorial campaign. The first was the disclosure by the *Boston Globe* that Francis Sargent had borrowed $40,000 from his wife, which the Director of Campaign and Political Finance, Norman Gleason, called a violation of the law. He said that while the law permitted unlimited personal loans from the candidate to his own campaign, it prohibited any loans from individuals that total more than the $1,000 gift limit. Sargent disputed this ruling, but negotiated a bank loan to pay off his wife. The incident, while relatively minor, suggested the independence of the new office charged with oversight of campaign finances. No attorney general or secretary of state, when he had the authority and duty to oversee political spending, had ever before made such a call during a campaign.

The second incident was disclosed after the campaign had ended by a special investigative team of reporters on the *Boston Globe*. They reported that Judge Francis Larkin, whom Sargent had appointed to the district court in Milford and who had wanted the Governor to promote him to the Superior Court bench, had delivered to Sargent's gate house an envelope containing $1,000 in cash three days before the election. In a note, according to the story, the judge said the contribution could be listed in the name of a relative. Sargent said that he returned the money. The case was investigated by the Massachusetts Supreme Judicial Court and Judge Larkin was censured.

The 1974 Attorney General's Race

One of the most talked-about campaign-financing stories in Massachusetts was in connection with the 1966 race between

Elliot L. Richardson and Francis X. Bellotti for the office of attorney general. During Bellotti's second try for attorney general in 1974, the 1966 case was remembered once again.

In the closing days of the 1966 campaign, it was brought to the attention of Richardson that a signed affidavit regarding his opponent had been filed in the Division of Insurance of Columbus, Ohio. The document stated that Bellotti had been paid $6,000 in 1963 and $6,000 in 1964, while he was Lieutenant Governor, for "legal services which cover representation in connection with routine matters arising with the Massachusetts Insurance Department." If those affidavits were accurate, Bellotti would have been in clear violation of the state's conflict-of-interest law.

Richardson called a press conference, released copies of the affidavits, and charged Bellotti with "moral insensitivity" and a "possible violation of the conflict-of-interest law." In the midst of the charges and countercharges between the candidates, Edward Brooke, who was Attorney General at the time, tried to conduct a quick investigation. In part because of the unwillingness of the insurance company to cooperate, Brooke was unable to complete the investigation before the election, which Richardson won by some 90,000 votes. It is generally assumed that the whole affair cost both candidates votes.

After the election the Nationwide Insurance Group sent representatives to Boston to amend the affidavits, saying that they were in error, filed as a result of a clerical mistake, and that in fact Bellotti had been paid for services rendered to the company which did not include contact with the Insurance Division and therefore did not involve conflict of interest. Brooke, then preparing to go to Washington as a newly elected U.S. Senator, felt that the company's amended affidavit was not a satisfactory explanation and sought to examine the books and records of the company for that period. But he was not able to complete this investigation by January, and Richardson, the incoming Attorney General, was put into the position of having to finish an investigation arising out of charges which he himself had made during the political campaign.

Richardson appointed a panel of three lawyers to supervise the continued activity, thereby insulating himself from that work. In March, the lawyers made their final report, in which they reached four conclusions: first, that the public records indicated a violation of law; second, that the amendments made by the company to the original affidavits were "meaningless"; third, that a full investigation had been required; and fourth, that such an investigation was conducted and did not reveal any evidence that in fact Bellotti had performed services for the company during 1963 and 1964 which were in violation of the conflict-of-interest law.

Cleared of the 1966 charges, Bellotti managed to win in 1974. But he said of the previous race: "That campaign scarred me permanently and it is never going to go away." Bellotti ran a fairly traditional campaign in 1974, taking care not to violate the law, but not going out of his way with disclosure either. As in previous campaigns, he had fierce support among the Italian-American community in the state. He also got contributions from attorneys whose firms would have business with the state, including Edward J. McCormack and David Perini, an attorney and head of one of the biggest construction firms in the state ($1,000 each); Jerome Rappaport, a large real estate operator in Boston, and Joseph Mulhern of Boston, who once had the biggest tax-rebate practice in Boston ($500 each). Bellotti also received $800 from the Massachusetts Dentists Interested in Legislation; $500 from the Massachusetts Probation Association; $1,000 from Garrett H. Byrne's Committee (Byrne is the District Attorney of Suffolk County); and $500 from the Bridgewater Corrections Officers' Union of the Massachusetts Correction Institute.

Bellotti said that he returned $12,000 in campaign contributions. "They were not illegal but I didn't want to take them." The biggest problem, Bellotti found, was the checks that came in the mail late in the campaign and were difficult to register in the required 72 hours. It was also sometimes impossible to identify the late donors who might have business with the state. "The problem here," declared Bellotti, "is that you simply don't know the names of all these people." Bellotti now thinks that the only sure way to avoid this kind of problem is to pass some kind of public-financing bill.

In the Democratic primary, in which the liberal vote was split between two reform candidates, Bellotti defeated five other candidates with 274,439 of the 809,848 votes cast. In the general election, his opponent was Joseph A. Spaulding, an attorney with a prominent Boston law firm. Spaulding had succeeded in defeating two candidates to gain the Republican nomination: William I. Cowin, a member of the Sargent administration who had the support of both Sargent and Senator Brooke, and Charles C. Cabot, Jr., who in addition to the famous Cabot name had government executive experience in both Washington and Massachusetts.

Spaulding raised and spent about a third of Bellotti's totals—
$233,729 raised and $227,100 spent by the Republican versus
$477,865 raised and $501,064 spent by the Democrat. Spaulding's large contributors included such blue-blood names as
Augustus P. Loring of Prides Crossing ($500); Raymond Emer-
son of Concord ($500); Katherine A. Russell of Manchester
($500); Louis W. Cabot of Wenham ($500); and, Bruce Crane
of Dalton ($1,000). Spaulding listed only one organizational
gift of over $500, from the One Percent Fund of Washington,
for $1,000.

Spaulding went far beyond what Common Cause of Massachusetts had called for in the way of a net-worth statement, and
beyond Bellotti's disclosures. He made available to the public
copies of his income tax returns and a statement of the value
of his real estate and investment holdings, all of which was
audited by a certified public accountant. He also disclosed that
he had a major investment in the Massachusetts Rehabilitation
Hospital, which does business with the state.

Bellotti answered the Common Cause income-disclosure form
by listing but not detailing his sources of income of more than
$500. "Disclosure is like a game," said Bellotti. "As a candidate
I don't see much point in it. I don't believe in being coerced
into anything. In fact, I've already released more than I think
I should have." Bellotti did release a statement which showed
that he had made $134,000 the previous year in his law firm,
and he said there was another $5,943 in interest and stock divi-
dends which he described as "nothing stuff." He also listed his
law office building and home at $140,000.

But if Spaulding went farther than Bellotti in an audited disclosure of net worth, there was no political gain in it for the
Republican. To the contrary: In debates Bellotti would simply
challenge Spaulding with the conflict of interest that would
exist in Spaulding's hospital ownership if he was elected attorney general. Spaulding's answer that he would take care of this
matter after he was elected crippled his attempts to come out
ahead on disclosure.

The *Boston Globe's* October poll, which showed Spaulding
21 points behind Bellotti, dried up his campaign funds. When
a poll just before the election indicated that the race was "too
close to call," it was too late. As it turned out, Bellotti won by
less than 1 percent of the vote (912,244 to 894,754, with the
Socialist Workers Party candidate getting 29,749 votes.) Both
candidates criticized the *Globe* poll. Spaulding complained bit-

terly during the campaign that the poll, by showing him trailing Bellotti badly until the last week, cost him a great deal in campaign contributions because people did not think he had a chance. In the days before the election, Bellotti bitterly attacked the *Globe* poll on television, saying that the voters didn't look at the "too close to call" line in the story but rather read the chart that said. he had slipped from a 21-point lead in mid-October to two points behind the day before the election.

Bellotti admits that the media campaign he directed at the *Globe* in the final days of the campaign may have provided him with victory. The *Globe* had supported busing and had published a long investigative series on Senator Edward Kennedy's Chappaquiddick episode which made many Kennedy supporters angry with the paper. "There was some vulnerability there with the busing position and the Kennedy story," Bellotti said later. He also felt he had successfully drawn a parallel with his 1966 experience, when late reports about his alleged conflict of interest—which subsequently turned out to be false—destroyed his chances.

Secretary of State

In the race for secretary of state, the state's reform movement provided the organization and recognition usually secured by money to defeat the incumbent, Democrat John F. X. Davoren. The reformers assembled as Mass Caucus '74, a group made up largely of anti-Vietnam war groups that had come together once before for a political campaign to elect Father Robert Drinan to Congress. The caucus met in Framingham Town Hall for a one-day session on March 23, 1974, for the purpose of selecting a candidate to beat Davoren. The caucus endorsement was won by State Representative Paul Guzzi of Newton, after two other reformers, Boston City Councilman Lawrence S. DiCara and state Representative John A. Businger of Brookline, were defeated and withdrew from the race. Their withdrawal was critical to the caucus's success; in the primary race for attorney general, for which the caucus had also endorsed a candidate, the loser had remained in the race and split the reform vote.

Guzzi won the primary, 398,684 to 303,097 for Davoren. "I am convinced that I could not have won the primary race if the caucus had not limited the field," said Guzzi later. "The caucus made it a one-on-one situation for me, where in the attorney general fight none of the others dropped out when [Edward F.] Harrington won the caucus endorsement. That ultimately killed him."

Guzzi said that the caucus was a kind of substitute money. "I had to organize early to win that endorsement and I had to go around the state to do it. What I got out of that was sort of a skeleton organization which helped my later organization in the primary and the final election. I received damn little money as a result of the endorsement. They gave me $1,000 right after the endorsement and we used their mailing list to raise money. We knew who they [those associated with the caucus] were, and the rate of return from them was very, very poor. We didn't get much money." But he said that instead of having to spend a great deal of money establishing a recognition factor throughout the state, this was done by way of the caucus.

The biggest gain of the caucus, however, was the number of workers who came to him. "It was as good as campaign money. Instead of an expensive mailing, we leafletted by hand and the organization that did the work was produced by the caucus. . . . We also had people holding signs on the overpasses at turnpikes. It was better than billboard advertising because it did not clutter up the landscape, and when they got through, they took their signs with them."

Guzzi spent a total of $141,462, much of it in the primary, during which he also borrowed $25,000. After the election, Guzzi received money from some of the committees of former House members to bail him out of the debt. Davoren spent $25,590 in his unsuccessful attempt to stay in office and reported receiving only two campaign gifts of over $500, which is unusual for an incumbent state officer seeking re-election.

Guzzi's Republican opponent in the final election, John M. Quinlan of Norwood, reported spending $110,365, almost as much as Guzzi. But Republicans have a difficult time winning that far down on the state ticket, and Guzzi achieved an easy victory, with 1,155,636 votes to Quinlan's 636,203. Quinlan's effort with the initiative petition apparently did not help him much despite the fact that his reform won an overwhelming victory on the ballot.

Assessing Campaign Reform

The 1974 election was a clear change from the days of Curley or Steffens, but the campaign reform law was not an unqualified success. At the top of the ballot, the reporting of contributions and expenditures seems to have been rather complete. But there were clear gaps in the reports of legislative candidates as to whether the money went into the candidate's own pocket or was spent on other campaigns. Campaign reporting at the bottom of the ticket was about as good as the candidates wanted to make it; and the pure volume of work involved in checking so many campaign reports made it impossible for the law to have any real impact at this level. Two common ways to evade the law were the use of different family names to get around limitations on individual contributions, and transfers of funds from one committee to another.

The real test of the new law and of the commitment to reform will be in how effective the independent campaign finance director can be. In 1974, he achieved some impact by calling two abuses to the public's attention before the election. The public notice of these alleged violations had its effect on other candidates, and to that extent the law might be called a success.

New recommendations will come before the legislature before the election of 1976, and among these will be public financing of the campaigns of the state officers. But there is a good deal of mixed feeling toward public financing. The Governor, a reformer in most areas, has not been enthusiastic. Public financing gained the express support of important Massachusetts politicians once before, only to be abandoned when the time came to work for it.

SEVEN

KANSAS:
REFORM AND REACTION

Al Polczinski

If Kansas had lacked an incentive over the past half-century
to reform its campaign-financing laws, the motivation was supplied in January 1973 by two judges of the Shawnee County
District Court in Topeka. The judges declared key sections of
the existing election laws unconstitutional, leaving the state
without any reporting procedures and with no limitations on
the amount of money candidates could spend for nominations
or elections.

Laws in effect since 1893 had required that every candidate
committee or organization keep accounts of contributions and
expenditures, filing annual reports with the secretary of state
"showing in detail from whom said moneys or property or other
thing of value were received, to whom said moneys or property
or other thing of value were paid, for what specific purposes
each payment was made, and the exact nature of the service
rendered in consideration thereof." A review of these annual
reports, however, reveals no detailed information and no clarity.
In some reports, contributors were listed only by last name
and amount contributed; several listed large anonymous contributions, such as from "friends" in various counties. There
was no uniformity in the reporting system, no enforcement,
and the requirement most vital to the voter—that reports be
filed prior to the election—was lacking. Reporting of expendi-

tures was equally haphazard despite the clear instructions of the state laws.

Judge E. Newton Vickers found these reporting statutes vague and unconstitutional because they failed to address the situation in which a candidate did not contract for or incur any obligation; he dismissed charges pending against 14 candidates who had not filed reports within 30 days after the primary or had failed in some other way to comply with the state's reporting law, stating: "In this day and age, when citizens should be urged to participate in their government by seeking public office, to reward their efforts with criminal charges for violating statutes which are uncertain and vague as to conduct required is not, to say the least, in the best interest of our state."

Also struck down, by Judge Adrian Allen, was a 1915 law limiting campaign spending to 10 percent of the first year's salary of the office sought. (Candidates for state senator or representative or for an office with an annual salary less than $1,000 could spend no more than $500.) During the 60-year history of the statute, the spending limitation had been presumed to apply only to the candidate's own funds. The spending ceilings were declared unconstitutional primarily on the argument that they violated state and Federal guarantees of equal protection by creating classes of candidates with different spending limits and special penalty provisions within the same classification. Candidates running for similar offices across the state were limited to different spending ceilings simply because the salaries for those offices varied from county to county or city to city.

Not involved in either court case was a statute requiring all candidate and political-party committees to file annual reports of all contributions received and money expended.

The court rulings spurred the legislature to action in 1973. A special joint committee—created to examine the whole area of campaign financing, financial disclosure, lobbying activities and government ethics—worked throughout the summer and presented its proposed reform legislation in 1974. Even without the two rulings, however, the Watergate scandals might have created enough pressure on legislators to update the state's antiquated election laws.

This also happened to be a time when public awareness of corruption was raised by the revelation of reported kickbacks connected with state architectural contracts, specifically $500,-000 in contracts to expand facilities at the University of Kansas Medical Center in Kansas City. News of these scandals had broken during the course of a special legislative-committee study on state contracts in the summer of 1972. What this committee uncovered was enough to create another committee the next year to look even deeper, take sworn testimony, and have Kansas Bureau of Investigation agents do some of its investigative work. On December 3, 1973, a Shawnee County grand jury began probing the same matters.

The 1974 legislative session had just opened the following month when the grand jury handed down indictments charging a conspiracy among 19 individuals and 5 architectural firms involved in the Medical Center project. Behind it all were allegations that the contracts were awarded on the condition of a 6 percent ($30,000) kickback to Governor Robert Docking's 1972 election campaign. Among those implicated were the Governor's brother, George Richard Docking, a Kansas City attorney who always served as his brother's campaign treasurer, and Richard Malloy, appointments secretary for the Governor, who also handled patronage. Named as co-conspirators but not indicted because of their cooperative testimony were Robert Brandt, the Governor's director of administration, and Kenneth McClain, appointed state architect by Docking and a partner, prior to his appointment, in the Kansas City architectural firm that landed the major contract.*

The 1974 Laws

In the light of the indictments, Watergate, and the court rulings, leaders of the House and Senate agreed to give top

---

* Oddly enough, the indictments didn't charge that the money ever was deposited or found its way into Docking's campaign, although the prosecutors alleged that that was what the kickback was intended for. After a Shawnee County District Court threw out the indictments later in 1974, the judge's action was appealed to the Kansas Supreme Court, which upheld the indictments and sent the case back to the county courts.

The trial of the first architectural firm, in October 1975, ended in dismissal of the charges against three of the defendants and acquittal of three others and the firm itself. Malloy, who allegedly received the $30,-000 kickback, also was tried in October. The trial ended with a hung jury, and the judge later sustained a motion of acquittal. Charges against Docking were dismissed. Nobert Sidorowicz and his architectural firm (Marshall, Brown, & Sidorowicz of Kansas) were convicted of conspiracy to commit bribery in January 1976 but have filed a motion for mistrial; the ruling is due within a day or two of this writing. One other firm, Marshall & Brown of Kansas City, Mo., pleaded no contest and was fined the maximum $5,000. All other individuals and firms either were acquitted or had the charges dismissed.

priority to campaign financing and government ethics in the 1974 session, and two bills setting new standards on these issues were to be passed before the 60-day session ended. The laws that emerged established strict limits for contributions and expenditures, required a four-step reporting schedule, and established guidelines of ethical conduct for state officers and employees, lobbyists, and candidates for state office. An independent 11-member Governmental Ethics Commission was created to settle disputes and monitor compliance.

The new bills' provisions were:

• Contributions from individuals and committees or organizations to any one candidate for statewide office were limited to $2,500 each for the primary and the general election. For offices on the district level (district court judge, district attorney, state board of education), the limit was placed at $500. Names and addresses were required for donors of $10 or more, and anonymous donations could not total more than 50 percent of the amount an individual could contribute to the candidate's campaign.

• Limits on expenditures were graduated according to the level of the office sought. For the governor–lieutenant governor team, the spending limit was $300,000 per campaign and no more than $500,000 for the primary and general elections combined. For other statewide offices, the limits were $150,000 per election and $250,000 overall; for district offices, $6,000 each and $10,000 for both; for the state Senate, $5,000 each election, but no more than $8,000 for both; and for the state House, $3,000 each and a $5,000 total.

• Reports of both contributions and any expenditures of $25 or more had to be filed seven days before the primary and general elections, 30 days after the primary, and on December 3 every year. Because the report due 30 days after the primary produced an overlapping of data on the primary and general elections, it was decided to require two more reports for the 1974 elections (by demanding separate primary and general election reports on the last two dates) and to have the 1975 legislature revise the reporting schedule for subsequent elections. Thus there were actually six reports required in 1974. All financial reports of a committee or a candidate were to be handled by a treasurer whose name was to be filed by the candidate within 10 days after he filed for office.

• The new law governing ethical conduct of state officers and employees, lobbyists, and candidates for state office replaced previous conflict-of-interest and financial-disclosure laws and added provisions for reporting lobbying activity beginning January 1, 1975. Legislators, state officers and employees earning $15,000 (except college teachers and state employees under control of the State Board of Regents), and candidates for state and legislative offices were all required to file statements of "substantial interest"—defined as ownership of an interest exceeding $5,000 or 5 percent of a business, receipt of $1,000 income from any business, receipt of gifts or honoraria totaling $500, holding the position of officer or director of any business, regardless of the amount of compensation, or receipt of $1,000 in fees or commissions from a business or partnership, such as a law firm, in any one year. State employees were also prohibited from accepting any "economic opportunity, gift, loan, gratuity, special discount, favor, hospitality, or service" totaling more than $100 in any calendar year.

• Lobbyists—defined as persons appointed or employed to lobby, or anyone who spends at least $100 in a year's time to lobby state officials—were required to register, to list employers, purpose of employment, and method of determining pay, and to file monthly reports of expenditures and recipients if the expenditures totaled at least $50 to any one vendor during the month.

• The Governmental Ethics Commission had the power to issue rules and regulations under the new laws, to render "advisory opinions," to conduct investigations and hearings, and to refer violations to appropriate enforcement authorities. Membership on the commission was composed of two appointees of the chief justice of the Kansas Supreme Court, three of the governor, two each of the Senate president and House speaker, and one each of the Senate and House minority leaders.

The first commission, appointed in April 1974, was made up of seven Republicans and four Democrats and included an associate professor of law, a college dean of student affairs, a banker, four former legislators, a newspaper publisher, a former Congressman, and a practicing attorney. Named as chairman was John Henderson, President of Washburn University in Topeka, who frequently had been mentioned as a possible candidate for governor or for Congress. Appropriations of $30,778 for the final two months of fiscal year 1974 (the first two months of the commission's existence) and $104,845 for fiscal year 1975 permitted the commission to hire Lynn Hellebust, a former member of the Legislative Research Department, as its executive director, later adding a secretary and attorney, and finally an accountant to audit reports and to draft a manual of accounting procedures for candidates to use in the 1976 election campaigns. (A request for a budget increase for fiscal year 1976 to provide the commission with a second auditor-accountant and one more secretary was denied.)

When the campaign-finance and ethics laws were signed by Governor Docking, he called their passage a step in the right direction but noted that his recommendations in his last legislative message had gone considerably further. Among Docking's proposals was one to limit contributions to no more than $500 in any one campaign, but the legislature set the limit at $2,500, citing advantages to incumbents if campaign contributions and expenditures were limited too severely. Instead, emphasis was placed on disclosure—of financial interests, of conflicts of interest, of lobbyist interest in legislation and in state officials, and of candidates' finances.

While there was some talk of the laws as an "overreaction," most legislators probably agreed with House Majority Leader Donn Everett, who stated during the debate: "I think the point is that the public out there doubts us—all of us. The polls said 83 percent of the public wants something done. With or without this bill, it's going to be tough for any of us to raise money. We need a bill in some form. . . . I agree . . . we are reacting, but we've got to go ahead."

Tight Money: The Elections

It was indeed tough to raise money for state political campaigns in Kansas in 1974, yet 1974 was also the year the state witnessed its first million-dollar campaign for a single office. Incongruous statements, but that was the kind of year it was for campaign financing, in Kansas as elsewhere. And central to these apparent contradictions was the way money was distributed among candidates and during the course of the campaign. There was more money spent on state elections in 1974 than in several elections past, for two main reasons: the large number of hotly contested races and the state of the Kansas economy, which was good. But while generous amounts were spent on some races and during some periods, most candidates found 1974 a lean year.

No harder-fought contest could be found anywhere in the country than the U.S. Senate race, which pitted Senator Robert Dole, a first-term Republican incumbent, against U.S. Representative William R. Roy, a two-term Democrat from the state's northeast corner. Dole's re-election had been given a number-one priority by the Republican Party, in part because he had been Republican National Chairman at the time of the Watergate break-in and it was felt that his honor was at stake. Although Dole was exonerated by the Senate Watergate Committee of any involvement, re-election by home-state voters was the toughest test he had to pass. When the final bills were tallied, Dole's winning campaign had cost $1,073,423; Roy had spent $737,669. Never before had one race in the state cost more than $1 million, and this one's total ran closer to $2 million.

Kansas Attorney General Vern Miller, the lone Democratic contender for governor, raised and spent very near the $500,000 limit allowed by the state's new campaign-financing law.

But these candidates—Dole, Roy, and Miller—were the exceptions. The richness of the Dole-Roy race was itself a cause of other candidates' problems because it siphoned off much of the Republican money. For almost all other state candidates, campaign money came in slowly, at times downright agonizingly, and in smaller amounts, although from greater numbers of people than before. The average collection by candidates for the Kansas House, for example, was just $1,085 each.

One of the reasons for the difficulty had to be Watergate and its psychological effect on citizens who were asked to support the everyday business of politics. "If anyone would say Watergate didn't have any effect, he would be naïve," Don Concannon, a candidate for the Republican gubernatorial nomination, said. Robert F. Bennett, Senate President who won the GOP primary and the governor's office, said Watergate did have an effect "not because it scared anyone away particularly ... but what Watergate did do is give them an excuse for not giving. Anytime you're seeking contributions," he explained, "you must remember the guy on the other side is looking for any excuse he can find not to contribute. I think many people were able to say 'With Watergate and everything, I just don't want to get involved.' Probably 90 percent of the time, what he was really saying was 'I don't want to give, but fortunately Watergate came around and now I have an excuse for that.' " Fundraisers in other states would concur with Bennett.

The new campaign finance-disclosure requirement, like Watergate, was used by some persons, mainly large donors, as an excuse not to contribute. And the indictment of state architects, in addition to its nonquantifiable effect on public confidence in government and politics, resulted in fewer names of architects showing up on contribution lists.

But neither of these was probably as important a reason for sluggish campaign giving in Republican gubernatorial races as the track record posted by their gubernatorial candidates in four previous elections. For eight years prior to 1974, Democratic Governor Docking had dominated the Kansas political scene, shattering all victory records as he won four consecutive terms. Not even a Republican had ever won more than two in this traditional Republican stronghold—where, however, the expansion of urban areas has meant increasing Democratic strength. In that eight-year period, Docking turned back challenges from the best the Republicans could field against him, some of whom ended their losing races well in debt.

Docking decided not to run for public office in 1974,* and the Democrat who hoped to succeed him, the incumbent Attorney General, had a popularity rating even higher than Docking's. Vern Miller had a reputation for toughness; one example was his successful challenge of the airlines and Amtrak on their practice of serving mixed drinks over or in Kansas, despite the state law prohibiting the sale of liquor by the drink. Two years earlier, he had carried every county in the state. The prospect of Republicans regaining the governor's office, therefore, was anything but rosy. Added to this was the large debt left by the 1972 nominee for governor, which the Republican Party assumed after the election; including unpaid operational expenses of its own, the state committee was saddled with a $107,000 obligation, seriously crippling its campaign readiness in 1974.

The party's financial condition discouraged more or less willing contributors who thought they would be tapped twice during the campaign, once by the candidate and once by the state committee. And if the Republicans lost the governor's race again, would their nominee come around for help to pay his outstanding bills?

The Primary

The big Republican money went to Bob Dole's Senate campaign rather than to any of the gubernatorial aspirants. By the August 6 primary, only $217,823 had been contributed to the four G.O.P. contenders, as opposed to $230,307 collected by Democrat Miller for his uncontested primary race. The money was only to appear toward the end of the general election campaign, when victory was in sight.

* There was widespread speculation that Docking's decision was connected with the architectural-contracts scandal, in which his brother was indicted. The governor and his family have strongly and consistently denied such suggestions.

With the party organization traditionally neutral in primary contests, each of the gubernatorial candidates had to fend for himself when it came to underwriting the campaign. Bennett opened his campaign with several disadvantages to overcome. Before the 1974 legislative session began, he had announced he would not run for governor, but he changed his mind when Docking took himself out of the running. Bennett was the last of the four men to file for the opportunity to battle Miller for the chief executive's office. Despite his leadership role in the Senate, he was not well known across the state. And he wore a beard—something Kansans had not seen on a governor's face since Populist Governor John W. Leedy left office in 1901.

Initially, the beard was Bennett's most controversial quality. He was told people were saying: "Well, he can't win anyway and with that beard, there's not a prayer of winning. If he doesn't want to work harder at winning than that, and he wants to keep his beard, he can finance his own campaign." In the end, the controversy that raged over the beard and whether he should shave it off not only provided him statewide identity but earned him invaluable free publicity.

Bennett's leadership post was an advantage, however. The possibility that he might lose the election and return to it—with its power over committee assignments, procedure, and legislation—tended to encourage his colleagues to support his bid (as did the chance that he would become governor and have influence over the selection of new Senate leadership). And his position helped him to draw from the Senate majority for his campaign chairman, his finance director, and his advisory committee. Bennett also received some contributions from Senate Republicans: $2,165 in outright donations and $2,730 of in-kind contributions in the primary. In the general election campaign, the amount contributed by senators totaled $6,375, of which $3,225 represented in-kind contributions.

His fund-raising was a personal, loosely organized effort. At the outset of his campaign, Bennett, a former Mayor of the Kansas City suburb of Prairie Village and member of an influential law firm, personally contacted friends who had supported him in the past. "I just made individual calls and asked them to contribute. In the primary this little cadre of old friends and contributors probably formed the principal source of my funds. They came up with the seed money," he said. "We had no specific strategy for raising money . . . it was catch as catch can," he added.

Campaign reports show that Bennett received more than half of his large contributions from his home base in Johnson

County, much of it early in the campaign. Large donations ($500 or more) made up a little more than a quarter of his primary total of $96,816. Bennett's largest single contributor for both the primary and the general election campaigns was Clarence Coleman, vice chairman of the board of directors of the Union National Bank in Wichita, who donated $2,500 in the primary and $1,500 more in the general. Other large contributions, some exceeding $2,000, came from various business executives and lawyers around the state.

Bennett won the primary by 530 votes, largely through a three-to-one edge in his populous home county. Runner-up was Don Concannon, an attorney who had been Republican State Chairman four years earlier and knew the traditional sources of money for Republican candidates. But Concannon was a maverick in his own party and did not have the support of these veteran party contributors. Instead, he relied heavily on professional friends for the largest of his campaign contributions. Almost half his $61,602 total came in donations of $500 or more from individuals and from four law firms.

As party chairman, Concannon had had statewide exposure to Kansas voters, but he had a disadvantage in being from remote Hugoton, population 3,000, near the Colorado border. It has become a much-quoted rule of Kansas politics in recent years that no one west of U.S. Highway 81 (the western half of the state) stands a chance of being elected governor because the state's population is concentrated in the eastern half. Furthermore, Bennett's base, Johnson County, is a center of Republican Party power.

The third man in the primary race was a newcomer to elective politics, but as minister of the largest Methodist church in Wichita, the Reverend Forrest Robinson also had a base of support. Robinson's fund-raising problems were profound, but his campaign was a uniquely post-Watergate example of substituting ingenuity for money.

The fourth candidate, Robert W. Clack, a professor of nuclear engineering on leave from Kansas State University in Manhattan, had no large contributions but himself. Clack had thought his campaign might cost him $20,000 and was originally prepared to put up that much money for the nomination to avoid soliciting contributions, but the new law limited him to no more than $2,500. As an appeal to what he thought consistent with the reform mood of the people, he did not ask for more than a dollar from anyone and would not accept any gifts larger than $10, although he received a few. When one offer of $100 came from a banker, he called the donor and asked if

there were other members of his family for whom he could
speak. When the banker said he could include his wife and
three children of voting age, Clack accepted $10 from each of
the five family members and returned the remaining $50.

Clack had hoped to rally Kansas conservatives who had identified with Barry Goldwater in 1964. He failed dismally, getting
only 17,333 votes to Bennett's 67,347 in the primary, and spending just $3,001. As a super-long-shot candidate with no strong
party ties, Clack felt that he was neither hurt nor helped by his
self-imposed contribution limitations. They probably made
little or no difference at all, he said later. The only consolation
Clack could take from his vote total was that each vote had cost
him only 17 cents, compared to Bennett's $1.25, $1.20 for Robinson, and $1.18 for Concannon.

The General Election

While the Republicans were sparring, Democrat Vern Miller,
without competitors for his party's nomination, was collecting
money. The largest chunk of it came from labor organizations,
whose support ran to more than $60,000, or about 12 percent
of Miller's total contributions. (Bennett, whose large backers
were mainly business and banking executives and fellow lawyers, did not receive a single large contribution from any labor
group.) Twenty-one of the first 26 contributions of $500 or
more that came to Miller's campaign from committees or organizations were from union groups. Six of the labor contributions were in the amount of $5,000 each, four of which arrived
in the week preceding May 1, when the $2,500 limit of the new
campaign-finance law went into effect. The top labor contributor was the District 70 Machinists Nonpartisan Political League,
which served as a clearing house in Wichita for contributions
from 13 lodges of the International Association of Machinists
and Aerospace Workers. Its records indicate that $16,750 went
to Miller's campaign, including two $5,000 collections. The
Kansas State Federation of Labor A.F.L.-C.I.O. donated $11,000,
including one $5,000 contribution on April 30. Contributing
at least $5,000 each were the Communication Workers of Amer-
ica Committee on Political Education, Washington; United
Steelworkers of America, Pittsburgh; and International Brotherhood of Boilermakers, Kansas City.

Miller's most generous individual contributor was long-time
friend Sherman H. Sampson, Wichita real estate developer and
nightclub owner, who gave $3,000 in April (before the $2,500
limit became effective). The Democratic candidate received a

large number of sizable contributions from building contractors and executives of firms involved in some phase of highway construction, including five in the maximum amount. Overall, Miller received more than half of his contributions from donors of $500 or more; Bennett just over a quarter of his.

Another difference between the Bennett and Miller campaigns was that state party money played a far larger part in the Republican's campaign than in the Democrat's. The 1974 year-end report of the Democratic State Committee, under new leadership after Docking announced he was leaving office, revealed contributions of only $34,401 and expenditures of $49,-541 for state campaign operations. Miller got only $11,366 of these funds, and toward the end of the campaign it was the candidate who contributed money to the state committee. In contrast, the Republican State Committee report listed $339,-260 in contributions and expenditures totaling $347,609. A sizable chunk—$48,000—of these funds went to Bennett's governor's race, partially offsetting Miller's labor support.

A curious pattern of campaign financing was engaged in by six senior executives of the First National Bank of Topeka, who chose to aid more than one primary candidate for the same office and to contribute to both Democratic and Republican candidates for governor in the general election. Rather than contribute as individuals directly to the candidates, the six passed money through two committees—one called Americans for Free Enterprise and the other Citizens for Good Government. The chairman of both committees was Maurice Fager, Senior Vice President of the bank; the other five were R. C. Clevenger, the bank's Board Chairman; T. R. Clevenger, President of the bank; William E. Drenner, Executive Vice President; Robert Guthrie and Frederick G. Weidling, Senior Vice Presidents. The six banking executives contributed all the money the two committees doled out, with the exception of $500 given by Clarence Munns, Board Chairman of a medical supply firm in Topeka.

On May 31, Americans for Free Enterprise donated $250 to Vern Miller, who was unopposed in the Democratic gubernatorial primary. On June 18, Citizens for Good Government gave $250 each to Bennett and Robinson in the Republican primary. On July 29, a week before the primary, Citizens for Good Government sent $250 to Americans for Free Enterprise, which promptly gave that same amount to Don Concannon in the GOP race.

Little more than two weeks after the primary election, Citizens for Good Government gave Democrat Miller $750. A week later, it gave $850 to the Kansas Leadership League, a major fund-raising arm of the Republican State Committee which poured considerable money into Bennett's campaign. Americans for Free Enterprise sent Bennett $750 on August 27 and $500 more on October 8. One day earlier, October 7, Citizens for Good Government had sent Miller another $500. The two committees also sent contributions to Senator Dole, to an unsuccessful Republican candidate for Congress, to two Republican candidates for attorney general, to a local candidate for county treasurer, and to the Republican State Committee.

Another duplication of contributions to opposing candidates, but on a far smaller and more common scale, was the $1,000 given to both Miller and Bennett by Kansas Bank Political Action Committee, the political arm of the Kansas Bankers Association.

Some major individual donors also gave to more than one candidate in certain races. Two Wichita business executives led all Republicans by distributing more than $12,000 each among various Republican campaigns on the state level and additional thousands to Federal candidates. Both gave money to each of the three top candidates for governor in the primary. Robert L. Williams, President of Imperial Oil Company, gave $1,000 to each of the candidates and contributed another $1,300 to Bennett in the general election campaign. C. Howard Wilkins, former President of the Pizza Corporation of America, also gave $500 to the three, and he and his wife each gave the maximum $2,500 to Bennett after the primary.

The gubernatorial campaign, in which the Democrat was heavily favored at the start, saw a shift in the odds, and accordingly in the contributions, as it progressed. Bennett, one of the most effective speakers to grace the Kansas legislative halls in some years, combined this ability with his extensive legislative and governmental experience to convince voters he could and would handle the executive role better than his Democratic opponent. Using a travel van for his campaign transportation, he got this message across to enough Kansans to trip up the popular Democrat. Bennett also ran television ads effectively comparing his legislative and executive credentials to Miller's law enforcement background, which probably turned the tide.

Miller, the man who almost everyone thought would be the next governor, seemed to make some mistakes. He failed to attack Bennett's legislative record or to point out how his campaign speeches differed from his voting record. Miller also was unable to shed a "super-sheriff" image. Although he was admired as a law-enforcement officer, voters were reluctant to give him the reins of state government. His campaign was mismanaged both financially and strategically. For example, his people spent money for bumper stickers when he was the best known (according to voter surveys) of any candidate on the ticket. In addition, he failed to use some of the Docking campaign advisors, who were far more effective than any Miller had, and therefore failed to inherit the broad support Docking received. Finally, just before the election, one of his celebrated drug raids backfired, and some of his undercover agents were in trouble with the law, an incident that hardly helped him.

Miller had spent almost all his funds by the first part of October and was forced to go on a desperate search for more. Meanwhile, as Bennett's stock in various state polls climbed, so did the rate of contributions to his campaign. When it was all over, he still had money in the bank, another example of money gravitating toward the winners.

A "New Image" Candidate

Perhaps the most interesting of all the gubernatorial candidates was one who didn't make it to the general election. In the political setting of Watergate, state scandals, and the drive for new election laws, the Reverend Robinson stepped up to a lectern in a crowded meeting room at the Ramada Inn in downtown Wichita and into the glare of television lights proclaimed, "Today, our great American experiment in democracy stands in jeopardy as an acute moral crisis pervades our entire system. To a frightening degree, increasing numbers of citizens are expressing mistrust of government and disrespect for many who have been elected to govern. Democracy cannot prosper in such an alien environment. The challenge before us is clear and cannot be ignored if our system is to endure. That challenge is for each of us to devote ourselves to the task of building a new basis for trust in government, initiated through a new commitment to those historic principles upon which she has prospered." Thus, more than a year before the general election and nine months before the primary, Robinson was the first to announce his candidacy for governor of Kansas, on the Republican ticket.

The 51-year-old pastor of Wichita's largest Methodist church was little known outside the Wichita area and realized he had to step out early if he was to capitalize on the Watergate mood. He declared for the governorship without any major political figure in his corner, without any prior organizational effort, before he knew who his primary opponents would be, and long before Democratic Governor Docking took himself out of the race.

He was not a total newcomer to politics. He confessed to a lifelong interest in it and, as a minister, had encouraged members of his congregations in three south-central Kansas cities to become involved in politics. Moreover, Robinson's father had been a Republican ward leader in Kansas when Herbert Hoover ran for President in 1928. By the time Alfred M. Landon was running for governor and later President, Robinson was seen everywhere with his father distributing campaign literature. In 1971 he was a member of a small group of Wichita Republicans who regularly to bury their party's past failures to elect a governor and to talk about the future. His possible candidacy was discussed in 1972, but Morris Kay, Majority Leader in the House and a former University of Kansas football star, gained the group's approval. Robinson was named co-chairman of the Kay campaign, a position that proved to be more title than role as Kay's campaign consultant from Missouri called the shots.

When Robinson was given a seat on the Republican State Committee in 1972, the itch to become a candidate began to grow. The media were already speculating about a long list of potential gubernatorial candidates for 1974, most of them past or present legislators, but including a few businessmen, a doctor, and a lawyer or two. By June 1973, Robinson was writing letters and talking to Republicans in key areas to learn what support there might be for his candidacy. "They all agreed it would be a long shot at that time; that I would have a real tough time of it but that it just might be the right time," he recounted. Only a few close friends encouraged him, but the desire to run and the belief that he might just win swayed him.

After he had announced his candidacy, Robinson and his campaign manager, Glen Hanson, a young former newspaper reporter, worked up a cursory budget. They had been told that it would require at least $250,000 for a man in Robinson's position to win the primary. What they hadn't been told was what to do if they raised only a quarter of that figure. When it became clear that they could never raise $250,000, they set a goal of $147,000, of which $96,000 was to go for media advertising. Even this estimate proved optimistic. "We knew from the beginning money would be the tough problem," Robinson said. "Our gamble was that the unique but X-factor of the ministry, the freshness of our approach and innovative campaign style might entice people to gravitate toward such a candidacy and make up the differential in money that other candidates would have."

In the hope of attracting support in the post-Watergate climate, Robinson announced limitations on contributions— no more than $1,000 from any one person, no more than $20 in cash, no more than $5 anonymously, and no money at all from labor unions or corporations. Robinson had trouble sticking to his pledge to take no corporation donations but did manage to hold fast. Any checks he questioned as corporate were traced down by his office bookkeeper, and if indeed they did come from a corporation as such, they were returned with a carefully worded explanation of his policy. The occasional corporate checks that turned out to have been drawn on a special fund under the sole jurisdiction of the person who signed the check were accepted.

But the possible public-relations advantages of these self-imposed limits were largely offset by the fact that Robinson's campaign lacked any organized fund-raising effort. The candidate was on the road and had little time for fund-raising himself, but whenever the money supply became short, he was forced to take time out for it. His campaign manager had none of the talents of a finance director, and his running mate was a disappointment in this department as well. Without anyone to coordinate a statewide campaign for funds, Robinson depended on small groups of people to raise money for him. There were such groups in Topeka, Kansas City, Salina, McPherson, Garden City, Dodge City, Liberal, Parsons, Pittsburg, Winfield, and of course Wichita, whose major effort was making calls and writing letters to people who might be expected to donate. In the first month, Robinson raised only $2,092, half of this a $1,000 contribution from Mrs. Olive Ann Beech, Chairman of the Board of Directors of the Beech Aircraft Corporation and a prominent member of Robinson's church.

Without money to purchase time and space with the mass media, the Robinson campaign had to depend on innovation. The first step was acquisition of a motor home, which not only provided him with housing while he was on the road but also served as a traveling billboard; with its campaign messages painted across the sides and the rear, it gave the candidate exposure a car or an airplane could not provide. One of the plus factors of being a minister, especially a Methodist minister in a state where one out of every ten people is a Methodist, was the entrée this gave him into so many communities. People were curious, if nothing more, about this minister-turned-politician. Robinson's local appearances often raised some funds, but usually not much (in the $15–$75 range). A regular schedule of meetings kept Robinson on the road getting needed exposure, however, taking him into more Kansas communities than any other candidate visited during the primary campaign. Personable but ham enough to seek and get attention, Robinson was equally adept at one-on-one campaigning and on the dinner circuit.

An idea concocted primarily to attract attention and obtain identity for his candidacy was a cross-state bicycle trip. The 716-mile bike hike began at Liberal in southwestern Kansas, stretched east and northeast through the state's midsection to near Kansas City, and then turned south to the home area of Robinson's running mate, Fred Braun, Jr. of Parsons. Robinson and Braun, with members of their families joining them from time to time, pedaled in relay fashion the entire distance on 10-speed bicycles, a trip that took five days in July, when daytime temperatures ranged from 95 to 105 degrees. At key cities along the route, there were luncheon or dinner meetings or some type of function planned to give the candidates maximum exposure.

"We neutralized attacks on us by those who said we did it to grab headlines by candidly admitting that's exactly why we did it," Robinson said. A huge success from the standpoint of free publicity, the trip landed the candidates on the front pages of 91 Kansas newspapers, most of which carried pictures with the stories, and on numerous radio and television interviews. Robinson was told by state Senator Bennett, who eventually won the primary, that if the election had been held the week after the bicycle trip, there would have been no way he could have come close to Robinson at the polls.

It was not until after the bicycle trip and the exposure it afforded that people began to think Robinson had a chance at the nomination. "Suddenly there was money coming in from all around the state, but unfortunately the last $7,000 came too late to get television time. The time had been bought up," Robinson recalled. A direct result of the lateness of these funds was that Robinson ended the campaign with four taped television spots in his desk drawer which never ran. Instead, he used the last dollop of campaign money for radio advertising.

In the space of little more than nine months and with a shoe-string budget, Robinson had come from nowhere to a point where he was able to garner nearly one-third of the Republican primary votes. Looking back on the campaign, Robinson did not think his limitation on campaign gifts was of much benefit. "I think more people thought we were foolish than thought we were wise or virtuous," he said. "If I ever do this again—and look how much easier I can say that—I'll start out with a strong finance organization." It is possible that a good finance committee, appointed early, would have aided Robinson despite the limitation, but he had the disadvantage of not having the political base that either Bennett or Concannon possessed. Among the four Republican contenders—who together raised less than the lone Democratic candidate—Robinson, with his ministerial background and meager statewide exposure, had to be considered a long shot under any circumstances.

Judgment and Revision: The Governmental Ethics Commission

During their first campaigns under the state's new campaign-finance law, candidates encountered extra paperwork and complained more about detailed reporting requirements that they found confusing than they did about additional controls. From the beginning, the Governmental Ethics Commission was inundated with questions and requests for interpretations, as many as 60 from a single source. Meeting on the average of twice each month, the commission issued 69 opinions, many of which contained answers to several questions, by the end of the year; 32 more were issued by March 15, 1975. No formal complaints filed during the 1974 campaign reached the hearing stage. Those complaints involving a candidate's statements, tactics, or campaign reports were resolved by consultation with opposing candidates, with the commission recommending corrective action.

Most of the early questions posed to the commission resulted in decisions on relatively minor points: for example, that contributions solicited to pay off past election debts were allocable to the reporting period in which they were reported; that the cost of refreshments served at a gathering for a candidate was considered an in-kind contribution only if it was substantial (over $25 in voluntary services, for example) and directly related to the provision of voluntary services; and that donation of over-the-limit anonymous contributions to a bona fide charity was an acceptable disposition of these funds.

Some of the rulings covered apparently fine points that never-theless could prove important to certain candidates or annoy-ing to all. One of these was the decision that materials or ser-vices purchased before the primary but for use solely in the general election campaign were to be allocated to the period in which the purchase was made. This meant that Democrat Vern Miller, for example, who had no primary opposition, could load up expenses during this period for materials that would really be used in the general election campaign. Another was a ruling that a candidate who used his own car had to list this as an in-kind contribution, based on a cost of 13 cents per mile, which could affect the conduct of district campaigns as well as require new accounting.

In one significant ruling, the commission informed the state committee of the Transportation Political Education League, political arm of the United Transportation Union, that as a political committee it would be required to list the names and addresses of all members who contributed each month to the league, regardless of the size of the contribution. Rather than comply with these directions and list the many 25-cents-per-month donors, the league decided to stop contributing to state candidates. The individual listing was required only when the union organization qualified as a political committee (meaning that its "major purpose" was to influence elections), however; unions themselves could continue to contribute as an entity instead of individually—which they did.

The commission also dealt with the long-standing practice of newspaper ads being placed by individuals to show their endorsement of a candidate. This was forbidden unless the individuals solicited contributions for the ad and turned them over to the candidate's treasurer, subject to the condition that the money was used for such an ad, or if they were willing to be considered a political committee and filed the necessary reports. Recognizing the practice as a traditional one, however, the commission said that during the initial election year, in cases where a group did not violate the act intentionally, it would permit the candidate to report such contributions, re-lieving the group from filing a report.

A sticky situation cropped up when the commission requested an opinion from the state attorney general in attempting to answer an inquiry on the status of persons serving on advisory boards. The attorney general found that because the 1974 legislature had decided to give these unpaid appointive mem-bers the same daily pay of a legislator ($35) they technically became state employees, who, under the new law, could not receive any "economic opportunity" of more than $100 a year. Confused by this ruling, and believing that the law could be construed to classify the salary they received as an economic opportunity and in violation of the $100 limitation, a number of lobbyists serving on these boards and commissions resigned. The commission settled the matter early in 1975 by ruling that lobbyists could continue to serve on the advisory bodies and still receive their normal pay as a lobbyist without violating the conflict-of-interest provision of the law. It also determined that members of these advisory bodies could not lobby their own agency and be paid for doing that, but that they could lobby on behalf of the advisory board (before a legislative committee) without being forced to register as lobbyists.

The most serious challenge to the new law came from two legislators who asked the attorney general for an opinion on its constitutionality, specifically that of the requirement for disclosure of clients and customers from whom state officials and employees (including legislators) received fees or commissions totaling $1,000 in any year. The legislators were concerned about the time-honored confidentiality of doctor-patient and lawyer-client relationships. "Many such clients and customers of those subject to the act complain that they did not approve of being publicly listed as having made the payments that require the disclosure to be filed," they noted, asking if listing clients' names and addresses in the required statement of substantial interest would result in an unconstitutional invasion of their rights. The attorney general's opinion noted that California's legislature had avoided a similar problem by amending its law to require disclosure of the "business entity or type of activity" which produced the income reported—but not names and addresses of individual clients. While the attorney general found a lack of any legal basis for a conclusion that the required disclosure was unconstitutional as a categorical invasion of privacy, he also saw a need for the legislature to consider writing "more strictly defined terms, so as to avoid the compromise of traditionally confidential relationships."

Early in 1975 the Governmental Ethics Commission, using its investigative powers, began post-election audits. The commission's accountant turned his attention first to statewide races of highest public interest. Standard inquiry forms were prepared and sent to persons listed as contributors and to firms listed as recipients of campaign funds in payment of goods and

services by the various gubernatorial candidates. As a matter
of policy, the commission staff was to conduct field audits if:
(1) formal complaints had been filed against a particular candidate or committee, (2) to clarify errors or omissions discovered
by an in-office audit, and (3) on a random basis. Many errors
have been found, but none apparently of a serious nature; the
main effect has probably been to annoy some contributors and
campaign treasurers.

Changing the Law

Gubernatorial candidates who had had their first experience
with the campaign-finance law found it to be "counterproductive" or "unnecessary" or "much ado about nothing." The
winner, while saying that he did not consider the philosophy or
thrust of the law too restrictive, suggested that improvements
could be made in its mechanics.

Not long after his inauguration, Governor Bennett said he
was disturbed by some rulings of the Governmental Ethics
Commission, especially those relating to ethical conduct and
lobbyist control. "What we wanted to do was to develop a law
that had as a major thrust certain obvious prohibitory functions and limitations and, then, a law which required disclosure,
feeling that these two would be the best answers to the problems," he explained. "We [legislators] were never interested in
people who give coffees or for that matter, even people who
give cocktail parties. What we were really interested in was
the individual who, in effect, provides an office staff for maintenance of an entire campaign or someone who gives a large
item like an automobile or an airplane and things of that
nature." Bennett also said he disliked the fact that he could
give a gift to or pay for the meal of a lobbyist who was a
personal friend, but this lobbyist could not do the same without getting in trouble with the law and reporting each such
expense even if it were simply a personal gesture of friendship.

Most legislators seemed to agree with Bennett's criticism of
what he considered to be an attitude on the commission or
among the commission staff "almost to bend over backwards to
enforce the letter rather than the spirit of the law." But the
commission did have some supporters, such as Representative
Tom Slattery, a Topeka Republican, who said in an August
1975 review of its work: "There may be some problems with
the law, but I think they are overemphasized. You do have to

keep records. Generally, I'd be complimentary of the com-mission and the law." Chairman John Henderson defended the commission's work, saying he thought it had been fair in its judgments. The intent of the legislature always was considered, he said, adding that he did not believe the com-mission had the authority to take it upon itself to expand or to narrow the law on the books.

During the 1975 legislative session, the sentiments expressed ranged from those who wanted to abolish the commission alto-gether to those who were for strengthening it and tightening the language of the new laws. Changes in the campaign-finance and ethics laws were among the last pieces of legislation acted upon before the late April adjournment. Some of the modifications enacted undoubtedly weaken the laws; others hold promise of shoring up previously weak points.

One major change came after the Chief Justice of the Kansas Supreme Court, citing a new judicial code which directs judges to refrain from political activity, indicated a desire to shed his authority to appoint the chairman and one other member of the Ethics Commission. The legislature provided that these 2 appointments be assigned to the governor, giving him the right to select 5 of the 11 members, although only 3 can be of the same political party.

A companion bill abolished the existing commission and created a new 11-member commission effective July 1. While several of the original members were appointed to the new commission, the thrust of the measure was to telegraph a mes-sage to the commission that legislators were displeased with a number of its more restrictive opinions. This move, together with the shift of greater appointive authority to the governor, was interpreted by some observers on the scene as a direct slap at Henderson, the commission Chairman. Before the bill won final passage, Henderson resigned, giving no reasons for his action. But there were reports that he felt his continued chair-manship might work a hardship on the university under his charge, to which he felt a strong responsibility.

Opposition to the complex system of reporting campaign contributions and expenditures nearly led to elimination of a vital part of that system—the report due 30 days after the pri-mary election. When the smoke of the session's final hours cleared, however, the report had been reinstated. But instead of being required 30 days after the primary, it will be required 10 days after and will constitute the final report of primary election costs and contributions. Subsequent reports due seven days before the general election and on December 3 will contain data relevant only to the general election campaign.

For coming election campaigns, the Ethics Commision was given authority to notify a candidate when he has missed a reporting deadline and to put this notice in the public record where it will be available to news media. The candidate will have five days in which to comply with the notice. In cases of gross errors found in reports, the commission will give notice to the candidate or committee, and a 30-day compliance period will begin with receipt of the notice, which is also entered on the public record. The commission hopes this public-notice procedure will be enough of a lever over the negligent party to effect compliance, since to ignore the notice will show clearly the intent of the candidate or committee to defy the law.

The commission had recommended fines for candidates who fail to file reports or violate spending limits of the law, but several legislators said they were not ready to set penalties for mistakes or late filings on the ground that they had not lived with the complex law long enough to make it work. Penalties were rejected by the 1976 session also.

The first annual report, issued by the commission in December 1975, announced that it had launched a public information program, had delivered 163 advisory opinions (as of October 31), and had reviewed 147 of the 772 political candidates and committees. (Of the candidates reviewed, 68 had failed to file the required reports or had made significant errors requiring follow up by the commission.) The report requested 2.5 additional auditors and one more full-time secretary to enable the commission to check more candidates' reports more thoroughly. It also made numerous substantive recommendations.

The 1976 legislature not only ignored the recommendations of the report but attempted to kill the commission. Efforts to reduce the budget from the Governor's recommended $133,245 to $53,637 were voted down in the House (67–55), as was an attempt to transfer the commission's duties to the secretary of state (72–36). An attempt in the Senate to cut the commission's budget to $51,937 was also unsuccessful. The present bill contains the Governor's recommended budget, which allows for only one additional clerk.

Among the changes that weakened the laws was one to establish a spending or contribution threshold of $500. If a candidate anticipated receiving or spending not more than $500 in either the primary or the general election campaign, would not have to file the required reports. It had been proposed that the threshold be set at $1,000, but under pressure from the Ethics Commission, the news media, and Common Cause, the legislature cut the figure in half.

One revision in the ethics law will allow a legislator or state officer to receive gifts valued at $10 or less from a lobbyist without having to be listed on the lobbyist's expenditure report. Another will permit lobbyists to list expenditures by category (such as food and beverage or transportation and lodging) rather than by the specific vendor (the name of the nightclub or restaurant, for example), a change intended to prevent embarrassment to legislators who may be concerned about constituents reading detailed lobbyist reports.

In response to the attorney general's recommendation that the legislature protect confidential relationships, business or professional associates of state officers, including legislators, were for all practical purposes eliminated from the provisions of the ethics law; the officials themselves remained subject to the law. For example, if a lawyer-legislator is asked by a client to represent him before some state agency, the lawyer must file a report of this representation. But if the client seeks out another member of the legislator's law firm (an "associate") to represent him, a report is not required. Also now excluded from the provisions of the ethics law are all members of state advisory boards who do not receive per diem pay and are reimbursed only for expenses incurred in the course of their service.

Other actions taken by the legislature included the following: Recommendations to extend provisions of the campaign-finance law to local levels of government were rejected, in large part because of the outcry by representatives from small communities, whose campaigns often are financed by trifling dollar contributions and who argued that the reporting procedure would be more bothersome than enlightening. The 1949 prohibition against wholesale or retail liquor dealers and their employees making contributions to political campaigns was repealed. And responding to an Ethics Commission opinion barring legislators or state officers from soliciting free tickets to university ballgames and other events and from accepting freely offered tickets if the value amounted to more than $100 in one year, the legislature decided specifically to allow state officials to accept up to $100 in free tickets to such events (although they could not solicit them).

public financing lay dormant in the 1975 legis-
A bill for partial public funding, sponsored by
both parties, had won approval in the House in
killed in the Senate. Governor Docking, in his
message to the legislature, had suggested a state-
ndum on public financing, but this, too, was re-
public-financing bill would have provided a tax
system on state income tax returns, with individuals
g which political party should receive their dollars.
$184,000 would go to the governor–lieutenant gover-
ns, with any remaining balance to be divided among
ve candidates. The bill died in the Senate because the
esponsible for its fate, Elections Committee Chairman
Booth (R., Lawrence), termed the Democratic-inspired
sal completely abhorent to him. He argued that candidates
cannot raise their own funds should not be candidates in
first place. Public financing of state elections was studied
an interim committee chaired by Booth during the summer
d fall of 1974, but the committee, not surprisingly decided
gainst recommending any public-funding proposal to the
.975–76 sessions.

Polls taken in Kansas during the past few years have indicated a lack of majority support for public financing of
Federal elections, and the same feeling most likely prevails
for tax support of state elections. Most Kansans seem to want
to watch the Federal process work in 1976 before considering
it again on the state level.

Kansans generally approved the bold steps taken in 1974.
The spirit of adventure waned in 1975, however, setting the
stage for a battle to keep what progress had been made. Only
time will tell whether Forrest Robinson was correct in the
observation, made during his gubernatorial campaign, that "In
the final analysis, the safeguard to honesty is not the campaign-
nance law or the conflict-of-interest law. The only safeguard
the character and integrity of the people who run for office
d are elected."

EIGHT

GEORGIA: THE POLITICS OF CAMPAIGN REFORM

Howell Raines

The Georgia Campaign Financing Disclosure Act of 1974 was born in late 1973 as a promotional gimmick for the gubernatorial candidacy of Democratic state Representative George Busbee of Albany. "Five or six of us were sitting around one night thinking about how we could get some publicity," recalled Busbee's campaign press secretary, Mike Dowling. "Watergate was bubbling along pretty good, and somebody said, 'Why don't we do something on ethics?' "

A few days later, at a press conference, Busbee unveiled a limited-disclosure bill whose basic provisions had been created by his campaign staff without reference to any model statute, such as those being circulated in Georgia by Common Cause or available from the Citizens' Research Foundation (or the Federal campaign law itself, which could have provided a sound working model for the mechanics of the reporting and monitoring processes). The Busbee bill applied only to candidates for governor and lieutenant governor, requiring them to file reports with the secretary of state, for public inspection, of all contributions and expenditures over $100. The bill also required that each candidate for these offices file a statement of personal financial assets and liabilities. Such statements would have to be filed annually by the incumbent governor and lieutenant governor. Although Busbee vowed to introduce and push the bill in the 1974 session of the General Assembly, which was to open on January 14, his staff had little expectation that it would become law.

Busbee's was by far the most modest of several ethics bills being proposed in the Senate. But by the time the session ground down to its final days in late February, Lieutenant Governor Lester Maddox, himself a gubernatorial candidate, had used his powers as presiding officer of the Senate to crush every substantive measure on the subject that had been introduced. The chief casualty was a well-researched bill sponsored by outgoing Governor Jimmy Carter which called for broad disclosure of personal and campaign finances and set up a strong ethics commission to police the filing process. Also buried in a Maddox-dominated committee was a spending-limitation bill introduced by state Senator Bobby Rowan, yet another gubernatorial aspirant. The Rowan bill would have put a $250,000 ceiling on gubernatorial campaign expenditures and a $250 limit on individual contributions. In lieu of these measures, the Maddox forces in the Senate drafted and passed a loophole-riddled bill which Carter promptly labeled a "farce." Its most glaring flaw was the failure to prevent the formation of independent "campaign committees," technically outside the candidate's control, which could supply money to the candidate without making any disclosure of the committee's receipts and expenditures. The bill required disclosure of the identities of only those contributors who gave $500 or more to the single committee controlled by the candidate.

Busbee, a skilled legislative mechanic, saw in the apparent Maddox victory a final chance to revive his bill, which had been stalled in the Senate along with the Carter and Rowan bills. He unearthed a little-used procedural rule that applies when the House substitutes a bill of its own devising for a measure already passed by the Senate; at that point, according to this obscure rule, the so-called House substitute must go directly back to the Senate floor for debate rather than being assigned to committee. This was the beauty of the rule for Busbee's purposes. As presiding officer of the Senate, Maddox had assigned all ethics bills to a committee dominated by two key supporters, Senators Gene Holley of Augusta and Culver Kidd of Milledgeville, who had shelved all the strong bills in committee and drafted the weak measure passed by the Senate with Maddox's blessing.

Busbee's theory was that if he could get his bill to the Senate floor, the Maddox forces would be reluctant to butcher it in an open fight. Using his influence as majority leader, Busbee had little trouble getting the House to pass his bill, in a slightly altered form, as the "House substitute" for the Senate disclosure bill. Rowan and Carter, their options exhausted, had meanwhile agreed to exert their influence in the Senate in behalf of the Busbee bill. Thus, on the last day of the session, the Busbee bill was transmitted back to the Senate. It had been broadened to include legislative candidates as well as candidates for governor and lieutenant governor but stripped of the provision calling for statements of financial assets.

The Maddox forces were painted into a corner. After the meaningless bill devised by his cronies had passed the Senate, Maddox had cunningly reversed his long-standing opposition to disclosure legislation. "Look, you can't get an ethical standards bill too tough for Lester Maddox," he had crowed, confident that the weak Senate bill would be adopted by the House. Maddox, of course, had not anticipated that the Senate would have to face the issue again. Thus, when the Busbee bill bounced back as the House substitute, Maddox could not afford to fight it openly, nor could he allow his allies to do so. Senator Holley, Maddox's chief campaign advisor and floor technician, resorted to the strategy of adding amendments that he hoped the House would find distasteful because they were so sweeping. One such amendment set up a five-member state ethics commission, with broad and ill-defined powers. Another senator allied with Maddox added a provision extending the bill's coverage to city and county officials, on the theory that House members would not want to regulate hometime politicians. But the Senate amendments zipped through the House by 102-to-0 just before the final gavel fell, and Georgia had its first campaign-financing disclosure legislation.

That any reform legislation passed at all is a tribute to the impact of Watergate on a clubby, conservative legislature which acted only because it felt, as one member admitted, that "the public demands it." Because the new law had been shaped by the struggle for advantage in the political campaigns to come, however, it was far from flawless.

The Law and Court Tests

"There are no major defects in this bill," Governor Carter said during the signing ceremony on March 5, 1974. "As far as the campaign this year, it will be as far-reaching a disclosure bill as exists anywhere in the nation." That estimate was far too optimistic, as forthcoming court tests and the experience of the campaign would demonstrate. Nonetheless, the law's basic provisions would stand and make the 1974 campaigns the most open ever held in Georgia.

The law required reporting of all contributions which in aggregate totaled $101 or more from "an individual, partnership, committee, association, corporation, labor organization, or any other organization or group of persons." A contribution was defined as "a gift, subscription, loan, forgiveness of debt, advance, or deposit of money or anything of value conveyed or transferred" to the candidate or his committee. The same $101 reporting requirement applied to expenditures. Contributions were to be accepted and disbursements made only by the candidate or a single campaign committee, with both required to file reports. Anonymous contributions were to be surrendered to the state treasury. The reports were to be filed on the 45th and 15th days preceding the primary, 10 days after the primary, 15 days before the general election, and a final report no later than December 31 of the year of the election. The first report was to reflect all receipts and expenditures for the year preceding the filing date. Penalties of $5,000 and up to one year of imprisonment were mandated for violations.

Comparison of the law to model statutes or Federal law revealed alarming gaps in its coverage. It failed to provide any mechanism for prompt reporting of large contributions received after the last pre-election filing (the Carter bill had done this). It did not require that cumulative contribution totals be shown for repeat contributors, nor did it require contributors to list any information other than a mailing address. Because contributors were not required to list occupations and principal places of business, only the most knowledgeable reader could determine the special-interest implications of a given contribution. It did not restrict contributions from persons or firms doing business with the state or in fields of endeavor regulated by state agencies. Political funding groups such as those maintained by corporations and unions were not required to make any reports whatsoever.

These and even more glaring flaws (which will be dealt with later) invited the political and legal attacks that were quick in coming. And the first political attack came from Maddox. In a campaign speech, Maddox noted that the legislature had adjourned without appointing the members of the State Ethics Commission created by the new law and posed the question as to whether the law could apply to the 1974 races in the absence of the commission. Governor Carter, not to be outdone by his archenemy at this late date, was on the verge of calling a one-day special session of the legislature to correct the defect when the attorney general ruled that the law would apply even in the absence of the commission. The flap came to naught, but it served notice that the law might have serious flaws as a result of its slapdash authorship and tortured passage through the legislature.

One person harboring such worries was Attorney General Arthur Bolton, who questioned the new law's standing under the Georgia Constitution, which states that "No bill shall pass which contains matter different from what is expressed in the title thereof." The law's title and preamble had never been adjusted to cover the amendments added in the Senate. For instance, the law's preamble stated that it would apply to state offices, but the Senate amendments had broadened its coverage to city and county officials. Moreover, the preamble did not serve notice that an Ethics Commission would be created in the body of the law. By late March, Bolton was saying that the Senate would "welcome some litigation" to clear up these doubtful points. Privately, he was known to consider the bill a nightmare of constitutional problems.

Bolton's wish for a court test was granted in early April by Leonard W. Weeks, an obscure candidate for the state House from LaGrange. The fact that Weeks was represented by a prestigious Atlanta law firm with ties to conservative political factions raised suspicion in some quarters that he might be acting in behalf of a more prominent figure, such as Maddox, but no such connection to any major candidate was ever proven! His suit argued against the law on the grounds both that it violated the state constitution and that it "chilled" First Amendment rights under the U.S. Constitution. A superior court judge concurred that the law was unconstitutional and enjoined the secretary of state from administering it. The Attorney General's office moved immediately to contest the lower court ruling in the state Supreme Court.

An interesting gauge of the degree to which the new law had caught on with the public—and more particularly with the state's political press—can be found in the reactions of the Democratic gubernatorial candidates. With the sole exception of former Lieutenant Governor George T. Smith, the major Democratic candidates vowed to obey the law regardless of the outcome of the court test. Smith denounced the measure as "a millionaire's law" because of its lack of spending limitations and said that, should the lower court be upheld, he would report only those contributors who did not object to voluntary disclosure. Two other candidates, Carter ally Bert Lance and former U.S. Senator David Gambrell, saw in the legal hassle a chance to make points against those legislator-candidates who had helped to pass the bill. Lance said he would disclose his campaign finances anyway and called on other candidates to do the same, "especially those who were responsible for passing this unconstitutional piece of legislation." Gambrell expressed disappointment that "several candidates who are claiming responsibility for getting the law passed are apparently not able enough in that capacity [as legislators] to have gotten a law passed which was clean and constitutional in the first place. I support the intent of the law and intend to comply with it whether it's upheld or not." Busbee, who had been campaigning vigorously on what he had come to call "my disclosure law," sought to duck these broadsides by claiming that the amendments added by Maddox's Senate allies had been intentionally designed to raise constitutional problems.

As the campaign ground along toward the first filing date of June 29, the situation was chaotic. Bolton petitioned the court for an expeditious ruling, which he said was essential to "maintain an orderly election process." The court heard arguments in late May and ruled on June 29, upholding Weeks's arguments concerning the conflict between the preamble and body of the bill. The court exempted city and county officials from reporting and struck down the State Ethics Commission provision, noting also that the law's vague language gave the commission impermissibly broad powers. But the majority opinion in the five-to-two ruling held that these defects did "not require a declaration that the entire act is unconstitutional. Its principal scheme is still intact."

Of particular interest in view of the national legal debate on campaign disclosure legislation was the court's ruling on arguments related to the U.S. Constitution. Weeks's attorneys had argued that "The recording and reporting requirements are intended to and will chill First Amendment rights without any legitimate purpose." The plaintiff called for the protection of what it argued was the right of confidential political associations, without which, it said, "present and potential members of an association would not exercise their right to associate for fear that public awareness of their membership will lead to reprisal or retaliation."

Assistant Attorney General H. Andrew Owen, who argued the case for the state, sought to show that there was ample precedent to establish disclosure legislation as constitutionally defensible. Owen relied heavily on the 1935 Burroughs-Cannon case, in which the U.S. Supreme Court had upheld the constitutionality of the Federal Corrupt Practices Act, finding that Congress's "conclusion that public disclosure of political contributions together with the names of contributors and other details would tend to prevent the corrupt use of money to affect elections cannot be denied."

In its majority opinion, the Georgia court concentrated specifically on the act's definition of a "contributor," in view of the plaintiff's argument that the act would infringe on an individual's or group's presumed right to contribute endorsements or advertising without the candidate's solicitation or, in some cases, without his knowledge. "The definition of 'contribution' presents no problem so long as outright contributions of money are involved," the court said. "Where the definition becomes difficult is in the area of publicity for a candidate—an area in which the bulk of the candidate's campaign expenditures will probably be made, but also an area in which the citizen is entitled to exercise freely his First Amendment rights in support of his chosen candidate. The exercise of such rights might take the form of payment for a newspaper advertisement benefitting a candidate, as well as volunteer propagandizing among one's friends, or putting up campaign posters. Our question is whether such activities are 'contributions.'" The court ruled it "constitutionally impermissible" to impede an individual's rights to engage in any sort of propagandizing or advertising activity in behalf of a candidate. However, the fruits of that activity, "whether they are called mere endorsements of a candidate or whether they are outright media publicity for him" become contributions. These contributions had to be reported. "An inquiry to the advertising medium used should enable the candidate or his committee to learn the identity of the sponsor and therefore report it as required," the court explained.

Thus did the Georgia court arrive at the core question of "whether a person has a constitutional right to remain anonymous in his support of a political candidate." Here they cited the 1953 U.S. Supreme Court case of the *United States* vs. *Harris*, a challenge of the Federal Regulation of Lobbyists Act, in which the court, relying heavily on the Burroughs-Cannon case, justified the limited intrusion on anonymity presented by the registration of lobbyists, saying "otherwise the voice of the people may all too easily be drowned out by special interest groups." The Georgia Supreme Court opinion held that although "anonymity in this regard is a constitutional

right, it is not absolute. . . . Any right to anonymity in this
regard must yield to the public's right to know who is 'behind
the scene.' "

Later in the summer, J. B. Stoner, avowed white racist running as a Democratic candidate for lieutenant governor, challenged in Federal court the act as amended by the Georgia
Supreme Court. Again Owens relied heavily on the Burroughs-
Cannon case in arguments before a three-judge panel in Atlanta,
which on August 2 ruled in support of the state law. A side
effect of this decision was to cut off tentative plans by Weeks's
attorneys to take their earlier reversal to the Federal courts. In
terms of the Georgia political campaigns, the Federal ruling
was anticlimactic, for the first two disclosures under the law had
already been filed.

The Democratic Gubernatorial Race

In Georgia, as in most Deep South states, the Democratic
gubernatorial primary is the major quadrennial political event,
a contest traditionally marked by heavy spending over a short
time span and by high per-vote costs. That pre-eminence was
intensified in Georgia in 1974 because the U.S. Senate race
brought forth no serious opposition to Herman Talmadge. Although the citizenry may have been amazed by the magnitude of
spending in the gubernatorial primary—$4.3 million by the
seven major candidates—analysis of the reports shows that
Georgia suffers from, if anything, too narrow a base of available
political money. Candidates are forced to draw on three major
sources: massive credit advances from banks; personal wealth
or that of close friends; and contributions from special-interest
sources or from a fairly limited group of perennial political
contributors. The competition for this limited supply of money
is intense, putting the donors in a strong position to extract
commitments from the candidates.

The impact of the new law—imperfect instrument that it
was—on the 1974 gubernatorial campaign cannot be over-
estimated. From the filing of the first reports on June 29 until
the August 13 primary, campaign finance became the major
issue among the 7 candidates who were generally conceded to be
the "serious" contenders out of a field of 12. The information
contained in the June 29 report and in the second, on July 29,
after being ground through the twin mills of candidate oratory
and prominent—if shallow—press coverage, had speedy and
dramatic effects on the candidates' fortunes. Former Lieutenant
Governor Smith, a strong contender in early polls, plummeted

when his reliance on land developers' money was publicized
Lester Maddox suffered a telling blow to his image as champion
of "the little people" when his first report showed that 60
percent of his contributions came in sums of $1,000 or more.
Bert Lance, who had spent months establishing himself as a
simple "country banker," began a long slide toward defeat
when his first disclosure showed a personal campaign contribution of more than $255,000. But most damaging to Maddox and
Lance, who were running first and second in the polls when the
first disclosure report was filed, was the revelation that they
were both heavily dependent on bank loans gained through
privileged credit treatment based on political and business ties.

Busbee's ultimate victory would owe much to the fact that
he developed into the most artful dodger of the campaign law
he had guided through the General Assembly. He escaped political damage on the loan issue by disguising the source of his
borrowed bank money; the system he used to do this was uncovered in the research for this chapter and is reported here for
the first time.

The Pivotal Role of Banks

It has long been common "insider" knowledge that Georgia
banks, particularly those in Atlanta and Augusta, play a major
role in campaign finance. In many respects, this tradition of
bank activism is the legacy of one man: former Citizens and
Southern (C&S) President Mills B. Lane, Jr. Lane openly used
the bank's influence and financial power in behalf of Ivan
Allen, Jr., the Atlanta Mayor credited with establishing that
city's reputation for good race relations in the turbulent 1960's.
Sources from within the bank and from former Governor Carl
Sanders' political organization confirm that credit from C&S
also played a role in financing Sanders' successful 1962 gubernatorial campaign. The tradition continued in the 1970's, with
C&S loaning money to the law firm of Atlanta's first Black
Mayor, Maynard Jackson, and other major banks from Atlanta
and around the state following the C&S example of political
involvement. Atlanta First National lobbyist John Stevens was
widely credited with torpedoing consumer-protection legislation
in the 1973 General Assembly session, and in that same year
Trust Company of Georgia, the "blue ribbon" bank identified
with Coca-Cola and other major Atlanta companies, directed a
large number of executive contributions into the Jackson
campaign. The banks' support has not been directed solely
to moderate and progressive politicians who seemed committed
to maintaining stable race relations as a base for business pros-

perity, however. Segregationist Governor Lester Maddox also
has enjoyed cordial and beneficial credit relations with major
Atlanta banks.

In terms of campaign finance, the granting of personal loans
to supporters has apparently been the standard mechanism for
injecting bank money into political campaigns. For instance,
former Governor Jimmy Carter has said that seed money for
his 1970 campaign came from supporters who raised about
$250,000 in personal notes. At times, bank support has taken
even more direct form. Atlanta's National Bank of Georgia
announced in early 1975 that it was under investigation for
possible illegal contributions of over $65,000 during a seven-
year period, although this money apparently did not figure in
the 1974 campaigns.

What cannot be known is the degree to which banks may
have relaxed credit standards or lessened normal pressures
for prompt repayment. There can be no doubt, however—and
this is confirmed by both bankers and politicians—that Georgia
banks repeatedly, indeed habitually, have made loans to politicians and their supporters with the knowledge that the money
would be used for campaign purposes. What have the banks
gotten in return for granting credit to politicians? Until a few
years ago, favored banks could get millions in interest-free
deposits of state money at the whim of the governor. Governor
Carter ended this notorious boondoggle shortly after his inauguration, but other more subtle incentives to the banks'
political activism remain. For instance, one would be hard
pressed to find any student of the Georgia legislature who
doubts that the almost total absence of effective consumer-credit
legislation in Georgia is related to the banks' willingness to lend
money to politicians for personal and campaign purposes. For
years, Georgia governors and banking officials winked at the
existing usury laws, while through a variety of "credit charges"
and other dodges, banks have jacked up interest rates far above
the legal limit of 8 percent. Finally, in 1975, banking lobbyists
were busily and successfully at work ramming through the
General Assembly a new banking code which in effect allows
banks to charge whatever rate of interest they like on consumer
loans. All this must be understood in the context of a state
government where casual conflict of interest violates no state
statute and is a political way of life. For instance, Jack Dunn,
Georgia's full-time Banking Commissioner, is in the real estate
investment business on the side, and the investments of firms in
which Dunn has an interest are financed by multi-million dollar
loans from C&S, one of the banks Dunn is supposed to regulate.

The 1974 disclosure law provided the first vehicle—the candidates' reports of donations and expenditures—by which bank participation could be documented by means other than the sketchy admissions of the banks and candidates involved. Those reports revealed that the role of banks is pivotal and dominant. It should be noted that possible legal obstacles to this participation were removed by a fortuitous change in the Federal banking law in 1972, which in essence provided that loans to candidates were legitimate if they were subject to the same credit regulations and procedures as other loans. A spokesman for the Atlanta office of the U.S. Comptroller of the Currency—the regulator of nationally chartered banks—acknowledged that even before the law was changed there was little likelihood of banks getting in trouble with politically motivated loans unless the transactions involved abuses so flagrant as to show up in routine audits of bank records.

The primary motivation for the involvement of banks in the 1974 campaign was an important piece of state banking legislation. In the 1973 and 1974 sessions of the General Assembly, the state's major banks had lobbied intensively for the bank holding company bill, which would have allowed the formation of statewide bank holding companies. A 1956 law had curtailed the expansion of the statewide banking system being developed by C&S and other large banks, limiting them to the acquisition of only 5 percent interest in banks outside their home counties. Busbee had sponsored the bank expansion bill while serving simultaneously as House Majority Leader and as a director of the C&S-Albany, one of 14 affiliate banks established by C&S before the 1956 law prohibited further expansion. Interest in passage of the bank-expansion bill was a clear incentive to C&S, First National of Atlanta, Trust Company of Georgia, as well as major banks in Columbus, Savannah, and Augusta, to become involved in several gubernatorial campaigns so that victory by any one of their candidates would bode well for the expansion-minded banks. C&S's interest in the bill was especially intense during the campaign period because it was then under court order to divest itself of its holdings in 25 "5 percenter" banks—holdings that C&S would be allowed to keep if the bill passed. (As it happened, a higher court later reversed the order, but this happened after the end of the campaign.)

Into this mix one final factor needs to be added: Hamilton Bancshares of Chattanooga—a holding company which has since gone into receivership—was at that time eager to buy banks in Georgia. It had sent its observers to the General Assembly sessions to test the climate for amending the bill to

allow out-of-state holding companies to purchase Georgia banks.
C&S, aware that Hamilton Bancshares had acquired an interest
in five Georgia banks under the old banking laws, was strongly
opposed to allowing Hamilton to expand its Georgia holdings.

The first disclosure reports, filed on June 29, showed heavy
involvement by Atlanta banks—as well as increased involvement by banks outside Atlanta—in the campaigns of Lance,
Maddox, Jackson, and Gambrell. Lance reported $350,000 in
loans from rural north Georgia banks, while his contributions
to that point from persons other than himself totaled only
$226,554. Maddox's $155,000 in loans from banks in Atlanta,
Augusta, and elsewhere in the state represented 58 percent of
his campaign budget to that point. State Senator Harry Jackson, a wealthy Columbus industrialist, had borrowed $148,500
from banks in that city, while raising only $83,205 in contribu-
tions. Gambrell reported a modest $30,000 loan, but as the
campaign ground on he would borrow another $90,000. Indeed,
of the five best-financed candidates, only Busbee reported no
bank loans in the initial reports.

Lance's Banking Ties

Lance's heavy reliance on bank loans and his position as
President of the First National Bank of Calhoun, Georgia, led
to repeated attacks on him as the "big bank" candidate—rather
than the "country banker" he wanted to look like—after the
June 29 report showed he had borrowed $350,000 from six
banks scattered around his north Georgia home. Indeed, Lance's
ability to borrow large sums of money provided the opening for
attacks on him as the "rich man's candidate." These attacks,
coupled with revelations of his personal wealth, would prove
politically fatal in the closing days of the campaign, but they
never penetrated the overlapping spheres of influence and common interests apparent on closer examination of Lance's loans.
What does emerge from such an examination is a classic picture
of how business alliances and financial resources can be brought
to bear on campaign finance.

Prudently declining to borrow from his own bank, Lance
turned instead to the nearby Citizen's Bank of Calhoun for a
$40,000 loan. The Board Chairman of that bank is Lance's
campaign advisor and sometime traveling companion, J. Mack
Robinson, a flamboyant businessman whose career has included
a fling as Yves St. Laurent's partner in a Paris fashion house.
Robinson is also a stockholder of the Roswell Bank, which
extended another $40,000 loan to Lance, and a board member

of the First National Bank of Atlanta, which lobbyed heavily for passage of the bank-expansion bill. Finally, according to Busbee's banking allies, Robinson was said to own stock in an estimated 19 small-town banks. The legislation favored by the banking interests would have the side effect of allowing people like Robinson with extensive bank holdings to form mini-holding companies of their own.

Lance himself, along with a key campaign advisor, State Highway Board Chairman Tom Mitchell of Dalton, provided the links to the banks that supplied the remaining $270,000 in loans. The Northwest Georgia Bank, located in the tiny town of Ringgold, accounted for two loans totaling $140,000. Under questioning about his loans, Lance acknowledged that he was a stockholder in that bank—where Mitchell, according to his official state Department of Transportation biography, was a director. Finally, three banks in Mitchell's home town of Dalton, each of which had Lance contributors on their boards, lent the candidate $40,000 each. One of these banks, the Hamilton Bank of Dalton, is part of the Hamilton Bancshares group. Its presence in the Lance loan list signaled Lance's amiable relations with Hamilton, dating back to the time when Hamilton owned 35 percent of Lance's own Calhoun First National. In 1958, Hamilton had allowed Lance, his family, and other Calhoun residents to buy control of the bank.

Lance's friendliness with Hamilton Bancshares raised a difficult situation for C&S. On the one hand, C&S bankers were attracted to Lance because of his background, and they had ties to the Lance campaign through his campaign chairman, L. L. Gellerstedt, an Atlanta contractor and C&S board member. But C&S skittishness about Hamilton was not allayed by the fact that Hamilton executives in Atlanta were spreading the word that Lance's election would mean amendment of the bank-expansion bill to allow Hamilton to move further into Georgia. This factor and, even more important, its past ties to Busbee influenced C&S to direct its main support toward him, even as C&S President Richard Kattel and Vice President Bennett Brown made respectable contributions ($500 and $400 respectively) to Lance. But C&S and its banking allies took care not to offend Maddox, either.

The Maddox Loans

It came as a surprise to many observers that Lester Maddox's initial campaign report listed $25,000 loans from both C&S of Atlanta and First National of Atlanta, twin pillars of that

Atlanta establishment which Maddox was forever accusing of trying to destroy him. But the fact is that C&S and First National frequently work in unison on matters of common interest, and Maddox had a history as a loan customer of C&S. Throughout his terms as Governor (1967–71) and Lieutenant Governor (1971–75), there were persistent rumors of a Maddox-C&S link. The rumors were rooted in fact. As proprietor of his whites-only restaurant, the Pickrick, Maddox was for years one of hundreds of small businessmen banking with C&S. But when he emerged unexpectedly as the Democratic gubernatorial nominee in 1966, Maddox began receiving the personal attention of C&S President Mills Lane and Lane's top aide at the time, Kattel. Here are the details of the transaction which cemented that relationship, first ferreted out of courthouse deed records and later confirmed in substance by Maddox and bank spokesmen.

The general election of 1966 proved indecisive when, because of the write-in candidacy of former Governor Ellis Arnall, neither Maddox nor Republican nominee Howard Callaway (later Secretary of the Army and, briefly, President Ford's campaign manager) received a clear majority. The election was thus thrown into the General Assembly, where the Democratic majority eventually elected Maddox.

While Maddox was awaiting legislative confirmation, which was by no means a certainty, deeds were signed giving him title to two valuable parcels of Atlanta real estate, income-producing restaurant buildings then under lease to a fast-food franchise. This sale was made by C&S acting in its role as trustee for the employee pension fund of Bibb Manufacturing Company in Macon. The bank also extended Maddox the $231,000 in mortgage loans to finance the purchase. As a down payment, Maddox said, he used the $42,000 which was "the little bit I had left from selling my Pickrick." Maddox and bank officials confirm that Lane personally figured in the transaction. That the sale was in the control of C&S, in its role of trustee, is supported by deed records. Even more interesting is the history of the Bibb Manufacturing Company, founded by Lane's grandfather. At the time of the sale, Lane, as well as two relatives who were also grandsons of the founder, were on the Bibb board of directors. A final intriguing element of the deal is that although the deeds were dated December 29, they were not filed in the courthouse until three weeks later—after Maddox had been elected by the legislature.

Maddox and C&S spokesmen insist that the transaction was routine. But the political component of an unpublicized business deal involving a bank president and a governor seems clear enough. And the political implications of Maddox's 1974 campaign loan from C&S become clear when one considers that the bank's registered lobbyist, Hubert Harris, Jr., acknowledged that "I made the loan myself."

Examination of Maddox's other 1974 loans further confirm the dominance of political considerations in dispensing loans to candidates. These included:

- A $25,000 loan from the politically active Georgia Railroad Bank and Trust Company of Augusta. It was cosigned by Senator Holley, who held appointment under Maddox as Chairman of the Senate Banking and Finance Committee, where the bank bill would be handled when it reached the Senate.
- A $25,000 loan from First Bank of Savannah, cosigned by wealthy state Senator John Riley, a key member of Maddox's Senate bloc and a director of another Savannah bank. The Savannah banks likewise had lobbied for the bill.
- A $30,000 loan from the Habersham Bank, cosigned by Lee Arrendale, Chairman of the State Prison Board during Maddox's term as Governor. A second cosigner was his brother, Tom, Board Chairman of the bank.
- The $25,000 loan from First National of Atlanta was cosigned by business partners A. N. Adcock and Leonard Morris of Tifton. Morris is a member of the State Merit System Personnel Board.
- The $25,000 C&S loan and an additional $25,000 from a suburban Atlanta bank were cosigned by real estate developers drawn to Maddox by his strong stand against land-use planning legislation.

Do such loans represent political support? "Hell, no," maintains Atlanta First National lobbyist John Stevens. "All we look at is the credit worthiness of the people making the loan. What they do with the money is up to them."

Such disclaimers notwithstanding, a political system rooted in bank credit did inspire Georgia politicians to seek out powerful and influential friends. While few candidates were so bold as state Senator Harry Jackson, who borrowed primarily from the Columbus Bank and Trust Company where he serves as a director, the awarding of bank loans in every case followed easily traceable lines of business alliance or political self-interest.

The most striking example of this was the case of Busbee, who in the primary period found himself in a position to enjoy

the financial benefits of bank financing and the political benefits of condemning the bank borrowing of his opponents.

The Busbee-C&S Loan System

George Busbee, who had taken the precaution of resigning
his C&S-Albany directorship in late 1973, was the candidate
most active in making bank loans the hottest issue of early
July. He took the offensive in earnest after repeated questions
from reporters had forced Maddox to reveal the identities of
his cosigners and had forced Lance into the telling admission
that "it so happens my financial statement is sufficient" to cover
his $350,000 indebtedness. In a major campaign speech on
July 9, Busbee labeled his opponent "Loophole Lance," alleg-
ing that his loans were a mechanism to allow the delaying of
contributions until after the last report was filed on December
31. (Attorney General Bolton had confirmed that the law was
flawed to the extent that a candidate would not be under any
obligation to report contributions after year's end.)

"In a time of unprecedented tight money," Busbee said,
"when the average citizen can't even get a home loan, when
a small businessman can't get an inventory loan, Mr. Lance
was extended loans of $350,000 for his campaign. He has been
quoted in the press as saying there were no cosigners on these
loans. If this is an accurate report, it means that he is making
a $350,000 contribution to his own campaign. If he has agree-
ments with friends to help pay off the loans after the final
disclosure report, the failure to report these agreements now is
a violation of the disclosure law, or at best an effort to circumvent the law. To refuse to give any details on how these loans
will be repaid shows a total disrespect for the people's right
to know the true source of campaign funding. I remember an
old saying in Dooley County which said: 'He who pays the
piper calls the tune.' The people of Georgia have good cause
to wonder who will call the tune in Georgia if Mr. Lance is
elected governor. Will it be undisclosed sources who will pay
off the Lance loans? If Mr. Lance, in fact, repays the loans
personally, the obvious question is presented: 'Is the governor's
office a plum which can be bought by a wealthy candidate?' Or
does the state have an interest in limiting the extent to which
its highest office can be bartered and bargained for by candidates
of unlimited financial means?"

At the same time that Busbee strongly projected himself on
the "right" side of this issue, he was reporting as "contributions" money that had its origin in loans to his supporters from

the C&S Bank of Albany, where Busbee had served as a director and where his campaign chairman, Senator Al Holloway, was still a board member. Of course, Busbee himself could have easily become mired in this issue, save for careful planning to disguise the role of C&S financing in his campaign. Of the $402,166 Busbee reported as "contributions" in his June 29 and July 29 pre-primary disclosures, $181,000 originated in loans from C&S of Albany and another $24,850 in a personal loan to Busbee from another Albany bank where two of his three top contributors were directors. Thus $205,850, or slightly over 51 percent of Busbee's reported contributions, originated in bank loans. Moreover, much of this money was backed by informal promises to contributors that they would be repaid as campaign resources allowed. These pay-back agreements first surfaced in campaign disclosure reports filed after Busbee had won the nomination in the September 3 runoff against Maddox.

The reports gave the appearance that the Busbee campaign had run in large part on high-risk, interest-free loans from supporters, in itself a funding device of questionable frankness, but they contained no clue as to the credit arrangement with C&S that undergirded the whole system. That arrangement is reported here for the first time.

The existence of the Busbee-C&S credit arrangement was first uncovered in the course of inquiries based on information contained in the Busbee disclosure forms when persons listed as contributors confirmed that they had signed bank notes with the understanding that the money be passed directly to the campaign committee. Asked about this some weeks after Busbee took office, the Busbee staff supplied a three-page memorandum drafted by Busbee's chief fund-raiser, Albany trucking executive J. Fred Taylor, and reviewed for accuracy by Busbee. Information from independent investigation, the Busbee memo, and the C&S bank provided the basis for the following account of a political funding system extraordinary for the cooperation it bespeaks between Georgia's major financial institution and a candidate.

According to Taylor, he and Busbee's law partner, William T. Divine, Jr., had primary responsibility for setting up the system. C&S-Albany President William Banks handled the bank's involvement. Busbee, Taylor added, was also "active" in the overall fund-raising effort. Taylor and other campaign staff members would recruit persons willing to sign personal notes on the understanding that the money go directly to the Busbee campaign. In most cases, the persons signing such notes were prominent businessmen, but signers also included two

House employees who lived in small towns some distance from Albany and the chairman of Busbee's Clayton County campaign committee, who lived in an Atlanta suburb where he worked as shipping supervisor for a paint distributor. C&S maintains that all signers met bank credit requirements. Indeed, C&S Public Relations Vice President A. D. Frazier insisted on characterizing the extraordinary loans as "routine," even though he acknowledged that his superiors had kept him in the dark about their patronage of Busbee.

Yet, in some cases, Busbee campaign staff members picked up notes at the bank, carried them to the contributors for signature, and returned them to the bank. That the arrangement was approved at the highest level is attested by the fact that two C&S directors were among those signing notes, and banking laws require that when directors receive loans, two-thirds of the board must approve the transaction. Kattel, President and Board Chairman of the parent bank in Atlanta and a Busbee contributor, is also a member of the Albany board.

Altogether, 36 persons signed such notes, most in $5,000 denominations. The notes generated $181,000 for the Busbee campaign. Also, loans were issued to eight Albany businesses controlled by the signers. Taylor, under his own name and through three businesses controlled by him, took notes totaling $30,000, and after the runoff received rebates of $29,500. Of the $181,000 advanced in this manner, the signers were later rebated $124,000 by the Busbee campaign, which they presumably used to retire bank debts they had incurred on behalf of the campaign.

Altogether, the Busbee-C&S loan system was the most sophisticated funding technique of the campaign, from both a financial and a public-relations standpoint. It represented a method of deferring campaign expenses so that the late contributions which come to the winning candidate—often from former adversaries—could be used both to pay campaign expenses and to reduce the investments of initial supporters. Unlike the Lance system, it did not have the drawback of leaving the candidate liable for a crushing debt in the event of defeat, but spread out that liability to friends and supporters willing to make a moderate gamble on the candidate's success. Perhaps most important, it protected both the candidate and the bank from charges of collusion, a point on which both were sensitive, and Busbee especially vulnerable, for his record as C&S's legislative advocate was well known. Had his intial reports revealed $181,000 in C&S loans he would have been subject to the kind of attack visited upon Lance and Maddox by himself and the other candidates. Moreover, the absence of C&S loans served to divert attention from the fact that the bank's employees and directors were making systematic contributions to the campaign, the magnitude of which will be examined below.

This financial aid to Busbee took place at a time when the bank's chief spokesman in political matters, lobbyist Hubert Harris, Jr., was telling newsmen that the bank had no favorites in the governor's race. Harris said he had advised the bank's senior officers to circulate a letter within the bank stating that policy. The reason: "In 1970, Carter wrapped us around [Carl] Sanders' neck and squeezed him to death with it. We didn't want that to happen to anybody." Even as Harris was assuring reporters that the bank was neutral, he was keeping a running tab on his bank's "investment" in Busbee, according to sources in the Busbee camp.

Is "laundering" too strong a word for this practice? Probably so, but it should be remembered that all three parties in the system—C&S, the Busbee campaign, the supporters who signed notes—knew that the money was originating as bank loans and being reported as routine cash contributions. At the very least there is the irony of the self-proclaimed author of campaign disclosure in Georgia participating in a system for minimizing the political impact of disclosure. It is interesting to speculate, too, on whether Busbee's loans, because disguised, were less an affront to the average consumer faced with "unprecedented tight money" than Lance's openly reported borrowings.

It should be noted that one motivation for candidates to seek substantial bank loans early in a campaign can be found in the pay-in-advance policies of most advertising media. This is not to say that candidates directed their borrowed money solely to advertising expenditures, but there is close correlation between loan volume and advertising budget in the Lance, Busbee, and Maddox campaigns. Maddox, who had borrowed $165,000 as of the August 13 primary, reported total payments of $135,324 to the advertising agency through which he purchased his television time in the same period, plus an additional $10,431 for production of his 30-minute television film. Lance had spent $250,000 on all media as of July 2 and was planning a $420,000 advertising budget for the primary. Busbee, whose borrowings totaled $205,850 in the first two reports, reported television-time purchases of $201,145. In explaining the $50,000 C&S loan taken out immediately after the primary—and, for the first time, reported as such—the Busbee campaign committee noted in its report that the money was needed quickly "to pay for advertising in the media for the runoff, which is a 'cash' item in advance." Since the relationship between borrowing patterns and media expenses has been noted in national campaigns, it seems worth considering that this motivation was operative here. Certainly no candidate had the capability of purchasing advertising time and meeting his other expenses in the primary on the basis of contributions alone.*

Contribution Patterns

Contributions to the major gubernatorial candidates reflected the strong influences of the candidates' personal wealth, local business community support for "favorite sons," and on special-interest considerations or political alliances. Of these elements, the kind of civic boosterism that inspires contributions to a home-grown candidate is not to be discounted: The three best-financed candidates—Busbee, Lance, and Jackson—all drew their basic contributory support from their home areas. Family wealth was the dominant factor in Gambrell's fund-raising, special-interest money in Smith's. Only Rowan among the major candidates rejected large donations. For the most part, contributions came in large denominations, and whether loans or outright gifts, they followed many of the same patterns, skirting or subverting disclosure.

Busbee's big early contributors were affluent businessmen and corporations in his home town of Albany, who accounted for over $175,000 of the $402,165 reported in his June 29 and July 29 reports. Strong secondary sources were the allies of Busbee's political mentor, former Governor Sanders, and executives and directors of C&S banking system. As we have seen, much of this Albany money was, in fact, loans reported as contributions. But even accepting the Busbee campaign's definition of them as contributions provides an interesting commentary on both the narrowness of Busbee's financial base and the campaign's less-than-frank approach to disclosure.

Of that $175,000 in Albany money, almost $89,000 had its source in three men—chief fund-raiser Taylor, Richard Coody, a contractor with extensive contracts for state buildings, and plumbing contractor John Gay. But in Busbee's campaign reports, the contributions from these 3 sources were reported un-

---

* Following the release of advance copies of this book, the Georgia chapter of Common Cause petitioned the State Ethics Commission to investigate the Busbee loans. In lengthy testimony before the five-member commission, Busbee admitted that his campaign had borrowed the money in the manner described above, but maintained that he had done nothing wrong. The commission, whose chairman was appointed by Busbee, concurred.

der 14 different personal and corporate names. (And the figure of 14 does not reflect Taylor's use of 3 versions of his signature —James F. Taylor, James Fred Taylor, and Fred Taylor—to report his $13,600 in personal contributions.) Contributions of money and in-kind services to which a dollar value was attached from corporations controlled by Taylor went like this: Taylor Enterprises, $810; Georgia Mack Sales of Albany, $8,325; Georgia Mack Sales of. Macon, $5,125; Interstate Truck Leasing, $8,565; Precision Fabricators, $5,000. Coody, under his own name and through four corporations, was responsible for $34,-685 in contributions, and Gay, under his name and through corporations he was associated with, brought in $21,326. Gay's business partner provided another $5,000, and the two supplied Busbee with campaign headquarters space in their Albany motel.

Busbee, of course, was able to meet the letter of the disclosure law without revealing the common links between these diverse individual and corporate contributions. The ploy became known only after an enterprising newspaper reporter plowed through state corporation records. Even then, Busbee maintained that there had been no violation of the spirit of the law. "Everybody knows that Fred runs Georgia Mack and those others," Busbee said. "There's no secret here."

C&S, unlike most other major banks, does not maintain a blind-titled executive contribution fund. However, comparison of bank officer and director lists with Busbee's contributor list reveals a consistent pattern of contributions from persons affiliated with banks across the state bearing the C&S imprimatur. In the two pre-primary reports, these contributions amounted to $27,400, making the C&S network of banks Busbee's leading institutional source.

Sanders accounted for Busbee's few major contributions from the Atlanta area. Most notable among these was $2,500 from developer J. B. Fuqua, whose financial relationship with Sanders was an issue in Sanders' unsuccessful 1970 campaign. After losing that race, Sanders had gone on to head a law firm handling such politically sensitive accounts as that of the Georgia Power Company for fees as high as, in the electric utility's case, $1 million per year. Sanders, a $3,400 contributor, and law partner Norman Underwood, a $1,000 contributor, figured primarily as behind-the-scenes strategists rather than fund-raisers, however. This is worth noting because Maddox's chief strategist and fund-raiser, Senator Holley, is a member of the same law firm, operating its Augusta office. One of the puzzles of the campaign, from a strategic standpoint, was that none of Busbee's or Maddox's opponents ever made a concerted effort to question the political propriety of the Sanders-Holley firm's dual involvement.

Busbee's primary reports also betray in seminal form a trait that was to become increasingly important after he emerged as the nominee—a willingness to appeal for and accept special-interest money from virtually any quarter. For instance, even before the primary, Busbee was allowing an Albany construction firm that did business with the state to carry campaign workers on its payroll. And Fred Taylor wrote fellow members of the Georgia Motor Truckers Association informing them that he was taking six months off from his business to work in the Busbee campaign because "If George is elected, the transportation industry will have a governor who knows this business and its problems and needs." He enclosed a copy of Busbee's voting record in behalf of more liberal weight limits, noting that legislator-lawyer Busbee had represented his trucking businesses for the past 15 years. After the campaign, Taylor confided that he was disappointed by the truckers' initial response to his letter, and that they gave sparingly in the 1974 primary because four years earlier they had given heavily to Sanders' losing campaign against Jimmy Carter. Interestingly, several of Busbee's staff members were relieved that the truckers did not give more at that early stage of the campaign; they were worried about the political impact if Taylor's letter with its blatant appeal to special-interest money should find its way into an opponent's hands. Liquor dealers, who Rowan charged were lobbying for the removal of incumbent Revenue Commissioner John Blackmon, contributed over $6,000 during the primary period. But the really heavy special-interest money from truckers and other sources would not begin to move Busbee's way until he reached the runoff with Maddox.

Bert Lance's contributions sprang from three main sources: his north Georgia home territory, affluent Atlantans, and allies of Lance's political patron, Governor Carter. In all, Lance attracted $354,793 in a fund-raising campaign launched with a $20,000 contribution of his own. The broadest-based effort was in north Georgia, where Lance received literally hundreds of contributions in the $10–500 range. The motivation for these contributions was simple enough—that section of the state had not produced a governor in this century.

Lance's real coup, however, lay in his ability to attract what Georgia politicians call "the Atlanta money," a traditional lode of campaign funds that is always the object of hot competition. (If nothing else, Lance's success in tapping this source gave a good idea of just how big it actually is.) The support Busbee gained from C&S executives and the few Sanders allies in Atlanta marked virtually the only exception in what amounted to a clean sweep of Atlanta by Lance. Even Sanders ally Fuqua and top C&S officials made at least token contributions to Lance.

It should be understood that this is special-interest money of a quite unique kind. It represents the established wealth and powerful businesses of the city that dominates the Georgia economy. Lance raised over $103,000 in the affluent northside residential area, where most of the city's leaders live, and his contribution roster read like an Atlanta Chamber of Commerce membership list. As this is money that usually moves in a unit, there could be no clearer signal of its direction than the listing of former Mayor Ivan Allen, Jr., the quintessential northside "silk-stocking" politician, as a $5,000 contributor. The northside influence accounted in large measure for the general affluence of Lance's contributor list, despite the many small contributions from north Georgia. Over a third of his contributions came in amounts of $1,000 to $5,000.

The Carter influence was a factor in Lance's strength in the northside. Although elected without their massive support, Carter and his wife had become extremely popular among wealthy Atlantans. Thus, wealthy benefactors of Carter's (at the time) dark horse Presidential campaign also figured prominently in Lance's financing: Attorney Phillip Alston, a Carter appointee to the Board of Regents, with his wife gave $6,000; Robert Lipshutz, also an attorney, whose office building now houses the Carter campaign, gave $2,500; Mrs. Robert W. Chambers, a principal owner of the *Atlanta Journal* and *Constitution*, both of which endorsed Lance, gave $5,000.

Lance also attracted northside contributors who generally support Republican candidates in national elections. For instance, textile manufacturer Nathan Lipson, a $1,000 Lance contributor, was among the state's leading contributors to the Committee to Re-Elect the President in 1972. Convenience-store magnate Dillard Munford, prominently associated with the Georgia branch of CREEP, was also a Lance contributor.

But Lance's own single biggest contributor was the candidate himself. Lance spent $235,253 out of his own pocket to run his campaign from June 1973 until February 1974, a beneficence made possible by his substantial personal wealth, voluntarily disclosed to amount to $3.1 million. Lance's total spending of $1,160,956 in the primary alone is probably a state record, although of course there are no reliable figures for earlier years. Even after he put close to a quarter-million dollars of his own money, plus $350,000 of personally secured loans, into the campaign, Lance's revenues fell $200,910 short of his final spending total. Lance confirmed in early 1975 that he had wound up paying the difference out of his own pocket. "I just had to go ahead and handle that myself," he said. (His campaign reports reflected only that the debts were paid, not that the money came from Lance.)

Many political observers, including some of his own advisors, believe that the disclosure of his multimillionaire status was responsible for Lance's loss to Busbee in the race for the runoff spot opposite Maddox. But Lance said he would make the same disclosure again. "There was no sense in my parrying about something like that," he said some months later. "I felt like it was just in keeping with the kind of campaign that I had run. If it cost the election, it cost the election. I will say this. I think there was too much emphasis on this. I was charged with trying to buy the governor's office. That's not the case. I was just being honest about what it costs to run for governor of Georgia."

In a sense, Lance represents a Deep South counterpart to national politicians like Nelson Rockefeller or the Kennedys— men willing to invest personal wealth seeking elective offices which will pay only a fraction of that investment in salaries. But Georgians are unused to such politicians, and Lance's explanation throughout the campaign that he and his wife just wanted "to give something back in service to the state which has given us so much" could not offset the steady erosion which set in after Lance, ignoring some of his advisors, had disclosed his personal wealth. He did come out of the campaign, however, with his personal reputation for honesty enhanced by his filing of the campaign's most detailed spending reports.

He also won the admiration of state Senator Rowan, the foe of big-spending campaigns. Rowan's colorful analysis is probably the best and most accurate summation of the political perils of their divergent approaches to campaign finance: "There was one tragedy in the campaign," he recalled. "Bert did lose for the wrong reason. It was a page-seven story, a private declaration that he made on his own accord. But just as sure as we're sitting here, Bert Lance was not in the runoff because he told his net worth. He peaked when he said he was worth $3.1 million, because the people of Georgia feel that money is what's wrong with politics. It's hard for them to orient to a politician like me saying he ain't taking it, but it's damn sure easy for them to orient to a politician saying he's got it." Lance's out-of-pocket contributions to his campaign exceeded the entire Rowan budget several times over.

In a sense, both Lance and Rowan were casualties of the new public awareness of the role of money in politics. At their opposite ends of the poles of campaign finance, each suffered from his forthrightness and its unique consequences. Whereas Lance probably created a deadly backlash against his candidacy when he disclosed his wealth, Rowan, who tried to capitalize on the campaign-finance issue, hamstrung himself with an unrealistically low budget.

Rowan's key message was: "If you don't take the big money you won't have the big obligation. If a man gives you $100, he'll work for you. But if he gives you $10,000, he'll expect you to work for him when you're elected." Rowan's rhetoric had a fine, populist ring, and he lived up to his promise to accept no contribution over $250, a figure derived from his campaign-spending bill. But he found that donations of such a small size simply could not generate enough income to match the $500,000 to $1 million budgets of his opponents. Rowan wound up raising only $125,497, including a $15,000 personal loan.

In retrospect, Rowan sees his candidacy as plagued by a circles-within-circles dilemma. In campaign finance he had a "good issue" which people responded to in his personal appearances. But he simply couldn't afford enough advertising to spread his good issue around in the short span of the primary campaign. "You might say I was killed by my own antibiotic," quipped Rowan. He now believes that the $250 limit could have been raised without sacrificing the effectiveness of his message. "If I were running again, knowing what I know now, I would look at a $1,000 limit. About half the people who gave me $250 would have given me a thousand. Maybe another quarter would have given me $500. I would have a limit and I would make it an issue because it deserved to be an issue, because you can look right now at the [Busbee] appointments, at what's happening in state government, and there's no need for you to throw away that political contributor list, because it's a vital part of state government. It ought not to be. The boards and bureaus of this state are not representative because their selection is based upon—for years—political contributions."

Second only to Bert Lance in expenditure of personal money was former Senator Gambrell. Himself a scion of a wealthy and socially prominent Atlanta family, Gambrell paid dearly for Lance's success in Atlanta and among Carter allies. Gambrell had been appointed to a vacant seat in the U.S. Senate by Carter, only to lose it in 1972 after serving two years. When it became apparent that Carter would back Lance, Gambrell struck out on his own. But by that time, Lance had so eroded Gambrell's expected base in Atlanta that Gambrell and his immediate family wound up putting $150,734 into a campaign which spent only $418,338.

The financing of former Lieutenant Governor Smith was extraordinary for its reliance on a single interest group. Smith, who had worked as a lawyer and lobbyist since leaving office in 1971, filed an initial disclosure which, upon close analysis, revealed that $70,860 of his $116,000 in contributions came from nine real estate men described as "either clients or good friends." Of that amount, $25,680 came from Jack and David Pendley, developer brothers with a long and controversial history of involvement with Atlanta-area politicians possessing zoning authority over their projects. In his second report, Smith's contributions had dwindled to $2,625; he also reported a $50,000 loan from a suburban Atlanta clothing firm, and it turned out that a principal in the firm was an official of a land-development group which had been involved in an SEC investigation of flamboyant Georgia speculator Fred C. Tallant. Smith made scant effort to avoid the appearance that his candidacy represented little more than a gamble by developers on gaining unprecedented access to state government. In fact, he noted that the economic recession had cut off a source of similar contributions from the mobile-home industry. "You've got to get your money somewhere," said Smith.

State Senator Harry Jackson of Columbus proved that a competitive campaign can be mounted by a candidate with access to the financial resources of a moderate-sized city, even if he lacks a genuine political base. By virtue of his position as a wealthy industrialist, Jackson was able to borrow $342,000, with $300,000 coming from the bank where he served as a director. The $140,922 in contributions that appeared in his two pre-primary reports reflected his access to the city's affluent circles: His average contribution was a high $791, with two prominent families accounting for $12,850 and $10,000 each. Jackson aimed his fund-raising pitch almost entirely at the local sentiment that Columbus, isolated near the Alabama line, is the stepchild city of Georgia. As a result, of his 199 reported contributions, only 21 came from outside Columbus.

Despite spending of over $500,000, Jackson finished sixth in the primary, winning less than 5 percent of the vote. He led however in per-vote cost, with $12.62 per vote, and was followed by Lance with $7.90 per vote; Maddox, who led the primary with 310,000 votes (38 percent), spent about $1.30 per vote; Busbee, second with 20 percent of the vote, spent about $3.20 for each vote.

As we have seen, these figures represent substantial expenditures of borrowed money. The primary, and then the runoff, left in their wake plenty of questions about how those debts would be retired by defeated candidates, but the disclosure law would provide few answers to such questions. As for the winner, repayment of his debts was more visible but no less disturbing.

Runoff and Payoff

A Busbee aide spent the morning after the August 13 primary calling Lance supporters in Atlanta who had turned down Busbee's earlier pleas. "I just said, 'All right, it's the fourteenth. Are you ready to roll?' They knew what I meant," he said.

The calls reflected Busbee's expectation that he would automatically inherit anti-Maddox contributors who had seen their primary favorites defeated. He was right. Busbee's post-primary reports showed that 30 contributors who had given Lance a total of $38,280 in the primary turned around and gave Busbee $34,600 after Lance's elimination; and of that group, 27 were from Atlanta's blue-ribbon contributors.

By making the runoff, Busbee attracted both those special-interest contributors dedicated to beating Maddox and those interested in hooking up with a winner, whoever he might be. Maddox had never been considered a friend of education, and the first category included the Georgia Association of Educators, representing the state's teachers, which sent Busbee $30,000 on August 19. In the second category were donors such as the Good Government Group of the Trust Company of Georgia, which gave Busbee $5,000 two days after the primary, and Hub, Inc., a firm making large pipes of the sort used in highway construction, which contributed $5,000 on the third day after the primary. The Good Government Group had parceled out small contributions to Busbee, Jackson, and Lance in the primary, while Hub had sat out the primary altogether.

Unlike Busbee, Maddox was finding few new friends. For example, only two noteworthy Lance contributors—Columbus banker Frank Morast and Atlanta developer Paul Duke—turned up on the Maddox list. Thus, Maddox was forced to call once again on the same tried and tested contributor groups—the wealthy rural businessmen like the Arrendales, his developer friends, and Augusta businessmen. One casualty of Maddox's money squeeze was his pledge not to accept more than $5,000 from any one contributor. Even though he was able to raise over $200,000 in contributions for the runoff period, this was not enough to offset his heavy advertising expenses, and he had to borrow another $75,000, the October 21 post-runoff reports revealed.

After Busbee crushed Maddox by a 60–40 margin in the September 3 runoff, the deluge of special-interest money began in earnest. These congratulatory contributions first showed up in the report of October 21, which covered the period from August 23—11 days before the runoff—to October 23. At this point the Busbee campaign committee had abandoned its practice of dating each donation, thereby obscuring the fact that most of these sensitive contributions arrived after Busbee had won the nomination and, in the absence of a potentially strong Republican candidate, become in effect Governor-elect. Busbee staff members later confirmed, however, that most of the special-interest contributions arrived after the runoff, and the December 31 final report shows that they continued unabated until the end of the year.

The most striking example of such contributions was supplied by the highway contractors, who had, for the most part, waited out the primary. By the end of the year, Busbee had collected over $45,000 from this group, virtually all in the last four months of the year. Truckers, who had earlier turned a deaf ear to Taylor's plea, brought in over $10,000—a result, according to Taylor himself, of discussions in the board meeting of the Georgia Motor Truckers Association on the necessity of maintaining ties with the new Governor. The earlier pattern of contributions from liquor firms or persons associated with them was intensified by Busbee's success. By the end of the year, these contributions totaled $17,770, thanks in large part to a Columbus liquor dealer who switched to Busbee after Lance lost.

Corporate and professional activity also continued unabated, accounting for almost $32,000 in contributions to Busbee, the great majority of them coming after he was the nominee. C&S executives and directors gave an additional $17,700 from August 23 onward, bringing their aggregate for the campaign to $45,100—over 5 percent of Busbee's total contributions. The state political funds associated with Dairymen, Inc.'s SPACE (trust for Special Political Agricultural Community Education) fund and the American Medical Political Action Committee gave $2,000 and $2,500 respectively. The Georgia Nonpartisan Committee for Good Government, political fund of the Atlanta-based Coca-Cola Bottling Company, gave $6,000.

The traditional political timidity of George unions was reflected in the late contributions of the state AFL-CIO Committee on Political Education. After sitting out the primary,

COPE gave Busbee $11,000 for the runoff, but the contribution was timed so that it would not show up on the August 23 report, the last before the balloting. The first disclosure of COPE activity came in the October 21 report. This caution is rooted in regional history, for unions have had an uphill battle in the Deep South. Their leaders have played their politics close to the vest, fearful of betting on the wrong horse and inciting punitive anti-union legislation beyond the right-to-work law already in effect in Georgia and most Deep South states.

The Georgia United Auto Workers, however, broke with this tradition. UAW leaders, who represent workers in Atlanta's auto-assembly plants, announced their support for Busbee early in the primary period, and the UAW political fund was Busbee's only consistent union contributor in the primary race. The UAW Community Action Program Council gave almost $7,000, and its public endorsement was used to good advantage to attract union voters in the primary. These sources, plus late contributions which included $2,500 from the Pittsburgh headquarters of United Steelworkers, brought Busbee's union total to $25,741.

The tide of congratulatory contributions ran so strongly that Busbee's final two reports, on October 21 and December 31, showed $564,833 in contributions collected between August 23 and year's end. The three primary-period reports had shown true contributions (as opposed to those originating in loan agreements) of only $342,104 over the span of the entire previous year.

How did the Busbee campaign use these late windfalls? In essence, it paid for the primary and runoff campaigns with the money that came in after victories in those elections. Busbee's total spending of $1,152,376 for the primary, runoff, and general elections includes the repayment of $182,550 to retire his personal indebtedness and partially reimburse participants in the Busbee-C&S loan arrangement (the rest of the debt being absorbed by the cosigners).

Exactly how much Busbee spent in pursuit of the nomination and how much in the general election campaign is difficult to assess because of his committee's failure to give specific dates for expenditures in the critical October 21 report, which covered the last days of the runoff and the initial weeks of the general election. However, staff members confirm that $900,000 had probably been expended by the end of the runoff. And much of the post-runoff spending was devoted to the rebates and other primary-related costs, for Busbee campaigned in only the most perfunctory manner against the Republican nominee, Macon

Mayor Ronnie Thompson. In 1974, as in the old days of the "Solid South," winning the Democratic nomination was tantamount to election.

A final question is whether or not Busbee, in his first months in office, demonstrated responsiveness to his campaign contributors.

In the case of the unions and teachers, he manifestly did not. He opposed pay-raise proposals from the Georgia Association of Educators for 1975–76 and denounced the teachers as greedy in his first budget address to the General Assembly. The unions were stunned when he endorsed new sales-tax legislation, but Busbee signed the legislation into law despite a personal appeal from Jim Thompson, the Atlanta labor leader who had lined up UAW support for him.

Busbee's corporate contributors, however, had no reason to complain, for immediately after his inauguration he moved to perpetuate the system of casual conflict of interest which has long prevailed in Georgia government.

J. Fred Taylor was named to the new post of "chief of staff." Although unsalaried, he took an office in the Capitol from which to oversee key appointments to state boards. Campaign adviser Norman Underwood, the lawyer-lobbyist from the Sanders-Holley firm, became Executive Secretary, the key position in controlling access to the Governor. Press aide Mike Dowling set up a public relations agency in Atlanta and registered as a lobbyist. His first clients were the Atlanta banks; C&S, Trust Company of Georgia, and First National of Atlanta paid him $4,000 to guide the banking bill through the 1975 General Assembly session, with the promise of a bonus when the bill became law. Sanders, himself the board chairman of yet another Atlanta bank, helped Dowling plan strategy in a meeting with friendly legislators in an Atlanta hotel. Taylor buttonholed House members in the halls of the Capitol during House debate to line up support for the bill, and it passed.

When the 1976 session rolled around, the bill had moved over to the Senate, where it was assigned to the banking committee, still chaired by Senator Holley. On the Senate floor, the bill had the support of Busbee's Senate floor leader, Terrell Starr—a member of the board of directors of C&S-Atlanta. With C&S lobbyist Harris and Dowling meeting with friendly senators to plan strategy, the bill zipped through the upper chamber. Busbee did not sign it for a few days, saying that he needed time to study its provisions, although they had hardly changed since he introduced the measure. He finally signed the bill into law without fanfare.

Taylor also lobbied successfully for a new law, sponsored in the House by Busbee's floor leader, raising weight limits on multi-axle trucks. Since there are few such trucks now in use in Georgia, the law will have the effect of generating sales for persons who, like Taylor, own truck dealerships. Busbee's initial choice for State Highway Commissioner was a road contractor whose firm had given $5,000 to the campaign after Busbee's nomination. The contractor turned the job down rather than divest himself of his $49 million in state contracts. Busbee appointed an attorney who had contributed $3,040 to the campaign as Revenue Commissioner. Most newspaper accounts linked incumbent Commissioner John Blackmon's removal to his unpopularity with the liquor interests that contributed to Busbee's campaign. Indeed, throughout his first 18 months in office, the new Governor seemed bent on proving the folk wisdom of his native Dooley County: Those who had paid the piper in the Busbee campaign clearly were calling the tune in the Busbee administration.

Campaign Debt

The campaign-finance law's lack of a provision for tracking campaign loans beyond the end of the election year was immediately recognized as its most glaring defect. Former Lieutenant Governor Smith cut to the heart of the problem: "After December 31, anybody can pay off his [a candidate's] bank notes, and nobody will ever know who it was." But the concern during the campaign, which centered on how the winner would retire his debts, was too narrow. The losers, bereft of any ability to attract post-election contributions, took advantage of this loophole to wrap their post-election financial affairs in secrecy. Of the more than $1 million openly borrowed by major Democratic candidates, repayment of only $110,000 could be substantiated by perusal of campaign reports. What has happened to this money? For the answer to this question, one must turn to the big borrowers themselves.

Maddox acknowledged immediately after his defeat that he was heavily in debt. After all, his reported expenditures of $750,397 included $240,000 in bank loans, plus an admitted $80,000 paid on his behalf by his advertising agency for television time. By late March 1975, Maddox said that debt had been reduced to $95,000 owed the banks and $42,000 due the ad agency, but the disclosure reports offered little more than a few sporadic clues as to where the money came from to reduce this debt. For instance, Maddox's reports showed repayment of a $50,000 loan from an Augusta bank and a $10,000 loan from a suburban Atlanta bank, but in neither case was there an indication of the source of this money. Senator Holley later acknowledged that he and a group of unnamed cosigners had paid the $50,000 note. Holley and Senator Riley confirmed that they had each repaid $25,000 notes cosigned with Maddox, although Maddox's reports failed to mention these transactions at all. Maddox himself confirmed that the $10,000 note was repaid by the Atlanta realtor who had cosigned it. The same bank seized a $5,000 campaign account to apply toward an additional $15,000 note, he said.

Maddox has been forced to return to the fried-chicken business in order to try to repay a debt he vows he'll retire "if they'll just give me a little time." He keeps a collection box in the lobby of his restaurant and is running newspaper ads appealing to former supporters for contributions. Only about $600 a month is coming in, however, and Maddox says that some of his cosigners are pressuring him to take sole responsibility for the outstanding notes. The experience has left him a bitter man. "A lot of people were supposed to help me whether we won or lost," he commented, "but it just hasn't happened that way."

From the banks' standpoint, the loans were apparently made with the expectation of repayment. But Harry Jackson makes it clear that the cosigners' relationship with his campaign entailed an agreement that there was no guarantee of repayment to the supporter. "Everybody who cosigned, cosigned with the understanding that they were making a contribution," said Jackson. He said his $342,000 in loans has been repaid with $120,000 of his own money, plus proportionate contributions from each cosigner. However, Jackson's campaign reports reflect neither the repayment of these loans nor the receipt by the candidate of any funds for this purpose.

Lance's loans totaling $350,000 are all still outstanding, and he is paying the debt service while he and his associates try to figure out how to retire them. Forgiveness of debt by any bank is out of the question, Lance said, as the act would constitute a "prima facie violation" of banking laws. For the moment, Lance reported, "We're just in a holding pattern. I pay the interest, and hopefully we'll do something about reducing the principal." But Lance made it clear that he feels his obligations under the disclosure law have been fulfilled: He does not plan to disclose publicly the disposition of his campaign loans.

In each case, the lack of a debt-tracking provision guaranteed that debts incurred to provide money to influence an election wound up as a private financial matter between the candidate and his creditor. Not only does this sacrifice the public's right to know the true source of this money, it also serves as an implicit encouragement to the attitude toward campaign borrowing expressed by Senator Holley: "We knew if he [Maddox] won, we'd have no trouble paying them off. We knew if he lost, it would be more difficult. The money just wouldn't come in like it would if we had won. But that's all right, because I wanted him to be governor. It was sort of like a horse race, but in a horse race, you get to bet win, place, or show. I only had one way I could go. I only bet to win and I lost."

In an unsuccessful campaign, the candidates who, like Maddox and Lance, gamble on victory and wind up with crushing personal debts are the losers, both financially and in terms of their future political independence. Ironically, it is the public which loses if the winning candidate has made similar gambles. For in a campaign system based on deficit financing, it is the congratulatory contributions of special interests which represent the winning candidate-gambler's jackpot.

Lack of Enforcement

A continuing series of incidents involving both petty and substantial disregard for the law resulted from the complete absence of enforcement. The campaign-finance law did not, as its preamble indicated it would, include any language to "provide for the investigation by the Attorney General of any apparent violations." In the absence of explicit instruction, Attorney General Arthur Bolton undertook no systematic review or regulatory activity, and the candidates succeeded in getting around the law through procedures that, in most cases, have never come to public scrutiny.

For instance, Maddox and several other candidates declined to list cosigners for their runoff loans even after the Attorney General had ruled, at the request of the Governor, that cosigners must be listed. Moreover, Maddox's October 21 report, filed after he was beyond political damage, revealed that on August 19 he had taken two additional loans for $25,000 and $50,000. Had these loans been promptly and properly reported, they would have been disclosed on August 23, during the heat of the runoff when the bank-loan issue was still a potential source of bad publicity.

Busbee, as noted earlier, was able to institute with impunity a practice of not providing specific dates for contributions or expenditures during the critical runoff period. The law does not specifically require dates, but a commission with rule-making authority would almost certainly have viewed the Busbee practice with a questioning eye. There was clearly an expectation on the part of the state that contributions would be dated, as the reporting forms contained a space for providing the "Date (month, day, year)" of each item.

Both Busbee and Maddox got away with a technique for channeling money through county-level campaign committees which seemed to fly directly in the face of the law's requirement that contributions be received and expenditures accounted for only by the central campaign committee. Typical entries noted only payments to or contributions from the county committees, thereby completely obscuring the source or dispensation of the money.

The most flagrant examples of this practice came, again, from the Busbee camp. In a three-week period at the peak of the primary race, Busbee reported payments totaling $10,500 to two campaign workers in Macon and Albany. Busbee admitted that the two men were, in turn, using the money to make cash payments for "routine campaign expenses," but he defended these unrecorded transactions as necessary to the efficiency of the campaign operation in the frantic closing days of the primary race. While issuing checks for every campaign expense is admittedly a slow process, the practice has the advantage of meeting the reporting requirements of the Georgia law. Busbee earnestly argued at the time that he did not intend to circumvent the law in this instance, but it is not his intent that is in question—rather, the use to which the money was put. And underlying this question is a deeper one. Was Busbee, as an attorney and an author of the campaign law, unaware that such unrecorded cash payments run counter to the spirit of that law?

In the absence of enforcement, Busbee and the Democratic nominee for lieutenant governor, Zell Miller, used the state party to obscure the source of $75,000 borrowed by their supporters from the Trust Company of Georgia. The money was split, with roughly two-thirds going to Busbee and one-third to Miller. Both listed the party as sole contributor. What they did not reveal was that this money was generated by supporters who co-signed a note payable to the party. According to state Democratic Party Chairman Charles Gray, the cosigners included the ubiquitous J. Fred Taylor, state Senator Al Holloway, state House Speaker Pro Tem Al Burruss, and a contractor who had supplied Miller with airplane transportation throughout the campaign. In short, the device of placing the money through the party served to disguise the activities of persons already involved in a highly visible and, in certain individual cases, controversial way.

It might be noted that the Georgia Supreme Court in its ruling concluded that the attorney general had the broad statutory authority to enforce the law in the absence of the Ethics Commission. However, Bolton, like his counterparts in many states, is reluctant to involve himself and his department in political matters. The merits of that reluctance aside, this lack of ongoing enforcement points up the critical need for a viable administrative and "watchdog" agency.

Money and the Minority Vote

In the closing days of the primary campaign, a heated debate broke out over alleged "buying" of black votes. It was a debate replete with demagogic racial overtones, as Gambrell and Jackson tried to make an issue of Busbee's liaison with state Representative (now state Senator) Julian Bond and other black legislators. Bond, it was charged by a Jackson aide, had participated in garnering for Busbee endorsements from "a number of black groups . . . all of which George Busbee paid for." The attack on Busbee and Bond was unfair, for all the major candidates—including Jackson and Gambrell—had freely indulged in the competition for the endorsements under a system involving the tacit understanding that the candidate receiving the endorsement would make "expense" payments to the endorsing groups.

The endorsement system has its roots in the era of segregated politics, when white candidates, fearful of dealing openly with blacks, made clandestine payments to black voters or political operatives through "bag men." According to state Representative Ben Brown, Chairman of the Georgia House's Black Caucus, "It was general [practice]. The old way was to go in and lay the $20 bills on the table and say 'All right, how many votes can you get?' "

The rise of black political power represented by the registration of 440,000 black voters in the state rendered the old system both inefficient and unacceptable to blacks no longer willing to deal in an under-the-table manner. The endorsement system is a continuation of the tradition of payments from candidates, with the critical differences that the money is channeled through committees charged with using it for legitimate election-related

expenses in the black community. It is a system that has the advantage of being open, but only the most politically naïve would
deny that in an unregulated campaign the system is subject to
abuse by both candidates and political brokers attached to the
groups.

The endorsement system became a political issue after Busbee
won the blessings of two of the most prominent black groups,
the Political Advisory Council of Savannah and the Glynn
County Democratic Club in the coastal city of Brunswick. The
mass meeting of the Savannah group late in the primary campaign was a major political event. Gambrell, Jackson, Lance,
Busbee, and Smith all made personal appeals for the endorsement with full press coverage. Promises of payment, for obvious
reasons, are not part of the candidates' presentations in such
meetings, but it is understood that the candidate who wins will
have to pay for printing of flyers for circulation in the Black
community and an election-day transportation system.

After Busbee won the Savannah and Brunswick endorsements, Gambrell and Jackson, knowing the underlying financial
arrangements, began challenging Busbee to reveal his "vote-
buying" expenditures. The arrangement was made to look more
sinister because the endorsements were timed so that the payments would not show up until the August 23 post-primary reports. The expenditures were not sizable in proportion to the
importance of such endorsements to the Busbee campaign, for
black supporters accounted for over half of the primary vote
which put him in the runoff with Maddox. Subsequent reports
showed payments of $4,202 to the Savannah group and $2,000
and $3,000 to the Brunswick group—the major part of a total of
$11,552 paid to endorsing groups, plus another $3,100 paid to
an ad hoc committee operating in the Atlanta black community.

Gambrell and Jackson, of course, were arguing that any such
payment was improper on its face, being in effect a payment for
a deliverable bloc of votes. Busbee maintained that the payments would be used for the proper purposes of "transportation
and poll workers and so forth." He was forced to admit, however, that his campaign had no control over the use of the
money once the lump-sum payments had been made.

This points up the core of the problem. Those unfamiliar
with the workings of Southern elections might be inclined to
side with the Gambrell-Jackson argument, but the fact is that
especially in rural areas there is a need for transportation cadres
and poll watchers to insure that black voters are not disen-
franchised by reason of their poverty, the inconvenient location

of voting places, and ballot manipulation. Given the prevailing political realities, the candidate who stands to benefit from the black vote is virtually the only source for the money needed to provide these services.

What is needed is a disclosure law broad enough to guarantee the integrity of the process. Had Busbee's disclosure bill been drafted on a model statute, he would not have been vulnerable to these attacks, for his bill would almost certainly have contained provision for reporting by political action committees. In that case, the propriety of the expenditures could have been substantiated by showing that the money had been used for legitimate "get-out-the-vote" activities. The endorsement system provides a good example of how a strong disclosure law can remove clouds of suspicion from what in an insufficiently regulated campaign are, indeed, practices of questionable propriety.

Repairing an Imperfect Law

After the runoff campaign, George Busbee singled out a limitation of campaign spending as the next frontier in campaign regulation in Georgia. Yet, in the General Assembly session that began almost simultaneously with his inauguration in January 1975, the Governor did not move aggressively to offer new legislation. The subject received not even passing mention when he outlined his legislative goals in his first state of the state message. In the absence of any leadership from the Governor, the politically ambitious Lieutenant Governor, Zell Miller, stepped forward as the champion of new legislation. Although it is not customary for the lieutenant governor to generate legislation, Miller called press conferences to announce that he would introduce amendments to the existing disclosure law to limit campaign spending and make some changes in the law's provisions, as well as a bill requiring lobbyists to file reports of their expenditures. Busbee was forced into the embarrassing position of having to step forward belatedly as an endorser of Miller's amendments to "my disclosure bill." The Governor did provide a signal service in influencing House Speaker Tom Murphy, never an enthusiast for any sort of reform legislation, to stand as a joint sponsor of the Miller proposal.

Even with the state's three top politicians supporting it, however, the General Assembly exhibited no great haste to act on the new disclosure legislation. After an easy passage through the Senate, which under Miller took on a new role as the more progressive chamber, the bill languished for weeks in the con-

servative House Rules Committee. Volunteer lobbyists from the
Atlanta chapter of Common Cause played the key role in breaking it loose by publicly charging that the committee intended to
bury both the spending limitation and lobbying proposals.
Thus prodded, the committee angrily voted both measures out,
and the amended disclosure bill, its spending limits intact,
passed on the final day of the session. The lobbying bill died in
a welter of weakening House amendments, a victim of rural
legislators' fondness for the lavish entertainments provided by
corporate lobbyists during their annual two-month stay in
Atlanta.

The disclosure law, retitled the Campaign and Financial Disclosure Act, now limits spending in all statewide and state legislative campaigns. Gubernatorial candidates can spend $400,000
in the primary, $300,000 in the general election, and $200,000
in each runoff, whether primary or general election. Thus, in a
typical year, a candidate for governor, running in a primary,
primary runoff, and general election, could spend $900,000. Can-
didates for lieutenant governor and all other statewide offices
may spend $175,000 in the primary, $125,000 in the general
election, and $75,000 in each runoff. State Senate candidates may
spend $10,000 in the primary, $10,000 in the general election,
and $4,000 in each runoff; state House candidates $6,000 in the
primary, $6,000 in the general election, and $3,000 in each
runoff. No limitations were placed on local and county officials,
but they were included under the disclosure requirements,
which call for reporting of all contributions over $101 and all
expenditures regardless of amount. Statewide candidates not
currently holding state or Federal office are allowed an extra 25
percent spending on the theory, according to Miller, that they
should be entitled to an additional allowance to offset the publicity advantages of officeholders.

The 1975 amendments had the effect of correcting some of
the more glaring defects in the 1974 disclosure act, while leaving others untouched. The most noteworthy improvements were
an effort to re-establish the State Ethics Commission on a sound
footing and broadening of the disclosure requirements to include all corporate groups and political action committees that
make contributions or expenditures on behalf of candidates. The
Ethics Commission will not be free of political influence in that
the secretary of state, lieutenant governor, and speaker of the
House will appoint one member each and the governor two.
But the commission will have substantial and clearly defined
powers, the most significant of which are the right to issue sub-

poenas for its independent investigations and the right to institute injunctive or prosecutorial actions in the superior courts.

The new law attacks the problem of bank-loan financing in
an indirect and sporadic way. It requires that cosigners of bank
notes must be listed, but there is no debt-tracking provision for
losing candidates beyond the end of the campaign year. Candidates who win an election are required to file annual year-end
reports only if their committees receive donations or make expenditures. It is doubtful whether this provision would require
the reporting of an unserviced or forgiven debt or the payment
of a loan which was handled as a personal financial obligation
by the candidate or his supporters.

The effort to correct the defects dramatized by the 1974 campaigns was very spotty, and the continuing omissions are equally
glaring: There is still no restriction on contributions by persons
or businesses holding state contracts. Contributors are still not
required to list any information other than name and mailing
address. There is no ceiling on the contributions that any single
individual or group may provide, despite the fact that Busbee
indicated during the campaign that the state should have "an
interest" in limiting the expenditures of wealthy persons like
Lance.

In its sections dealing with Ethics Commission enforcement,
revelation or cosigners, and disclosure by corporations and
political organizations, the law clearly reflects an effort to correct the abuses of the 1974 campaigns. But because these changes
were executed within the framework of the existing statute, the
perpetuation of defects resulting from that law's sloppy construction was assured. Like Georgia's original disclosure law,
this new version represents a compromise between the public
pressure for reform and the political expedients that prevail in
a legislature with only a scant and reactive interest in reform.

NINE

PENNSYLVANIA: THE FAILURE OF
CAMPAIGN REFORM

Gerard J. McCullough

The year 1974 opened in Pennsylvania with both gubernatorial candidates agreeing voluntarily to high standards of conduct in campaign finance, and with the Democratic administration and the G.O.P. leadership in the state House promising
substantive reform of the Election Code. It ended with four
minor changes being made in the code and with Governor Milton J. Shapp testily informing a news conference that persons
holding state contracts would be among those invited to a $500-
a-ticket post-election fund-raiser to pay off more than $300,000
in campaign debts. Why did Pennsylvania fail to respond to the
demands for reform of campaign finance that followed Watergate?

Part of the answer no doubt lies in the political history of the
state. Pennsylvania has had a tradition of questionable campaign fund-raising techniques that began in the 1850's with
Simon Cameron, the state's first great Republican boss. Cameron is credited with developing the "Pennsylvania idea," the
notion that wealthy industrialists who benefited most from
G.O.P. policies should pay the price for political representation.
Cameron's successor, Matthew Quay, ruled the G.O.P. for 30
years from the office of State Treasurer. His contribution was a
technique called "shaking the plum tree"—requiring political
contributions from banks in return for interest-free state deposits. (When Auditor General Robert Casey suggested in 1974

that state deposits be used to aid banks in minority areas, the suggestion was rejected.) Quay's successor, Boise Penrose, whose statue graces the front lawn of the Capitol, is said to have originated the "squeeze bill," a piece of legislation detrimental to a particular industry, usually introduced around election time. A large contribution to the G.O.P. would keep the bill from becoming law. Perhaps the greatest contribution to fund-raising techniques came from Philadelphia contractor Matthew McCloskey, former Treasurer of the Democratic National Committee, who is credited with inventing the $100-a-plate fund-raising dinner in 1934. These dinners broadened the base of political financing to include small businessmen, lawyers, government employees, and others with a vested interest in government.

Another part of the explanation for the failure of reform lies in the fact that, while the Governor and an overwhelming majority of legislators expressed support for various types of campaign reform, there was no serious study of the problem by either executive or legislative branches. The Shapp administration, which had used the study route to explore other important issue areas before drafting legislation, did not do so for campaign reform. The Pennsylvania General Assembly debated partisan proposals at length but did not consider (on the basis of, for example, experience in other states) the impact of those proposals for campaign financing.

And part of the answer lies in the political present in the state. The pressures to retain the traditional system of financing, rooted in the party organizations, turned out to be stronger than those for reform born of the Watergate climate.

The 1937 Election Code

The Pennsylvania Election Code of 1937, the law regulating campaign financing and the objective of proposed changes, is a typically loophole-ridden piece of legislation. It requires that all money must be under the control of the candidate or the treasurer of an authorized committee and prohibits both corporate contributions and—in contrast to most states—direct union donations. Its basic disclosure provisions include the filing of reports that are available for public inspection and that include the names of contributors and the dates and amounts of contributions, as well as a detailed listing of expenditures, with checks or vouchers for those of $10 or more. The weaknesses in the disclosure rules are that reports need be filed only *after* elections (30 days following a primary or general election)

and that neither the addresses nor the occupations of contributors must be listed, making it difficult to trace sources of
money and impossible to gain any information in time for the
vote. While all contributions theoretically must be reported,
in practice ticket purchases to political fund-raisers were exempted as not being actual "contributions."

Administration is in the hands of the politically appointed
commonwealth secretary, a cabinet-level position traditionally
filled by a former state chairperson or other prominent party
official. Enforcement is by local prosecutors and the state attorney general. Failure to file an election expense account is a
violation per se of the Election Code, punishable by a fine of
up to $1,000 or imprisonment up to two years; a successful
candidate cannot be sworn into office until his accounts have
been filed. In addition to these criminal restraints, the public
can file a petition for a court audit of any political expense
accounts within 20 days after the last day for filing. If the audit
shows a violation of the code, the court certifies its decision to
a local district attorney for possible criminal proceedings and
to the state attorney general, who may institute *quo warranto*
proceedings to determine the candidate's title to his office.

Administration and enforcement of this code have been very
lax. The tradition of appointing party officials as commonwealth secretary guarantees a person who understands the practical complexities of the election law, but it does not guarantee
unprejudiced administration. Furthermore, in interpreting the
disclosure provisions of the Election Code, Pennsylvania courts
have uniformly held that inadvertent errors in election expense
accounts do not justify certification of the case for prosecution,
which is considered to be warranted only if it can be shown
that the inaccurate reporting occurred through fraud or corruption. As a result, in the entire 38-year history of the Election
Code, there had not been a single reported criminal prosecution against either a candidate or a political committee for failure to account accurately for campaign-finance activities. Nor
had there been a serious re-examination of the Code until 1973,
when the legislature was prompted to act by the early Watergate disclosures.

The 1973–74 Attempts to Reform the Code

In the spring of 1973, three proposals for reforming campaign
financing were announced in Harrisburg—one in the House,
one in the Senate, and one in the Governor's office. Republican

state Representative Patrick A. Gleason introduced a bill to tighten the Election Code by requiring financial reports before as well as after each election and including the names and addresses of all contributors; limiting general expenditures, media expenditures, and contributions; and providing tax credits of up to $25 for political contributions. State Senator Edward L. Howard, also a Republican, introduced a bill with disclosure and contribution and spending ceilings similar to Gleason's and also including a provision for establishing an independent elections commission to supervise the financing of campaigns. The Governor's package, which he billed "the most comprehensive election-reform legislation program in the Commonwealth's history," was modeled on the Federal Election Campaign Act of 1971. The bill adopted the Federal reporting dates (five annually); provided for limits on general spending, media spending, contributions, and the spending of a candidate's own funds; and left enforcement with the commonwealth secretary but made violations a third-degree felony punishable by fines of up to $10,000 or five years in prison.

The three bills reflected their authors' concern with campaign financing. Gleason and Howard had been among the minority of legislators pushing for new forms of ethics and open-government legislation, including lobbyist-disclosure bills, a "sunshine" law, and a bill to require financial disclosure by legislators. Gleason said that he began working on campaign-finance legislation in 1971, when the Federal act was passed, but his ideas received little support in the House Republican Caucus until 1973, when Watergate made campaign finance a potential election issue, especially for the G.O.P. Howard, a reform-minded Philadelphia suburbanite and banker who financed most of his own 1970 campaign, said the need for reform of election finance was brought to his attention mainly through the national efforts of Common Cause. Howard had read a pamphlet distributed by Common Cause in Harrisburg in 1973, and he asked the state chapter of the organization to draft a model reform bill for him. Shapp's proposal was a direct response to Watergate, according to Lawrence J. Beaser, the Governor's chief counsel, who drafted the law. Beaser said Shapp called him at home one night after becoming upset by the latest disclosures on TV about CREEP and ordered Beaser to draft a strong campaign-finance bill.

The interest in campaign reform evidenced by these three was not shared by many others in the Pennsylvania legislature, however. The Gleason bill, although co-sponsored by 13 Republicans and 2 Democrats, gathered dust for nearly a year in the House State Government Committee, whose Chairman, state Representative Guy A. Kistler, told inquiring reporters that he did not consider campaign-finance laws "an important issue." Howard could not find a single co-sponsor for his reform measure in the 50-member state Senate; when the bill was introduced, it was referred to the Senate State Government Committee and forgotten. And Shapp tried unsuccessfully for eight months to find a single Democratic Senator to sponsor his bill in the upper chamber, which his party controlled. Finally, on January 14, 1974, the Governor's proposal was introduced in the House under the sponsorship of state Representative John P. Murtha, who at the time was running in a special election for a vacant U.S. Congressional seat. The Murtha bill, with 33 Democratic co-sponsors, was also referred to Kistler's committee and dropped from sight.

The failure of all three bills can be attributed largely to the political makeup of the committees considering them and of the houses in which they were introduced. The State Government Committees in both houses are second in power only to the Appropriations Committees and as a result are composed of senior legislative leaders, many from "safe" districts. Such legislators not only have the largest stake in the existing system, but they have the power to resist drives for reform that other legislators may be more susceptible to because of strong constituent pressure (even if they do not personally favor reform). The State Government Committees can thus be seen as a first line of defense against legislation that might make life harder for incumbents.

Sentiment was stronger for campaign reform in the Republican-dominated House than in the Democratically-controlled Senate. Because its members are re-elected every two years, the House tends to be more responsive to public pressure, which was reacting to Watergate. The strong opposition of Chairman Kistler to any form of campaign-finance legislation was not shared by a majority of House members, although his control of the committee handling the Gleason legislation doomed it. The Senate, whose members are elected every four years, is more impervious to constituent pressure. Governor Shapp was also up against a general Democratic belief that because of anti-GOP sentiment caused by Watergate, re-election was assured without making an issue of campaign reform. Most Democratic senators are elected through the party organizations in Philadelphia, Pittsburgh, Scranton, Erie, and Westmoreland

County, industrialized areas where the Democratic nomination is equivalent to election. The Democratic bosses set the slates, and the Senate is usually a reward for long and faithful service as a committeeperson or ward leader. Powerful county chairmen such as Peter J. Camiel in Philadelphia and Leonard Staisey in Pittsburgh were reluctant to experiment with new campaign-finance laws, for the simple reason that the ability to raise funds by the old methods—contributions from payrollers, lawyers, contractors, etc.—is a large component of their control over city politics. Shapp got an income tax bill passed in 1971 by agreeing to let Camiel name the state court judges for Philadelphia, but the Governor apparently was not willing to bargain for his campaign-finance bill.

Senators also generally need more funds than House candidates, because they represent more than four times as many people. Reported costs of running for the Pennsylvania Senate range from $15,000 to $50,000, depending on whether there is a primary; for the House from $5,000 to $10,000. The disparity is due mainly to the costs of mailings, which constitute the major expense of all legislative elections in Pennsylvania and which are deemed necessary whether or not the race is competitive. For most local candidates campaign expenditures are limited to travel and telephone costs, a brochure, a mass mailing, a small amount of advertising in local newspapers, and election-day payments to canvassers and poll watchers.

Thomas F. Lamb, a Democratic state Senator who retired at the end of 1974, explained the Senate's resistance to finance reform this way: "The senators are realistic men who have more experience in practical politics than most House members. They know the difficulties that are involved in raising funds. They know that some people might not want to contribute if they have to be listed by name and address. The senators just weren't willing to put those kinds of restrictions on themselves."

In early 1974 pressures were building to move the campaign-finance bills out of committee and onto the floor for enactment. The two gubernatorial candidates, Shapp and Republican Drew Lewis, both called for reform of the Election Code when they announced their candidacies in January. And the public sentiment for reform, which was likely to affect House members, all of them up for re-election, was growing.

These pressures were most acute in the House G.O.P. Caucus, where increasing numbers of members feared that an anti-Republican tide could sweep them out of office in 1974 as easily as the Nixon landslide had swept them in. "The spillout of Watergate in our party was one of moral outrage and fear of destruction," said House Majority Leader Robert J. Butera later. "As a result, the advocates of reform were catapulted into a position of policy leadership. We were acting from a mixture of good motives and fear." The aim of the House Republican leadership was to pass a campaign-finance reform bill before the legislative recess for the May 21 primary election. This would mean that when the legislature returned in the summer the pressure for reform would be on Shapp and the Democratic-controlled Senate.

The obvious vehicle was the Gleason reform bill, but Butera recognized that it would be difficult to get this bill around committee Kistler and that the Gleason bill was comprehensive enough to raise too many objections from too many members. Kistler was at one end of the spectrum of House sentiment on the issue, representing a minority of House members who were totally opposed to any form of campaign-finance legislation. In the middle of the spectrum were most members, who believed that full disclosure was necessary, but who opposed the concept of limits on contributions or expenditures, and who questioned public financing. At the far end of the spectrum were those who accepted all three basic concepts—disclosure, limits, and public financing. The Gleason proposal addressed itself to all three areas, and thus was certain to meet opposition almost everywhere.

In order to get reform legislation moving, House leader Butera took the matter out of Kistler's hands by dropping the Gleason bill and appointing state Representative Daniel E. Beren, a fellow Montgomery County delegate and one of the most able legislators in the House, to draft a new package of bills. Following low-keyed hearings in five cities, the Beren subcommittee drafted 18 bills aimed at tightening the Election Code's reporting provisions and eliminating questionable financial practices. Key aspects of the bills dealt with:

- Ethics—requiring all companies awarded nonbid state contracts to report annually political contributions from officers, partners, and directors.
- Disclosure—requiring that all candidates and political committees file quarterly reports of campaign debts, that all purchases of tickets in amounts over $100 to political fundraisers be reported, that finance reports, including contributions and expenditures, be filed 15 days before elections and that they contain the full name and mailing address of con-

tributors, that candidates name a single campaign treasurer, that all contributions over $50 be paid by check or money order, that campaign spending records be kept for the length of term of the office involved, and that copies of finance reports be available from the commonwealth secretary at cost rather than the existing $1-per-page charge.

* Enforcement—requiring that the Commonwealth Court of Pennsylvania (the appelate administrative court) conduct random audits of finance reports, that a civil action be established for campaign violations in addition to the criminal action provided for in the 1937 law, and that candidates refusing to comply with reporting laws be barred from taking office.*

After a two-day debate in early May, most of the Beren bills were passed unanimously by the House. Further, an amendment lowering the reporting limit on political ticket purchases to over $25 (from Beren's $100-plus) was adopted. Two controversial amendments introduced on the floor but not incorporated into the bills were provisions for contribution and spending limits and for an independent elections commission, with bipartisan representation, staggered terms, and the power and funds to conduct audits. Commonwealth Secretary C. Delores Tucker, who is also Vice Chairman of the Democratic State Committee, campaigned vigorously against the commission, arguing that one publicly monitored official with statewide jurisdiction would be "a better vehicle for true reform than a commission" since this officer would be more accountable to the public. She noted that there had been no prosecutions for finance violations because the 1937 code did not give the secretary enforcement powers and implied that she would be willing to use the powers of enforcement in a bipartisan manner if they were granted.

The speed and unanimity with which the House acted on Beren's measures led Democratic Representative William Shane to remark on "an unprecedented reformist zeal that I hope will linger until after the May 21 primary." The "reformist zeal"—or increasing nervousness about re-election—did linger in the House as G.O.P. candidates prepared for the general election. In early June the House passed unanimously a bill to place a 15 cents per citizen limit on spending by candidates, to

---

* This was a fine distinction from the prohibition in the 1937 law against the swearing into office of those who have failed to file accounts.

limit individual contributions to 10 percent of this ceiling, and to establish an independent election commission—measures that had been passed over before the primary.

But the House's zeal did not carry through the halls of the Capitol to the state Senate. On the same day that the House passed these measures, the Senate State Government Committee was dismantling the Beren bills. The committee flatly rejected the bill that would have required campaign-finance records to be kept for the tenure of office—that is, four years for the senators—preferring the 1937 law's two-year requirement. In other action, the committee struck down the House amendment requiring reporting of ticket purchases in excess of $25 to political fund-raisers and restored the anonymity of $100-a-plate dinners by requiring reports only for purchases of more than $100. The Senators also deleted a provision requiring the pre-election disclosure of campaign expenditures, but retained disclosure of contributions 15 days before the election.

Most of the other bills were simply never reported out of committee. Democratic Senator Lamb announced to the press that only those bills the State Government Committee expected to be passed would be sent to the Senate floor. The Governor, meanwhile, declared in press conferences that his administration was pushing for even stronger measures than those passed by the House—measures based upon Shapp's own campaign-finance proposals, which had first been announced in 1973 and introduced in the House (but not the Senate) in January 1974. When asked why his bill was not being pressed in the Senate, Shapp stated that the strategy of his administration was to amend the Beren bills in the Senate State Government Committee on the basis of his own measure. Lamb, however, disputed Shapp's statements, saying that he had never been approached by Shapp, that the Senate Democratic leadership had never agreed to incorporate the Governor's measure onto the House bill, and that this was not in fact being done.

When the full Senate voted on July 10, five of the measures were passed unanimously and sent to the Governor's desk. A sixth measure, the key bill calling for finance reports to be submitted both before and after elections, was also passed but with a significant amendment, which—passed by a voice vote with lightning speed—eliminated a reqiurement in the 1937 Election Code that vouchers be filed for all expenditures of more than $10. The effect of the Senate amendment was to weaken the reporting provisions of the code and to return the pre-election disclosure bill to the House for concurrence, thus eliminating the possibility that the measure would be voted on again prior to the election.

The provisions for spending and contribution limits had been buried in committee, and one of the bills passed by the Senate, requiring reporting of the names of those who gave more than $100 to political fund-raisers, was vetoed by Governor Shapp. Shapp argued that the existing Election Code already requiring the reporting of all contributions, including ticket purchases of $100 or less—failing to mention that the Code was ambiguous with respect to the ticket purchases to political fund-raisers, or that his own election bill, which he continued to say he was working for, would have exempted from reporting requirements ticket purchases of less than $200.

The net effect of the two-year struggle to reform the Pennsylvania Election Code was the signing into law of four minor bills requiring:

- That firms holding nonbid contracts with the state annually report the political contributions of their top officials.
- That a candidate designate a single treasurer to handle the funds of all committees set up to promote his candidacy.
- That candidates who refuse to comply with campaign reporting laws be barred from taking office.
- That the commonwealth secretary's office make copies of finance reports available at cost.

The first two measures represented small but significant steps in improving the state's disclosure laws, but the bills left unplugged gaping holes in the 1937 code. Candidates are still required to report only once, 30 days after the election. There are no new provisions for enforcement, which has been very ineffective.

Democratic Fund-Raising in the 1974 Governor's Race

The campaign-finance reform legislation that was being considered in the legislature affected the conduct of the governor's race. Milton Shapp's bill was about to be introduced in the Pennsylvania House (thence to fade into legislative oblivion) when the Governor announced his re-election fund-raising drive on January 11, 1974. Shapp promised that his campaign committee, which would also raise money for Lieutenant Governor Ernest P. Kline, would abide by the provisions of the Governor's bill, including Federal reporting dates (March,

June, and September 10, 10 days before an election, and January 31), spending limits amounting to $1.2 million each for primary and general elections, media spending at 80 percent of the limit, contribution limits of 5 percent of the total ceiling, and limits of 25 percent of the ceiling for use of a candidate's own funds. The only variation from his bill in Shapp's own campaign was that he promised to limit individual contributions to $5,000, rather than the $60,000 (5 percent of $1.2 million) allowed in his bill. Shapp's opponent also announced a program of voluntary disclosure, while differing with some of the incumbent's self-imposed rules.

Shapp declared at the outset of his campaign that "fund-raising will be extremely difficult this year because of the bad connotations connected to the national misuse of funds during the 1972 Nixon campaign." As an antidote the Governor proposed to keep his own campaign spending to an "absolute minimum" and to make every effort "to collect contributions at the grass-roots level from average citizens with no vested interest beyond an interest in good state government." He was more successful with the first goal than with the second.

Shapp's spending in 1974, while hardly an "absolute minimum," was just over half of what he had spent to get elected in 1970 and little more than a third of his reported spending in 1966, when he first made—and lost—the race for governor. Shapp, then a wealthy electronics manufacturer, spent $3.8 million of his own money in 1966, and in 1970 another $2.7 million, most of it his own; but in 1974 total spending for the Shapp-Kline committee was $1,459,527 (none of it Shapp's own). Shapp had only token opposition in the primary (from state Representative Martin P. Mullen, a morality candidate who chastised the Governor for vetoing antipornography and anti-abortion legislation) and spent under $300,000 of his total before that election. His spending for the general election was thus close to the $1.2 million limit in his bill.

The Shapp-Kline committee's main effort to limit spending was to shorten the length of the traditional pre-election media blitz. Radio advertising (costing $17,000) began only three weeks before the general election and television advertising (at $149,000) two weeks prior to the voting. Another $66,000 was spent for billboards. Richard A. Doran, the Governor's executive assistant and chief political strategist, who had also been active in Shapp's big-spending 1966 and 1970 campaigns, said he was "ruthless" in eliminating unnecessary expenditures, in part because "People can spin out of control when you have to raise so much money for an election. I decided early in the campaign that I would rather decrease expenditures than let the fund-raising get out of control."

As an incumbent with high popularity, Shapp could afford to limit spending. His major political achievement in three years as Governor had been to consolidate the diverse elements of the Democratic Party into an effective mechanism for re-election. There were natural ties between the Governor, a program-oriented activist who had entered politics with the election of President Kennedy, and the liberals who had been his earliest supporters. Shapp also strengthened his ties with organized labor by cooperating with the A.F.L.-C.I.O.'s efforts to win improved unemployment and workmen's compensation benefits. And he nailed down his position as an undisputed boss of the statewide Democratic organization by installing his own man, Dennis E. (Harvey) Thiemann, as state Democratic Chairman and by giving local Democratic leaders in Philadelphia, Pittsburgh, and Scranton much power over state patronage. Thus Shapp emerged in 1974 as a candidate for re-election with the strong support of the liberal Americans for Democratic Action, the state A.F.L.-C.I.O., and all 67 Democratic county chairmen.

He was aided immensely by his role in settling a nationwide strike by independent truckers in early February. While the Nixon Administration remained paralyzed by Watergate, Governor Shapp was the only high-ranking official with the initiative to meet with the truckers, who had made a truck stop on Interstate 80 in Pennsylvania their strike headquarters. Shapp won the truckers' trust and then went to Washington, where he worked out an agreement on diesel prices and freight rates that ended the shutdown. As a result of his handling of the strike, Shapp's popularity reached an all-time high. A March poll conducted for him by Cambridge Survey Research, Inc. showed that 64 percent of the voters (including 49 percent of the Republicans) gave Shapp a "favorable" job rating—the highest given at the time to any statewide or national figure. (Before the strike, Shapp's favorable rating had hovered between 36 percent and 42 percent.) It also showed a 56–23 percent lead over his rival. On the basis of this poll, Doran mapped out the Shapp campaign as a low-keyed, low-budget affair, relying on traditional Democratic support and stressing the Governor's achievements as a "proven leader."

The Shapp-Kline committee had less success in carrying out the Governor's promise to "collect contributions at the grass-

roots level" than it did with keeping spending down. While
Shapp himself disliked raising money (and hadn't had to do so
in his previous campaigns, when he used his own), he did establish a well-coordinated fund-raising effort. It was headed by one
of his most trusted political associates, former state Secretary
of Revenue Robert P. Kane, and assisted by another Shapp
veteran, Nancy Mawby, who had been active in the fund-
raising operations of the Democratic State Committee. There
were a number of early efforts to stimulate grass-roots contributions, including direct-mail and telephone solicitation using
the fund-raising lists of the 1972, 1973, and 1974 Democratic
telethons. "We tried it early in the campaign when we were
fresh and had a lot of energy," Nancy Mawby said. "None were
very successful. We even tried soliciting door to door in Allentown, but we raised only about $300. The key problem was a
lack of manpower." Ultimately, the committee relied on large
transfers and large contributions of $500 or more for nearly
70 percent of the money it raised.

While Shapp's incumbency and popularity could have helped
him gain the small, individual contributions he said he wanted,
it simultaneously insured the availability of the large donations
that were the basis of his campaign chest. Cabinet members,
other high-ranking state officials, and a handful of wealthy
businessmen formed the core of financial support for Shapp.
Although Pennsylvania is one of the few states where it is illegal
for labor unions to contribute directly to political candidates
or committees, there was no lack of contributions from union
"political education" committees.

Of the $340,728 raised in the three and a half months before
the primary, $35,100 came in large transfers from business and
labor organizations and from other political committees; $148,-
100 came in large contributions ($500 or more) from individ-
uals; and another $25,000 came as a personal loan from Jack
I. Greenblat, an Allentown businessman appointed by the
Governor to the State Tax Equalization Board. The amount
raised in contributions of less than $500 was $132,528. Of the
$845,023 raised between the primary and the general election,
$300,000 came in the form of transfers from committees and
$236,674 in individual contributions of over $500; the amount
raised from smaller contributions was $235,984.

Shapp tried to establish the integrity of his campaign, and
his administration, in part through provisions in a three-page
code of conduct issued in January for all campaign staff and
volunteers. One provision of the code was that "contributions

made to this campaign in any amount will be accepted only with the understanding that they imply no commitments or favorable treatment of any sort from this administration"; another stated that "No state employee's job will be placed in jeopardy because a political contribution is or is not made." There was no evidence during the campaign that the Shapp-Kline committee aggressively sought funds from state employees or from persons with a financial stake in the operations of state government. But there were a number of contributions from persons doing business with the state and at least 50 donations of $200 or more from middle-level state officials. Lawyers and law firms, some holding bond-counsel contracts with the state, dominated the list of larger contributors, which included at least two dozen architects and engineers, a leasing firm, Harrisburg lobbyists, an excavating firm, an auto supply firm, a demolition firm, and about three dozen building and service contractors.

The full scope and character of the Governor's fund-raising operations cannot be understood by looking only at the Shapp-Kline committee, however. Before the campaign, an agreement was reached among Robert Kane, Shapp's chief fund-raiser, Sam Begler, the Governor's patronage chief and long-time political operative in Pittsburgh, and Harvey Thiemann, the Governor's hand-picked state chairman, that there would be three separate fund-raising operations in 1974. The Shapp-Kline committee would conduct its activities, as would the Democratic State Committee, while Begler would establish his own operation for Shapp in Allegheny County (Pittsburgh). It was further agreed that the committee would not solicit contributions from rank-and-file state employees, but that the Democratic State Committee would be free to do so. During the campaign the Democratic State Committee transferred $300,000 to the Shapp-Kline committee, and Begler's organization, called Allegheny County Pennsylvanians for Shapp-Kline, provided $20,000 to Shapp-Kline and $20,000 to the Democratic State Committee. (It also provided manpower and walking-around money for election day.) The effect of the agreement was to provide the Shapp campaign with one "up-front" organization, identified with the Governor and operating under strict disclosure requirements, and two less visible and more traditionally oriented fund-raising operations.

Serious questions were raised about the Democratic State Committee's handling of government employees when its treasurer, William R. Casper, was indicted in the summer of 1974 by a Butler County grand jury on 24 charges of macing, criminal conspiracy, and criminal solicitation. Casper, though under indictment and later convicted in a trial that began in early 1975, continued to serve as the chief fund-raiser for the state committee and as Butler County Democratic Chairman. Witnesses at Casper's trial testified that he had met with state officials in the Butler County highway shed prior to the 1974 election and ordered them to extract contributions from state employees. Foremen and equipment operators were assessed $120 (with $20 going to the county and $100 to the state), while laborers contributed $60 ($20 to the county and $40 to the state); contractors who leased snow-removal equipment to the state paid an average of $100 per machine. This was considered to be common practice, but one that had never before been proven. During the election campaign, Shapp and Democratic State Chairman Thiemann defended Casper's continuance in his posts, arguing that he had not been proven guilty.

In any case, the Casper incident—the details of which did not become clear until after the election—was a minor event in comparison with a Republican assault on Shapp's integrity as Governor and as a candidate in 1970. The forum for these charges was a six-month investigation by a Select Committee on Contract Practices, chaired by Representative Gleason, one of the original authors of the Republican campaign-finance bills. Two investigative attorneys from the staff of former Philadelphia District Attorney Arlen Specter were hired by the Republicans to conduct the committee investigation and were provided with the full resources of the G.O.P. staff in the House. Their inquiry formed the basis of public hearings which began in the summer of 1974 and continued through October, climaxing with a pre-election appearance by the Governor himself on October 7.

The Gleason hearings followed a series of committee investigations on alleged corruption in the Shapp administration during the previous two years (1973–74), when the Republicans controlled the House. During these years, a House Liquor Control Committee investigated Shapp's appointees to the Liquor Control Board and found evidence of political favoritism. A Select Committee on the Administration of Justice investigated a wiretapping incident that had led to the firing of two Shapp cabinet members. The House Consumer Protection Committee questioned the state Insurance Department's handling of a case involving a financially troubled Pittsburgh firm with indirect ties to Shapp. These hearings raised questions about the integrity of Shapp's administration, but never produced a major scandal or touched the Governor directly.

The Gleason hearings, which were widely publicized, similarly failed to prove any outright corruption and never got close to the Governor. Their main allegation was that a close associate of Shapp, Frank C. Hilton, who had directed the Governor's 1970 campaign and was later appointed state Secretary of Property and Supplies, had received a large kickback from a Pittsburgh man in return for designating him as broker on a state insurance contract. The committee criticized Shapp for failing to act on the matter until September, when Hilton was called to testify before a Federal grand jury in Pittsburgh. (Hilton was later indicted.) Shapp defended the delay, stating that Hilton had lied to him and the press about the matter.

While the Gleason committee unearthed some interesting facts about the repayment of Shapp's 1970 campaign debt, it could prove no criminal wrongdoing. One subject of inquiry was a committee organized after the election to retire an estimated $1,675,000 borrowed by Shapp and his wife to finance the campaign. It is a normal practice for such post-election fund-raising efforts to be handled by the Democratic or Republican state committees, which operate year in and year out and which are required to file annual financial reports with the state; other political committees are required only to report 30 days after an election in which they participate. As Shapp's committee, called Pennsylvanians for Progress, was a candidate rather than a permanent committee, it was not required to (and did not) file any reports. The provision in the Beren bills for quarterly reports on campaign debts was addressed to closing just such a loophole.

A second aspect of Shapp's debt-repayment explored by the Gleason hearings was that large contributions were received through post-election "victory" dinners from law firms, architects, engineers, and contractors doing business with the state. But although the receipt of large quantities of funds from some firms was documented, the Gleason committee failed to present evidence of criminal extortion. Shapp himself, testifying before the committee, noted that "it was 1970 and we followed the practices of 1970."

Despite their direct focus on Shapp's integrity and that of his administration, the Gleason hearings probably did the Governor little harm with the electorate as a whole. While perhaps losing him votes in some parts of the state, they may have gained him support in others, particularly the sophisticated Philadel-

phia area. After six months of inquiry before the public television cameras, including testimony by the personable and
popular Shapp, Gleason couldn't come up with much to discredit the Governor.

Financing the Republican Challenge

Shapp's Republican opponent, Drew Lewis, permitted Gleason to do the dirty work of attacking the Governor and his
record, while he concentrated instead on projecting a positive
image and running a typically post-Watergate campaign—at
least most of the time. As a challenger, he also had to spend
more time raising money.

Lewis agreed with Shapp at the outset on the ground rules
by which they would conduct their campaigns. Though their
reporting dates were different (Lewis said he would make
monthly reports), both agreed voluntarily to essentially the
same disclosure provisions—to make a full accounting of all
contributions (by name, address, and amount) available to the
news media prior to the election. Lewis would not accept
Shapp's proposal that individual contributions be limited to
$5,000 or that total spending be limited to $2.4 million, however, calling the latter an "incumbent's protection act." And
Shapp did not accept the Lewis proposal that individuals contributing more than $3,000 to a gubernatorial candidate be
prohibited from receiving nonbid contracts with the state.
Lewis, who also called for reform of the Election Code, stipulated that he would accept no cash contributions of more than
$50 and that he would identify large contributors by specific
occupation and very large contributors by their major holdings.
After the election, he said that by following these guidelines
rigorously he had eliminated the "$5,000 to $20,000 cash contributions, the ones that get you into trouble." He had also
run a very different campaign than he probably would have in
previous years.

Perhaps never before in the history of Pennsylvania Republican politics has a candidate emerged more likely to succeed at
financing a gubernatorial campaign. A 42-year-old business executive, Drew Lewis, had built his statewide political reputation
on his skills as the Pennsylvania G.O.P.'s top fund-raiser, a
"key man with access" who had bailed the party out of a $600,-
000 debt in 1972. When he was managing Congressman Richard S. Schweiker's race for the U.S. Senate in 1968, Lewis had
recognized that the perennial debt of the Republican State

Committee made the financing of a statewide campaign a night-mare. In 1970, when Lewis decided that he would like to run for governor, he chose to become active in the financial affairs of the state committee rather than seek the state chairmanship, reasoning that the chairmanship would only involve him in factional disputes, while the prerequisite for a successful 1974 campaign was a debt-free state organization.

A Harvard M.B.A. who at 40 was named President of Snelling and Snelling, the world's largest employment agency, Lewis spent three years dissolving the Republican debt. As Chairman of the Republican Finance Committee, he revamped the accounting procedure, installed new personnel, and dreamed up novel ways of encouraging contributions. (One very successful technique was to ask potential contributors to "sponsor" portions of the debt by writing checks to the committee for the exact amount of certain outstanding bills. When the bills were paid, the contributors received a letter of thanks and a copy of the receipts.) By 1973 the Republican State Committee was operating in the black for the first time in seven years.

Lewis had won the respect of many county leaders and the friendship of industrialists and bankers who formed the financial backbone of the party. But this did not assure him the Republican nomination in 1974. Traditionally the candidate for governor had been chosen by a small group of old-line Republican county chairmen representing large voting blocs in the eastern and western portions of the state, and these men were backing other candidates. Lewis recognized that he would have to execute a flanking movement around the G.O.P. bosses in order to get the endorsement of the 136-member state committee at its annual meeting in February 1974. Using his chairmanship of the Finance Committee as a vehicle, he took to the road in early 1973 and made appearances around the state in a dual role—to raise money for the Republican State Committee and to win the G.O.P. nomination without the support of the bosses.

To finance his year-long pursuit, he established a special committee called the Friends of Drew Lewis, operated by campaign strategist Rich Robb from an office at Snelling and Snelling. In the 13-month period between December 22, 1972, and January 28, 1974, when Lewis formally announced his candidacy, the Friends of Drew Lewis and Montgomery County (suburban Philadelphia) Republican Committee spent a total of $143,423 promoting Lewis. Montgomery is Lewis's home county and he has been the man behind the scenes in the county G.O.P., especially as a fund-raiser, for many years. The bulk of the money ($123,867) was raised by the Friends, most of it in $500 and $1,000 contributions from Lewis's personal friends in the Philadelphia area and from wealthy Republicans in Pittsburgh. Expenditures by the Friends committee included salary and expenses for Robb ($30,240) and consulting and production fees ($25,887) to media consultant Roger Ailes, the man credited by Joe McGinnis in *The Selling of the President* with remaking Richard Nixon's image for the 1968 campaign.

Most of the remaining money went toward a $100,000 advertising campaign scheduled to coincide with Lewis's formal announcement in January. The campaign's original aim was to build name identification for Lewis and to scare off potential Republican challengers. But as it turned out, anyway, Lewis's Republican rivals all dropped out of the race for various reasons, and three months later Lewis, unopposed, won the state committee endorsement by acclamation. By that time, he had already dissolved the Friends committee, established a full-time fund-raising operation called Lewis for Governor, and set his sights on Milton J. Shapp.

The task of defeating the Governor in the wake of the truckers' strike and Watergate, was not going to be easy. Although most Republicans were certain in January 1973, when the Friends committee was organized, that the man who won their endorsement would be the next governor, and polls that month bore them out, a Market Opinion Research poll taken in March 1974 gave Shapp a 60 percent to 20 percent lead over Lewis and found that only 19 percent of those polled recognized Lewis's name. In addition, Shapp enjoyed a Democratic registration margin of more than 300,000, control of the state Democratic fund-raising apparatus, a patronage payroll of 28,118, and a $900,000-a-year state government publicity network.

Lewis's major problem was to offset the low recognition factor that plagued him even more than his Republicanism. He gambled that nine intensive months of television could translate his fresh image, his lack of a political record (a plus in 1974), and his calls for governmental integrity and good management into enough votes to upset Shapp. He recognized that it was impossible to raise enough money (estimated at over $5 million) to buy nine months worth of television, and moreover that direct advertising was not the way to convince the voters that he was a candidate of substance. Television news, he reasoned, was the source of the public's political evaluations and decisions.

Building his campaign strategy on this hypothesis, Lewis divided the state into six campaign areas, corresponding exactly to the six major television markets in the state: Philadelphia in the east, Pittsburgh in the west, Erie in the northwest, Scranton–Wilkes-Barre in the northeast, Johnstown-Altoona in south-central Pennsylvania, and Lancaster-Harrisburg in central Pennsylvania. He then drew up a campaign itinerary that enabled him to spend one day a week in each of these areas. The usual format was an airport press conference, followed, if possible, by trips to the local television stations. The rest of the day was devoted, in descending order of priority, to newspaper and editorial meetings, Lewis for Governor fund-raising, meetings with Lewis workers, Republican fund-raising events, and person-to-person contacts and speeches.

According to the Lewis timetable, the day of campaigning was judged a success if the local television news cameramen showed up at the airport in the morning. Lewis was 100 percent successful for nine straight months in five of the six television market areas, Robb said later. But in Philadelphia—which includes the vote-rich, heavily Republican suburban counties of Montgomery, Delaware, and Chester—Lewis was less than 30 percent successful.

To supplement his free appearances on radio and television news shows, Lewis bought about $1 million worth of media advertising. And to pay for advertising and the $50,000-a-month operating expenses of the campaign committee, Lewis conducted an ambitious and sophisticated fund-raising operation based at the Republican State Committee headquarters in Harrisburg. Lewis himself concentrated on the large contributors, devoting one full campaign day a week (Tuesdays) to shaking the money tree. The staff at the Republican State Committee, which he had organized during his tenure as Finance Chairman, was responsible for grass-roots fund-raising.

On balance, the fund-raising efforts of the Lewis campaign must be judged a limited success. Lewis said after the campaign that there was "ample money" to support his committee's activities and to buy advertising. Total campaign expenditures by the Lewis for Governor Committee and the Republican State Committee in 1974 were about $2.3 million, a figure adjusted to take into account the frequent transfers between the Lewis committee and the various fund-raising organs of the state committee. The Lewis committee itself reported spending only $1.2 million, but most of the money raised by the state committee and its various fund-raising organs was also used to promote the Lewis candidacy. The funds came from both traditional and nontraditional sources.

Absent from the lists of contributors to the Lewis campaign were architects, engineers, bond counsel, builders, service contractors, and other vested-interest givers who normally hedge their bets by contributing heavily to both party candidates in a gubernatorial election. To a certain extent, Lewis had preempted such contributions by seeking the nomination against the wishes of the old-line Republican leaders. Though out of power in Harrisburg, the party still had access to such money through the control powerful Republicans exercised over the state Public Utility Commission and the state Turnpike Commission, but these leaders did not use their financial influence in the 1974 gubernatorial campaign. Another factor in the absence of such contributions was apparently Lewis's conscientious effort not to ruin his political reputation by tying himself up with what he considered to be questionable sources of political money.

In keeping with the candidate's self-imposed regulations and announced commitment to electoral reform, the Lewis campaign made a noteworthy effort to broaden the base of his financial support. In the ten-month period between January 1974 and the November election, the Republican State Committee sent out more than a million pieces of mail soliciting funds for itself and the Lewis for Governor Committee. This large and unprecedented direct mail solicitation raised $336,920, with an average contribution of $22.53.

Probably more impressive than the amounts raised, however, were the direct-mail techniques devised by William A. Murray, a professional fund-raiser recruited by Lewis in 1973 to work full-time for the Republican Finance Committee after 18 years of experience as a direct mail fund-raiser with the Boy Scouts of America. Murray and his assistant, John M. Woznisky, another former Boy Scout fund-raiser who later became Executive Director of the Republican State Committee, did a considerable amount of experimenting with different combinations of fund-raising lists to come up with a good base of contributors. Murray reasoned (correctly, it turned out) that those most likely to send mail contributions to a Republican candidate were not necessarily registered G.O.P. voters but those who were in the habit of buying things by mail. To test this hypothesis, Murray worked with about two dozen purchased mail-order lists—including Ruby Red Grapefruit (a mail-order produce firm), Mark Cross writing instruments, *Holiday* Magazine, and Boyds

City Dispatch (a personal-property listing)—which were "wedded together" by Murray with lists of traditional Republican contributors and G.O.P. registration lists in selected counties. The mailings were carefully charted, and there was an effort to follow up each with telephone solicitation. Murray, who now works as a consultant to the Republican National Committee, said after the election: "There weren't too many state committees going in the direction that we did with direct mail. It is incredible how far behind they are. Our only problem was that you can't really do this kind of testing effectively during the election year. But until Drew became better known as a Republican candidate we couldn't really give people a reason to contribute."

On the traditional side, large individual contributions and loans from wealthy and socially prominent Republicans accounted for about half of the money raised in the election year. Individual contributions of $500 or more totaled nearly $500,-000, while loans accounted for almost $600,000. The biggest gift contributions came from Richard Mellon Scaife ($42,500), Fitz Eugene Dixon, Jr. ($21,000), and John T. Dorrance, Jr., Chairman of the Board of Campbell Soup Company ($17,500). Scaife, 42, an heir to the Mellon banking, oil, and industrial fortune, had served as Treasurer for the 1972 Committee to Re-elect President Nixon in Pennsylvania, and was best known for having contributed $1 million to Nixon, using 332 checks for $3,000 each and 2 checks for $2,000 each. Dixon, 50, of Lafayette Hill, an heir to the Widener family fortune, was a well-known socialite who maintained racing stables and owned 25 percent of the Philadelphia Flyers.

Some large donations were made through standing Republican county committees authorized by Lewis in filings with the commonwealth secretary to raise money on behalf of his candidacy in order to avoid the Federal gift tax on contributions of more than $3,000 to any one committee. Campaign finance records voluntarily submitted to the press showed that some $155,-200 in large contributions made their way to Lewis through these local committees; for instance, his three biggest donors—Scaife, Dixon, and Dorrance—wrote checks of $2,500 and $3,000 to more than a score of different county committees. Money from the committees was usually transferred to the Lewis for Governor organization, although sometimes the local committee spent money directly for Lewis. All transfers were reported voluntarily by the candidate. A handful of other Lewis committees were also used to avoid the gift tax. In one of the more humorous episodes of the campaign, former Republican Congressman John H. Ware, a 66-year-old utility executive, wrote checks of $1,000 each to the Young Pennsylvanians for Drew Lewis Committee and the Concerned Elderly Citizens for Drew Lewis for Governor Committee.

In June, Shapp's campaign manager, Kane, charged that the "indirect contributions" from the county committees "hint at the possible laundering practice which is arising from the investigation of Watergate." William R. Dimeling, Lewis's counsel, argued that the use of county committees as a tax shelter was actually an improvement over past statewide campaigns in which a large number of "phoney" committees were formed to handle large contributions. "What we were trying to do by using the existing county Republican committees was to provide a more accurate and established means of accounting for the big money," said Dimeling. "Administratively, it was a pain in the neck to use the small committees, but Drew felt it was the more open way to go about it."

Potentially much more controversial and damaging to Lewis's reform candidacy was the revelation by the press that Lewis had received loans totaling half a million dollars from Scaife and Dixon. At the beginning of October, Drew Lewis received a telephone call from *Philadelphia Bulletin* reporter Joseph R. Daughen, asking him to explain where his committee got enough money in September to reserve some $500,000 worth of television advertising for the fall campaign. Daughen had been studying the monthly financial reports of the Lewis for Governor Committee and had concluded that there wasn't enough cash on hand to put the money up front for that much television time.

The answer to Daughen's question was simple but potentially damaging to Lewis, who was attempting to escape the stigma of Watergate by basing his campaign on the themes of openness, independence, and integrity. In early September, faced with an almost total lack of campaign money, Lewis had arranged loans of $250,000 apiece from Dixon and Scaife. The details of the loans had been worked out by state Senator Richard Frame, the G.O.P. state chairman, and the money had gone indirectly to Lewis's campaign through a special committee called the G.O.P. Media Account, which paid for the advertising.

Dixon and Scaife had accepted as collateral a written pledge that they would have first call upon the net proceeds of three planned G.O.P. fund-raising dinners in October. The loan agreements stipulated that the dinner proceeds be divided "immediately" into two equal shares and—together with interest calculated at an annual 14 percent—turned over to Dixon and Scaife within 20 days. If the full amounts were not paid off within 20 days of the last dinner, the agreement provided that half the outstanding balance and interest be paid by November 30, and the final balance by December 31. In the event of a default, the state committee would also be obligated to pay attorneys' fees of 5 percent of the amount in default.

As aware as Lewis was of the possible impact that publicity about the two huge loans could have on his image, he was equally aware of the danger involved in trying to keep the loans from the news media until 30 days after the election, when the Election Code would require a full accounting by all of Lewis's political committees. Lewis had planned to disclose the loans on October 20, the next scheduled date for his voluntary monthly financial statement and 17 days before the election. Disclosure on that date would fulfill his promise to the news media but would not give Shapp time to prepare advertising that could make the Republican candidate's dependence on G.O.P. fat cats—especially a former Nixon fat cat—into a campaign issue.

Daughen's questioning changed the timetable. Lewis and Robb agreed early on October 5 to provide Daughen with full details of the loan by arranging a meeting in Harrisburg between the reporter and Frame. When the Daughen story ran Wednesday, October 9, on the front page of the *Bulletin* and was subsequently sent across the state by the A.P. and U.P.I., Lewis was ready with his answer. Fund-raising had been one of the major problems in his campaign, he told reporters, and the drying up of contributions in the post-Watergate atmosphere had forced him to turn to large contributors. "Either I take the heat for large contributions, or I don't have a campaign, so I take the heat," he said. Lewis also declared that it wasn't the size of a contribution that mattered, but the motives of the giver. He said that several persons who contributed to Shapp's campaign had received lucrative contracts from the state. "What can I do for Scaife? He doesn't need anything from me or the government," he said.

The effect of the revelation about the bank loans was difficult to assess. The press generally accepted Lewis's explanation, and a poll conducted after the election showed that Lewis had made a favorable impression on 62 percent of the voters and an unfavorable impression on only 15 percent; only 1 percent of the objectors mentioned the bank loans. But the same poll tallied the composition of the state electorate at 40 percent core Democratic and only 23 percent core Republican, and concluded that the principal objection to G.O.P. candidates was their identification with big business.

A more serious problem in Lewis's campaign was that he failed to generate an issue, a reason to replace the incumbent with him. He criticized Shapp's increased spending as Governor and lack of improvement of basic services, but these traditional Republican charges never caught fire with the electorate. As for charges that the Shapp administration was a corrupt one, those were left to the Gleason committee and to the candidate for lieutenant governor, House Speaker Kenneth B. Lee.

Lewis's carefully planned media strategy also had a fatal flaw, perhaps not unrelated to the lack of issues in the campaign. He lost in the five-county Philadelphia area, which Shapp won by a 225,000-vote margin. (Shapp, as expected, took the city by almost that much, while Lewis carried two of the neighboring Republican counties by narrow margins and lost two others, one also normally Republican.) And it was there that Lewis fell short in coverage on the local newscasts, as he was never able to convince either the Philadelphia news media or the suburban electorate that he was a candidate of substance offering a meaningful alternative to Shapp. Lewis lost the election by 300,000 votes overall, with 46 percent of the vote to Shapp's 54 percent. His media strategy—devoting both campaign time and his advertising budget to television—had to be judged a general success, as it helped familiarize voters with his name, which only 9 percent of the people recognized in January 1973; and despite Watergate, Lewis carried 39 of the state's 67 counties and made serious inroads into traditional Democratic strongholds in the western part of the state. Defeating an incumbent is indeed a difficult proposition.

Reform—Rhetoric and Reality

Despite the rhetoric of reform and commitment to disclosure, the money sources for the 1974 election weren't all that different than in the past. In richer Republican times, Drew Lewis, a successful fund-raiser could have raised more than he did. His direct-mail campaign tapped new sources and his openness probably eliminated others, but he still managed to collect over $2 million altogether, mostly from wealthy individuals, and to spend $1 million for media. And Shapp turned to traditional vested-interest givers to provide the money to counter Lewis's media offensive. Shapp didn't need his own money this time. "Running for the U.S. Senate is a rich man's game because you have little patronage and no contracts to give out," said one Democratic strategist. "But running for governor is an entirely different story. A governor controls a $4 billion annual budget and has hundreds of jobs to dispense. There are lots of people who want a piece of that action. If you're a really viable candidate for governor you can literally stand on the street corner and people will come up and put money in your pocket."

The very limited changes in Pennsylvania's Election Code suggest that the next election may be no more "reformed" than this one—maybe less so, once Watergate fades into memory. For the relative openness of the 1974 campaign was a result of voluntary disclosure by the candidates, not state requirements for reporting of contributions and expenditures before the election. The rules on the books are still the unenforced and virtually unenforceable ones of the 1937 code. The failure of the state Senate to pass any but the most minimal measures sent to it by the House, and the lack of commitment of the Shapp administration to pass its own measures, despite repeated declarations, are testimony to the strength of the state's entrenched political organizations, with their vested interest in the status quo.

TEN

OHIO: A TALE OF
TWO PARTIES

Brian T. Usher

Shortly after midnight of election day 1974, Republican James A. Rhodes called a press conference in a Columbus hotel to concede his "defeat" at the hands of Governor John J. Gilligan. Believing that he had failed in his comeback bid for a third term as governor, the 65-year-old Rhodes went to bed as an apparent retiree from Ohio politics. A few hours later, a happy aide woke Rhodes to tell him he had won after all by a slim 11,000-vote margin.

Dan Rather of the CBS network was telling the nation it was the greatest gubernatorial upset in the country that year. From the standpoint of campaign-finance reformers, it was not only an upset but an ironic triumph of the admittedly old politics over the self-professed new politics. In the post-Watergate atmosphere of heightened interest in political money, the liberal Democrat Gilligan ran as a champion of campaign reform and said he had "disclosed every dime" given to his campaign. But Ohio voters turned to Rhodes, who had ducked the reform issue in 1974 and had flirted for years with the edges of the campaign-finance law.

Ohio is not like other major industrial states. Ohio, John Gunther wrote, "basically ... is nothing more or less than a giant carpet of agriculture studded by great cities." Ohio has no Chicago, no New York City, no Detroit to dominate her. About three-quarters of the state's nearly 11 million people are grouped in 9 major urban enclaves—including troubled Cleveland, aging Cincinnati, white-collar Columbus, brawny Toledo, progressive Dayton, and rubber-based Akron—and scores of medium-sized cities; the rest live in rural areas. The state's people are oriented geographically to three different great U.S. regions—the East, the Midwest, and the South—and this fragmentation has had a fundamental effect on Ohio politics and political finance: Republicans have been much more adept historically in overcoming geographic barriers to build a statewide party and coordinated finance system, while Democrats have been bogged down in rivalries among their city empires. This is a basic reason why Republicans have dominated Ohio politics for the better part of two decades.* Democrats, although fielding winning "personalities" at times, had failed to finance a strong statewide party until Governor John Gilligan began to do it for four years after his election in 1970.

The State Parties

Almost thirty years ago, under party patriarch and former G.O.P. National Chairman Ray Bliss of Akron, Ohio Republicans established a strong centralized method of raising funds that has been copied and envied by parties in other states. The center of the system is the Republican Finance Committee, which is established by, but separate from, the party's major ruling body, the Executive Committee. Counterpart finance committees in the state's 88 counties are selected by county executive committees. All money solicited by these committees first goes to the state committee in Columbus, which keeps half for operating expenses (to run state headquarters and provide services to local candidates and organizations) and returns half to the executive committee in the county where it was raised. In this way the state party's health is not dependent on the whims of local county chairmen; instead, the local leaders rely on the strong central party with its sophisticated political services. The annual operating budget for state headquarters ranges from $500,000 to $1.5 million depending on whether statewide, legislative, and county offices are up for election (even-numbered years) or only city offices (odd-numbered years).

While the Finance Committee is in charge of raising all money, the Executive Committee, headed by the state chair-

---

* Figures on party affiliation, however, show a Democratic advantage in sheer numbers. In 1974, 1,113,797 people voted in the Democratic primary, 655,047 in the Republican.

man, decides how to spend it. The chairman holds great power over local committees, candidates, and even elected officials in a system that has contributed significantly to the independence of the state party from the fortunes of candidates and office-holders. The continuity of power has also helped to solidify the system: Kent McGough, the present State Chairman, is only the third in the 28 years since the system was adopted (Bliss was the first, and John Andrews, who stepped aside for McGough in 1973, the second).

The Democratic Party in Ohio has been much less solid, and has traditionally depended upon a strong governor to pull it together temporarily, tending to fall on bad times when the state government is in Republican hands. This was the case between 1962 and 1971, when the statehouse (under James Rhodes), legislature, Supreme Court, all boards and commissions, and most other statewide offices were controlled by Republicans. One obvious result of Republican domination was the lack of patronage to encourage party workers and, in the time-honored Ohio tradition of political donations by state employees, the money that flows from it. During the second Rhodes administration in the late 1960's, Democratic State Chairman Eugene P. O'Grady ran the party from an aging hotel room with worn rugs, bare light bulbs, and a mimeograph machine, on a budget of about $50,000 a year. Democrats were not without their successes in the 1950s and 1960s, but winners tended to be powerful, charismatic vote-getters like Frank Lausche, who as Senator and Governor never attempted to build a party or financial structure.

The situation changed after the victory of John Gilligan as Governor in 1970 and of Democratic candidates for attorney general, auditor, and treasurer. Gilligan brought the disparate local Democratic parties together in a loose confederation, using the patronage of his office to build party coffers and manpower pools. During his administration the state party averaged about $1 million a year in funds raised and spent and operated out of a plush $2,000-a-month office with 20 to 30 paid staff members.

Democratic candidates traditionally have raised money directly rather than going through their party as Republicans do, and thus they do not depend so much on party support. In 1974 as before, much of the money from Democratic contributors, especially labor money, was going directly to Gilligan and other statewide and legislative candidates. The state Democratic Party did engage in some slate spending, mainly for a $250,000 "sample ballot" in the general election, which was mailed to most registered Democrats and was credited with helping to pull through several candidates.

The traditionally potent Republican Party collected almost twice as much as the unusually strong Democratic Party in 1974 —about $2.9 million, as against $1.5 million. But because Republicans sent about half their proceeds back to the county level, state headquarters and candidate expenses were about on a par.

The Republicans also had a special committee to raise money for statewide candidates (thus avoiding the Federal bookkeeping required on funds for Federal candidates), to which donors could earmark their gifts for particular candidates. But the total raised by the Republican Resources Committee, $441,071, was at least matched by direct contributions to Democrats. Most of this committee's proceeds went directly to the Rhodes campaign, to the displeasure of other Republican candidates in tough races. Neither state party gave much financial aid to its nominee for U.S. Senate, because the race between Democrat John H. Glenn and Cleveland Mayor Ralph J. Perk was never considered to be close. (It wasn't; Glenn won by 1,012,537 votes—the largest margin in state history.)

The coffers of neither party were as full as they might have been for the 1974 elections. Both found businessmen reluctant to donate early in the year because of Watergate and a new campaign-finance law that required disclosure of donors and amounts. In addition, Democrats, who had just recently built up their fund-raising capability, reined in one aspect of it— soliciting contributions from state employees—after the practice was criticized in a February 1974 report by the General Accounting Office. Because of this curb on their activities, the Democrats had to borrow $160,000 from a bank to keep their expensive headquarters operating in the middle of an election year.

Both parties were embarrassed by GAO audit reports, but the Democrats were more severely affected. The General Accounting Office questioned the legality of such traditional practices as hiring on the basis of political loyalty in Gilligan's departments that received Federal funds (a violation of Federal law); the purchase by State Department of Transportation employees of $204,400 in tickets to a 1972 fund-raising dinner (about half the total raised), reportedly on solicitation by department officials; and the performance by state employees of fund-raising activities on state time and using state equipment.

In August the GAO also accused the Ohio Republican Party of circumventing the spirit of the 1971 Federal law by reporting "too many" contributors in reports. This, the GAO said, was an effort to obscure and hinder identification of major donors. No prosecution of Republicans was recommended, but the GAO did recommend that the U.S. Attorney General prosecute Democrats for the 1972 practices.

The reason Attorney General William B. Saxbe, an Ohio Republican who had defeated Gilligan for U.S. Senate in 1968, did not prosecute the Democrats is not entirely clear. It appeared, however, that the GAO's reports on both parties in several states were drawing quiet protests from Congress and from national party leaders in both camps. It has also been hinted that there might have been agreement not to pursue either side. (It is noteworthy that Congress stripped the GAO of its auditing power in that area under the new Federal campaign law.)

Election-Law Reform

Both parties were forced to deal with the issue of campaign-finance reform in 1974, as were politicians in almost every other state. Perhaps predictably, the debate was highly partisan. Republicans tend to be more disciplined on such issues because of their centralized fund-raising system and the fact that G.O.P. officials generally hail from relatively homogeneous constituencies, mostly small towns or suburban areas. Democrats, with their diffuse financing system and wide variety of constituencies —urban, suburban, Black, white, ethnic, rural, old-line, liberal, and mixtures thereof—are generally less disciplined. But when it comes to campaign financing, the party lines are firmly drawn.

The law on the books early in 1974 had long been a patchwork of vague and loophole-ridden sections under which a variety of questionable practices flourished unchallenged, among them the laundering of funds by the use of multitudes of campaign committees for one candidate, the donation by state and local government employees to "flower funds"* and the solici-

---

* "Flower fund" is the name given to a political slush fund contributed to by the employees, sometimes from their salaries, of state or local office-holders. It is so named because it also serves the purpose of buying gifts or donating flowers for funerals or sick persons, including employees or allies of the officeholder. The fund is used for the officeholder's campaign in election years, and replenished in off-years.

tation, often under pressure, of state contractors for campaign funds. Several loopholes remained after the Ohio legislature passed a reform bill in April 1974, and basic aspects of campaign financing remained the same, but at least Ohio had taken a few steps along the road to reform. The steps weren't easy.

A special session of the legislature on campaign-finance reform called by Governor John Gilligan in November 1973 adjourned after weeks of haggling without passage of a bill. Legislators could agree on some reforms, such as pre-election disclosure and spending limits, but they could not satisfactorily negotiate the crucial question of limits on contributions. With a divided legislature—Republicans controlled the Senate 17 to 16, while Democrats had a 58 to 41 margin in the House—the session lapsed into partisan bickering as each party tried to gore the other's sacred-cow contributions. (Republicans were at times especially intransigent because they didn't want Gilligan to claim credit for a new campaign-reform law as he had earlier in 1973 with a new ethics law for public officials and candidates, which provided for disclosure of sources of personal income and spelled out certain bans on conflicts of interest.)

Republicans proposed to hamstring union group contributions with an "earmarking system" for candidates; Democrats wanted limits on individuals and political parties—the mainstays of the Republican money machine. The "earmarking system" would have required that unions and other large organizations have their members designate the recipients for contributions to a political-action fund. The Democrats believed the proposal was a ploy to destroy group contributions because such designations would entail technical, strategic, and administrative problems. There were shreds of philosophical differences in the party positions: Freedom of the individual seemed to underly the G.O.P. idea of "earmarking," while the Democrats believe that the only way the "little man" could make his presence felt in the system was through mass action. But the feelings stirred up by the debate were political not philosophical. Republicans railed at the "buying" of influence among public officials by strong pressure groups such as unions, claiming that the insulation provided by political party fundraising was the most virtuous way of financing campaigns. The Democrats, rejecting parties as laundry mechanisms and as special-interest groups themselves, argued that organized giving through unions or other groups was the best way for most citizens to match the political influence of wealthy ones. As both sides explored the holes in the other's theory, the session dissolved in bitter acrimony, and campaign reform was dead for 1973.

But spurred by national events and by some active reformers, the split legislature dodged the thorny questions and adopted a quite modest reform bill on April 4, 1974. The law took effect July 23, after the May primary, but covered the fall campaign. The main features of the new law were pre-election disclosure for all candidates and parties; a single, centralized campaign committee for each candidate; and spending limits for state and local elections. Names, addresses, amounts, and dates were to be listed for contributions and expenditures over $25, along with the purpose of expenditures. Reports were to be filed with the secretary of state for statewide and Congressional offices, with county boards of elections for district offices. Spending limits were set at 10 cents each for the total state population for the governor's race ($1,065,201 in 1974); 1.5 cents per Ohioan for other statewide offices; 12 cents each, divided by the number of districts (33) for the Senate ($38,734); 15 cents each, divided by the number of districts (99) for the House ($16,139); and $50,000 for the Supreme Court and $35,000 for the Court of Appeals. The new law also prohibited contractors from receiving nonbid state contracts from an officeholder who had gotten more than $1,000 from the contractor in contributions (although those engaged in competitive bidding could give as much as they chose); strengthened the ban on extracting contributions from employees with rewards, punishments, or threats related to job security, and created the Ohio Elections Commission, a five-member board to police the new law, with powers to investigate complaints and to recommend prosecution to appropriate authorities. Four of the five members were to be appointed by the secretary of state, two from a list of names supplied by each major party; the four then jointly were to appoint a chairman.

Because of the strong partisan division on this issue, and the veto each party had over the wishes of the other due to the split legislature, the legislators left the financial angels of both parties untouched by contribution limits. They also left major loopholes that allowed: candidates legally to pocket campaign money (as long as they paid income tax on it), for there was no specific ban on converting funds to personal use; laundering and "pass-through" of funds such as through the parties or special committees like the Republican Resources Committee; continuation of the exemption of the $25-per-ticket social events, which Rhodes and many others had used to leave often large sums of money unaccounted for on contributor lists; circumvention of spending limits for candidates by party spending on slate advertising and by spending of committees "in opposition" to certain candidates (neither of which would be counted in the spending limits); and candidates to spend their own money on their campaigns up to the limit for their races (thus dropping a $5,000 ceiling under the old law).

The existence of these loopholes prompted the stated election chairman of Ohio Common Cause, Avery S. Friedman, to call the law "grossly inadequate"; Friedman added that the "self-congratulations" among legislators on the new law made further reform a "terribly remote possibility." State Senator Tony P. Hall, the Democratic nominee for secretary of state, said the bill "is only a shell designed to fool the public into thinking the legislature has enacted true reform." After the election, Republican State Chairman McGough described it as "a very weak law" which had "almost no effect on our operations."

Triumph of the "Old Politics"

One person who defended the new law throughout the campaign was Governor Gilligan, who had pressed for its passage even when it had to be watered down. One who couldn't have cared less about campaign reform was his opponent, former Governor Rhodes, whom Gilligan had defeated in 1970.

Rarely in Ohio electoral history has there been a greater contrast between two candidates for governor. They differed in personal backgrounds, politics, and state administrations. Gilligan comes from a basically affluent, intellectual, big-city (Cincinnati) background and is a scholarly, articulate liberal. Rhodes comes from a southeast Ohio rural-poor background. Gilligan was a university professor by profession, while Rhodes had barely one semester at Ohio State University and fought his way up the political ladder in the old-style, ward-heeling, patronage, campaign-fund-shuffling manner. Rhodes defies ideological labeling, but has been basically true to the Republican business-oriented line without being an intellectual conservative; his political allies have long been local politicians and businessmen. Gilligan is an urban-oriented liberal who has long cultivated ties to big labor unions. In his two administrations in the 1960's, Rhodes concentrated on building highways, state parks, university and vocational education buildings, while holding the line on state taxes and devoting very little attention to state services such as prisons, mental health, and human resources. Gilligan, in his term as Governor (1971–74), pushed for reform of the state tax structure and the introduction of an income tax, while trying to upgrade some institutional services long ignored by governors of both parties.

The two candidates also had strongly contrasting personalities. Gilligan's irritated many in his own party and among the general public, to whom he appeared cold and aloof, with his professorial way of lecturing in TV appearances and press conferences. The state press corps and statehouse politicians adopted the term "arrogance factor" to speak of the effect of Gilligan's personality on his own chances for re-election. The Governor's aides would privately wring their hands about the problem, and to combat it his campaign even made a TV ad showing Gilligan in human at-home situations with his gracious wife, Katie. Rhodes hardly needed such ads. He was generally perceived as the gregarious but wily old pol, surprisingly energetic for his 65 years, with a friendly, down-to-earth manner, ribald jokes, and fast, charming double-talk. Jules Witcover of the *Washington Post* dubbed Rhodes the Casey Stengel of the gubernatorial fraternity. While Gilligan was seen by some of his political friends to be highly ethical and honest almost to a fault, Rhodes' background was considered somewhat unsavory, including stories of campaign-fund problems in the 1950's and general political wheeling and dealing.

The two candidates' campaigns reflected their different styles and ideologies. Gilligan, deciding to make his a pace-setter in "going beyond the law," disclosed his financing periodically and voluntarily during both the primary and general election campaigns (the new disclosure law didn't go into effect until the general election). He imposed a $3,000 limit on individual contributors (a husband and wife could give a total of $6,000). The Gilligan campaign compiled, at the cost of $14,000, computerized reports of recipients and expenditures listed in chronological and alphabetical order—making research and disclosure by the press much easier. Fund-raising was carried out by a network of county finance organizations established by Ohioans for Gilligan, the central campaign committee, which, according to reports, saw that no individual contributions exceeded the announced limits.

While individual contributions were limited, organization giving—in keeping with Democratic party traditions—was not. The major organization support of Gilligan was from labor groups, which donated $387,086, or about 37 percent of his general-election total. This sum included donations from national and out-of-state union groups, including Leonard Woodcock's United Auto Workers CAP Council in Detroit ($25,000) and I. W. Abel's United Steelworkers in Pittsburgh ($12,000). Gilligan had long cultivated ties to national labor leaders, having worked with them to unseat U.S. Senator Frank Lausche in the 1968 primary (Gilligan lost in November to William Saxbe). That year he received more labor money than any other senatorial candidate except one (Wayne Morse). As Governor, Gilligan appointed the man backed by Woodcock and Abel, Howard M. Metzenbaum, to finish Saxbe's term after he resigned to become Attorney General in December 1973. Gilligan nursed some national party ambitions and figured to be acceptable to both liberals and labor factions in the wake of the Democratic debacle in 1972.

Another significant segment of donors in the Gilligan campaign were government employees, about 645 of whom gave a total of $45,000, including $16,735 from a $100-per-person golf outing for middle and upper management state employees. Gilligan's appointees to state boards were also among his donors, as were state contractors and vendors. But Gilligan finance staffers steered away from heavy solicitation of state employees after the GAO report charged the Democratic Party with violating the law in its 1972 fund-raising practices.

With the advantage of incumbency, Gilligan had his share of *quid pro quo* givers, but his campaign-finance director, Patrick Holland, and deputy campaign director, William J. Bannon, declared that the Governor tried to avoid any systematic exploitation of businesses that might profit from state contracts. "That doesn't mean that kind of soliciting did not go on," Bannon, a former state Democratic finance chairman who after the election became Midwest coordinator for the Presidential campaign of Senator Jackson, said after the election. "It probably did at the local level among county party people or local solicitors. But the Governor instructed the campaign-finance people not to do it." Bannon added that such agreements, out of control of the central campaign, could have caused embarrassment to the pro-reform Governor had he been re-elected.

Despite Gilligan's reform-mindedness and setting of voluntary limits on individual contributions, his campaign did not meet the goal of financing a big campaign from small contributions. Even though a substantial sum—$586,982—did come in gifts of less than $500, the entire Gilligan campaign (primary and general) still got 60 percent of its money in 392 separate contributions of $500 or more. Here is a breakdown, according to Holland's computer printout:

CONTRIBUTION RANGE	NUMBER OF CONTRIBUTORS	TOTAL	PERCENT OF TOTAL
.01–$25	3,514	$ 51,910	3.5
$25–$50	951	$ 44,447	3.0
$50–$100	2,115	$209,577	14.2
$100–$500	1,001	$281,048	19.1
$500–$1,000	250	$236,545	16.0
$1,000–$1,500	26	$ 36,136	2.5
$1,500–$3,000	88	$217,437	14.9
$3,000 and over	28	$395,300	26.8
Primary and general total	—	$1,472,400	100.0

The category of $3,000 and over was composed almost entirely of labor contributions.

The profile of Rhodes's contributions does not look too different from Gilligan's in one respect: He got 67 percent of his donations in amounts of $500 and above—as compared with 60 percent for Gilligan—for $580,016 of his total. But in his methods and sources of funding, the Republican waged a very different fund-raising campaign. First of all, Rhodes had the advantage of his party's long-established statewide fund-raising apparatus. He profited not only from Finance Committee fund-raising, which drew money from around the state, but from contributions directed to him through the special-purpose Republican Resource Committee, his major backer through mid-October. State Chairman McGough, a mild-mannered party technician, worked in tandem with the candidate to raise money. They complemented each other in both function and personality: Rhodes came on as the aggressive candidate willing to be responsive to those who signed on, McGough as the solid fellow who made sure Rhodes's campaign was well-organized, despite its appearance as a lean, undermanned operation in Rhodes' own business office in Columbus.

The former Governor and the party chairman went to traditional Republican sources—businessman, industrialists, chiefs of regulated industries—and about 75 industrial and business leaders gave $106,000 to the campaign. The Ohio Manufacturers Association gave $7,350 through its political action committee. The Timken family, owners of the Timken Company of Canton, gave Rhodes a total of at least $16,000 (W. R. Timken is chairman of the Ohio Republican Finance Committee). Members of the Berry family of Dayton, owners of the L. M. Berry and Company advertising firm, gave Rhodes at least $10,000. Kent and Kelvin Smith, Cleveland industrialists and their families, gave $9,000.

Nursing-home operators, coal and strip-mining operators, and oil and natural-gas interests were among industries with special problems of regulation under the Gilligan administration that contributed to the Governor's opponent. Nursing-home operators, who were pressured to meet stiff regulations for fire protection, gave or lent Rhodes about $34,000. Strip-miners, working since 1971 under a strict law pushed and enforced by Gilligan, gave about $21,000. Executives of oil and natural-gas companies, subject to environmental controls, gave about $15,000.

The largest, and most controversial, support for the Rhodes campaign came from the highway lobby. The bulk of this money came late in the campaign, when, after polls showed the previously favored Gilligan seriously slipping, Rhodes decided to launch a major media attack. Highway contractors gave most of the $100,000 in eleventh-hour loans and much of the $460,000 in gifts received after October 16. At least 40 persons representing more than a dozen highway construction firms gave or lent more than $145,000. In addition, Political Education Patterns, the political arm of the Operating Engineers Union, whose members man road-building equipment, gave $10,000. The Ohio Contractors Political Action Committee gave $6,500, the Auto Dealers Investment Group, $2,000, and the Political Resources Organization for Interested Truckers (PROFIT) gave $4,500. Several of the individual donors had earlier given to Rhodes through the Republican Resources Committee in response to a solicitation by Frank P. Converse, the President of Great Lakes Construction Company of Cleveland. In a June letter to his fellow highway contractors, Converse appealed for checks to be mailed to the Resources Committee, earmarked for Rhodes, and addressed to Rhodes's business office in the same downtown office building as his headquarters. The replies were to be sent to the attention of P. E. Masheter, who had been Highway Department Director in the two previous Rhodes administrations.

Although Rhodes and highway builders deny any *quid pro quo* in the solicitations and donations, Rhodes's later actions in favor of highway contractors strongly suggest that some

understanding did exist. In February 1975, as one of the
first acts of his third administration, Governor Rhodes sent
to the legislature a $1.6 billion bond issue for transportation,
part of a four-part constitutional revision plan to make Ohio
"depression proof" by providing jobs, mostly in the construction industry. Almost all the transportation money—$1.4 million
—would go to highways, making the issue the largest highway
proposal in Ohio history. When the Democratically controlled
General Assembly failed to approve his proposal, which as a
bond issue had to be placed on the ballot by the legislature or
by initiative petition, the Governor vowed he would put the
package to a vote even if he had to pass petitions for the
300,000 necessary signatures.

Even before Rhodes introduced the bond-issue proposal,
Ohio Contractor (the publication of the Ohio Contractors
Association) proclaimed that his third inauguration day, February 13, 1975, "ought to be declared a holiday by the Ohio
construction industry. . . . Ohio's construction industry is on the
verge of a major expansion. It is a happy future to look forward to." They could look forward to it in large part because
the highway-supported media campaign had succeeded in getting elected the man called by one political writer "Governor
Roads."

Throughout the campaign Gilligan pursued a strategy of
exploiting Rhodes's record of campaign practices, past and
present. Rhodes, meanwhile, showed little concern with the
issue of reform and sloughed off opposition charges. The Rhodes
record first became an issue on June 26, when the *Cleveland
Plain Dealer* reported that a comparison of Rhodes's 1970
U.S. Senate finance report and his 1974 primary report showed
at least $16,640 "missing" or not accounted for in itemized
expenses. Rhodes and his campaign treasurer stated that the
money had been spent for political polls and consultants, but
declined to produce evidence of work performed or canceled
checks. According to Chairman McGough, the 1970 Rhodes
for Senate committee had $107,533 left, which it gave to the
state party. The party in turn spent $31,740, with Rhodes's
approval, and gave his Senate committee a check for $76,149
in June of 1971. But the 1974 Rhodes for Governor report
showed only $59,509 transferred from the Senate committee.
J. Gordon Peltier, Rhodes's campaign treasurer and long associate, said the $16,640 was used for political purposes before
August 1972, when the Rhodes for Governor committee was
formed. After reviewing the situation, Secretary of State Ted

W. Brown, a Republican, ruled that the law did not require Rhodes to account for money spent before he filed as a candidate in 1973. Indeed, the law at that time did not require such accounting, but the new Ohio campaign law that took effect in June 1974 did cover such "interim periods" by requiring annual reports.

Another charge about Rhodes's previous campaign practices concerned his handling of campaign funds in the 1950's while he was state auditor. The *Akron Beacon Journal*, in an October article, charged that, according to Federal sources, Rhodes had tapped his campaign funds 14 times for $54,982 for personal expenses between 1954 and 1957 and failed to pay taxes on the money. (It is not illegal under Ohio law to convert campaign funds to personal use as long as the candidate pays income tax on the revenue.) The Internal Revenue Service forced Rhodes to pay $15,762 in back taxes, the article said. The newspaper report repeated charges that had been made in a 1969 *Life* Magazine article, but in greater detail. Rhodes ducked most of the questions on his IRS problems, calling the charges a rehash, which they were, although not irrelevant to the 1974 election.

An issue that drew considerable attention during the campaign was Rhodes's failure to report in his June 1974 disclosure statement the names of any contributors to a November 1973 $25-a-plate chicken lunch in Columbus, which raised $158,864. The donors' names were not reported on the ground that Ohio law (then and now) exempts gifts of $25 or less from reporting requirements. But Rhodes's argument that the chicken lunch sold 6,355 single tickets to contributors (that is, that no one gave more than $25) strained credulity, especially after newspapers delving into the question discovered that letters had been sent to businessmen asking them to purchase and sell "at least ten tickets" and "as many as you can afford." Also revealed was a letter signed by Gordon Peltier, Rhodes's finance director, advising the chairman of the luncheon that ticket distributors could "write a check for more than one ticket" and not disclose the names so long as the total "represents individual ticket purchases."

State Senator Tony P. Hall, a Dayton Democrat who was running for secretary of state, jumped on the issue, urging Secretary of State Brown to investigate and subpoena all records, including canceled bank checks. Brown questioned Rhodes's aides about the lack of record-keeping and confirmed that one $50 contribution came from Charles A. Orwig, an oil company

executive, but he ruled that, in the absence of court interpreta-
tion, the $50 Orwig contribution was a pair of contributions
from Orwig and his wife. He also ruled that there was no
evidence of unreported larger contributions and said he would
not conduct a "fishing expedition." Hall, disgusted that Brown
would not pursue an investigation "unless we gave him the
smoking pistol," in September filed the first complaint with
the new Ohio Elections Commission. Because of the time
necessary to investigate, the newness of the commission, and the
fact that it met only once a month, it was not until after the
election that the commission voted, three Republicans to two
Democrats, that it had no jurisdiction on alleged violations
before July 23, the date when it was formed. But the publicity
surrounding the issue had some effect, for in his post-election
report, Rhodes listed all contributors (even $25 ones) to a $25
Jim Rhodes Rally held in October 1974.

In another controversial solicitation during the primary,
Rhodes aide Richard Krabach, a cabinet member in the first
and present administration, sent letters to out-of-state corporation executives asking "your group" to give $1,000 in the form
of "personal checks" for "each of your installations in Ohio."
Although Ohio law forbids corporate contributions to candidates, one form letter was sent to the Managing Editor of the
Des Moines Register and Tribune, A. Edward Heins, addressed
to him as a corporate board member. Rhodes said the Krabach
letter was an appeal to individuals only despite references to
"your group" and "installations in Ohio." No investigation
was made by any agency.

Gilligan made increasingly pointed attacks on the various
questionable Rhodes campaign practices. On July 5, after the
press published articles reporting possible irregularities, Gilligan wrote a confidential memo to his top staff suggesting that
Rhodes's primary report (filed in June) should be scrutinized
to "raise every conceivable question" for possible "leaking to
certain reporters" and for campaign ammunition. Gilligan
noted his campaign's difficulties with collections because of
insistence on full disclosure and urged his staff to investigate
Rhodes to "make sure every potential contributor to Rhodes
is convinced in advance that in one fashion or another, perhaps
before a grand jury, that their contributions will become public
knowledge." In speeches and television ads Gilligan declared,
"Jim Rhodes has refused to disclose his campaign finances
despite the fact that thousands of dollars of his campaign funds
have been reported missing in the 30 years he's been in office.

Ohioans are tired of the slush-bucket campaign practices of the past. Jim Rhodes is going to find out the people will no longer tolerate them."

Rhodes's response to all charges was to "stick with the issues" of schools, taxes, and Gilligan's mismanagement" of the state-house—a strategy that worked better than Gilligan's. The "people" did seem to tolerate Rhodes's financing practices. In any case, most of the stories about those practices appeared in the press in the summer of 1974, before most people were very interested in the campaign. Rhodes's massive media effort overcame any damage Gilligan might have done, and inflicted mortal wounds to Gilligan's campaign in the process. Engineered by Bailey Deardourff and Eyre, this media campaign was made possible by the last-minute outpouring of money to Rhodes, mostly from highway builders and regulated industries. Rhodes had collected only $408,361, half of his final total, by October 16. But his post-election report filed on December 20 showed that he ran up a large debt buying media time, borrowing more than $100,000 in the last 20 days of the campaign from 19 persons and paying it back in early December with late contributions, many of them dated just before or after the election. Although Gilligan outspent Rhodes with a general election total of $1,032,981 to Rhodes's $856,490 (including loans), only 43.5 percent ($450,285) of Gilligan's budget went for media, compared to Rhodes's 69.2 percent ($592,513). Most of the Rhodes media money was spent in the populous Cleveland market.

Strategists for both sides have said that it was this media campaign that neutralized the Democratic vote, either prompting switches to Rhodes or persuading large numbers to stay at home. Instead of extolling the Republican's virtues, Rhodes's slickly executed ads raised disturbing questions about Gilligan's handling of the Governor's office. For example, one showing a sheep being shorn of its wool reminded voters that Gilligan had once quipped at a state fair that he "sheared taxpayers, not sheep" (a facetious reference to the image the Governor may have gotten by helping to enact an income tax in his first year in office). Another ad about a "shell game" spoofed Gilligan's contradictory statements about a budget surplus. The ads were short, punchy, and often misleading, but they were credited with confusing enough Democrats who already had no particular love for Gilligan.

Even as he attacked Rhodes on the integrity issue, Gilligan had to deal with the charges of misconduct in his administration raised by the GAO investigation. The Governor carefully avoided assuming a defensive posture, and left the refutations to party spokesmen. After the election, on December 27, Attorney General William J. Brown advised Gilligan that "no prosecution was warranted" in connection with allegations of the GAO that state employees had committed misdemeanors by soliciting contributions in 1972. "The simple fact is that the people we talked to in our investigation believed they were acting within the law in soliciting and selling dinner tickets," said Brown. "It's been done for years under both Democratic and Republican administrations in Ohio." The GAO report, which Republicans attempted to use as a foil to questions about Watergate and Rhodes's finance practices, nevertheless exposed some of Gilligan's sore spots. Gilligan had attempted to show that his administration was not just "business as usual."

When Rhodes won the election, it seemed to prove his assumption that traditional issues of education, taxes, and personalities would sway voters—not campaign reform. A post-election survey conducted in key precincts by the *Akron Beacon Journal* did in fact bear this out: According to its findings, strong Gilligan backers and some Republicans were wary of Rhodes on the "integrity" issue, but key Democratic and independent voters decided on more traditional issues. Voters who switched from Gilligan to Rhodes often cited beliefs that Gilligan had not delivered on items such as highways and school aid; some mentioned the Governor's personality and a general lack of confidence in government. The main post-Watergate effect seemed to be a cynicism toward politics in general, which hurt Gilligan more than Rhodes because many independents and Democrats in the Cleveland area, especially in the Black wards of East Cleveland, failed to be excited by the match. This was true of those who had voted in 1970, not just traditional nonvoters. Ironically, Gilligan lost the election in the industrialized Democratic northeast part of the state, mainly Cuyahoga County (Cleveland), center of the Rhodes media effort, where his 1970 backers either stayed home or voted for his opponent. In Cleveland city proper, Gilligan lost 50,000 votes from his 1970 total, while the Republican total remained the same. (Gilligan's statewide deficit was 11,000 votes, less than 1 percent of the total.)

In perhaps the ultimate irony of a paradoxical campaign, it was Gilligan's campaigners—not the Rhodes people as envisioned in Gilligan's July 5 memo on campaign strategy—who faced a grand jury in the aftermath of the election. After

Rhodes took office, his administration and Franklin County (Columbus) prosecutor George C. Smith conducted an investigation into post-election hiring practices in the Gilligan administration before he left office. The grand jury investigation, begun in April 1975, resulted in charges against 14 campaign workers who were placed on the state payroll for a number of weeks after the election, received state pay, but did not report for work. They worked instead as part of the Recount Planning Group, a successor to Ohioans for Gilligan which was organized to carry on a recount of the election and which operated from late November to mid-January. Ten of those charged made a deal with the prosecutor and pleaded guilty to "theft by deception" of state funds, a misdemeanor, and returned the money they had received. Three pleaded not guilty and were later convicted of grand theft, for "stealing" a sum over $150. They were sentenced to six months in jail but are currently free pending appeal. The charges against one worker were dropped. In addition, the Recount Planning Group itself was indicted for permitting the "theft by deception"; the only individual referred to in the indictment was William Bannon, Gilligan's deputy campaign director, who supervised the group, but was not on the state payroll. The group was found guilty and fined $5,000. Bannon was only mentioned as chairman and not indicted. No campaign or administration officials were indicted by Smith, who said there was "not one scintilla of evidence" that Gilligan knew the workers had not reported to state jobs. Yet the incident was extremely embarrassing to Gilligan from several standpoints, and his frustration was complete.

The Legislature: The Labor Factor

The battle for control of the 33-member state Senate was the second most important struggle for power in Ohio in 1974. Democrats—who had not controlled both houses of the legislature since 1960—had taken the House of Representatives in 1972, but Republicans had retained the Senate, 17 to 16. Most of the action in 1974 among the 18 races (the other 15 senators were midway through their four-year terms) centered around 6 key districts in the major urban areas of Cleveland (2 districts), Columbus, Dayton, Lorain, and Canton. Democrats won all 6 with healthy infusions of labor money and took control of the Senate (21 to 12), while staying in power in the House (59 to 40).

The hallmark of the legislative races was the outpouring of a half-million dollars—a third of the total spent by all candidates —in contributions to general-election campaigns by special-interest groups (that is, labor unions, who gave almost a quarter-million, and other lobbies and special interests). Lobbying-group contributions in fact made up the major portion—in some cases up to 90 percent—of funds raised by many powerful legislative leaders and committee chairman of both houses. Lobbies gave still more through the two parties and through special campaign committees set up by the party caucuses in each house. Virtually all of the $14,704 collected by the House Democratic campaign committee was given by lobbying groups (and was passed out by Vernal G. Riffe, Jr., Speaker Pro Tem of the House, who was to unseat the former speaker in a post-election caucus). A quarter of the House Republican campaign fund of $46,866 came from special-interest groups, as did more than half of the $13,991 collected for G.O.P. senatorial contests. About half of the Democratic Senate fund of $12,750 came from lobbying groups. Interestingly enough, a $1,000 gift had more impact in the 1974 legislative race than previously because of the spending limits established under the new law—$16,139 for the House and $38,734 for the Senate.

Ten of these special-interest groups donated about 70 percent of the entire half-million dollars; the totals listed below include lobby gifts to the Republican and Democratic legislator commit-tees for each caucus in both houses, as well as direct gifts to legisla-tors' campaigns:

United Auto Workers CAP Council	$87,146
Real Estate Political Action Committee	$51,712
Communications Workers of America	$40,085
Ohio A.F.L.-C.I.O.	$39,630
Ohio Medical Association	$37,896
Savings and Loan League of Ohio	$32,850
Ohio Contractors Association	$22,420
Ohio Education Association	$21,113
Auto Dealers Investment Group	$18,950
Ohio Trial Attorneys	$16,751
Total	$368,553

Groups representing bankers, dentists, and osteopaths were more conservative, giving $100–$150 per candidate, mostly to strong incumbents, key committee chairmen, and leaders. Manu-facturers and highway contractors gave heavily to Republicans and to influential Democratic leaders. Educators gave to friends on both sides of the aisle, with larger gifts going mostly to Democrats in key races. Overall, Democrats raised a greater proportion of their funds from special-interest groups than did Republicans, who could fall back on the strong party apparatus and wealthy individuals among their constituents. The more influential legislators of both parties tended to get special attention even if they were expected to win easy victories. Senate Majority Leader Oliver Ocasek, whose opponent was indicted during the campaign (and later convicted, as well as beaten almost four to one) received 57 percent of his $11,850 in contributions from lobbying groups; House leader Vernal Riffe, who was solid in his home district, received $12,817 in contributions from such groups; and state Representative C. J. McLin, a leader of the House Black caucus and the most powerful Black politician in Dayton, received $10,080 in gifts from almost every lobbying group in the statehouse and from a host of top Dayton businessmen, although he was considered unbeatable and Republicans had stopped fielding candidates against him. (His 1974 opponent, independent Sinthy E. Taylor, spent a grand total of $77.04 and lost by 15,336 to 2,672.)

Labor money was not only the largest category of special-interest support, it was also probably the element that made the difference in the election. Labor's participation in campaigns in Ohio has been developing over the years and had been strengthened through the efforts of Governor Gilligan, who began systematically to solicit labor contributions for candidates other than himself after his election in 1970.

Labor has always been politically active on issues that affected it directly, such as minimum wage, unemployment insurance, and workmen's compensation. In 1958, Ohio labor mobilized to defeat a "right to work" Constitutional amendment—considered a direct threat to unionism in general. However, it was not until the late 1960s and the 1970s that labor began to take an interest in other issues, such as tax reform, which affect their constituents directly as citizens but not as union members. At the same time, unions in Ohio as well as elsewhere began to collect more money for their political-action funds and thus had more to deliver to candidates. The United Auto Workers, historically one of the most liberal unions, had formed an early and close relationship with Gilligan. The A.F.L.-C.I.O. was also friendly, although feuds between Gilligan and Ohio A.F.L.-C.I.O. President Frank King ended only in May 1974 when Gilli-

gan backed a successful convention move to depose King. As Ohio
U.A.W. and A.F.L.-C.I.O. leaders have developed more political
sophistication, the unions have become involved in lobbying on
almost all important legislation coming before the General Assembly.

Organized labor contributed more than $230,000 in 1974
to legislative campaigns, mostly in important contests expected
to be close; $70,000, mainly from the U.A.W., A.F.L.-C.I.O.,
and the Communications Workers (C.W.A.), went to the six
Democratic Senate candidates in key races. Transportation
workers and other smaller unions gave small amounts to almost
all Democrats. Positions on issues and past voting records are
considered by labor leaders when deciding on endorsements,
but once an endorsement is secured by a candidate, the degree
of financial support is usually in direct correlation with the
difficulty of the race. Labor-backed candidates in safe districts
got only modest sums even if they were powerful legislative
leaders like Vernal Riffe or Senate Majority Leader Oliver
Ocasek.

Democratic challengers in the key races received large donations from unions. In the Dayton district race, Neal F. Zimmers,
Jr., a 32-year-old county court judge, raised the most of any
Democratic legislator to defeat incumbent Republican Senator
Clara E. Weisenborn, a garden columnist for a Dayton newspaper. Almost all of Zimmer's money came from unions—
$7,000 from the A.F.L.-C.I.O., $6,000 from the U.A.W., and
$2,515 from the C.W.A. (Weisenborn raised $20,750, with
$7,300 coming from party sources and substantial gifts from the
Ohio Manufacturers, Medical Association, Bankers Action New
Committee, and other committees.) The same pattern held in
the other four races in which incumbent Republican senators
lost to Democratic challengers. The big-three union givers—
the U.A.W., A.F.L.-C.I.O., and C.W.A.—pumped from $1,000
to $3,000 each into races won by Democrats Anthony J. Cele-
brezze and J. T. McCormack in Cleveland, Robert Freeman
in Canton, and Donald Pease in Lorain county. The one
Democratic incumbent in a key race, Senator Robert O'Shaughnessy of Columbus, hung on to his seat with a healthy assist
from the major union groups.

In his loss to Celebrezze (the son of the former Cleveland
Mayor and H.E.W. Secretary), incumbent G.O.P. Senator Paul
R. Matia of Westlake, a Ceveland suburb, faced one of the most
interesting political-finance challenges in the legislative races.

A 36-year-old liberal Republican who had been chief sponsor of Ohio's new election law, Matia announced on May 8 that he would not accept gifts from statehouse lobbying groups because "the obvious purpose of these contributions is to influence the successful candidate when he is in office. I think this is wrong and the only way to stop it is for candidates to refuse contributions." As a result, he raised just $17,695, compared to Celebrezze's $26,551 (including $3,000 each from the U.A.W. and A.F.L.-C.I.O., $2,679 from the C.W.A., and $1,000 each from the Teamsters and educators). Other legislative candidates limited gifts from lobbyists, but none went to the extent Matia did, nor did any have such a difficult race. After the election, which he lost by 48 to 46 percent, Matia said he was convinced the financing situation caused his defeat. Although Matia encouraged lobbying groups to have individual members in his home district contribute directly to his committee, "I had no takers with very few exceptions," he recalled. "They prefer to give it in a big lump as a group so they can use it for just one purpose—influence legislators."

Republican legislators and some business lobbyists feared labor unions might have gained too strong a hand in the General Assembly elected in 1974, in which Democrats had been boosted into power on union money. Robert L. McAllister, registered lobbyist for the Ohio Association of Realtors, said at the beginning of the 1975 legislative session, "I have already told my people that if one of our bills comes up against opposition from labor, forget it. I can't do anything about it."

An interesting footnote to this fear of labor influence was the failure of two major lobbying efforts by labor leaders early in the 1975 session. The A.F.L.-C.I.O. and the U.A.W. had made a deal with Governor Rhodes in which they agreed to support his four-point bond-issue package for placement on the ballot in return for Rhodes's support of a labor package of unemployment and workmen's-compensation benefits. But a band of Democratic senators—including those who were backed heavily by union money in the key races—balked at the Rhodes-labor deal, and the bond issue failed to make the primary ballot. Several Democrats, including Zimmers, McCormack, and O'Shaughnessy, said they did not mind supporting the bills directly, but were not about to deliver the bond issues just because of labor's deal with Rhodes. Democratic Senate leaders joined in opposing two of the four bond issues, and all four were then dropped at Rhodes's suggestion. Instead, he placed them on the November 1975 ballot by petition, and in the fall campaign most Democratic senators, the A.F.L.-C.I.O., and the U.A.W. publicly opposed them.

The Effect of Campaign Reform

Ohio politicians performed many contortions in the name of campaign-finance reform in the wake of Watergate. In an effort to show that "safe-district" congressmen need not take contributions, U.S. Representative Charles Vanik, a Cleveland Democrat, vowed at the start of the year that he would not solicit, accept, or spend any campaign money for re-election. But Vanik found that others spent in his behalf (in slate spending), and he had to spend money to send money back. He reported it all. Many state candidates made pre-election disclosures voluntarily in the primary when none was required, some in response to a Common Cause request. They disclosed their income taxes and personal assets in press conferences. They made campaign-finance reform a major issue in their campaigns, and the Ohio legislature, with much fanfare, passed a modest reform bill.

Disclosure of contributors was measurably improved in 1974, especially after the new law took effect. The first mandated pre-election disclosure on October 24 gave Ohioans, through the media, their first glimpses into the way candidates financed campaigns. Requirements for centralized bookkeeping in one committee for each candidate made research easier and therefore disclosure more likely. Candidates and their fund-raising assistants said afterwards that it was probably one of the cleaner elections in Ohio history, although that is almost impossible to measure. Some candidates or their aides said money, especially cash, was offered to them under the table on the condition of nondisclosure, but they refused to take it. "It used to be a badge of courage for some of these guys to take money under the table, but this year, they would have been considered dumb," said William Bannon, deputy director of Gilligan's campaign. Many money-raisers still believed that some of this went on anyway.

But despite the atmosphere of reform and the effects of the disclosure law, the patterns of campaign finance did not appear to shift significantly. The amount of largesse declined slightly in many situations, but basically the same sources continued to provide it. And some circumventions of the law continued.

Enforcement of the law didn't begin until after reports were filed in December 1974. The Elections Commission received hundreds of complaints of minor violations (such as failure to file or to report all contributions) and had to make interpretations of language in the new law regarding these matters. It recommended prosecution in only six cases of minor candidates or groups; most cases were dismissed after the commission found most had "no willful intent" to violate the new law, with its little-known and largely uninterpreted provisions.

While politicians worried and fumed over the issue of campaign finance, it seemed to have no particularly strong effect on voters in state races. Although cynicism about politics did appear to cause a drop in voter turnout in some areas, voters seemed to be deciding elections on questions other than campaign reform. John Gilligan and Paul Matia were two candidates who came out strongly on the reform issue, and both lost. Two other candidates running on reform platforms, both challenging strong incumbents, also lost. One was Democratic state Senator Tony P. Hall, who challenged Secretary of State Ted Brown and spent three times as much as Brown—a third of it labor money—in attempting to show that the incumbent was less aggressive in pursuing Republicans than Democrats on alleged election-law violations. The other was Republican George C. Smith, a county prosecuting attorney from Columbus, who also challenged an incumbent Brown—Attorney General William J. Brown, a Democrat—with charges that the official conducted a "coverup" on the GAO report on the Ohio Democratic Party. Smith also tried to make an issue of the Attorney General's practice of soliciting contributions from "special counsels," attorneys hired by him to perform state service in their home towns because it is cheaper than hiring permanent state staff. Brown netted about $190,000 from three major fund-raising dinners given in his first three years in office, about 60 percent of that coming from special counsels and their law partners, who got a total of $1,598,346 in state fees over those years.

Incumbents were re-elected in every other race but one. In that contest, Richard F. Celeste, a Democratic state Representative from Cleveland with heavy labor backing, upset a third Brown, John W. Brown, a 16-year veteran of the office.

Money obviously did affect the elections. Rhodes spent a little less than Gilligan, but seemed to spend more effectively on media ads in the key markets. Democrats seized power decisively in the immensely important Ohio Senate races, with organized labor groups proudly pouring large contributions into the key races. Winning Democrats throughout the state outspent Republicans, who were plagued with contributor problems, especially early in the year.

Whether the 1974 distribution of funds will continue, reversing the traditional Republican advantage in that area, remains to be seen. After Gilligan's loss, the state Democratic Party fell into debt and had to move to smaller office space with only a handful of staffers, including a new state chairman acceptable to, but not handpicked by, Gilligan. But while the Governor's defeat caused financial problems for the party, the Democratic confederation was still intact with the survival of several state officeholders and a takeover of both houses of the legislature. The Republicans, similarly, can be expected to recover from fund-raising difficulties related to Watergate.

An even more important question than the amount and distribution of funds is whether the influence of special-interest money will continue to be seen in governmental decision-making. The incident in which Democratic senators balked at the deal between Rhodes and labor, despite the fact that labor support had helped them reach the Senate, gives some hope. But Governor Rhodes's swift introduction of a huge highway bond issue and his moves to loosen restrictions on strip-miners and nursing homes—two regulated industries that contributed heavily to his campaign—suggest that independence from such groups is yet to come in Ohio. The play of factions seems as prevalent in Ohio's politics as it is in the state's geography.

ELEVEN

NEW YORK:
LOOPHOLES AND LIMITS

Sam Roberts

Campaign financing in New York state's 1974 elections was influenced by four firsts: These were the first statewide contests after Watergate; the primary election was the first to be held in September (rather than June) in decades; the name of Nelson Rockefeller was not on the gubernatorial ballot for the first time in 20 years; and these were the first elections run under a new and stricter spending law.

More than $11 million was spent by gubernatorial and senatorial candidates. At the same time, under the pressure of the press and their opponents, candidates attempted to outdo each other on financial disclosure and voluntary requirements that went beyond the new law—which on several occasions also appeared to have been violated, in spirit if not in letter. The issue of candidates' independence (or lack of it as charged by opponents) was a central one in the major campaigns. Financing itself—which had not been taken seriously by the electorate in the four previous races involving a highly vulnerable Rockefeller—became a key issue in both the gubernatorial primary and the Senate election. But in both contests, media campaigns mounted by the big spenders enabled them to become winners by overcoming criticism from their rivals.

The New Law

The election law passed by the legislature and signed by Governor Malcolm Wilson in May 1974 provided for limits on donations and on total expenditures by a candidate, for

277

stricter reporting requirements, and for enforcement by a bi-partisan commission. Under the law, a statewide candidate could spend no more than $105,000 of his family's money in the primary and no more than $250,000 in the general election (5 percent of the total allowed); persons not related to the candidate could contribute no more than $21,000 to a single campaign or $150,000 to all campaigns in one calendar year. Loans would be counted as contributions if unpaid by primary or election day. Total spending was pegged at 50 cents per registered voter for statewide offices, or about $4 million; $40,000 in each election for state Senate, and $25,000 for Assembly candidates, with family money accounting for no more than 50 percent of these funds. In contrast to the national trend, the new law also permitted corporate contributions for the first time, although it limited them to $5,000. There was, in addition, a ban on cash contributions of over $100. Enforce-ment was by a new New York Board of Elections, which was empowered to subpoena witnesses to hearings and impose $1,000 fines for each violation but was not required to act on complaints within a specified time limit. The board was re-sponsible for setting reporting requirements, which it fixed in 1974 as August 16, September 3, 16, and 30, October 11 and 28, and November 25. The board was granted an initial outlay of $750,000, including the $25,000 annual salaries of each of four part-time commissioners (two Republicans and two Democrats) appointed by Wilson in June. Six days before the September primary, the board issued a strict fair-campaign code, designed, according to the board chairman, "to outlaw dirty tricks." The rules prohibited personal vilification or attacks based on race, sex, religion, or ethnic origin; misrepresentation of political positions; "political espionage"; and fraudulent literature or representation by one candidate's employees as supporters of another.*

In comparison with the law on the books in early 1974, the Election Procedures Reform Act seemed to be a real "reform." The old law, which had practically never been enforced, pro-vided for unrealistic spending ceilings based on the number of votes cast in the previous election, and for reporting only 10

---

* A suit brought by three Assembly candidates charged with campaign-law violations resulted in the voiding by a Federal court, in July 1975, of the prohibition against attacking a candidate's race, sex, religious, or ethnic background, and of the ban on misrepresentation of party affiliation or positions. The court found these restrictions "repugnant to the right of freedom of speech." None of the other provisions have yet been chal-lenged.

days before and 20 days after the primary and general elections. There was virtually no monitoring system; the secretary of state's office insisted that it served merely as a filing agency and only occasionally forwarded to the attorney general the names of those who failed to file.

Although the contribution and spending limits in the new law could not be described as unreasonably restrictive, they did constitute a brake on past practice in New York. For example, in 1970 the mother of U.S. Senate candidate Richard Ottinger contributed $1.7 million to her son's unsuccessful campaign; Rockefeller spent some $7.5 million, most of it reportedly family money, in his gubernatorial re-election effort; and Andrew Stein, a Manhattan Democrat, was reported to have spent $250,000 in his first campaign for the state Assembly, 10 times the amount he would be permitted under the new law. The law could be expected to prove especially onerous to candidates who had to rely on an expensive media effort to increase their public recognition but whose financial support was derived mostly from their own families and a few well-to-do friends. However, it was difficult to imagine anyone but a Rockefeller feeling constrained by the $4 million ceiling on spending for statewide offices.

Of course there were weaknesses—some apparent at the law's inception, others which came to light as the campaign progressed. Aside from the spending limits, which might be considered too high or too low depending on one's point of view, there was the question of enforcement. The new Board of Elections was clearly not an independent body but an avowedly partisan (if bipartisan) one, consisting as it did of former Supreme Court Justice Arthur Schwartz, who was counsel to the Republican State Committee; Remo J. Acito, counsel to the Bronx Democratic Committee; Donald Bettaliata, counsel to the Suffolk County G.O.P. committee; and former Democratic State Chairman William McKeon. The board was naturally reluctant to involve itself in controversy or to be boxed into making decisions at all, and few surprises could be expected from it during the campaign.

Enforcement was difficult, too, simply by virtue of the fact that the board, which was not appointed until June, had to get organized very quickly to administer the law. The counsel to a commission appointed by Rockefeller in 1973 to study campaign reform, whose report had helped form the basis for the new legislation, had predicted that "there will be a fair amount of confusion," and he was right. After the first filing date, on August 6, a clerk at the board's Albany headquarters described the office as a "nuthouse" and conceded that the board would be deluged with the second campaign reports before it had an opportunity to do anything more than file the first.

The fact that the new financial restrictions took effect in the middle of the primary campaign also affected the way some candidates observed the spirit of the law. Both major gubernatorial candidates raised substantial amounts before June 1, when the law went into effect, and these sums were not subject to limits on either candidate and family donations or spending.

The Race for Governor: Through the Loopholes

Despite the strictures imposed by the new Election Procedures Reform Act, Congressman Hugh L. Carey of Brooklyn spent more than $4 a vote to capture the Democratic primary in a campaign to which his brother contributed, lent and guaranteed loans of over $1 million of the total $2.5 million spent. About $300,000 of that was "repaid" by primary day through a series of questionable new loans. How could this happen? Carey's rival, longtime front-runner Howard J. Samuels, had to ask himself the same question after it was all over.

Things looked pretty good for Howard Samuels in early 1974. Three times before, Samuels, who was identified with the liberal or "reform" wing of the party, had sought the Democratic gubernatorial nomination and failed. But in his most recent attempt, in 1970, the former upstate industrialist had almost wrested it from the candidate backed by the "regulars," former U.S. Supreme Court Justice Arthur Goldberg. Goldberg managed a narrow party victory that year but suffered an embarrassingly severe loss in November to Governor Rockefeller, who won an unprecedented fourth term by his biggest margin ever. Perhaps the bosses had made a mistake.

Shortly after that defeat, Samuels was selected by Mayor John V. Lindsay to head the new New York City Off-Track Betting Corporation. (Samuels had bolted Democratic ranks to support Lindsay the year before.) OTB was a base from which Samuels could keep his loyal inner circle and troops together as he projected himself to the public as an executive who could apply the administrative skills of big business to usually inefficient and overextended government. He did both. Dozens of veterans of Samuels' political campaigns and other Democrats were placed on the payroll of OTB. And his reputation as the chairman and president of a scandal-free, revenue-producing public-benefit corporation put Samuels well in front of the race for governor before it ever began.

Like other candidates, Samuels spent a lot of time in 1973 and early 1974 raising funds. More than six months before the September primary, Samuels announced that he had received almost $200,000 in contributions from 951 New Yorkers. Although he sought to demonstrate his broad-based rank-and-file support with the fact that 70 percent of the donations (that is, number not amount) were for $25 or less, there were also a number of substantial gifts. Among the largest was $25,000 from Edgar Bronfman, the Seagram Distillery executive who had been a regular Samuels supporter. Later, Stewart Mott, the horticulturist, philanthropist, and General Motors heir, contributed $15,000 and lent the Samuels campaign another $45,045. Other big pre-primary donations included $25,000 from Arthur and Karen Cohen of Arlen Realty, whose buildings housed some OTB parlors; over $24,000 from builder Sigmund Sommer; $19,000 in gifts and loan guarantees from industrialist Charles Dyson; almost the same amount from John Tishman of the well-established realty firm that bears his family's name; and sizable amounts from the Alexander's Department Store family, garment-center executives and their companies, and other assorted individuals and firms. Of the total $170,000 in loans received by March 1974, more than $95,000 came from Samuels himself.

By June, the candidate disclosed that he had raised $750,000 since his campaign committee was formed in May 1973, 16 months before the primary. Most of that went for travel, communications, advertising, and telephone bills. Samuels' own loans and contributions to his campaign topped $190,000 by the June 1 effective date of the new financing law and would pass the $220,000 mark by the time of the primary.

Samuels' first noticeable opponent was Westchester Congressman Ogden Reid, whose family had published the now-defunct *New York Herald Tribune.* Only the year before, Reid had infuriated Rockefeller forces by switching parties and winning re-election as a Democrat. By the time 3,500 "friends" had consumed 135 quarts of liquor and created a miles-long traffic jam to his home where he opened his campaign in December 1973, Reid had already spent more than $100,000 and hired the first string of what was to be a battery of high-paid consultants, including Matt Reese and Associates of Washington, and at least nine salaried professionals.

By the end of February, Reid disclosed—voluntarily—that he had collected over $500,000 in loans and contributions and spent $470,000. He listed $16,655.31 in out-of-pocket expenses in an accounting period which dated back to February 1, 1973.

Like Samuels, Reid sought to emphasize the wide support he had received from small contributors by noting that 79 percent of his 393 contributions were under $100. But an even greater percentage of his *total receipts* for the period actually came from only three sources: Several Reid committees received a total of $90,000 from the candidate and his wife; another $100,-000 from Mr. and Mrs. Leonard Davis, longtime friends of the candidate (Davis is president of the Colonial Penn Insurance Companies); and a $200,000 loan from the Manufacturers Hanover Trust Compny guaranteed by Meshulam Riklis, the aggressive president of the Rapid-American Corporation conglomerate and chairman of Reid's fund-raising committees. There was one other large contribution: Seagram's Edgar Bronfman, who had contributed $25,000 to Samuels, gave the same amount to Reid.

Despite the amount of money raised and spent by Reid, however, he was not taken seriously as a candidate. Some thought he really planned to run for the Senate, either in 1974 or 1976; others that he was simply trying to establish himself as a Democrat. Many felt that he hadn't been in the party long enough to warrant its nomination. In any case, Reid dropped out of the race just before the convention and declined an offer of the Senate designation, which was going to be contested in the primary anyway.

Another candidate in the gubernatorial contest was generally taken even less seriously than was Reid. He was Donald Manes, the savvy and ambitious young Borough President of Queens, whose candidacy was sometimes dismissed as a stalking-horse or as a publicity-seeking stunt for a future city or state race. It says something about New York politics and campaign financing, however, that Manes could spend approximately $300,000—with about two-thirds of that from loans guaranteed by himself and a few friends—and still not be considered a serious candidate.

When the Democratic State Committee met in Niagara Falls on June 13 to select its nominees for statewide offices, Samuels was way out in front, and he got the designation. His fund-raising and his studious cultivation of party bosses over the years stood him in good stead, and the backing of the reform New Democratic Coalition (NDC), which he had gained earlier, provided a solid bloc of votes. But the regular support, which may have been broad, was not deep.

One of Samuels' challengers for the nomination was Hugh Carey, who was barely even recognized by the public outside his Congressional district, let alone considered a serious candidate. But the party leaders did take him seriously—the main reason probably being the campaign report Carey had just filed for the period January 1–May 31, which revealed that he had raised $692,000 ($660,000 from his brother) in five months —almost the amount it had taken the front-runner a year to amass. The bosses decided to give Carey 25 percent of their votes, which by party rules ensured him a place on the primary ballot. Samuels, although he had the support of a solid majority of the state committee, was unable to budge the bosses from this decision. Queens Democratic boss Matthew Troy, Jr. dubbed it "bossism in reverse" when the leaders ignored Samuels' pleas and allowed Carey in. What they really did was refuse to stop what seemed to be a rising Carey tide—one that they probably could have contained only at the cost of too many twisted arms. Their main fear was that the funds Carey had already proved he could attract would be turned against the party machine in local primary races. Since the Congressman had insisted he would run anyway, the maneuver eliminated the more politically —and financially—painful petition route to the primary,* which could encourage other anti-organization contests.

Money was not the only factor in the decision to give Carey a primary berth, however. Some party leaders, who were less than ecstatic about Samuels but were maneuvered into endorsing him because of his delegate strength, figured that Carey had a better chance against Governor Wilson. Many—if not most—of the party leaders at Niagara Falls preferred the "regular" Carey to the "reform" Samuels anyway, and had only backed Samuels (who had challenged them in the past) because they thought he was a winner. Once they had a chance to bail out, they took it. And then there were others with the misguided notion that handing Carey his 25 percent would afford him enough face-saving to switch to some other slot on the slate and leave the top spot to Samuels. But Carey was in the race to stay.

Unfortunately for the Samuels people, they didn't realize it. They had underestimated—dismissed might be a better word —Carey from the beginning, and the Democratic leaders' partial support of him did not change that strategy. The failure of Samuels to recognize Hugh Carey as a serious contender proved

---

* Under New York law, a candidate may qualify for the primary ballot either through selection by the party state committee or by securing the signatures of a certain number of qualified voters (the number of signatures depending upon the office sought) on nominating petitions. Under Democratic Party rules, candidates who get at least 25 percent of the state committee's votes in a designating convention gain a place on the primary ballot.

to be his fatal blunder. But it was easy to see how he made the mistake.

While the Samuels camp was preparing for formal entry into the race (he declared on February 13), the 55-year-old Congressman was being shepherded around by publicist Paul Buiar to kingmakers and image-molders who knew very little about him. They were aware that in 1969 he had hinted that he would mount an independent mayoral race but bowed out when 2 of his 14 children were killed in a car crash. They knew his wife was dying of cancer. They knew that he still had debts outstanding from his 1972 Congressional race. But very few of those early chaperones to Carey's political affairs and virtually none of his rivals knew anything about his brother. "If you go back," a still dazed Samuels campaign manager, Ken Auletta, recalled right after the election, "the big mistake in the campaign even more than underestimating Hugh Carey was in underestimating Edward Carey." Samuels' researchers quickly discovered that brother Ed was more than just "in the fuel oil business," but how rich the candidate's older brother was they did not imagine. He had not helped Hugh Carey before, as far as was known. Public records on his privately held companies were practically nonexistent.

But financial sources have estimated annual sales of the Carey Energy Group at about $1 billion. The keystone of the interlocking corporations is the New England Petroleum Corporation (NEPCO)—a major supplier of fuel to utilities in New York state and New England—of which Ed Carey is the sole stockholder. In fact, Edward Carey is the nation's largest independent oil producer. His savvy enabled him to profit from environmental laws by being among the first to lock up contracts for low-sulphur fuel and to capitalize on the energy crunch by breaking the Arab boycott with Libyan oil. Between pipelines awaiting approval from politically attuned agencies and especially family pride, he also had an obvious interest in his brother's election.

Once they had a better idea of Ed Carey's wealth, the Samuels people still didn't think he'd be able to use it under the new law. "In the spring of 1974 we saw Ogden Reid as the main opponent," Auletta recalled. "We looked at the new law and we were ecstatic—a family could put in no more than $105,000, and his brother had already put in 92 percent of Carey's total. We just said this almost guarantees the primary. From the day the law passed until it was signed, Edward Carey put in $375,-000—which we later tried to equate with Maurice Stans' satchel in 1972. We said how the hell is he going to report this? He reported it differently on his voluntary reports to the Democratic State Committee and to the state Board of Elections." And "after [Hugh Carey] got his 25 percent from the state committee," Auletta remembered, "we said he's not going to be able to come up with any money. The thing we were hearing was that he had terrible financial problems." The Samuels assessment, of course, turned out to be far from the truth. With Ed as a backer, Hugh Carey didn't need anyone else—at least not for a while.

The Carey campaign was launched at the end of the first week of January, when Ed Carey called the Bank of Commerce and guaranteed a $750,000 loan for the fledgling campaign apparatus, which was run like a venture-capital acquisition of the Carey Energy conglomerate. NEPCO Vice Presidents Patrick McKew and James McGregor were named as campaign treasurer and financial legal watchdog over finances, respectively. James H. Tully, a law partner of brothers Hugh and Dennis Carey in the firm that represented NEPCO, was installed as campaign committee chairman. A flock of NEPCO employees, from executives to secretaries, were granted voluntary leaves to create a campaign machinery from scratch.

One of the Carey campaign's first expenditures was $20,000 for a carefully circulated survey by Chicago pollster Leo Shapiro, which showed that Samuels did not have the primary locked up. Next, the Carey camp signed a $37,000-a-month contract with media-man David Garth, whose varied string of winners included John Lindsay, Los Angeles Mayor Thomas Bradley, Senators Adlai Stevenson of Illinois and John Tunney of California, and Governor Brendan Byrne of New Jersey. Garth immediately placed the Congressman on a diet that lost him almost 25 pounds, and on May 1 launched the first of 60 television and radio spots that would cost $1.5 million by the conclusion of the campaign.

Television proved to be the answer. What with Watergate reaching a climax in the Judiciary Committee's impeachment hearings and the subsequent resignation of Richard Nixon, there was no way that a relatively tame primary between two men of similar views was going to make news or create controversy. Carey, more than Samuels at first, needed the recognition and then popular acceptance that television commercials could accomplish. For days in early spring, Carey walked with a hired television crew a few steps in front of him through the Brooklyn Navy Yard, an upstate center for the deaf, and a tree-lined row of rehabilitated housing in hopes of walking off with the nomi-

nation. The first series of spots, costing $200,000, was launched
to impress political pundits and party potentates before the convention as well as to gain voter recognition and publicize
Carey's record in Congress. The ads carried themes such as
"When you try hard enough, you can get government to work
for people," and descriptions of Carey as "a decorated war hero
who spoke out for peace" and "a Catholic who is fighting for
Soviet Jewry." The advertisements played on a public skepti-
cism formed by Watergate and on Samuels' elaborate plans to
reform state government, with the warning: "Before they tell
you what they want to do, let them show you what they've
done."

Meanwhile, some Samuels strategists made the irreversible
tactical error of practically writing off the primary to conserve
their political and financial strength for the fight against Wilson
in November. And they allowed themselves to fall into the trap
of appearing to be incumbents in a year when that was particularly unpopular. "Governor Samuels in '74," the slogans
said. For those who even vaguely remembered how many times
Samuels had run, it seemed as though he was already in office
and should make way for a fresh face. The only other face left
in the gubernatorial primary race by then was Hugh Carey.

By the time Samuels' people realized their mistake in failing
to promote their candidate and meet the Carey media challenge,
there was neither the time nor the money to correct it. By mid-
summer, Samuels had spent slightly over $1 million and was los-
ing momentum, yet he still did not place a priority on media
spending. In August, with the declination date weeks gone and
Carey clearly a serious candidate, Samuels finally realized he
was in a horse race. Previous agreements to avoid vituperative
attacks that would make unity impossible after the primary col-
lapsed under the strain. Samuels' rhetoric increased in direct
proportion to his desperation. And, perhaps inevitably when
the tide is running the other way, everything he tried backfired. Samuels related high utility prices to Carey Energy profits,
to the Carey campaign; and some supporters released scurrilous
memos connecting Ed Carey with the "rabidly anti-Israeli, anti-
Jewish and anti-American" Libyan leader Qaddafi. Retaliating,
the Carey camp noted quietly that Samuels had failed to pay
New York city income tax for two years while a city official, that
Samuels himself had exceeded the limit on personal contributions (but he was within the range of candidate contributions),
and that Samuels had used "city time, city personnel, and a city
agency" to build his own personal political organization, without which he would not be running for governor.

When Carey commercials bombarded the airwaves in late summer, Samuels charged that Carey was mounting an "extravagant weekend media blitz. If Mr. Carey is buying time on an oil credit card," his opponent stated, "the public is entitled to know it now." And Samuels' campaign manager, looking back, says he thought then: "Obviously, his brother is putting in all the money and the last two weeks of the campaign will be a contest not between Hugh Carey and Howard Samuels, but between Hugh Carey and the law. I was still confident it was going to be a tremendous embarrassment." If the Carey campaign was unable to repay enough of Ed's loans by September 10, the candidate could be in the uncanny position of winning the primary and subjecting himself to almost automatic prosecution under the election law.

But Edward Carey was to pull yet another surprise. For months, his company accountants had been masterminding a financing system that seemed to fall just this side of the law. In addition to supplying different sets of statistics to the state Board of Elections and the Democratic State Committee, they prepaid television advertising and other bills before the June 1 operative date of the spending law, were slow to identify the occupations of some key contributors who turned out later to be oil company executives, and created an accountant's nightmare of campaign committees through which funds were transferred for no apparent reason. So effective were the accountants in carrying out the process and keeping it within the confines of the law that the Carey campaign was practically unaffected by attacks from Samuels. Responding to a charge by Samuels that Carey had received large loans just before the effective date, in violation of the spirit of the election law, Carey campaign treasurer Patrick McKew declared that the funds were needed for television commitments and pre-convention campaigning and flatly denied that any money had been "hidden." If anything had been played down, in fact, it was that from March 1 through May 31, only eight persons other than Edward Carey contributed $1,000 or more. That list was topped by oil-man Leon Hess ($6,000), Louis Russek ($5,000), and Carey's law partner Richard Manning ($3,000).

When Carey submitted his August finance report, it indicated that more than half of his almost $475,000 in receipts during June and July was in the form of loans from his brother. (It also disclosed that he had outspent Samuels by 50 percent—a revelation made particularly significant since Carey collected his $1.5 million in about half the time it took Samuels to accumulate $1 million.) By early August, Ed had lent or guaranteed loans totaling $1,175,000 to the campaign, $225,000 of it since June 1. His last big primary-campaign loan, for $122,-500, was made on August 13 and was followed up a week later by a final loan of $20,000. But the Samuels camp's hope that Carey could not get below the $105,000 family-donation limit by the September primary was not to be fulfilled. About $300,-000 would be contributed to bring Ed Carey well within the legal limit. Where it came from and how it arrived are still the subjects of controversy.

Starting in August, liquid assets from obscure sources began gushing into Carey's campaign coffers. Much of the money was in the form of loans—leading skeptics to surmise that the lenders were offered the no-risk proposition that they might some day be repaid by Edward Carey. It was difficult to attribute the sudden surge and the enormous proportions simply to spontaneous outpourings of support. Eventually, the bulk of them would be identified as having some connection to the still secret Carey Energy Group, its subsidiaries, and its customers. But the specific link was not clear until after the primary. On August 21, the day Edward Carey advanced his last $20,000, like amounts were lent by four other individuals: Jack McGregor, the NEPCO Vice President; Richard Manning, a Carey law partner; Kevin Cahill, the candidate's personal doctor, whom he would later nominate as a state health advisor, and Jane E. Haswell, Edward Carey's daughter. On August 30, Harold Fisher, a friend, politically prominent attorney, and gubernatorial appointee to the Metropolitan Transportation Authority, and his son Andrew each lent $20,000; Richard Weinand, another NEPCO official, lent $18,000.

But that was only the beginning. Between August 31 and September 3, more than $200,000 in loans alone materialized from divergent sources who seemed to sense an increasing air of urgency to bring Edward Carey within the legal limit. Oil lawyer Samuel Nakasian lent $21,000, and $20,000 each was produced by Lehman Brothers partner James Glanville and Abraham Lindenbaum, a politically potent real estate attorney who was an intimate of the officially neutral Mayor of New York, Abraham Beame. Another $10,000 each came from two other Lehman Brothers partners, Alan McFarland and Lewis Glucksman. Pierre Senecal, President of the NEPCO Canadian subsidiary, lent $9,500.

By September 9, the day before the primary, enough loans and gifts had been accumulated to bring Ed below the $105,000 family-contribution limit and, campaign officials said, even under the $21,000 personal limit. Included in the last-minute largesse was $21,000 each from brothers Dennis and Martin Carey, $20,000 each from Corbin Robertson, Sr. of Houston, Joseph Savoca of Commonwealth Oil of Puerto Rico, and John C. Gorman of Eller Terminals, another NEPCO subsidiary. Arthur Erb, an associate of Gorman, lent another $18,000, $20,000 more came from Andrew Calamari of the Carey law firm, and $5,000 each flowed in from K. K. of Hong Kong, NEPCO Washington representative Robert Trevisani, a car-wash company with a Park Avenue address, and each of three companies—Navaho Offshore Services of Italy and the Compania de Navigation and General Engineering of Panama—controlled by Franco Salenbeni, the Milanese man whose agency built NEPCO's Bahamian refinery.

Three days before the primary, Samuels demanded that his rival release a list of last-minute contributors to the public, rather than simply following the letter of the law by mailing lists of $1,000-plus contributors to the state Board of Elections on a daily basis during the final week of the campaign. Samuels named his own benefactors, among them retailer Robert Levinson, who lent $10,000 in the last few days on top of $16,000 previously lent or guaranteed, and the Committee on Political Education of the International Union of Electrical, Radio and Machine Workers in Washington, which contributed $10,000.

The same day the Carey money was being counted, the votes were also being tallied. With surprising ease, Carey delivered a stinging rebuke to both the Democratic State Committee and the NDC with which it had joined in an unusual alliance. He defeated Samuels—who was so confident that he had already chartered a plane for a post-primary campaign swing upstate—600,000 to 387,000. Slightly more than 25 percent of the state's eligible Democrats bothered to vote. As it turned out, not one committee-backed candidate won, except the lone Democratic incumbent, Comptroller Arthur Levitt. But the bosses' "defeat" in the governor's race had to be seen in light of the fact that after endorsing Samuels in June, key party leaders had either covertly campaigned for his opponent or simply sat on their hands.

When the books closed on the primary campaign, Carey had outspent Samuels by $2.5 million to $1.6 million. Of that total, media expenditures accounted for over $750,000 from the Carey camp and only $120,000 of Samuels' expenses.

Why was Carey able to survive the Samuels salvos on campaign spending when it was such a sensitive issue? Ken Auletta offered this view: "One of the great ironies was that Hugh Carey actually benefited from Watergate much more than Howard, because it looked like he was running against an established candidate. He effectively boxed us in. As for the money issue, it was one of the great puzzlements. So many of the late loans were related to NEPCO. We tried to put that out, and it was so late in the campaign that it wasn't believable. The press had a lot to do with it. There was an unconscious bias. A lesson I would learn is that if you're going to use negative stuff, use it early. If you wait till the last minute, it looks like a large part of the information is coming from one camp. And to break away from the daily coverage to do an investigation, and to look like the *Daily News* or *New York Times* is taking sides by running an exposé is in a way like injecting yourself into a campaign. The press didn't do its job."

But Auletta and other Samuels supporters hadn't thought it would take the press to bare and neutralize Ed Carey—and thus destroy his brother's chances. They believed the law would obviate the need for muckraking. When Ed Carey was miraculously repaid, the issue of his loans died with Samuels' candidacy, although it was unsuccessfully resurrected later by an equally desperate Malcolm Wilson. A few days before the November election, Wilson aides suggested that the $750,000 bank loan guaranteed in January 1974 had violated the election law. In January 1975, almost a year after the loan was guaranteed, the Board of Elections stated that there was nothing wrong with consolidating the loan because it was received before the June 1 effective date of the election law.

The General Election

The main objective of the Republican-controlled legislature in 1974 when it moved the state primary from June to September was to ensure that the traditionally divided Democrats would be so thoroughly at odds after a long primary battle that they could never regroup for the November election. (The stated goal of the switch was to save campaign costs.) This strategy was to backfire—as did so much in the 1974 elections. In fact, Hugh Carey emerged from his long primary campaign against Howard Samuels with enough momentum to unify all the various and usually warring Democratic factions and to go on to a strong victory in the general election.

Part of his new strength was reflected in a change in financing: His brother was no longer Carey's sole means of support and gave very little to his campaign. Other sources of funds opened up, although the cash flow was not as great as it might have been in pre-Watergate days. In New York, as elsewhere, 1974 did not look like a Republican year, and Malcolm Wilson —who had remained in the background for 15 years as Rockefeller's Lieutenant Governor, and seemed even more bland as Governor—didn't have much going for him. He'd become Governor automatically when Rockefeller resigned in January (ostensibly to head his own Commission on Critical Choices, probably to run for President) and somehow had the aura of a lame duck from the start. So Carey, who like Wilson was a Catholic and thus a good bet to recapture for the Democrats those Catholic voters who had recently backed Republicans, was immediately the front-runner.

Traditional sources such as unions, real-estate interests, and the Democratic Party gave or lent significant sums to Carey, as did oil interests. The state party, which had raised about $132,-000 from the national party's June telethon and about $10,000 in an auction the same month, gave Carey about $115,000 in funds that were difficult to trace to individuals because they were funneled through dozens of local committees. Organized labor gave $400,000, the largest share from the waterfront unions which have long exercised virtually unchallenged political clout in Carey's home district. Public-employee unions gave over $50,000, and the traditionally Democratic and liberal International Ladies Garment Workers Union $40,000. Among regulated industries, notable donations came from six liquor distributors, who gave $25,000, and from insurance executive Leonard Davis, who gave $25,000.

Corporate contributions played a new role in the 1974 election. For years, politically connected companies or those that sought political connections for state road-building, construction, insurance, and other contracts had quietly contributed cash or services in the form of postage stamps, lumber for billboards, attorneys' time, troops to collect petition signatures or distribute literature, and office space. Finally, following various unsuccessful prosecutions and wholesale evasion of the ban, the election law was amended in 1974 to permit corporate contributions. Unlike unions, however, whose political-action arms could supply unlimited resources, corporate donors were restricted to $5,000 per campaign. But because the new provision so directly contradicted what the corporations had been warned about for years, and since it was enacted in the midst of widespread prosecutions and disclosures for similar secret donations to the 1972 Republican Presidential campaign, company officials were understandably wary about changing their ways.

"They were so nervous," one Democratic fund-raiser recalled, "that every time you solicited from a corporation you had to send them a copy of the law."

Most corporate campaign contributions were from small, privately held firms whose executives were unburdened by any requirements to consult stockholders or boards of directors. This was particularly true of Carey's donations, which came mostly from firms that had an affiliation or commercial link with the oil empire presided over by his brother. By election day, Carey had collected approximately $100,000 from roughly 100 firms, including foreign companies, that were involved in the refining, shipping, and brokerage of oil. In fact, the bulk of Carey's special-interest money came from oil and related industries.

In some cases, the corporate-contribution provision created a complication for independent analyses of receipts—already complicated by the plethora of political committees and the sometimes inexplicable transfers of funds among them. For instance, Brooklyn real-estate mogul Donald J. Trump, who has frequent contacts with city and state agencies and departments, contributed about $25,000 through seven companies obscurely described in official filings by names like Boro Office Corporation and Nautilus Hall but all firms controlled by the Brooklyn builder through holding companies. Specific links like these or connections involving foreign-based firms were often difficult to establish without the cooperation of the candidates themselves. It was clear in some cases that such cooperation was provided only because the candidates feared adverse publicity if they refused to divulge the specific identity of donors.

Much of the Carey campaign's financing, in the general election as in the primary, came from loans. Just after the primary, the Carey camp borrowed $50,000 from a politically prominent banker, Abraham Feinberg of the American Bank and Trust Company, and $35,000 from well-connected attorney William Shea (for whom the baseball stadium is named). Although overwhelmingly positive polls helped perk up the pace of contributions as the election approached, Carey was forced to turn to loans, direct and indirect, to help finance a media campaign whose cost was about the same as the primary blitz. The Bronx Democratic County Committee, whose Chairman, Patrick Cunningham, was to become Democratic State Chairman after the election, borrowed $50,000 to pass on to the Carey campaign. Some $50,000 in loans was guaranteed by investment bankers Herbert Allen and his son, who specialize in municipal bonds (and who had already contributed over $25,000), and by film executive and lawyer Arthur Krim. Another $50,000 loan was guaranteed by two Rochester aviation executives. James P. Wilmot and Raymond Hylan. James H. Tully, the former Carey law partner who would become State Tax Commissioner in the new administration, lent $10,000. Some Wilson backers also gave to Carey late in the campaign.

Carey's manager, Jerry Cummins, described the new donor interest in his candidate: "Very early in the campaign, we had a very difficult time getting money because nobody thought we were able to win. Especially before June 1, without someone to have given Hugh Carey enough to put himself across, Hughie was a dead man. Then, a lot of people didn't understand the law. We went to them and said that Ed Carey under the law has got a problem. Up to that point, people said, 'What the hell do you need money for? You've got all the money you need.' Even after the primary it was difficult because of the new law. People had already given to other campaigns, and there was a tendency to stay away because people felt they would be put under a microscope. And any time people will find an excuse they will use it. So many people had already gotten in trouble giving money (in the Watergate scandal) that they wouldn't give anything—or they would give $1,000 when they used to give $5,000. Our major problem was that guys were scared from the past and some used it as an excuse. And our most effective fund-raising tool was when they thought Hugh Carey could win."

Malcolm Wilson spent a fraction of the amount his predecessor had disbursed in 1970 and was unable to raise anything close to the $3 million he had assured party officials he would collect. But although his campaign was sometimes short of funds —as was Carey's—money didn't decide this election. For one thing, Wilson spent a little more than Carey, $2.7 million to $2.5 million, although Carey had invested in a lot of media during the primary that helped propel him to the governorship. The vote totals, 2.9 million for Carey compared with 2.1 million for Wilson, meant that it cost Carey roughly 80 cents a vote to win this election (as against $4 in the primary), Wilson $1.20 a vote to lose it. "I don't think you can blame it on money in itself," Republican State Chairman Richard Rosenbaum remarked later. "I don't think we really had much chance to win, after 16 years, the economy, inflation, Watergate, and the pardon. There were too many unsurmountable obstacles."

More than half of Wilson's receipts came from the Republican Party, whose state and local committees reportedly gave over

$1 million—much more support than Carey got from the Democrats. The distribution mechanisms were similar for both parties. The funds appeared on contribution lists as block grants, with no hint of their original individual or corporate sources. Individual party committees reported their receipts, but there was no way of knowing what proportion of a single contribution was actually earmarked for the Wilson campaign. The $145,000 from Nassau County Republican boss Joseph Margiotta's machine, $75,000 from the Governor's Club, and $600,000 from the state organization and its dinner committees provided stark proof of the ability of a party in power to attract financial support. Wilson also benefited from substantial contributions from Republican businessmen, including trade associations and executives of companies specifically subject to state regulation, such as the Saratoga Harness Racing Association, which gave $7,500, and four executives of the American Home Assurance Company, who contributed $5,000 each. Wilson also got about $60,000 from corporations, most of it in amounts well under the $5,000 limit.

While Wilson did not end up in debt, Carey did. The new Governor had $1,585,000 in outstanding pre-primary loans, another $480,000 from the general-election race, and an estimated $250,000 in bills for printing, telephones, and other items. It was thus a good thing for the Democrats that contributions kept coming in after the election victory. Still, further fund-raising was necessary in order to repay the deficit. Carey held a $500-a-plate inaugural ball at the Waldorf-Astoria, which collected almost $500,000, and a $100-per-person buffet affair at Lincoln Center's New York State Theater, which raised another $135,000. Special interests, wealthy individuals, and prominent state officials were among those on the guest list. Perhaps the most ingenious idea on the part of the Carey camp was to print a political and governmental guide to New York that would be financed with $3,000 contributions from each of about 300 contributors, which was expected to decrease Carey's campaign debt by almost $1 million. Carey named a six-person executive finance committee to work on repaying the rest of the debt. Lacking, however, was the same sense of urgency that accompanied repayment of Edward Carey's loans in the final days of the September primary. No such deadline applied after the election.

Ramsey Clark: Less Is More?

When Ramsey Clark decided to enter the New York senatorial primary early in 1974, very few people (including some of his own workers) thought he had a chance. And when he won that primary in September, once again very few people thought he could beat incumbent Republican Jacob J. Javits. This time they were right, but Clark came rather close—2 million votes to Javits' 2.3 million. The soft-spoken, transplanted Texan who was Attorney General under Lyndon Johnson didn't raise quite as much as his opponents in either race, but Clark's fund-raising method may have earned him more votes than the more usual approach could have bought him.

Aside from Edward Carey, who persistently tried to stay as far from the public eye as possible, Clark was the only major figure in the 1974 statewide political picture to put campaign financing on the front page. His strategy was simple. No campaign contribution would be accepted from any individual if it exceeded $100. Clark had even toyed with the idea of a $10 ceiling but was convinced by nervous fund-raisers that it would not be practical.

After a few early entrants dropped out of the race, the Democratic primary was a contest among Clark, State Committee designate Lee Alexander, the Mayor of Syracuse, who was virtually unknown outside that city, and Abraham Hirschfeld, an immigrant and a self-made millionaire garage-owner. While Clark talked about his independence, Alexander wound up being tied to an unpopular establishment without reaping any of the advantages that the Democratic designation might have provided in other times. Within a week before the primary, he had reported raising just over $50,000, more than half of it in the form of a $27,000 loan from Arnold Grant, a New York City attorney and ex-husband of former city Consumer Affairs Commissioner Bess Myerson. Syracuse realtor Henry Bersani lent another $5,000, and most of the rest was contributed by local business and professional men from New York City and Syracuse—including $1,000 from ubiquitous builder Christopher Boomis.

By the time Hirschfeld was through, he had spent almost $500,000 in a complicated series of loans and repayments through other loans, including loans of $100,000 each from his wife and from Ace Wire and Cable Company Board Chairman Jack Firestone. He also relied on a less sophisticated version of the media blitz that had won Westchester Representative Richard Ottinger the Democratic Senate nod in 1970, to evolve from an unknown former state party treasurer into a candidate who captured almost 25 percent of the vote. With only three candidates in the race, however, 25 percent was not enough. Hirschfeld had sunk most of his money in media and never was able to project anything more than the image of a heavily accented, candid, well-meaning man voters might like to discuss politics with over a backyard fence but not necessarily send to Washington. "All I had was television," Hirschfeld would lament later, "and it was not enough."

Clark raised $230,000 from 11,500 people by primary day—all reported to be in the form of contributions of $100 or less—and on that day he was carried in on the crest of the anti-establishment sentiment that swamped virtually every State Committee candidate, polling over 400,000 votes to Alexander's 250,000 and Hirschfeld's 200,000. And Clark, whose victory was expected just before the election but whose margin was a surprise, looked longingly to the general-election race, when his campaign-financing practices would present an even starker contrast with his Republican rival.

By this time, Javits knew he was facing what he would describe later as the toughest fight of his political life. How long would Carey's coattails be? How many Republicans would be too embarrassed by the antics of their national leaders to make their way to the polls? How accurate was the assessment of a Clark supporter that "the 'undecideds' are good for five points, and the unenthusiastic Republicans are another three points for us, and maybe Carey is good for another five. You add all that up, and it's a horse race." Tentatively on the plus side was the Conservative Party candidacy of Vietnam war widow Barbara Keating, who was expected to erode the Democratic vote. And there was lingering hostility over Clark's controversial visit to Hanoi—hostility that was muted only slightly by Javits' sojourn to Havana on a Senate-sanctioned trip in the middle of the campaign. Javits, armed with the Liberal Party line on the November ballot, also had an additional advantage that had become commonplace for New York state Republicans: He had no primary challenges and could sit back for several months collecting money and watching the Democrats squabble over who would wind up opposing him.

By primary day, when Clark had a surplus of $12,000, Javits had raised well over $450,000—more than half of it from a gala fund-raising dinner the previous spring—and spent about $150,-000. Almost $290,000 of his receipts, according to Common Cause, came in the form of contributions of $500 or more, including over $100,000 from 26 persons who each contributed $3,000 or more. By the end, Javits raised and spent over $1 million, Clark about $850,000.

Javits' big donors were mostly the Republican businessmen who had supported the Senator in his past campaigns. Maybe

they were giving less than usual (the Senator's campaign manager, John Trubin, said donations were at least 25 percent
behind previous years, mainly due to Watergate, the economy, and disclosure laws), but most of them were there. It was
reported, in fact, that Javits established at least 10 campaign committees to take advantage of the Federal law limiting contributions to $5,000 to any single committee. (Samuels and other
statewide candidates did the same to allow donors to keep individual contributions below $3,000 to avoid the gift tax.)
Political committees of more than a dozen national unions gave
Javits $1,000 or more. And the National Republican Senatorial
Committee contributed $10,000.

But one major source of receipts was missing. The Republican State Committee, which had been counted on for around
$300,000, begged off because it did not want to subject itself to
the strict disclosure requirements of the Federal campaign-
financing law. Since that statute covered services as well, it
meant that the State Committee switchboard and photocopying
capacity were no longer available to Javits as they had been in
past campaigns. "The Federal law became somewhat complicated and technical," Republican Chairman Rosenbaum observed. "If you put up a billboard with two Federal faces, you
would have to split the costs. And contributors would have to
divulge information that they might not have wanted to divulge. Because of the Federal regulations, we tried to encourage
people to contribute to Javits directly."

Whether big contributions were "off" in 1974 or not, their
continued predominance in Javits' campaign was a major Clark
target. "Has he learned nothing from Watergate?" Clark asked
of his Republican rival. "Senator Javits says he must raise and
spend at least a million dollars in order to acquaint the voters
with his record, and the reason he needs so much is that his
record is so extensive. But if the public still doesn't know the
Javits record after his 18 years of free mailing privileges, there
must be something unimpressive about that record." Time after
time—in press conference, news release, and interview—Clark
would hammer away at that theme. Analyzing the $500,000
Javits had raised by September, Clark charged that more than
75 percent was from contributions of $1,000 or more, 25 percent
came from banking and security interests, and more than 5 percent from food and pharmaceutical executives whose industries
the Senator's subcommittee regulates. Clark caustically noted
that Javits held an $8,000 contribution from the Maritime
Engineer's Beneficial Association for a month before returning
it—two days before he voted against a bill to require that more

foreign oil be carried on American ships. Clark listed dozens of corporations whose executives "have contributed larger amounts to his campaign than I accept from anyone" and asked rhetorically: "Why do they contribute? Because they know they have a friend in Washington." Clark slammed the Senator for accepting over $5,000 from George and Ruth Farkas in 1968 and then helping Mrs. Farkas become U.S. Ambassador to Luxembourg. And he repeatedly assailed him for accepting a $15,000 contribution from Vice President–designate Rockefeller, on whose confirmation Javits would have to vote.

Even in a year when campaign financing was more on the mind of the electorate than ever before, and despite what was probably the closest thing to public funding in New York state politics, Ramsey Clark's Senate bid failed. Why didn't the public buy Clark as a candidate? For one thing, Javits was an extremely popular Senator among Republicans and Democrats alike. He had few natural enemies, which could hardly be said of Clark—whom many considered a radical, someone outside the mainstream of American politics. Javits had generally been considered unbeatable by any Democrat, so perhaps the surprise was not that Clark didn't beat him—even in an anti-Republican, Watergate year—but that he came so close.

It can be debated, but probably cannot be concluded, that the $100 limit kept Clark from winning the election. After all, he raised $850,000, and by choice spent little on television (which might have made a difference). "I think as one among a number of issues campaign financing was a plus," Clark's campaign manager, Victor Navasky, reflected later; "but it was not enough of a plus to cancel out the fact that Javits was Jewish when the Palestine Liberation Organization was coming to New York, that Javits had a very strong constituency. And it didn't overcome any incipient fear people had about Ramsey and about his trip to Hanoi and other stands. It's a lot of baggage to come into a campaign with. If we had lots of money and been willing to spend it on TV—which wouldn't have been Ramsey —we might have done something else."

Was the $100 contribution limit a mistake? "On balance, almost everybody thought it was a great thing," Navasky observed. "Psychologically, it was a unifying force—it was a rallying point, it gave a theme to the campaign that interrelated with other things. It also affected expectations—that salaries would be low, that money should not be wasted. And it helped get a lot of volunteers. We ended up raising most of our money through the mails," Navasky continued. "Traditionally, we would go to an investment banker. To get a guy who could get on the phone and raise $10,000 wouldn't do us any good. So we got Paul Gottlieb of American Heritage and raised $500,000 by direct mail. The advantage is that you're advertising while you're fund-raising. . . . We also had a recognizable constituency, a liberal constituency that you can reach economically by using liberal magazine mailing lists. On the first mailing of 400 we made $20,000, and it kept pyramiding. But when you do that you don't have your 'real money' until the last month of the campaign. And you never know when you raise money through the mails how long it would last."

By the end of the campaign, Navasky recalled, "even if we had wanted to do an ambitious television we didn't have the cash to do it. In the end we found ourselves with $150,000 for TV, but we hadn't been able to reserve the time. Ramsey didn't want to use TV at all." That $150,000 was less than a third of what Javits spent on television time and production.

By November, the Clark campaign had received contributions from 30,000–40,000 individuals, all of which had to be carefully computerized to comply with reporting requirements. Another problem unforeseen when the $100 limit was conceived was making sure the contributors kept their donations to $100 each for the primary and general elections. "When you're in trouble you go back to them [the early supporters]," Navasky recalled. "We couldn't do that. Then Ramsey added his condition of no loans. And you couldn't give $100-plus tickets to a benefit. We wanted to keep to the spirit and we were also concerned that Javits would come in [and criticize the campaign for failing to adhere to the standards set by Clark]. Ramsey said let them in for nothing. So since we had too many people who already gave $100, we let them in for cost. In an infuriating way, we stuck to that. In the ticket-selling wing, someone would want to buy tickets in another name. Some of that inevitably goes on. But we returned checks from unions and individuals and also corporate accounts. Over $20,000—in a hundred individual checks—was returned. The real benefit of it all was vis-à-vis Javits. It embarrassed him into spending less and raising less."

Javits campaign manager Trubin disputed Navasky's assessment of the impact of the $100 limit. "It was a conversation piece," the affable lawyer replied. "You had to respond to it. It was a useful tool to Clark—and probably we were affected by it somewhat. But we were sticking very closely to what we could handle. If we had the money, we would've probably committed and spent more. We were very careful. And at the end, we didn't have any more newspaper ads because we didn't have the money. We were running against the tide and we had a lot to overcome. It was a bad year for incumbents all over. Jack's victory was a very significant one in that climate and under those circumstances."

Other Perspectives

None of the other statewide races were affected by money as were the gubernatorial primary and Clark's race. The Democratic primary for lieutenant governor (a post for which citizens vote separately in the primary but which is linked to the governor in the general election) was a three-way race. Major candidates were Manhattan Assemblyman Antonio Olivieri, who spent $120,000—almost half from himself and his family—and gained 220,000 votes; Mario Cuomo, a lawyer who spent $115,-000 and got 285,000 votes; and Mary Anne Krupsak, an upstate Senator, who spent just over $40,000 and won with 375,000 votes. Thus if money mattered at all, it seemed to matter in a strange way, for spending proved to be in inverse proportion to the number of votes received. There was a limit to the effectiveness of commercials, newspaper advertisements, and stuffed mailboxes for a race that many considered to be insignificant for anyone but the odd man out to win. In this case, of course, the odd man turned out to be a woman—who became the first of her sex to be elected to major statewide office since an election for secretary of state 50 years before.

The gubernatorial candidates were in a political bind when it came to the primary for lieutenant governor. Neither wanted to run the risk of alienating any portion of his constituency by endorsing one of the three contenders, yet each wanted the strongest candidate to win in order to enhance the ticket's chances of victory in November. Samuels was faced with an even more complicated problem in making a choice: Both he and Olivieri had been endorsed by the NDC; Cuomo, however, was the State Committee candidate. Convinced that coupling his campaign with Cuomo's would help him capture the Democratic nomination as well as the more important prize in the general election, Samuels decided to endorse the Queens lawyer and create a joint campaign committee with him. But what he wound up doing was alienating two constituencies: Olivieri and the reformers were miffed because Samuels had spurned the designated NDC candidate; and Cuomo became irate because Samuels, seeking to have the best of both worlds, was printing joint campaign literature and palm cards with Olivieri, as had been agreed earlier, as well as with Cuomo. Samuels' ties to both Cuomo and Olivieri, which in the long run did not do any of the three much good, simply served to highlight the fact that Krupsak was someone fresh and seemingly independent—a distinction that otherwise would probably have benefited Cuomo, who was making his first bid for political office.

The winner of the primary for attorney general, Robert Abrams, the reform Bronx Borough President, tried to make an issue of campaign financing in his general-election race against long-term incumbent Louis Lefkowitz. Abrams urged the attorney general to survey all state officials to determine whether they had received gifts or loans from Rockefeller, whose personal largesse to his official family was revealed in the middle of the fall campaign. (Lefkowitz complied with Abrams' request by asking for a ruling from his rarely convened advisory committee on ethics.) Abrams also accused his Republican rival of "election-year cynicism and hypocrisy" for reportedly supporting a prohibition against campaign contributions from staff members of elected officials while at the same time accepting some donations from his own staff. Abrams, who received several contributions from former staffers of the Borough President's office, said Lefkowitz had received contributions from almost half of his 328 assistant attorneys general—including more than $100 each from 19 of his 24 bureau chiefs. Whether the public was impressed was not clear. Abrams lost toLefkowitz by 2.6 million to 2.2 million—a respectable showing against a man generally considered invincible.

Questions of illegality and misuse of campaign funds were raised several times during the 1974 elections. Perhaps in less sensitive times they would have been overlooked. In one case, only days before the primary, the state Senate Crime Committee began an inquiry into an alleged payment from Matthew Shipman, Assemblyman Antonio Olivieri's campaign manager, to a delegate at the June Democratic designating convention who was wavering on the vote for lieutenant governor. A day after the delegate gave the committee a statement, Olivieri fired Shipman for "an error of judgment" with an "inference of impropriety" for having handed the delegate a blank $1,500 check at the Niagara Falls convention (for what was intended to be a joint political mailing).

In late July, the *New York Times* quoted two ranking Democrats as saying that U.S. Senate contender Abraham Hirschfeld was ready to donate $50,000 to Allard Lowenstein's Nassau

County Congressional campaign (Lowenstein had decided to run for Congress after bowing out of the Senate primary). It also developed that Hirschfeld allegedly had earlier offered up to $10,000 each to Clark and Lowenstein, but denied that it was to induce them to leave the race. Lowenstein said he had received $5,000 from Hirschfeld; Clark acknowledged having received $200 from Hirschfeld and his wife, but promptly returned it upon realizing, after the disclosures, that it did not "reflect friendship." Since the man who allegedly offered the $50,000, an attorney friend of Hirschfeld, also worked for Samuels, the controversy spilled over into the gubernatorial campaign. Both Samuels and Carey called for an investigation, however, and the Board of Elections cleared all the participants of wrongdoing by late August.

At about the same time, the Board of Elections ruled that there was no impropriety proven in allegations that petition carriers for Court of Appeals candidate Jacob Fuchsberg and interim Manhattan District Attorney Richard Kuh were paid by the number of signatures they collected. Chairman Arthur Schwartz of the board, which angrily warned partisans not to bounce "spurious claims of misconduct" off the board, happened to be on a list of six former Bar Association presidents and three retired judges who had endorsed Kuh for a full term.

One factor in the awareness of campaign-finance details was recent local scandals, which combined with Watergate and new laws to create an atmosphere of caution. A series of incidents embarrassing to those involved (and sometimes costly in terms of money and position) had begun in June 1973 when 70-year-old Wall Street investment banker John L. Loeb was fined the maximum $3,000 for illegally disguising $48,000 in contributions to Senator Hubert Humphrey's unsuccessful bid for the 1972 Democratic Presidential nomination. Loeb insisted that it was "a mistake made unwittingly and promptly corrected" when he funneled his donation to the Humphrey campaign committee through the personal checking accounts of eight employees of his investment firm.

In December 1973, several of the state's most powerful Republicans, including Assembly Speaker Perry Duryea, were indicted for financing and executing a scheme to siphon votes from Democratic Assembly candidates by creating a bogus Action Committee of the Liberal Party to circulate literature for Liberal officeseekers in a dozen marginal districts. Although the charges were dismissed in January 1974, on the ground that the law under which the Republicans had been indicted was unconstitutional, the taint of the indictment was enough to curb any political ambitions Duryea may have had (he was widely believed to have been eyeing the governor's office) and made campaign treasurers more wary of practices that had been commonplace in the past.

Early in 1974 Watergate Special Prosecutor Leon Jaworski announced the indictment of George M. Steinbrenner III, Chairman of American Ship Building and a general partner in the New York Yankees, for illegally contributing company funds to the campaigns of former President Nixon and members of Congress, both Democrats and Republicans. After initially loudly proclaiming his innocence, Steinbrenner pleaded guilty and was fined $15,000.

In late spring, Representative Angelo D. Roncallo, a Long Island Republican, was tried on charges of extorting funds from a local contractor for the benefit of the Republican Party. Acquitted, Roncallo declared during his re-election race: "I get a $3 check from a guy in South Dakota and I have to find out what he does to assure no possible conflict of interest."

Meanwhile, much publicity surrounded the indictment of Brooklyn Representative Bertram Podell, a generally liberal Democrat, for using his influence to help a Florida airline win a lucrative Bahamas air route and taking $41,350 in bribes in the guise of legal fees and campaign contributions. Podell convinced the Democratic organization of his innocence and ran for re-election (thus having the dubious distinction of then being the only Congressman in the country seeking re-election while under indictment) but lost the primary. On October 1, Podell stunned his supporters by pleading guilty to conspiracy and conflict of interest.

Such scandals helped to encourage some voluntary efforts to curb abuses and promote public awareness. The most publicized was of course Ramsey Clark's self-imposed $100 contribution ceiling. Another was the agreement arranged by the Democratic State Committee under which statewide candidates would divulge their campaign finances more often than required by law. This disclosure program was limited to the primary and required candidates to make updated lists of campaign contributors available to the State Committee, which in turn made them available to other candidates. The arrangement worked moderately well, except that Ramsey Clark refused to participate and Hugh Carey's reports were occasionally confusing since they were not always compatible with figures his committees filed with the state. Another effect of the scandals was a greater scrutiny by the press, which devoted more time and space to campaign financing than ever before.

Independent, good-government groups also tried to shine light on the subject. Just before the primary, the New York Public Interest Research Group, an independent offshoot of Ralph Nader's similar Congressional-inquiry project, issued individual booklets about the voting records, community standing, and financial situation of 191 members of the state legislature. Common Cause monitored campaign contributions, in part as a first step in a full-fledged scrutiny of state government and support of the same kind of reforms enacted by referendum in California. Because it lacked time and manpower, however, the group did not continue the monitoring project through the final financial reports.

The Board of Elections probably had some effect on ensuring compliance with the new campaign-finance law, although its efforts could not be called aggressive. Many candidates in legislative contests were unacquainted with the specific filing requirements and failed to file some reports or simply left out information such as addresses and occupations of contributors. After its confusion early in the campaign, the commission notified by mail those not filing within five days of the due date and sued dozens of candidates who still failed to file. It eventually succeeded in getting forms from most candidates.

In May 1975, the Board of Elections decided that Carey had not violated the new election-law limits on spending and contributions. But the board's two Republican members, expressing concern over the Carey campaign's finances under the old law that expired June 1, 1974, stated: "In our opinion, the evidence supports a finding that there was a reckless disregard of the limitations contained in Section 455 of the law . . . wherefore it is our considered judgment that there is reasonable cause to believe that a violation of the law warranting criminal prosecution has taken place." The split along party lines left the accusations unresolved, however, and the board made no other findings in that matter.

The Funds Factor

A month before Helen Carey died of cancer, David Garth, whom the Carey camp was hoping to hire, leaned across the aisle of a Washington-bound shuttle and asked Hugh Carey whether he was sure that he wanted to run for governor. "Helen, tell him," Carey said turning to his wife. "No matter what

happens," Helen Carey predicted, "he's going to go all the way."
Garth met not much later with Carey's brother Edward, who
asked how much it would cost to become the Democratic gubernatorial nominee. "I said it will take around $2 million,"
Garth recalled. "I said it was possible but a real long shot."

Helen Carey's prediction that her husband would go all the
way and Garth's assessment that victory was possible both
proved to be correct. But neither was within the realm of accomplishment without the money that made Carey's campaign
the most expensive in New York in 1974. It cost $5 million in
the primary and general elections to propel Carey from his
Brooklyn apartment to the executive mansion in Albany. Without the recognition and image of independence that a more
than $1.5 million media campaign was able to buy, Carey would
have run out of the money.

When it was all over, there was plenty of comment on the
new law, which theoretically should have prevented a campaign financed the way Carey's was. As Samuels campaign manager Auletta stated, "In a sense, we took the primary for
granted. We did it, in part, based on a law that we thought
was ironclad." Republican State Chairman Rosenbaum complained about the Carey loans, especially in the general election, and asked: "If you can borrow whenever you want and
not pay anything back by the election, what's the point in having limits?" This complaint was echoed by Auletta, who suggested that the elections board be replaced by an independent
commission packed with certified public accountants. "I also
don't see any reason why unions are excluded from limitations
—I don't understand the difference between them and corporations, and they also negotiate with government." Auletta
added, "I don't think the $105,000 limit [on contributions from
a candidate and his or her family] is unreasonable, but you
might have to question whether there should be some limit on
gifts from people in allied industries." Even Carey's campaign
manager Cummins, had complaints: "It's a bad law—not one
lawyer or one person can tell you in toto what you can or cannot do." Cummins also spoke of the Federal law: "And the
new Senate limits are unrealistic, when they don't get money
from other sources, like the Presidential candidates." That same
complaint was raised by Javits campaign chief Trubin, who
noted the problems involved in increasing Javits' base of post-
election contributors to pay off almost $80,000 in debts with
individual contributions of $1,000 or less (as the new Federal
law required). On the other hand, Ramsey Clark did manage

to raise about $850,000. The Clark camp, noted campaign manager Navasky, also had to impose restrictions of its own when "people wanted to take out unauthorized ads and such and we just didn't let them."

The new law was clearly not ironclad. Subtleties and distinctions were shaped by the perspectives and needs of individual candidates, and formal opinions by the election board and pending court cases made it still more flexible. Spending limits appeared to be altogether too high in a law replete with loopholes involving loans, family funds, and repayment provisions. Monitoring of campaign contributions and speedy decisions on candidates' complaints are crucial to the effectiveness of the stricter controls and also need improvement.

There were the predictable calls for further reform in the 1975 legislature, but no action was taken. Among the innovations that went nowhere were an income-tax credit of up to $10 a year for political contributions, proposed by Governor Carey, and a model bill produced by two respected civic groups, which recommended partial public financing, lower expenditure limits, more stringent curbs on loans and contributions, a ban on campaign receipts from labor unions and corporations, a pre-election pamphlet to be sent to all voters, and a single depository for all of a candidate's campaign funds.

While the Carey and Javits campaigns clearly showed that money still talks, the inability of money alone to influence the outcome was also noted by Malcolm Wilson's campaign manager R. Burdell Bixby, who candidly stated: "If we divorce the candidate from the campaign operation, there isn't a single thing I would have done differently. I have been frustrated many times, but I started in the Alf Landon campaign so I'm not unaccustomed to frustration." Frustration was perhaps the name of the game in 1974, for candidates who tried to stir up voters about their opponents' fund-raising techniques, for candidates trying to comply with the law, and for voters trying to learn the truth about campaign financing. Fund-raising was probably more open than before, with fewer improprieties and more information than ever in the past. But the room for improvement was still almost universally considered to be vast.

TWELVE

EPILOGUE

ASSESSING CAMPAIGN REFORM: LESSONS FOR THE FUTURE

David S. Broder

The 1974 general elections were unique and significant in American political history, if only because they occurred just three months after the first American President was forced to resign from office as a result of improprieties and illegalities stemming from his own campaign. The Watergate scandal which toppled Richard M. Nixon from office had many dimensions, but it was triggered by a break-in at the Democratic National Committee by operatives of Nixon's 1972 campaign committee who had been supplied with secret political funds. Within the first three days of its seemingly interminable life, the Watergate case turned public attention to the sources and uses of campaign cash. And by the time it had reached its climax in August 1974 with Nixon's resignation, the impression was firmly lodged in the public mind that money—political money—was at the root of this evil, too.

It could have been expected that an awareness of the power, if not the evils, of political money would be a central feature of the 1974 campaigns. The fact that many states had passed new laws regulating campaign financing within the two years since the last major election—and since the beginning of Watergate —ensured that the issue would play a role. The 10 reports in this volume suggest, however, that the changes wrought by recent electoral reforms were not as extensive as the furor created by Watergate might have indicated. To recount some

highlights of the campaigns is to acknowledge the power of
money itself and the seemingly more ambiguous power of a
public consciousness of it:

• In Maryland, Governor Marvin Mandel used the advantage
of his office to dry up funds for any opposition by raising almost
a million dollars at a campaign-kickoff dinner held more than
17 months before the election. Almost 10 percent of the money
came from unions—active here as elsewhere on behalf of Democratic candidates—and much of the rest came from businessmen
who had profited mightily from their dealings with the state.

• In Florida, where the incumbent governor went well beyond
the terms of the state's new law in limiting individual contributions to his campaign to $100, the outcome of most races was
proportional to the expenditure of money. Incumbents pre-
vailed—as they did in most states. A statewide official deeply
mired in scandal was renominated and re-elected, in large part
because he was able to extract campaign funds from those he
regulated, while his challengers found no alternative sources
of money.

• Texas—whose campaign-finance practices are legendary and
where a scandal two years before Watergate brought a major
housecleaning of the state government—persisted in its traditionally extravagant ways. More than $8 million was spent on
campaigns in the state, even though there were few serious contests in the primary or the general election. The biggest winner,
Governor Dolph Briscoe, was originally elected in 1972 as a
reform candidate and in 1974 was the largest single contributor
recorded in the state—advancing $645,000 in gifts and loans to
his own re-election campaign.

• In California, reformers won a major initiative battle by
outspending their combined labor and business opponents and
passing Proposition 9, in many ways the toughest campaign
finance and conflict-of-interest statute in the country. At the
same time, Edmund G. Brown, Jr., the Democrat elected Governor in 1974 and a principal backer of Proposition 9, raised
over $1.5 million in the primary and almost $2 million in the
general election from the traditional sources: wealthy individuals, business and labor, public-employee groups, and others
with a large personal stake in the policies of state government.

• In Massachusetts, a long history of corruption alternating
with reform efforts resulted in the passage in 1973 of a comprehensive campaign-finance reform act. Before signing the law,
which closed a loophole exempting testimonial dinners from
campaign-finance reporting, Governor Francis Sargent held a

number of $100-a-plate testimonials. He offered to return the money raised at the affairs if the state legislature would pass a public-financing bill, but it failed despite supposedly wide support.

• In Kansas, a scandal involving awards of architectural contracts to campaign contributors heightened the impact of Watergate, but its chief effect was to make funds scarce for every race except the U.S. Senate. In that climate of scarcity, six senior executives of a Topeka bank formed two committees with the wonderfully euphemistic names of Americans for Free Enterprise and Citizens for Good Government. The committees gave identical contributions to the major contenders for both the Democratic and the Republican gubernatorial nominations and later sent larger donations in parallel amounts to the nominees of each party.

• In Georgia, the man who won the governorship was the principal sponsor of the new campaign-financing law—and also the most skillful in evading its disclosure requirements and concealing the fact that his campaign was being aided by the same kind of bank loans for which he was criticizing his opponents. The banks were particularly interested in the election because of a bill before the legislature that would permit greater bank expansion—a bill supported by the major banks and originally introduced by the winning candidate (also a bank director at the time).

• In Pennsylvania—where business, labor, and state employees have traditionally been rich sources of political funds—there was great talk of reform, but the entrenched political machine managed to head it off. While Governor Milton Shapp's reelection committee honored his pledge that "no state employee's job will be placed in jeopardy because a political contribution is or is not made," the Democratic State Committee did solicit state employees and transferred $300,000 in collections to the Shapp committee. The State Committee's chief fund-raiser was indicted (and later convicted) on charges that he extracted campaign "contributions" of $60 from each laborer in the state Highway Department, $120 from each foreman, and $100 per machine from contractors.

• In neighboring Ohio, labor unions contributed lavishly to the re-election campaign of an incumbent Democratic governor, providing almost $400,000 (or 40 percent of his campaign budget) and virtually all of the contributions exceeding $3,000 he received. But Governor John J. Gilligan was defeated, in part because his opponent, former Governor James A. Rhodes,

was able to exploit a strong historical relationship with the
highway and construction industry—whose members financed
most of his successful last-minute television blitz. Gilligan had
been an apostle of campaign-finance reform, while Rhodes
faced serious questions in the Ohio press about the handling
of funds in his past campaigns. But the Ohio voters, even at
the height of what Spiro Agnew called the "post-Watergate
morality," managed to rise above principle and overlook that
difference between the candidates.

• In New York, former U.S. Attorney General Ramsey Clark
managed to raise $850,000 under his self-imposed $100-per-
contributor limitation, but was badly outspent on television
and lost to an incumbent senator, three-fourths of whose contributions came in blocks of $1,000. And challenger Hugh
Carey became Governor after a stunning primary victory in
large part because he had a brother who was in a position to
give or lend $1.2 million to his campaign. The brother, fortu-
nately for the Careys, had a set of accountants who were canny
and quick enough to arrange $200,000 in loans from other
sources in a three-day period just before the primary, which
enabled Edward Carey to escape the penalties of the new law.

This recital may sound discouraging, but it needs to be kept
in perspective. The very fact that so much can be reported
about the finance practices in these 10 states is in itself a direct
by-product of the legislative reform efforts that preceded the
1974 campaign. A comparable study of state campaign finances
would probably have been impossible before this, for most state
(and Federal) campaign-finance laws were very limited in their
application, riddled with internal inconsistencies, and adminis-
tered by appointees of the very politicians whose campaigns
were to be scrutinized. As Herbert Alexander has noted, the
10 reports in this book are in fact a tribute to the success of
disclosure.

Beyond making possible a book such as this, what have the
reforms of the last few years done for campaign financing in
the United States? How well has disclosure worked to help the
electorate make intelligent choices among candidates? How
have limitations on contributions and expenditures altered the
traditional pattern of funding? What has been the role of public
financing in creating a new atmosphere for electoral campaigns?
Just what do these accounts tell us about the wisdom, success,
and prospects of campaign-financing reform? A reassessment of
goals by both legislators and the courts will have to take into
account the kind of information reported in this volume.

Most of the disclosure laws discussed in this book do help shed light on campaign-financing practices and should help eliminate blatant abuses. With some exceptions, they provide for a consolidated financial accounting of individual campaigns to be filed in timely fashion, both before and after the primary and general elections, with a public office accessible to press and public scrutiny. For the most part, too, the new laws outlaw cash transactions of any significant size—thus closing one of the most notorious loopholes in local campaigns. (Texas is one state that continues to permit cash contributions.) While it is virtually impossible to prove a negative point, the experienced observers who wrote the chapters in this book failed to find any evidence of significant unreported cash contributions flowing into the 1974 campaigns. The Maryland and Georgia chapters spotlight the potential abuses in the cash distribution of election-day "walking-around money," but there appears to be no widespread problem of unreported cash expenditures in other states.

These studies do raise some important questions, however, about the overall utility of disclosure as a device for regulating campaign-finance practices. One question concerns the volume of reports and the capacity of the news media to handle them. While the press in many of these states devoted unprecedented attention and reportorial resources to campaign finances in 1974 (stimulated, no doubt, by the Watergate climate), several correspondents report that the mass of data generated by the new laws all but choked the information system. As noted by William Endicott, *The California Journal*, which conscientiously covers politics and government in that state, complained that the volume of reports "makes it difficult, if not impossible, in many cases to ferret out the significant contribution or trend of contributions from the eye-washing detail offered, one suspects, more in faithfulness to the letter of the disclosure law than to the spirit." Plenty of information may be available, but it may not be possible to evaluate it.

California was one of many states where traditional special-interest groups apparently vied in devising reporting euphemisms for themselves. The savings and loan associations operated as the Good Government Committee. Pacific Telephone Company executives became the Citizens for Responsible Government. The Consumer Action Committee turned out to represent the professional astrologers. And painters, decorators, and sandblasters, of all people, styled themselves the Environmental Action Committee. Under Proposition 9, which went into effect after the 1974 elections, such groups would have to report their sponsors, but only in a separate filing; the committees themselves would continue to be legal.

The amount of record-keeping required annoyed some candidates—for instance, those in Kansas, who moved after the election to revise some of the reporting regulations. Florida was another state where complicated reporting requirements drew some protests, and a reduction in the number of reports is likely. In Texas a proliferation of candidate committees, including 46 for the governor's re-election campaign, made it almost impossible to keep track of contributions and spending. For the most part such shortcomings can be dealt with, if there is a will to do so, through a rationalization of reporting rules and closing of loopholes.

The more serious question about disclosure raised by these reports concerns the unpredictability and the seeming arbitrariness of public reaction to financial candor. The theory underlying most reform efforts in the field of campaign finance is one that draws a sharp distinction between the unselfish, well-motivated small contributor and the selfish big giver with ulterior motives. It is this theory which is used to justify not only disclosure provisions but also the limitations on the size of contributions. The courts have ruled that these considerations in many cases justify limitations on privacy and free expression involved in campaign-reform laws.

But there are very few examples in these comprehensive reports that fit the reformers' model, in which the law forces disclosure of secret financial obligations or conflicts of interest and the alerted public recognizes the danger of electing a particular candidate to public office. Two California legislative races did seem to show this pattern: In one, the winning candidate revealed the special-interest (mostly business) contributors of his opponent, and in another, publicity about an investigation into an incumbent's failure to report campaign funds in the past helped lead to his defeat (although he was subsequently cleared of the charges).

But such examples are few and far between as compared to the number of cases in which the voters seemed to ignore the obvious implications of financial disclosures. California voters shrugged off the knowledge that two men with large landholdings and development plans invested more than a half-million dollars—virtually his entire pre-primary budget—in a single candidate. The voters elected that man as state controller—the office which, among other things, supervises land and property assessment procedures in the state. There are also a disturbing number of instances in which the voters turned their backs on candidates, like the Massachusetts candidate for attorney general, strongly identified with the cause of campaign-finance reform.

There is additionally the troubling problem cited in Georgia, among other places, of the extreme cost of candor to a particular candidate. One gubernatorial aspirant in that state, who appeared to have strong credentials, was crippled by his willingness to concede that he was a millionaire three times over and that he had advanced $250,000 toward his own campaign. Another candidate in that same race voluntarily limited contributions to $250—and was effectively dealt out of the battle for the nomination because he could not finance a campaign that began to match his opponents'. The eventual winner, meanwhile, was securing loans that he did not report but which helped him win the race.

Disclosure, it appears from the evidence in this book, may be a necessary ingredient in an effective strategy against the corrupting influence of money on politics, but it is not sufficient to guarantee against impropriety. Its chief advantage is that it focuses press and public attention on the candidates' actual or potential conflicts of interest. Its drawback is that it does not, by itself, seem to insulate the candidate from those influences.

The success of measures designed specifically to do that—contribution and spending ceilings—is by no means clear in the states profiled here. There is documentation in virtually every chapter of the predominant role of lobbies and special-interest groups in campaign funding, especially of legislative races. If there is any safe axiom in American politics, it is that our legislators get the funds with which they run from the very people who have the greatest direct stake in the legislation they will pass. The arrangements are not subtle. Fund-raising dinners are held during the legislative sessions, and the distribution of campaign contributions is often done personally by the same lobbyists who are negotiating with those legislators on provisions of specific bills. The cynical remark of a Florida lobbyist, who had been "invited" to one of those mid-session "appreciation dinners" given by and for a key legislator, was that "you've got to appreciate someone for their past service—or their future service." At that point, the difference between a contribution and a bribe becomes so blurred as to be almost invisible.

The difference was perhaps least clear in Maryland, whose $2,500-per-election contribution limit did little, if anything, to inhibit wealthy individual and special-interest giving, or the influence it often seemed to buy. Florida, where special interests contributed almost two-thirds of the money collected by winning legislators (apart from candidates' and party funds), had a similar limit. In Massachusetts, contribution ceilings did seem to work as part of a comprehensive effort to clean up state politics. The winning gubernatorial candidate there, Michael Dukakis, went even further than the law required and sent back contributions from state employees or those who did business with the state.

Of these states, Florida also had spending ceilings ($600,000 for the governor's race, $850,000 in the event of a runoff), but Massachusetts and Maryland did not. The tendency for money to be spent when it is available, noted by Jerome Kelly in Maryland, suggests that limits may affect elections. But the accounts of other states with limits—Kansas ($500,000 for primary and general elections for governor), New York (about $4 million for statewide offices), and Ohio (about $1 million)—indicate that the evidence is far from conclusive. The Supreme Court has, of course, struck down spending ceilings except when used as part of a public-financing system, so that these examples may not turn out to be very relevant. The question of where to put limits, in cases where they may constitutionally be used and are desired by legislators, will remain, however.

Overall, these studies suggest no strong conclusion about the adequacy or inadequacy of campaign finances, when measured against some theoretical standard of what an election for a certain office "should" cost. The amounts spent on legislative races, for example, vary enormously from state to state—from the $1,000 average in Kansas to the $230,000 expended in one high-intensity district in California. In only a few races did the issue of exceeding statutory limits arise. There are a number of references to scarcity of funds—a problem that ceilings were to have helped to resolve—particularly for Republican candidates. Some candidates—for example, the minister who decided he wanted to be governor of Kansas—obviously were balked by their inability to command financial backing. But this observer is unable to say with any certainty that we are spending "too much" or "too little" on state elections. In an apparent majority of the cases where candidates complained about a lack of funds, they seemed actually to collect plenty.

If no firm conclusions can be drawn on the effect limitations have had in reducing the influence of big contributors and slowing the race for funds, some can be drawn about their success in encouraging the participation of smaller donors, thus opening up the political process. It is clear, unhappily, that few of the voters who are quick to complain about politicians' "selling out" to their contributors—are themselves ready to put money into the political process. On the basis of the evidence presented here, one would have to conclude that the vast majority of Americans, while appalled by what they learned from Watergate and their own state scandals about the corruption of politics by large campaign contributors, did not accept any personal responsibility for providing their politicians with an alternative source of funds. Even the $100 ceiling voluntarily imposed by popular Florida Governor Reubin Askew did not alter the pattern of giving significantly: Of the state's 3.5 million registered voters, fewer than 9,000—one-fourth of 1 percent— chose to contribute to the "people's campaign" the Governor had pledged to conduct. As former Florida state Senator Louis de la Parte commented, "You can put 1,000 average voters in a room and say, 'How many of you have ever contributed to a campaign, any campaign?,' and not one of them will have contributed. Then you ought to be able to ask them: 'Then where in the hell do you think the money came from?' "

Like several other politicians in this book, De la Parte believes that the ultimate answer to campaign-finance problems must include some form of public financing. None of the 10 states discussed here incorporated public financing in the laws that were applicable in the 1974 campaigns, and at the time these chapters were written only Maryland had any form of public-financing law—scheduled to go into effect for its next state election in 1978. Just as the public has been less than eager to contribute directly to campaigns, it—not surprisingly—has not clamored for the chance to funnel its money through the government to the candidates either. Efforts to enact public-financing legislation, as in Massachusetts, often produced the verbal support of lawmakers but not enough votes for passage. Stirrings of interest in public financing were nevertheless reported in many states, and the argument for such experiments is implicit in much of the information developed here.

The experiences of these 10 states help to bolster the argument that, if the United States is going to attempt to introduce public funds into the campaign-finance mix, the experiment ought to begin at exactly the opposite end of the ballot from the Presidential race—which is now the only election in the country that Congress has singled out for such a tax subsidy. The place to begin might be at the level of the state legislature, where candidates today typically have no alternative but to go to special-interest groups for whatever money they need. Despite Watergate, the evidence is far from persuasive that there is any inherent difficulty in raising adequate sums for the Presidential general election campaign from perfectly legitimate, disinterested, small private contributors. Even the least successful candidates of modern times, Barry Goldwater and George McGovern, have been able to raise impressive amounts of money in small contributions from people who shared their vision of America. Although most candidates now running for the Presidency have supported and accepted public funds and say they rely on them, experience indicates that they are not essential to these races. The case for public subsidy of Presidential campaigns is in my judgment weak, and the case for substituting tax dollars for available private contributions nonexistent.

But the same thing cannot be said of candidates at the bottom of the ballots, most of whom lack the visibility to attract small private contributions. The housewife or electrician or small businessman who has a desire to serve in the legislature will not, on the evidence furnished in this book, get much help from his party or from her neighbors in financing a race. If the candidate is able to get money at all (which is not likely if an incumbent is the opponent), it will come from the highway builders, or the liquor dealers, or the public employees' union, or some other group—probably operating with a euphemistic label—which has a direct interest in how that candidate will vote on issues vital to its economic well-being.

A new look at public financing is just one of the probable results of a revision of campaign-finance statutes in the light of the Supreme Court decision. The reports in this book indicate that if the states are going to deal rationally and constructively with the problems of paying for politics, some other policy problems should be taken into account as well.

One is the advantage of incumbency in all aspects of the campaign and the steps that might be taken to make races involving an incumbent more competitive. Many of those incumbency advantages are probably inherent in the possession of public office and cannot be erased. They may be justified as a reward for the burdens of office and the inevitable degree of controversy associated with having to vote and act on issues which divide a constituency. Those ineradicable advantages include the knowledge of issues an officeholder acquires, the name familiarity that derives from previous campaigns and the possession of public office, and the opportunity for personal service to constituents that most incumbents enjoy.

But there are other advantages of incumbency that can be offset by deliberate policy, in order to make campaigns more

competitive. One is access to private contributions. A handful
of states have tried to offset the incumbent's advantage by putting a ceiling on his treasury lower than that on the challenger's
—a provision that is irrelevant without spending ceilings. It is
questionable whether the courts would permit such a provision
even under public-financing-related ceilings. Another, possibly
more feasible alternative is to provide direct financial or in-kind
assistance to the challenger, designed to offset the incumbent's
advantages. Such benefits could range from the direct provision
of public funds to free mailings to the challenger's prospective
contributors or free media time. Agreement in principle that
the goals of finance-reform legislation ought to include more
competitive races would allow experimentation with a number
of devices, and a test in the states of their effectiveness.

A second problem that demands special attention from serious students of campaign-finance reform is the use of loans to
circumvent and sometimes evade the strictures of the law. In
state after state, there are reports of individuals, businesses,
banks, and others providing large-scale advances in order to
assist their favored candidate. Often the sources of these loans
or the guarantors are disguised from public view. There are
instances where loans have not been repaid and become, in
fact, contributions. Even where repayments are made, the access
to the loan at a particular point in the campaign—typically,
when large-scale media advertising costs are faced—determines
whether or not a candidate can succeed. Serious attention needs
to be paid to the question of regulating these loans—as to both
size and timing—if campaign reform is to be made more meaningful.

A third, closely allied problem is that of late contributions
to campaigns—particularly the contributions that come in after
the election is over and the winner is known. Those contributions, documented in several of the states, are naturally and
properly the objects of special suspicion as to the motivation of
the giver. Anyone with a disinterested desire to see someone
elected would normally lend his financial support before election day. Those who wait until late in the campaign—probably
in order to avoid being listed in the final pre-election disclosure
statement—or who give to the winner after the votes are in
automatically attract raised eyebrows.

In policy terms, the question could well be raised as to
whether special restrictions might apply to contributions given
after the closing date for the last pre-election disclosure. Perhaps the amount of these contributions should be limited more
strictly than those given well in advance of election day. Per-

haps certain sources with direct and obvious interests in the actions of elected officials should be restricted from playing the late-contribution game. Whether or not such controls are applied, several states clearly need to amend their statutes just to "catch," for reporting purposes, the late givers. Since political fund-raising is continuous, the reporting requirements need to be made comprehensive in their own time span, lest certain givers escape scrutiny altogether.

These reports highlight another problem which is all too familiar to students and practitioners of politics: the weakness of the political parties. Ohio is one of the few exceptions to the generalization that the parties provided little in the way of campaign funds for their candidates in 1974. In most instances, it is striking to note, the authors of these studies automatically refer to the passage of campaign funds from the original givers through the political parties to the ultimate candidate-recipients as "laundering." It is assumed in most instances that the purpose of such a process was not to immunize the candidate from a sense of obligation to the real giver but, rather, to conceal from the public the source of funds in a particular race.

Given the condition of the parties in most states, that may be a valid assumption. But it is not an inherent condition, and any consideration of campaign finance which ignored the potential for parties to play a positive role in raising and distributing funds for their nominees would be seriously incomplete. For those who believe—as this writer does—that parties can be of great value in increasing competition, in combating special-interest influence, and in defining meaningful policy choices, their relegation to the category of "laundries" is sad, even if accurate. Any complete strategy for improving campaign-financing practices in this country must include an effort to expand the fund-raising role and capacity of the political parties.

The obvious means is by channeling public funds through parties rather than directly to candidates, as is already done by some states. Another way to affect party participation is to permit parties to contribute significantly more money to candidates than individuals can, where contributions are limited.

In considering the prospects for meaningful change in the campaign-financing system, the contributors to this volume were all aware of the political forces at work in their states. In fact, the most striking feature of the reform legislation described here is its generally limited nature. The reports on most states reveal the tendency of legislatures to enact reform statutes that are far short of the models most reform proponents have in mind. Model statutes, such as the ones drafted by Common Cause, embody certain philosophies which lawmakers may or may not endorse. In addition, any model statute must be adapted to the needs of the jurisdiction to which it will apply. But such laws do represent a rational approach to the problem posed by campaign financing, an approach that might constructively serve as a starting point for consideration of legislation on the state level. Few states—California being a notable exception—in fact used model statutes. Most, like Georgia, plunged ahead, often merely making politically expedient changes in the election law.

The state laws described here approximate the terms of a comprehensive model law, to some degree, in their disclosure requirements. Some, but not all, limit the source and size of campaign contributions. A few, but not many, put ceilings on campaign spending. None had public financing in 1974. Because of these shortcomings, the impact of these statutes is as often to distort the election process as it is to "clean up" the campaigns. There are legitimate reasons to oppose certain aspects of campaign-finance reform, as the Supreme Court has confirmed. Thus, the states should not be criticized simply for not including certain of these provisions in their laws. But a rational and comprehensive approach to this complex area of law, as is found in the model laws, is necessary wherever serious reform is undertaken, and that kind of approach has been the exception rather than the rule.

The most significant lack in most of the state statutes is that which renders almost every other provision moot. Fewer than half the states covered here appear to have effective, independent enforcement agencies. More typical is the Ohio Elections Commission, whose members are appointed on recommendation from the two major parties and whose main activity, according to Brian T. Usher, has been delivering findings of "no criminal intent" or "no jurisdiction." What Sam Roberts says of New York applies to many, if not all, of the other states: "The New York state election law that was on the books in the winter of 1974 was loosely worded and even more loosely enforced." For example, the reform law passed in the Texas legislature in 1973, after scandals had shaken the state house, lacked an independent enforcement agency. And as the aftershock of that scandal faded into history, there seemed little disposition to toughen the law. In a few states where the enforcement agency provided by law took its responsibilities seriously in 1974, the upshot has been political criticism and, in

the case of Kansas, the forced resignation of the chief enforcement official.

It is an axiom of politics that compromise is of the essence
in the legislative process, and it is hardly surprising that the
statutes described in this book fall short of the political scientists' ideals. Unfortunately, the deviations do not seem random.
The most notable lack is of any change that would disturb the
overwhelming advantage enjoyed by incumbents in financing
their re-election campaigns. In Pennsylvania, for example,
Gerald J. McCullough reports that both parties in the legislature have established their own campaign committees "which
regularly raise money from lobbyists, labor unions, state employees, and others." Those same legislators killed a provision
of a reform bill that would have required disclosure of ticket
purchasers at their favorite $100-a-plate dinners.

That kind of example raises the question as to whether better
legislation in this area can be achieved from some agency other
than the sitting legislature—for example, through initiative
petitions put to the voters. Political scientists and practicing
politicians have made strong arguments against the use of the
initiative in complex, technical fields like campaign-finance
regulation. Proposition 9 in California, while having the advantage of being far more comprehensive than any of the legislation
derived from state legislatures, still is not devoid of important
policy and practical problems. The notion of a 20,000-word
law being submitted to a yes-or-no decision by the voters troubled even some of the proponents of Proposition 9. That is
hardly the ideal way to legislate in a sensitive area.

Yet it does seem obvious that in asking incumbent legislators
to write the rules under which they and their opponents will
conduct the next election, we put a heavy burden on human
nature. It may be prudent to watch the legislatures over a
longer period of time and see if they improve on their post-
Watergate reform laws or, as some of these reports suggest,
begin to dismantle them.

But it seems to me possible that just as the courts were finally
forced to intervene on the apportionment issue, because incumbent legislators could not be counted on to reapportion
themselves out of office, there may be a need here for outside
agencies to take a larger hand in campaign-finance legislation.
What may be useful are a variety of experiments with mixed
commissions of private citizens, party officials, and legislators,
charged with examining existing laws and recommending improvements. Where state constitutions permit the use of the

initiative to bring "model laws" directly to the voters, that option can be kept in reserve if the legislature balks at enacting a balanced and comprehensive statute. Even where that option does not exist, the prestige of the commission recommendations may be a useful force in closing the loopholes which still exist in so much of the legislation enacted in 1973–74.

Model statutes—for example, those drafted by Common Cause and the Citizens' Research Foundation—can provide some guidance to those seeking specific numbers and requirements. Common Cause has issued a national model statute including specific figures and strict regulations covering all the basic aspects of reform: disclosure, contribution and spending limits, public financing, and enforcement. (Some of these provisions will have to be revised in the light of the Supreme Court decision.) CRF's statute includes strict disclosure and enforcement requirements and provides as well for an institution to encourage wider public participation, both monetary and voluntary, in elections and to channel money to candidates and political parties.

The reporters who furnished these accounts of the rules and regulations and the actual practices in their states in 1974 have demonstrated the intractability of the problem of cleaning up our elections. But everything they have found indicates how vital it is to persist in the attack on the corrupt practices which have done so much to damage Americans' faith in their own democracy.

APPENDIX

THE CITIZENS' RESEARCH FOUNDATION'S MODEL STATE STATUTE ON POLITICS, ELECTIONS, AND PUBLIC OFFICE

Herbert E. Alexander and J. Paul Molloy

In the summer of 1973, under the auspices of the Citizens' Research Foundation, the authors began to draft a *Model State Statute: Politics, Elections, and Public Office.** Published by the Foundation in February 1974, it proposes three techniques to improve the political system and ensure greater citizen vigilance and participation: new rules to assure open and honest politics, new institutions to enforce and implement those rules, and new incentives for individuals to use their political power. In other words, it is a model law to "prevent abuses in the conduct of public office, the election process, and political activity through law, impartial enforcement, and affirmative state action to assure universal citizen participation, awareness, and vigilance."

The model is both comprehensive, with 15 different titles, and separable, to enable states to choose or modify those titles and provisions best suited to their individual needs. In toto,

The introduction is adapted from Herbert E. Alexander and J. Paul Molloy, "The People and Politics," *National Civic Review*, September, 1974. Copyright © 1974, National Municipal League.

* A grant from the Edna McConnell Clark Foundation financed the Model's preparation and publication.

the model represents an attempt to balance negative or restrictive and positive or constructive aspects of legislation. While large contributors are discouraged by a special tax on their contributions, small contributors are sought out by a positive action program. While free broadcast time or newspaper advertising space is offered candidates for public office, it is done so on the condition that they limit expenses. While political committees are required to keep accurate records and file reports, clear guidelines are spelled out and state assistance, in both funds and services, is provided.

The balance of the model is perhaps best reflected by the two new institutions it envisions. First, an independent State Commission on Public Offices is established, with five members who serve staggered 10-year terms. The commission is appointed by the governor with the advice and consent of the Senate, and no more than three members can be of the same political party. This is the "watchdog" and "enforcer." All political contributions and expenditures are reported to it several times before and after an election as well as on a regular periodic basis for ongoing political committees. The commission has the duty not only of receiving the information but of making sure that it is correct. "Who is giving what to whom" is the commission's standard of public reporting because it is the public's right to know. The commission performs the same function with respect to lobbying reports, and it also makes public notices of awarded government contracts of $1,000 or more.

The model's commission also receives personal financial statements from candidates for public office and from elected and appointed public officials. Those statements are kept up-to-date and remain confidential unless or until the commission has reason to believe that an individual has been guilty of a conflict of interest. It can then, and only then, use the data in court.

Disclosure of personal finances of candidates or public officials is not required by the model because our society rightly values privacy of personal matters. A society that strips all personal privacy from individuals who are or who want to be public officials must pause to wonder just what standards those public officials would tend to use when assuring a citizen's right to privacy. Moreover, mandatory public disclosure would cause some qualified candidates to forego running for office.

On the constructive side, the model establishes the State Voters Assistance Board. The board's primary function is to promote greater political activity by the people, political committees, and political parties. It has three members, appointed by the governor with the advice and consent of the Senate and serving full time for five-year terms. Its basic role is to breathe new life into politics by lowering political costs, acting as a catalyst for popular participation in politics, and encouraging more light than heat in political discourse.

For example, the model provides for universal voter registration, a function which for too long has been a barrier to voting for some and an unnecessary expense for candidates and parties. The board has the ultimate responsibility to see that everyone who is eligible to be registered to vote is registered, and the changes in registration are easily accomplished. The board is also responsible for a number of voter information programs, including a voters' digest, which goes to every voter before an election and gives basic information about candidates, issues, and where to vote. It is similar to those now disseminated in Oregon and Washington and is designed to lower campaign costs and better inform the voters.

Television costs often become disproportionately high in statewide campaigns. One of the board's voter information programs authorizes it to buy blocks of TV and radio time as well as print advertising space for allocation among those candidates who are willing to limit their campaign expenses for such items. The model prescribes an equal and fair allocation for major and minor parties and candidates, resulting in lower campaign costs and, it is hoped, a better-informed public.

The model looks ahead and requires that each CATV system reserve one channel for exclusive use by the board. The board would permit public-interest groups, political parties, and public officials to use that channel on an ongoing basis so that the public could be aware of politics, politicians, and public issues at times other than just before election day.

To further reduce costs for political parties and candidates, the board is authorized to maintain production facilities within the state for both audio and video tapes. Parties and statewide candidates are also given a telephone-recorded message line and access to mailing labels for primaries and a free mailing during the general election period. These are small items, perhaps, but in the aggregate such assistance will go far to relieve financial pressures in campaigns.

Campaigns and politics still will cost money. As a matter of fact, the greater the outreach of democracy, the greater the cost. Every political party and candidate would prefer to raise all the necessary funds in small contributions, but today that cost has become prohibitive. To enable every participant to have a greater stake in the political process than ever before and at the same time to alleviate the cost of encouraging people to give to politics, the model establishes four "systematic individual political contribution programs," which the board must promote, approve, and supervise. Simply stated, the four programs give every citizen not only an opportunity but also an incentive to become a small contributor and provides the mechanisms to accomplish this end.

Three of the four programs use the payroll-deduction system for regular withholding, and one system, a public purchase plan, uses a Christmas Club approach through banks, giving the self-employed, retired, or nonemployed the opportunity to participate. In two of the programs, the public purchase plan and the payroll-deduction plan, scrip (political-contribution certificates) is used. The scrip is regularly provided to the contributor and can be given by him only to a political committee. There is a built-in incentive because the political-contribution certificates have a greater value than the original purchase price.

A third program, the trust-account plan, is a joint venture between an employer and employee. The employer matches the employee's withholding, and both sums are turned over to a trustee bank, which keeps the money until the contributor specifies the recipient candidate or committee. While in these three programs the individual retains control over his contribution, the fourth program recognizes the common-purpose political action fund (COPE, BIPAC, etc.) and permits the use of payroll deductions for such funds, provided that the fund meets certain democratic standards set forth in the model.

Finally, the board is given responsibility for a grant program designed to strengthen political parties. Political parties, defined as those that have received 5 percent of the votes in one of the two preceding statewide elections, are eligible to receive two types of grants, public-issue grants or community-service grants. The public-issue grants are designed to provide money for parties to develop programs to meet the needs of society within a certain subject area—for example, education, transportation, agriculture. The community-service grants are to provide seed money for the parties to develop community-service programs using volunteers. Those programs could be as diverse as the interests among party supporters. For example, a political party could run daycare centers, job-training programs, consumer-assistance centers, government-assistance centers. The range of services would differ from community to community and would run the gamut from programs to alleviate poverty

to civic beautification. Above all, the programs would give the
political party an ongoing purpose and outreach into the community to detect problems before they reach crisis proportions
and to give the people an opportunity to be a part of politics.

Quite apart from the money problems of politics, elections,
and the conduct of public office are the ethical standards we
as a society believe should apply. The model contains specific
prohibitions against conflict of interest, corruption, unfair
political practices, and tampering with an individual's political
or civil rights. Nevertheless, it also recognizes that some varia-
tions and practices are not illegal but simply "hardball politics."
During the course of a campaign, charges about the fairness of
actions or statements abound, and in such cases the State Voters
Assistance Board is responsible for arbitration. Within three
days of hearing a complaint, the board must in writing give its
opinion as to fairness under the act.

Summary of the Model Statute

TITLE I—PURPOSE AND DEFINITIONS

Section 101 states the purposes of the Act in a way to create
a "spirit of the law" which will be consistent with the goals of
honest and open politics, valid elections, and honest government.

Section 102 defines key terms or words that are used throughout the Act. The terms are defined in a way to avoid loopholes,
and often the definitions are interrelated. Where necessary,
certain terms are defined within the context of the substantive
provisions of the Act; however, this section takes that fact into
account and does not purport to define all the terms used in
the Act.

TITLE II—STATE COMMISSION ON PUBLIC OFFICES

Section 201 establishes a five-member commission with appointment and removal provisions designed to create the maximum possible independence from political parties or elected
officials.

Section 202 defines in considerable detail the duties of the
commission—which are primarily maintenance, regulation, publicity, and enforcement of the reporting and disclosure of political finance. The commission also has a duty to oversee reports
of lobbyist expenditures and personal finances of elected officials. Various reports are mandated by this section so as to
provide data to better understand political finance.

Section 203 gives the commission the broad powers necessary to do its job consistent with the "duties" given it throughout the Act but particularly by Section 202. It can issue orders, seek injunctions, assess penalties, conduct investigations, cause criminal actions to be brought by the attorney general, and if the Attorney General is involved can on its own bring criminal actions. This section also gives the commission normal housekeeping powers—purchases, contracts, hiring and firing, etc.

Section 204 details specific rules of procedure for the commission to follow. Subsection (a) involves proceedings to determine violations and (b) involves rule-making. The procedures have been carefully drawn because of the need to provide due process of the highest quality in an area as sensitive as politics.

Section 205 defines the scope of the commission's jurisdiction and makes it clear that the attorney general also has jurisdiction to ensure enforcement of the Act. Legal remedies are specified, and a provision is included to advance actions brought under the Act for prompt adjudication before the courts of the state.

Section 206 gives citizens standing to file complaints of any violations before the commission. The commission must respond to such complaints.

Section 207 directs the commission to undertake a one-time special study, although based on its duties (Section 203) and its powers (Section 204) the commission could undertake similar studies in the future. Specifically, the study is an evaluation of election administration and the number of offices filled by elective (rather than appointive or career) personnel.

Section 208 simply authorizes funds for the operation of the commission and permits the commission to enter into contracts with local governments that opt to come within the scope of the Act.

TITLE III—DISCLOSURE OF POLITICAL FINANCES

Section 301 brings all political committees within the scope of the Act. Subsection (a) covers committees operating at the state level; (b) covers committees operating within local jurisdictions which opt for coverage by the Act.

Section 302 requires political committees to file a statement of organization with the commission, guards against a loophole that would allow individuals to spend money outside of a committee, details the data that should be contained in the statement of organization, provides for reporting of changes in the statement, and permits the commission to change the requirements by regulation following a public hearing on such changes.

Section 303 directs the commission to classify committees according to types or purpose (i.e., candidate committees, party committees, public-issue committees, or incumbent committees); fixes dates upon which each type of committee must file periodic financial reports; makes certain individuals responsible for the activities of the committee (as relates to compliance with the Act); and specifies that for candidates for Federal office, substitution of copies of the Federal reports is permitted.

Section 304 relates to requirements for committee organization. Candidates must have only one committee with overall responsibility, and all committees must have at least one responsible official who is a legal resident of the state. Political committees outside the state (but making contributions within the state) must have a committee organized within the state. Other rules relating to the type of political committee are set forth.

Section 305 places responsibility for record-keeping and accountability by a committee. Contributions must be fully identified (amount, date, and source), no cash over $20 may be accepted, authorization for expenditures must be in writing, and loans must be bona fide with certain individual officials assuming responsibility for repayment. Records are segregated for each campaign, and the Social Security number is used for identification purposes.

Section 306 sets forth the procedure for filing reports, details what the reports must contain, and provides for the reporting of late contributions. In addition, the commission is mandated to develop a centralized system to ease the record-keeping burden for each committee.

Section 307 relates to transfers (contributions by one committee to another committee) so as to discourage individuals from earmarking funds to avoid disclosure of real source.

Section 308 prohibits earmarking of funds by contributors.

Section 309 lists the penalties applicable to violations of Title III.

TITLE IV—ETHICAL CONDUCT OF CANDIDATES AND PUBLIC OFFICIALS

Section 401 requires publicly elected officeholders, candidates for public office, and political appointees to file with the commission personal financial statements if they earn $10,000 or more a year.

Section 402 details the data required in personal financial reports (which are held in confidence in the absence of a finding of a conflict of interest by the Commission).

Section 403 requires all paid lobbyists to register and file reports with the commission. Detail for the registration is provided, and the commission is directed to set forth, by regulation, detail required by reports. Such reports must include contributions by the lobbyist or employer. The commission is directed to make public lobbyist reports.

Section 404 makes unlawful a number of transactions which are or would lead to conflict of interest. While there is some overlap between the prohibitions in Section 404 and the more numerous illegal acts in Title VI, there is no inconsistency and the prohibitions in this section tend to be more precise and comprehensive vis-à-vis conflict-of-interest situations.

Section 405 authorizes the commission to provide public officials or lobbyists with written advisory opinions which will have the effect of being a complete defense against violations based on the same factual situation.

Section 406 lists penalties applicable to violations of the provisions of Title IV.

TITLE V—POLITICAL EXPENDITURES AND CONTRIBUTIONS

Section 501 requires that expenditures by a political committee be authorized by a responsible individual; prohibits certain corrupting expenditures; but places no overall limit on expenditures other than those which may be voluntarily entered into by a committee in exchange for free broadcast time or other services by the state pursuant to the voter information programs available under Title IX of this Act.

Section 502 relates to "nonindividual" political contributions (corporations, unions, etc.). While the section flatly prohibits such political contributions, it then spells out certain areas where political contributions or expenditures are permitted. While the section closes off political contributions to candidates or political parties, it recognizes that corporations, labor unions, etc. have a legitimate right to political expression and permits such entities to campaign on issues, to communicate within their membership with no holds barred, to match employee contributions (Title XI) and to make direct contributions to the State Voters Assistance Board (Title VII). For public advocacy or campaigning on issues, an entity must "fly under its own colors" by forming a committee and registering with the commission.

Section 503 relates to political contributions by individuals. There is no limit on the size of a contribution an individual may make, *but* large contributions are discouraged by placing a progressive tax on contributions, which must be paid by the recipient committee. All contributions in excess of $20 must be made by check (or other negotiable instrument requiring the contributor's signature).

Section 504 relates to public employees and their involvement in political activity. In general, it recognizes that public employees have a right to participate in the political process, but it spells out permissible activities and places others within the discretion of the commission on a case by case basis.

Section 505 prohibits one individual from making a contribution in the name of another.

Section 506 requires that a pecuniary value be placed upon all "in-kind" contributions in accordance with guidelines to be established by the commission.

Section 507 requires that all credit obtained by a political committee be either from a bank or businesses whose ordinary business is the extension of credit except for services rendered or goods sold. This provision is intended to eliminate the use of loans for indirect contributions.

Section 508 relates to government contractors and consultants. While such individuals may make contributions, they have to do so via political-contribution certificates (issued by the state pursuant to Title XI), and provision is made for every government agency to report all contracts to the commission if the contracts are in aggregate $1,000 or more to the same individual or entity during a fiscal year.

TITLE VI—UNFAIR AND UNLAWFUL CAMPAIGN PRACTICES

Section 601 relates to "unfair" campaign practices by placing the board in the position to be a public arbitrator of alleged unfair practices. The board must comment in writing within 72 hours on the fairness and propriety of the alleged unfair practice. Broad guidelines are provided in the section, but basically the board must decide on a case by case basis with the public being the final judge of "fairness."

Section 602 prohibits anyone from depriving anyone else of his or her civil rights. (The penalties are stated as misdemeanor or felony and classified—A, B, or C—for the unlawful acts in this title. The classification is defined and penalties affixed in Section 623.)

Section 603 prohibits anyone from interference with anyone else's rights in elections—voting, campaigning, acting as an election official, etc.

Section 604 prohibits interference with anyone who is helping anyone else obtain his or her rights by giving him or her such rights.

Section 605 prohibits interference with anyone who is simply helping someone else obtain his rights.

Section 606 prohibits and enumerates corrupt practices related to elections.

Section 607 prohibits anyone from withholding a government benefit, whether direct or as the result of a government contract or program, from anyone in an effort to influence his vote or exercise of any political right.

Section 608 prohibits a government employee from misuse of his position for political purposes.

Section 609 prohibits the use of government property for political purposes except for use of buildings for open meetings.

Section 610 prohibits anyone from tampering with public records.

Section 611 prohibits bribery by defining the elements, limiting defenses, and spelling out what constitutes a *prima facie* case that an action is unlawful.

Section 612 defines and prohibits the unlawful rewarding of public servants.

Section 613 prohibits a public servant from taking a fee for something he should be doing free.

Section 614 prohibits trading in public office and political endorsement.

Section 615 prohibits trading in special influence.

Section 616 prohibits anyone from threatening a public servant.

Section 617 prohibits retaliation against a public servant, witness, or informant.

Section 618 prohibits anyone from disclosing confidential information obtained as a public servant or participant in a government proceeding.

Section 619 makes it unlawful for anyone to speculate on the basis of official action or information for a period of one year following his employment as a public servant. Also contained is a prohibition against any official taking an action to benefit himself as a result of speculation.

Section 620 makes it unlawful for anyone to impersonate a public servant.

Section 621 prohibits anyone from misapplication of property which has been entrusted to him as a fiduciary, or in his capacity as a public servant, officer of a financial institution, or a paid or unpaid associate of a political committee. This section would cover not only the ordinary misappropriation of funds situation but would also be useful for enforcing the Title XI contribution program systems and proper use of committee funds (which in many cases will include public funds).

Section 622 prohibits deceptive writings and is broad enough to cover situations like the use in the 1972 campaign of Muskie's letterhead to discredit Muskie, Humphrey, and Jackson.

Section 623 enumerates the penalties which shall be applicable for the various types of offenses contained in Title VI (felonies and misdemeanors—Class A, B, or C).

TITLE VII—STATE VOTERS ASSISTANCE BOARD

Section 701 establishes a three-member board appointed by the Governor and confirmed by the Senate which is nonpartisan, full-time, and independent. (Its independence is considerable but not as great as the commission in that removal for neglect of duty may be accomplished by the Governor.)

Section 702 defines the basic duties of the board—which are primarily to promote political activity (i.e., information to the public, financing of political candidates and parties, voter registration, and citizen awareness of and participation in the political process).

Section 703 gives the board fairly broad powers but makes it clear that enforcement powers are with the commission.

Section 704 mandates the commission to resolve disputes arising out of contracts of the board or board rulings whenever the board is a party to such a controversy.

Section 705 authorizes the board to use certain income (direct contributions and assessments on large contributions) for specific purposes and contains a general authorization for funds to be appropriated.

TITLE VIII—UNIVERSAL VOTER REGISTRATION

Section 801 gives the board the responsibility for assuring that everyone is registered to vote who should be. In addition, the board must maintain on a current basis a centralized file of all eligible voters and service local election districts.

Section 802 requires citizens to register to vote. In short, the effect of this section is to make voter registration the function of the state board, rather than relying upon political parties or other groups to encourage citizens to register to vote. Subsection (a) requires the citizen to register but does not directly penalize him if he does not do so. Subsection (b) requires the board to cooperate with local election boards and places upon the board the duty of getting everyone registered.

Section 803 establishes cooperation between the U.S. Postal Service and the board for the purpose of keeping the registration file apprised of change-of-address information.

Section 804 sets up an automatic purge of the rolls of dead voters by requiring the state bureau of vital statistics to notify the board of deaths of individuals age 18 or over.

Section 805 details the information data that must be provided as part of the registration. This section also takes into account registration by party and permits either permanent or temporary changes 30 days prior to an election.

Section 806 relates to the voters whose eligibility is questioned at the polls. (The voter is allowed to vote by secret ballot, and the commission then decides on the validity of the vote after the election.)

Title IX—Voter Information Programs

Section 901 directs the board to publish two weeks prior to each general election a voters' information digest and to distribute it to all the voters in the state. The section specifies some of the information to be contained in the digest and provides that the board shall by regulation establish rules for obtaining other information.

Section 902 authorizes the board to purchase blocks of television and radio time for use by candidates on an equally allocated basis for those candidates who voluntarily enter into agreements to limit their spending.

Section 903 mandates that educational television and radio stations set aside time for allocation by the board to political candidates—both during campaign periods and on a year-round basis.

Section 904 directs each CATV system within the state to set aside one channel of its system for transmission of such programs as the board may request (and determined pursuant to Section 905).

Section 905 authorizes the board to allocate free broadcast time (available under Sections 903 and 904) to public officeholders, political parties, and/or political committees to use as they determine.

Section 906 establishes production facilities within the state for use by candidates and parties to record audio and video tapes.

Section 907 authorizes the board to provide telephone services (recorded messages) for parties and statewide candidates.

Section 908 authorizes the board to develop, in conjunction with the state commissioner of education, a public-issue and governmental-process curriculum for elementary and secondary schools. (The schools do not have to use the curriculum, but it will be available for those schools that do want to use it.) The section enumerates elements which should be included in the curriculum development. In addition, the board shall prepare a legislative digest for use by the schools on a weekly basis during the legislative session.

Section 909 establishes a library of political comment to be operated by the board and to serve as a repository and clearing house for material published by candidates and parties.

TITLE X—PUBLIC GRANTS TO POLITICAL PARTIES

Section 1001 authorizes grants to political parties. The amount of grants is set at 50 percent of the funds the board receives from direct contributions and assessments on large contributions to candidates and committees. Eligibility requirements are set for parties, and there is a requirement that all eligible parties be allocated an equal amount.

Section 1002 relates to one of the two types of grants—public-issue grants. The section defines areas for public-issue grants, procedures for obtaining them, and limitations on their use. It also makes clear that the end product is the sole property of the political party.

Section 1003 relates to the other type of grant available—community-service grants. It sets up procedures, places limitations, and defines what a community-service grant is—i.e., basically a community-service program run by the party, using volunteers.

Section 1004 gives the commission the power to audit the use of grant funds and builds in an automatic evaluation role with respect to the continuation of the public grants to political parties.

TITLE XI—SYSTEMATIC INDIVIDUAL POLITICAL CONTRIBUTION PROGRAMS

Section 1101 sets forth four types of contribution programs designed to get more people involved in political giving and charges the board with the responsibility for promoting and supervising such programs.

Section 1102 authorizes the board to issue political-contribution certificates, which are scrip having a greater value than its purchase price and available through participation in two of the four contribution plans to be promoted by the board. Political-contribution certificates can be purchased only by individuals, and there are limits on their use. (Only a political committee can spend them, and only the purchaser can give them to a candidate or committee.) Details concerning the certificates and their use are contained in this section.

Section 1103 relates to the payroll-deduction plan for the purchase of political-contribution certificates. The board must approve each plan which must be available to all employees and not subject to coercion.

Section 1104 relates to the public purchase plan for the purchase of political-contribution certificates, using a Christmas Club type of approach at banks and financial institutions. Board approval of the plan is necessary.

Section 1105 deals with common-purpose political-action funds such as COPE or BIPAC, by authorizing the board to encourage such funds but setting standards to insure that membership knows how its money is used and has a voice in electing the fund's officials.

Section 1106 relates to the trust-account plan, which is a joint venture between employers and employees whereby a bank trustee holds money from both in an employee's account. The proceeds from that account will be paid out only on instruction from the employee and only to a political candidate or committee. The employer may match the employee's withholding for such an account up to 100 percent. The board must approve all such plans.

Section 1107 authorizes the board to use a number of incentives or promotions for encouraging the development of and the participation in individual systematic contribution programs. The section also deals with the procedures to be used by the board in fixing the value of political-contribution certificates.

TITLE XII—TAX INCENTIVES FOR CANDIDATES, PARTY OFFICIALS, PUBLIC OFFICIALS AND INDIVIDUAL CONTRIBUTORS

Section 1201 permits candidates and party or public officials to deduct from their ordinary income out-of-pocket expenses in connection with their campaign or holding of office for income-tax purposes.

Section 1202 gives all taxpayers a tax credit for 50 percent of a political contribution up to $25 a year. The section also

contains a provision that prevents getting a double tax credit
(Federal/state) based on the same contribution or increment
of a contribution.

TITLE XIII—OPTIONAL COVERAGE FOR LOCAL AND COUNTY OFFICIALS

Section 1301 authorizes local governmental units to opt for
coverage under all the provisions of this Act.

Section 1302 deals with procedures to resolve situations involving overlapping jurisdictions (with part wanting in and part
wanting out).

Section 1303 is a cost-sharing provision for those local governmental units opting in. It is based on the number of elected
offices and violations.

Section 1304 is a local-option provision for getting out once
a jurisdiction has opted in but then changed its mind.

TITLE XIV—MATCHING GRANTS TO CANDIDATE AND PARTY COMMITTEES

Section 1401 authorizes the board to provide grants to eligible
candidate and party committees based on the first $25 of a
contribution.

Section 1402 deals with the amount of grants and the payment
procedures to eligible committees.

Section 1403 relates to eligibility requirements for a committee to receive matching grants. In general, a committee must
raise either $1,000 or .001 times the population which can vote
for the office sought (whichever amount is greater) before it is
eligible for matching grants. (Party committees must receive
a certain percentage of their income from contributors of under
$100; candidate committees must reach the amount noted above
using such contributions.)

Section 1404 directs the board to apportion available funds
equally between pre-nomination and post-nomination periods.
It also provides the formula for allocating available funds
among candidates or committees. In general, candidate committees receive funds in pre-nomination periods and party committees receive funds in the post-nomination periods. No
committee can receive more than its allocation limit, and
unused allocations are carried forward to the next election
period for reallocation by the board.

Section 1405 establishes procedures for the board to use with
respect to overpayments.

Section 1406 prohibits individual gain from committee funds other than for service rendered or goods sold.

Section 1407 is an authorization for funds to be appropriated to carry out the grant program in this title.

TITLE XV—MISCELLANEOUS PROVISIONS

Section 1501 is a general repeal clause. It is written with several leads so that a legislature can add the specific law repeal by this Act.

Section 1502 is a savings provision which is broad enough to protect ongoing action in any area affected by this Act on the day of enactment. It also contains transition authority for the commission.

Section 1503 is a separability provision assuring the continued effect of the Act if one part is found by a court to be wanting.

Section 1504 makes the Act effective upon enactment but makes allowance for specific dates to the contrary for any provisions where the statute permits start-up time or contains another date.

DATE DUE			

Campaign money   195190